CANADA'S northland has received the attention of hardy explorers, traders, administrators, churchmen, teachers, and adventurers, for many generations. The fur-trade has long been the chief factor linking the northland's scattered settlements with established communities elsewhere. The gold rush to the Yukon just before the turn of the century increased the number of white settlers in that territory. More recently, the quest for gold in the vicinity of Yellowknife has stimulated a new northward movement of population. The discovery of oil near Fort Norman, of pitchblende and other important minerals on the eastern shore of Great Bear Lake, has given further impetus to the exploration and peopling of the far northwest. Furthermore, the second World War brought about the close co-operation of the United States and Canada in creating the establishments necessary for the defence of the northern frontiers of this continent.

Looking to permanent development, the Canadian Social Research Council, with the support of the Rockefeller Foundation, made a preliminary survey of this region in 1944, more especially of the Mackenzie District and Yukon Territory. The results some of these researches are embodied in this new volume. Each of the contributors is a specialist in his field, and the fruit of their researches will be a valuable source of material on the North-West for many years come.

The New North-West

The New North-West

EDITED BY

C. A. DAWSON

PROFESSOR OF SOCIOLOGY
McGILL UNIVERSITY

TORONTO
THE UNIVERSITY OF TORONTO PRESS
1947

Preface

CANADA's northland has received the attention of hardy explorers, traders, administrators, churchmen, teachers, and adventurers, for many generations. The original inhabitants were Indians and Eskimos, who lived by hunting and fishing. The Hudson's Bay Company and other trading companies developed a market for the furs collected by these native peoples, and the fur trade was long the chief factor linking the Northland's scattered settlements with established communities elsewhere. The gold-rush to the Yukon just before the turn of the century increased the number of white settlers in that territory. More recently, the quest for gold in the vicinity of Yellowknife has stimulated a new northward movement of population. The discovery of oil near Fort Norman, of pitchblende and other important minerals on the eastern shore of Great Bear Lake, has given further impetus in the exploration and peopling of the Far North-West. Furthermore, the Second World War has brought about the close co-operation of the United States and Canada in creating establishments for the defence of the northern frontiers of this continent. This noteworthy trend of events led to the survey which was undertaken by the Canadian Social Science Research Council in 1944, and which resulted in the publication of a series of articles in the *Canadian Journal of Economics and Political Science*. These and other articles are now brought together by the decision of the Council in a single volume.

This book was made possible by the financial support of the Rockefeller Foundation which sponsored the survey plan of the Canadian Social Science Research Council and enabled the Council to enlist the co-operation of the authors who contributed by the preparation of these articles. I am indebted to Professor H. A. Innis, President of the Social Science Research Council, who has been actively associated with this project from its inception. The Council and others engaged in this venture wish to express their appreciation for the co-operation of the *Canadian Journal of Economics and Political Science,* and in particular that of its editor, Professor V. W. Bladen of the University of Toronto. The aid of Dr. Charles Camsell, Deputy Minister of Mines and Resources, was very important. Major-General W. W. Foster, Special Commissioner for Defence Projects, was equally helpful.

v

I am particularly indebted to Mr. R. A. Gibson, Deputy-Commissioner, Bureau of Northwest Territories and Yukon Affairs. He made available the aid of his Department in giving an accurate presentation of the facts. In this connection, a member of his staff, Mr. J. L. Robinson, now Associate Professor of Geography at the University of British Columbia, was most helpful in checking data presented and helping to make many necessary corrections. Dr. E. S. Archibald, Director of Experimental Farms Service, gave most helpful assistance, and permitted the publication of an article on agriculture by a member of his Department. For the co-operation of the *Canadian Geographical Journal* in connection with the reproduction of articles and charts, the editor is very grateful. To the members of Canadian government staffs in the far North-West, to the managers of mines, transportation companies, and a host of others, the authors of this volume are indebted in innumerable ways.

Finally, a special word of thanks is due to Dr. H. C. Hanson, General Manager of the Alaska Rural Rehabilitation Corporation, at Palmer, Alaska.

C. A.D.

Contents

Illustrations

Part One

C. CECIL LINGARD

Administration of the Northland

THE Canadian Northland embraces both the Yukon and the North West Territories, a total area of 1,516,758 square miles. The Yukon Territory, which forms the extreme north-west portion of the mainland of Canada, extends northward from British Columbia to the Arctic Ocean and eastward from Alaska to the District of Mackenzie. The North West Territories, which have diminished in area time and again during the last seventy-five years, today embrace the vast mainland portion of Canada lying north of the sixtieth parallel of latitude between the Yukon Territory on the west and Hudson Bay on the east, together with the islands in Hudson and James Bays and in the Arctic Archipelago.

OUTLINE OF THE HISTORY OF GOVERNMENT IN THE NORTH WEST TERRITORIES, 1870-1905

The history of administration of the Canadian Northland has its beginning in the passage on June 22, 1869, of a Canadian "Act for the temporary government of Rupert's Land and the North-Western Territory when united with Canada."[1] One year and a day later the imperial government transferred both these territories to Canada and in 1880 transferred all the islands claimed by Great Britain in the North American Arctic.[2]

This vast empire, designated as the North West Territories, was not destined to remain long intact. The creation of the Province of Manitoba in 1870 out of a small portion known as the Red River Settlement was but the first of a series of provincial establishments and expansions that were ultimately to reduce the North West Territories to their present area. Until 1875, however,

[1] *Statutes of Canada*, 32-3 Vict., c. 3 (1869). Rupert's Land included, according to the Hudson's Bay Company's claim based on the Charter of 1670, the whole watershed of Hudson Bay and Strait. The North-Western Territory, after the extension of British Columbia's boundary to its present limits in 1866, comprised the region between Rupert's Land, British Columbia, and Alaska. The Canadian government, it may be added, claimed the territory in the basin of the Saskatchewan and Red Rivers on the grounds of early French activity, although the Hudson's Bay Company always held it to be a part of Rupert's Land embracing the Hudson Bay watershed.

[2] Order of Her Majesty in Council admitting Rupert's Land and the North-Western Territory into the Union, June 23, 1870; V. K. Johnson, "Canada's Title to the Arctic Islands" (*Canadian Historical Review*, vol. XIV, 1933).

3

the provisional act of 1869 provided for the government of the remainder of the Territories, which were ruled from Fort Garry (Winnipeg) by the Lieutenant-Governor of Manitoba and his North-West Council, with the newly established Department of the Interior maintaining oversight from the capital at Ottawa.

The distinctive political career of the North West Territories commenced with the passage by the Canadian Parliament of the Northwest Territories Act[3] of 1875, which thirty years later still served as the pattern of legislation directing the administration of the more remote Northland.   The Act of 1875 provided that the administration of the Territories should be placed in the hands of a resident Lieutenant-Governor assisted by an appointed North-West Council and invested with both executive and legislative powers.   The legislative powers included taxation for local purposes, property and civil rights, administration of justice, public health, police, roads, highways, and generally all matters of a purely local and private nature.   An ingenious clause provided for the gradual evolution of the Council into an elected Legislative Assembly.

The years that followed 1888, the date of the first session of this elected Legislative Assembly, were significant in the political history of the then North West Territories, which were divided for postal and administrative purposes into the provisional Districts of Assiniboia, Saskatchewan, Alberta, and Athabaska in 1882, and of Yukon, Mackenzie, Franklin, and Ungava in 1895.[4] It was not to be expected that pioneer settlers in the first four above-mentioned districts should long remain content with the limited powers possessed by their Territorial Assembly.   Following a series of memorials to Ottawa which increased in frequency and directness with the accelerated growth in population of the North-West, the federal Parliament passed a number of North West Territories amendment acts[5] which finally resulted in the concession to the Legislative Assembly of a complete system of responsible government within the territorial status in 1897.[6]

By the commencement of the present century it became evident that nothing short of the provincial status would satisfy the pioneering communities spreading over the Canadian prairie Districts of Assiniboia, Alberta, and Saskatchewan under the unprecedented flood of immigration then pouring into the West. The story of this provincial autonomy movement, the product both of financial embarrassments arising out of the territorial status and of constitutional aspirations for a provincial status in no way inferior to that

[3]*Statutes of Canada*, 38 Vict., c. 49 (1875).

[4]The District of Keewatin was created in 1876 and withdrawn from the government of the North West Territories on that date.

[5]*Statutes of Canada*, 51 Vict., c. 19 (1888);   54-5 Vict., c. 22 (1891); 60-1 Vict., c. 28, s. 8 (1896-7).

[6]*See* C. C. Lingard, *Territorial Government in Canada* (Toronto, 1946).   Chapter i presents an outline of the political development of the North West Territories from 1875 to 1900.

enjoyed by other members of the Canadian Confederation, has been told elsewhere in great detail.[7] Suffice it to say here that two new prairie provinces, Saskatchewan and Alberta, came into being on September 1, 1905,[8] with their southern and northern boundaries fixed at the forty-ninth and sixtieth parallels of north latitude respectively. Extending from British Columbia on the west to Manitoba on the east, they embraced the Districts of Assiniboia and Alberta and the major portion of the Districts of Saskatchewan and Athabaska, the only provisional districts having representation in the Legislative Assembly of the old North West Territories.

The Reorganized North West Territories Defined. The creation of the Provinces of Saskatchewan and Alberta in September, 1905 necessitated the passage by the Parliament of Canada of an act providing not only for the delimitation of the remaining North West Territories but also for their administration. This act, known as the "Northwest Territories Amendment Act, 1905,"[9] stated that "the Northwest Territories shall hereafter comprise the territories formerly known as Rupert's Land and the Northwestern Territory, except such portions thereof as form the Provinces of Manitoba, Saskatchewan, and Alberta, the District of Keewatin and the Yukon Territory, together with all British territories and possessions in North America and all islands adjacent to any such territories or possessions except the colony of Newfoundland and its dependencies."

Under this Act, the District of Keewatin, adjoining Hudson Bay on the west, and the Yukon Territory, lying directly north of British Columbia, were both excluded from the newly defined North West Territories. Apparently it was the intention of the government to retain Keewatin as a separate district until such times as its contiguous portions might be added to Manitoba and Ontario. However, the federal authorities changed their mind on July 24, 1905, when a proclamation was issued under an order-in-council placing Keewatin (enlarged by those portions of the Districts of Saskatchewan and Athabaska not to be included in the Province of Saskatchewan) within the jurisdiction of the reorganized North West Territories.

On the other hand, the Yukon—one of the provisional districts established in the North West Territories in 1895—which had been proclaimed the Yukon Judicial District by the Governor-in-Council on August 16, 1897, had been earlier separated from the said North West Territories and constituted the "Yukon Territory" by an Act of the Canadian Parliament, passed in June, 1898, even while the famous Klondike gold-rush was in the process of making it one of the great gold-producing regions of the world.[10]

[7] *Ibid.*

[8] See *Statutes of Canada*, 4-5 Edw. VII, cc. 3 and 42, for the Alberta and Saskatchewan Acts of 1905.

[9] *Ibid.*, 4-5 Edw. VII, c. 27, s. 3 (1905).

[10] *Revised Statutes of Canada*, 1906, c. 50; *Statutes of Canada*, 61 Vict., c. 6, s. 2 (1898), cited as the Yukon Territory Act.

The North West Territories were, however, to undergo a further loss of territory in 1912 when the older Provinces of Quebec, Ontario, and Manitoba were extended northwards.[11] Quebec was enlarged to include the District of Ungava—that is, all of Rupert's Land lying south of Hudson Strait and Ungava Bay and east of Hudson and James Bays. Ontario and Manitoba were given the remainder of Rupert's Land lying south and west of James and Hudson Bays as far as the sixtieth parallel of north latitude. Thus, by the year 1912 the original area of the North West Territories had been reduced to that of the present day, while the boundaries of the three remaining Districts of Mackenzie, Keewatin, and Franklin were revised and delimited as now existing by an order-in-council of March 16, 1918, effective on January 1, 1920.

GOVERNMENT OF THE YUKON TERRITORY, 1898-1944

Prior to the creation of the Yukon District as a separate Territory for administrative purposes by the Yukon Territory Act in June, 1898, a detachment of North West Mounted Police, under the command of Inspector Constantine, had been sent to the Yukon (1895) to represent various departments of the federal government. The growth of the mining industry in the two succeeding years necessitated the appointment of a customs officer and a gold commissioner and the removal of the recording office from Fortymile to the site of the present Town of Dawson. Also, a member of the Executive Council of the then North West Territories had spent several months in the District enforcing regulations respecting the importation and sale of intoxicating liquor.[12] However, with the arrival of tens of thousands of people in the Klondike region at the time of the gold-rush of 1897-8, the federal authorities took steps for the establishment of a separate local system of government.

Intended merely as a temporary measure to provide for the maintenance of order and the administration of the new mining community, the Yukon Territory Act followed in general the principles of the Northwest Territories Act of 1875. Provision was made for the appointment of a Commissioner as the chief executive officer to administer the government of the Territory under instructions given him from time to time by the Governor-in-Council or the federal Minister of the Interior. To aid the Commissioner, a Council of not more than six persons (including the judges of the Territorial Court) was to be appointed, possessing the same legislative powers to make ordinances for

[11]*Statutes of Canada*, 2 Geo. V, cc. 45, 42, and 32 (1912).

[12]*Journals, Legislative Assembly, Northwest Territories*, Session 1898, p. 8; "Minutes of Meetings of the Executive Council of the Territories," 1897-8, orders-in-council nos. 83, 90, 94, and 95 (dated January 11, 1898); Department of the Interior, *The Yukon, its History and Resources* (Ottawa, 1916), p. 14. In 1894 the federal government had sent Inspector Constantine into the Yukon to report upon the need for law and order. F. C. Fetherstonhaugh, *The Royal Canadian Mounted Police* (New York, 1938), p. 70.

the government of the Yukon Territory as were exercised at that time (1898) by the Lieutenant-Governor of the North West Territories acting with the advice and consent of the Legislative Assembly thereof. Moreover, while the federal Governor-in-Council was given power to make ordinances for the peace, order, and good government of the Territory as well as to exercise residuary jurisdiction beyond that possessed by the Commissioner-in-Council, the latter was restricted in its authority to impose taxes or duties, alter punishment for offence, and appropriate public money, lands, or property without the authority of Parliament. Provision was also made for the disallowance of ordinances by the Governor-in-Council within two years after their passage and for the continuance in force in the Yukon of the existing North West Territorial laws relating to civil and criminal matters until amended or repealed by competent authority.[13]

Because of the uncertainty on the part of the federal government respecting the nature, nationality, and political experience of the pioneer inhabitants, the Act of 1898 lacked any provision for popular representation in the Yukon Council. The following year, however, an amendment to the Yukon Act was passed giving natural born and naturalized male British subjects in the Territory the right to elect two representatives to the Council for a term of two years and requiring its sessions to be open to the public.[14] The Commissioner-in-Council was also empowered by the amendment Act of 1899 to make regulations respecting shops, taverns, public health, and local improvements and to impose licence fees and other charges connected therewith as soon as the two elected representatives took their seats. Furthermore, the Commissioner and his Yukon Council were given authority to bestow upon any elected municipal corporation the power to levy taxes upon the inhabitants for local purposes.

The next significant phase in the political evolution of the Yukon Territory was the attainment of parliamentary representation in the House of Commons. It was not unnatural that the mining community, which possessed an estimated population, in the spring of 1900, of over 5,000 in Dawson and a total of about 10,700 in the surrounding creeks, should seek representation in the federal Parliament at the earliest possible opportunity. Indeed, a mass meeting of citizens of the Yukon on March 23, 1900, ratified a petition to the Ottawa government asking for the right to elect two members to Parliament in order

[13]*Statutes of Canada*, 61 Vict., c. 6 (1898); *Debates of the House of Commons*, 1898, vol. II, cols. 6728-31.

[14]*Statutes of Canada*, 62-3 Vict., c. 11 (1899); *Debates, House of Commons*, 1898, vol. II, col. 6729. The sections of the Act of 1899 respecting the two elected representatives did not go into effect until July 13, 1900, when an order-in-council to that effect was issued by the federal government. The membership of the appointed Yukon Council during the years 1898-1900 comprised the Superintendent of the N.W.M.P., the Judge of the Territorial Court, the registrar of lands, the legal adviser, and the gold commissioner, all of whom served without salaries, being already government employees in other capacities in the Territory. Mr. William Ogilvie was Commissioner of Yukon Territory at this time.

that "important and pressing questions relating to the Yukon Territory may be properly brought before the House of Commons by members . . . acquainted with the conditions" of the mining country.[15]

When the question was raised in the House of Commons in June, 1900, the Prime Minister, Sir Wilfrid Laurier, advised delay in granting parliamentary representation until after the census of 1901, when the exact condition of the Yukon population and country would be better known. Especially did the government want to be informed of the total number of British subjects and aliens in the Territory. Moreover, the two members requested in the petition was not in accord with the unit of representation in the Dominion, which at the time was one member for about 22,000 electors.[16]

Despite a motion by Sir Charles Tupper, ably supported by Sir George Foster, urging immediate provision for Yukon representation, the government postponed the matter until the session of 1902 when the Yukon Territory Representation Act was passed, constituting the Territory an electoral district with the right to return one member to the House of Commons. Under the Act, every male British subject (exclusive of Indians) of twenty-one years of age with twelve months' residence in the Territory received the right to vote, and the first election of a member to the national Parliament was required to be held on or before January 1, 1903.[17] Actually, the Yukon elected its first member to Parliament in December, 1902, in the person of Mr. James H. Ross who had resigned the office of Commissioner to contest the seat.

Meanwhile, in response to local agitation, the Yukon Council had forwarded a memorial to Ottawa asking among other things for representation in the Senate, the addition of five elected members to the Council, the right of the Yukon Council to adopt all ordinances independently of the federal government, apart from the latter's power of veto, and the right to establish breweries and to control the Yukon liquor traffic.[18]

The great material interests involved in the mining community and the considerable amount of local taxation levied upon the inhabitants seemed to justify increased popular representation in the Yukon Council which at the time consisted largely of federal government officials. At any rate, Parliament passed an amending Yukon Act increasing the elected representatives in the Territorial Council to five members, thereby making that body of ten (exclusive of the Commissioner) half appointed and half elected.[19] Another

[15]*Debates, House of Commons*, 1900, cols. 7773 and 7780.

[16]*Ibid.*, 1900, cols. 6615 and 7778-9.

[17]*Ibid.*, 1900, cols. 7780-5; 1902, vol. II, col. 3306; *Statutes of Canada*, 2 Edw. VII, c. 37 (1902). Numerous sections of the Act detailed the method of carrying on elections in a sparsely settled pioneer community. The qualifications of voters were set out in the same terms as in the Northwest Territories Representation Act.

[18]J. Castell Hopkins, *The Canadian Annual Review of Public Affairs*, 1902, pp. 88-9.

section of the Act gave the Yukon Commissioner-in-Council, subject to the provisions of any ordinance of the Governor-in-Council, the same powers to make ordinances for the government of the Territory as were at that time possessed by the Lieutenant-Governor of the North West Territories, acting by and with the advice and consent of the Legislative Assembly. Included in the powers of the Commissioner-in-Council was the authority to make ordinances for the control and regulation of the sale of and traffic in intoxicating liquor in the Territory. Further provisions of the Act defined the power of the Governor-in-Council to make ordinances for the peace, order, and good government of the Territory, provided that in case of conflict between the ordinances of the Commissioner-in-Council and of the Governor-in-Council those of the latter should prevail, and declared that ordinances passed by the Governor-in-Council should not remain in force longer than the end of the next ensuing session of Parliament unless approved by resolution of both Houses. This latter provision was intended to restrict the great powers of the Governor-in-Council to dispose of large mining interests and other matters by order-in-council without parliamentary sanction.[20] Of course, the federal government possessed the veto power with respect to ordinances of the Yukon Commissioner-in-Council.

Despite the election of five local representatives to the Yukon Council in January, 1903, the citizens immediately renewed their agitation for a wholly elective Council. Dr. Alfred Thompson, who had been striving in the Council during 1903-4 to have a memorial forwarded to Ottawa in favour of a fully elective body, stated in the House of Commons as member for the Yukon, in 1905, that every election platform that had been formed in the Territory during the last four years contained such a plank.[21]

A resolution from residents of the Yukon, tabled in the House of Commons the following year, reiterated this "oft-repeated request . . . for a wholly elective Council" and urged "its speedy granting" as "absolutely necessary to ensure the good government and continued prosperity of the business and mining industries" of the Territory. Resolutions or memorials introduced repeatedly at meetings of the Yukon Council by the elective members on behalf of this reform step in the movement of greater self-government were (in the words of the resolution) "opposed, or their purport and imperative urgency minimized, solely by the actions and votes of the appointed members of the Council."[22]

[19]*Statutes of Canada*, 2 Edw. VII, c. 34 (1902). Dr. Alfred Thompson, the Reverend John Pringle, and Messrs. J. A. Clarke, Max Laudreville, and Robert Low were elected to the Yukon Council on January 18, 1903.

[20]*Debates, House of Commons*, 1902, vol. II, cols. 3126, 3834, 4485, and 4533.

[21]J. Castell Hopkins, *The Canadian Annual Review of Public Affairs*, 1904, p. 352; *Debates, House of Commons*, 1905, vol. IV, col. 7060.

[22]*Debates, House of Commons*, 1906, vol. IV, col. 6547.

Speaking in support of the resolution, the member for Yukon sketched the administrative history of the Territory from 1897 and stated that the people were not asking for provincial status but rather for a system of government similar to that which prevailed in the old North West Territories prior to the passage of the Alberta and Saskatchewan autonomy bills, that is, a popularly elected legislative assembly in charge of local affairs. Recognizing that the decline in population of the Yukon (from 21,000 in 1901 to a variously estimated 8,000 to 12,000) might have a bearing on the question, Dr. Thompson pointed out that a very large proportion of the population were male adults, perhaps 900 out of every 1,000, capable of voting. Moreover, they had shown since 1900 that "they were capable of using without abusing representative institutions."[23]

In his reply to the case for the Yukon the Minister of the Interior, the Honourable Frank Oliver, declared it to be a fair supposition that conditions of government which were applicable to a larger population in the Yukon were not altogether inapplicable to a smaller one; indeed, conditions in the Yukon in 1906 were hardly those which ordinarily demand a change.[24] On the other hand, Mr. R. L. Borden, leader of the Opposition, urged that action be taken forthwith to give the people the right which they most ardently desired, not only because they were capable of governing themselves, but also because future prospects of prosperity in the mining industry were such as to justify giving representative government to a territory which had attained the requisite degree of permanence.[25] However, a delay of two years ensued and the usual election of five members to the Yukon Council for the customary two-year term took place on April 17, 1907.[26]

The "Act to Amend the Yukon Act," assented to July 20, 1908, to meet the wishes of the people for a fuller measure of self-government, provided for a wholly elective Council of ten members with complete legislative power within certain defined limits. The Council was required to sit separately from the Commissioner in annual sessions for a three-year term, although the latter might order a dissolution and a new election at any time. While all money bills for the appropriation of any part of the public revenue of the Territory or the imposition of any tax must originate in the Council, no such bill, vote, resolution, or address might be adopted unless it had first been recommended to Council by message of the Commissioner.

Provision was also made for a sessional indemnity of $600 and actual travelling expenses for each member of the Council; the auditing by the Auditor-General of Canada of all receipts and expenditures of Territorial

[23]*Ibid.*, cols. 5103-7.
[24]*Ibid.*, cols. 5110-11.
[25]*Ibid.*, cols. 5113-15.
[26]J. Castell Hopkins, *The Canadian Annual Review of Public Affairs*, 1907, p. 615. The other five members of the Council were still appointed by the federal government.

funds and of appropriations of Parliament for the Territory as authorized by the Commissioner to be expended with the advice and consent of the Yukon Council; the appointment of an Administrator by the Governor-in-Council to execute the functions of the Commissioner during his absence or inability; and the like appointment of a Public Administrator as official guardian in and for the Territory. Furthermore, to permit the completion of the two-year term of the existing Council, provision was made for the Act to go into force on May 1, 1909.

It is evident that the Yukon did not receive responsible government. While the elected representatives of the people possessed legislative power within well-defined limits, the Commissioner was responsible to the federal government alone in respect to his wide executive and administrative functions. The people's representatives might initiate and pass legislation for the Commissioner's approval, disapproval, or reservation for the assent of the Governor-in-Council, but they possessed no control over its execution. Clearly, the success of the system would largely depend upon the wisdom, good sense, and executive ability of the Commissioner on whom the federal authorities depended for efficient and intelligent administration of the Yukon Territory.[27]

The elective Yukon Council of ten, comprising two representatives from each of the five electoral districts of North Dawson, South Dawson, Bonanza, Klondike, and Whitehorse, continued to function until the spring of 1918 when the decline in the population of the Yukon to that of a few thousand people led the federal government to reduce and reorganize the whole administrative machinery of the Territory.[28]

In April, 1918, Interior Minister Meighen introduced a bill to provide for the ratification of steps already taken in March to abolish the offices of commissioner, administrator, director of surveys, assistant gold commissioner, mining inspector, legal adviser, and various mining recorders and clerks, and for the transfer to any officer of the Crown of any or all the duties of the offices so abolished. The bill also empowered the Governor-in-Council to abolish the existing Yukon Council and to appoint a Council of two or more members by warrant of the Governor-General under his Privy Seal.[29]

[27]*Debates, House of Commons,* 1907-8, vol. VI, cols. 10529-41.

[28]The population of the Yukon Territory had declined from 27,219 in 1901 to 8,512 in 1911 (of which 1,528 were Indians), and 4,157 in 1921. The census of 1931 gave the population at 4,230 (including 2,730 white inhabitants) and that of 1941 a total population of 4,914. Cited in J. Castell Hopkins, *The Canadian Annual Review of Public Affairs,* 1911, p. 11; *Debates, House of Commons,* 1911, vol. I, p. 593; *ibid.,* 1922, vol. III, pp. 2456-7; *ibid.,* 1937, vol. II, p. 1440; *Report of the Department of Mines and Resources,* 1943, p. 91.

[29]*Statutes of Canada,* 8-9 Geo. V, c. 50 (1918); *Debates, House of Commons,* 1918, vols. I and II, pp. 464, 682, and 2221. The duties of the offices abolished were delegated to the Gold Commissioner, George P. Mackenzie, with an annual saving of $150,000 in the cost of administration (J. Castell Hopkins, *The Canadian Annual Review of Public Affairs,* 1918, p. 748).

After conferring with the Yukon Commissioner and the Yukon member of the House of Commons, the federal government decided to maintain the elective feature of the Yukon Council and to reduce its membership from ten to three. Consequently, Parliament passed another amending Yukon act in 1919 providing not only for an elective Council of three, but also for a reduction in the sessional indemnity from $600 to $400 and for the extension to women of the franchise for elections to the Council.[30]

In view of the creation of a new mining district as a result of the Mayo silver strike, the Territorial Council in 1923 forwarded a memorial to Ottawa asking for an additional Council member and an increase in the sessional indemnity. The government, however, rejected both requests, believing that the three representatives and the indemnity of $400 were ample until the population increased.[31]

The governmental machinery of the Yukon Territory today bears the stamp of the policies of 1918-19 when the number of officials was materially reduced and offices co-ordinated in the interests of economy and the accompanying decline in mining population. The local government is composed of the Commissioner or Controller as the chief executive and an elective Legislative Council of three members with a three-year term of office and a procedure identical with that outlined above with respect to the larger Council of ten. The Controller at Dawson, Yukon Territory, administers the government under instructions from the Governor-in-Council or the Minister of Mines and Resources.[32]

The Controller with the advice and consent of the Yukon Council, and subject to the provisions of any Act of Parliament applying to the Territory and of any ordinances of the Governor-in-Council, has power to make ordinances dealing with the imposition of local taxes, the sale of intoxicating liquor, the preservation of game, the establishment of territorial offices, the establishment and maintenance of prisons and municipal institutions, the issuing of licences for shops, taverns, saloons, auctioneers, etc., the incorporation of certain types of companies, the solemnization of marriage, the administration of justice, including the constitution and maintenance of territorial courts of civil jurisdiction, the definition of the powers of sheriffs and the imposition of fines or penalties for the enforcement of territorial ordinances,

[30]*Statutes of Canada*, 9-10 Geo. V, c. 9 (1919); *Debates, House of Commons*, 1919, vol. I, pp. 5, 592-4.

[31]*Debates, House of Commons*, 1923, vol. IV, pp. 3943-4.

[32]*Revised Statutes of Canada*, 1927, vol. IV, c. 215; Department of Mines and Resources, *The Yukon Territory* (Ottawa, 1944), p. 5. The present Controller is Mr. G. A. Jeckell; the three elected members of the Yukon Council are John R. Fraser, Ernest J. Corp, and Alexander A. Smith, representing the electoral Districts of Dawson, Mayo, and Whitehorse, respectively. The present Member of Parliament for the Yukon is the Honourable George Black, K.C.

the expenditure of territorial funds and such portion of any moneys appropriated by Parliament for the Territory as the Controller is authorized to expend by and with the advice of the Council, and generally all matters of a merely local or private nature in the Territory. Thus, the Yukon Council enjoys most of the legislative powers of provincial legislatures excepting chiefly the right to incur debt.

A brief sketch of the work of the Yukon Council will further illustrate the principal fields of local government and administration in this frontier mining community. While many ordinances dealing with the protection of miners, employers' liability, pollution of streams, benevolent societies, highways, ferries, forest fire prevention, hotels and road houses, liquor licences, taxation of unmarried men and women, poll tax, the construction and repair of local roads and bridges, succession duties, game, fur export, etc., during the earlier years, have been fashioned after those which had been in effect in the old North West Territories, subsequent legislation has been largely devoted to their amendment in the light of changing economic and social conditions. During recent years the impact of the aeroplane, the Alaska Highway, and associated projects have called for additional ordinances and amendments respecting highway traffic, the protection of Eskimo ruins, the work of scientists and explorers, greater control of hunting and trapping, the imposition and collection of taxes on income, gasoline, and fuel oil, the maintenance of children of unmarried parents, the prevention of venereal diseases, and the prohibition of fee-charging employment agencies.[33]

The three major items of local government, second only to mining which remains the special concern of federal officials, are roads, education, and public welfare. The Yukon Council has annually devoted a considerable portion of its territorial expenditures to the building and repair of roads and bridges connecting new mining camps with Dawson, Whitehorse, and other centres of the industry and, in addition, has frequently memorialized the federal government for special grants in aid of vital transportation.[34] Likewise, the Council has voted funds for public health and the maintenance of hospitals at Dawson, Whitehorse, and Mayo and passed ordinances concerning the appointment and duties of health officers and rules for the prevention of disease.[35]

[33]*Consolidated Ordinances of the Yukon Territory*, 1914, *passim*; *Ordinances of the Yukon Territory*, 1942, 1943, 1944; *Annual Report of the Department of the Interior*, 1936, pp. 37-8; *Report of the Department of Mines and Resources*, 1939, p. 82; *ibid.*, 1941, p. 72; *ibid.*, 1943, p. 72.

[34]See Professor H. W. Hewetson's study on transportation in the Northland in Part VII. Mr. J. H. McNeill of Dawson is the present superintendent of roads. In 1939 and 1943, for example, expenditures on maintenance and repair of roads out of Territorial funds totalled $53,378 and $43,587 respectively (*Report of the Department of Mines and Resources*, 1939, p. 85 and *ibid.*, 1943, p. 74).

[35]See, for example, *Consolidated Ordinances of the Yukon Territory*, 1914, c. 40.

The authority of the Territorial Council to make ordinances in respect to education is determined by the Yukon Act which empowers the majority of the ratepayers of any portion of the Territory to establish such schools as they think fit and to fix the necessary rates. Moreover, a minority of ratepayers in any district or portion of the Territory may establish Protestant or Roman Catholic separate schools, in which case they shall be liable only to such rates as they impose upon themselves.[36]

The School Ordinance, which is administered by the Territorial Commissioner (or Controller), provides for a Council of Public Instruction with powers to prescribe text-books, courses of study, and standards of instruction, and a Superintendent of Schools to establish rules and regulations concerning education and perform such other duties as may be assigned to him by the above authorities. Special provisions exist for the establishment of school districts and the election of trustees, assessment and taxation, the language of instruction, and religious instruction (if desired by the ratepayers) during the last half of the school day.[37] At present, the Yukon Council makes grants in support of education to high, public, and separate schools at Dawson, public and high schools at Whitehorse, and public schools at Carcross and Mayo.[38]

As might be expected in a pioneering mining community lacking responsible government and provincial institutions, a great deal of the administration of Yukon affairs remains in the hands of the federal government. While the Departments of Public Works, Post Office, Transport, Justice, Revenue, Labour, Health, R.C.M.P., Defence, etc., co-operate with the Department of Mines and Resources with regard to the various problems of government respecting the Yukon, the Lands, Parks, and Forests Branch of the latter Department is directly responsible for all business arising from the general administration of the Territory under the Yukon Act and the ordinances passed by the local Council.[39] Moreover, the same branch has charge of the disposal of lands under the Dominion Lands Act, the administration of the highly important Yukon Placer and Quartz Mining Acts, and the collection of revenue in the Territory. Although seven or more federal departments maintain officials in the Yukon, the Controller (Mr. J. A. Jeckell) at Dawson represents all departments in addition to carrying on his duties as chief executive of the territorial or local administration under instructions from the

[36]*Revised Statutes of Canada*, 1927, c. 215, s. 28.

[37]*Consolidated Ordinances of the Yukon Territory*, 1914, c. 79.

[38]Department of Mines and Resources, *The Yukon Territory*, pp. 25-7.

[39]Prior to December 1, 1936, the Department of the Interior had charge of the general administration of the Yukon. On that date, the Department of Mines and Resources came into being under authority of the *Statutes of Canada*, 1936, c. 33. The new Department assumed work of the former federal Departments of Mines, Interior, Indian Affairs, and Immigration. Its Lands, Parks, and Forests Branch, under R. A. Gibson as Director, is subdivided into four bureaux which include the Bureau of Northwest Territories and Yukon Affairs.

Governor-General-in-Council or the Minister of Mines and Resources.[40]

The most important field of federal jurisdiction in the Yukon has to do with mining legislation and administration. Originally the federal government regulated mining operations by order-in-council, as in 1897-8 when it issued regulations governing placer mining and the diversion and use of water from any stream or lake in the Territory for mining purposes.[41] As orders-in-council were subject to frequent change, thereby leading to much uncertainty, it was not unnatural for the Yukon Council to urge upon the federal government the passage of stable and permanent mining laws as well as the curtailment of hydraulic concessions. Indeed, a special committee of the Yukon Council was appointed on September 6, 1905, to fashion a draft law governing mining in the Territory with a view to having it passed as an act of Parliament the following year.[42] Consequently, while the Yukon was still in the throes of a vital transition from the crude hand methods of placer mining to hydraulic operations and the more expensive forms of mining production, Parliament passed the Placer Mining Act of 1906. That this Act and the Yukon Quartz Mining Act of 1924 have functioned so successfully may be in large measure due to the fact that the federal authorities wisely fashioned their provisions upon the views of the mining interests and employees assembled in meetings all over the Territory.[43]

Although the history of transportation and communication appears elsewhere in this study,[44] it should at least be recorded here that the federal government through its various departments has played a major role in the evolution from dog-team and canoe to highway, steamboat, railroad, and aircraft transport—a factor of the utmost importance in the development of a mining country. From the earliest years, Ottawa has voted annual grants (often in excess of $100,000) to the Yukon Council for the construction or repair and maintenance of mining roads in the Territory, while its yearly appropriations on behalf of postal and telegraph services frequently exceeded $150,000 and $275,000, respectively. The federal government's telegraph system, inaugurated in 1899, connects the major Yukon centres with British Columbia, while the North West Territories and Yukon radio system links Dawson and Whitehorse with Edmonton. The government provides air-mail services daily except Sunday between Whitehorse and Vancouver or Edmonton, while the Canadian Pacific's commercial air service has brought the Yukon within a few hours' flying time of these terminals which connect with Trans-Canada Air Lines.

[40]Department of Mines and Resources, *The Yukon Territory*, 1944, p. 5.

[41]*Statutes of Canada*, 61 Vict. (1898), vol. I, p. xxxix.

[42]J. Castell Hopkins, *The Canadian Annual Review of Public Affairs*, 1905, pp. 396-8.

[43]*Debates, House of Commons*, 1941-2, vol. IV, pp. 3395-6, George Black, Yukon M.P., giving a survey of mining laws. See Department of Mines and Resources, *The Yukon Territory*, 1944, pp. 29-32, for a synopsis of the placer and quartz mining laws and regulations.

[44]See Part VII.

Finally, reference must be made to the Alaska Highway. Its construction as a strategic military road during 1942-3 is remarkable both for the engineering skill and dispatch of the Americans and the vision, mutual confidence, and co-operative enterprise of the governments of Canada and the United States.

In view of the fact that the Yukon is a big-game country and the fur trade an important industry, the hunter and trapper (other than native-born Indians and Eskimos) carry on their operations under licence and regulation of the Yukon Game Ordinance, while exporters of furs from the Territory must pay an export tax. In the interests of the native population and the preservation of game, the Territorial government has established the Peel River Native Game Preserve (1923) and the Kluane Game Sanctuary (1943).[45]

The fine reputation of the Yukon as a law-abiding community, unequalled by any other mining region in the world, has resulted from the nature of the judicial administration and the admirable enforcement of law and order by the Royal Canadian Mounted Police. From the establishment of the Yukon as a separate territory in 1898 provision has always existed for the continued application of the laws relating to civil and criminal matters and the ordinances in force in the old North West Territories until repealed or altered; and of every act of the Parliament of Canada except as otherwise provided in any such act. Moreover, the year 1898 saw the establishment of a Territorial Court of three judges (reduced to one in 1912) possessing high qualifications and barred from holding any other office except that of membership in the then appointed Territorial Council. The Yukon Act also laid down court procedure and provided for jails and places of confinement in close conformity with the system in the North West Territories. As early as 1899 the Supreme Court of British Columbia was constituted the Court of Appeal for the Yukon, while in 1902 an amendment was passed permitting appeals to the Supreme Court of Canada in mining cases and controversies amounting to $2,000 or over.[46]

While the Governor-in-Council may appoint police magistrates for Dawson and Whitehorse, the Yukon Commissioner, each member of the local Council, each judge and every commissioned officer of the R.C.M.P. have *ex officio* all the powers of a Justice of the Peace when in the Territory. In the administration of criminal law, provision exists for summary trial by a judge without the intervention of a jury in offences of theft, wounding, indecent assault, escaping from lawful custody, and assaulting or resisting a public officer. In any case of trial with jury six jurors only are required. A person convicted of

[45]Department of Mines and Resources, *The Yukon Territory*, 1944, pp. 33-4; *Statutes of Canada*, 4 Geo. VI, c. 45 (1940). Lands in the Territory are disposed of by sale, lease, or homestead entry under regulations approved by order-in-council. See the Northland reports on settlement by Professors Griffith Taylor and C. A. Dawson in Parts II, III, and XI.

[46]*Statutes of Canada*, 61 Vict., c. 6, ss. 10-21 (1898); *ibid.*, 62-3 Vict., c. 11 (1899); *ibid.*, 2 Edw. VII, c. 35 (1902); *ibid.*, 2 Geo. V, c. 56 (1912).

capital offence is safeguarded against the execution of the death sentence by the judge or stipendiary magistrate trying the case, through a provision which requires the latter to forward full notes of the evidence to the Secretary of State and to await the pleasure of the Governor-General. At the present time a stipendiary magistrate presides over the Territorial Court with powers to exercise all the authority and function of a Judge of the Court.[47]

Ever since the opening of the Yukon the enforcement of law and order has been the responsibility of the Royal Canadian Mounted Police. Although the force stationed in the Yukon Territory at the beginning of the century totalled 227 men, scattered in small detachments along the mining creeks, perhaps a quarter of that number has sufficed since 1914. While the Mounted Police have been the subject of much praise for the manner in which they have rendered life and property as safe as in the most law-abiding communities in the nation, they have also assisted other federal departments of government in the collection of royalties, customs and excise, the recording of census, and the enforcement of health regulations, etc.[48]

As numerous federal departments share in the administration of the Yukon and frequent changes have taken place in keeping records, it is impossible to give an overall picture of administrative revenues and expenditures for the Yukon during its fifty years of development. The following incomplete statements and tables may, however, offer a fair estimate.

TABLE I

APPROPRIATIONS FOR GOVERNMENT OF THE YUKON TERRITORY

Financial Year Ending March 31	Salaries and Expenses of Administration	Grant to Yukon Council for Local Purposes	Special Grant for Roads, etc.
1910	$170,750	....	$ 37,500
1916	128,000	$125,000	100,000
1918	320,000	120,000	
1920	215,000	170,000	
1923	160,000	65,000	
1929	60,080	45,000	70,000
1934	45,000	70,000	
1935	42,000	60,000	
1936	42,000	60,000	
1937	42,000	70,000	65,000
1938	50,000	70,000	63,000
1944	44,000	60,000	

While Table I concerns appropriations for Yukon purposes by the Department of the Interior to 1936 and subsequently by the reorganized De-

[47]*Ibid.*, 1 Edw. VII, c. 41 (1901); *ibid.*, 3-4 Geo. V, c. 13 (1913); *ibid.*, 4-5 Geo. VI, c. 30 (1940-1); *Revised Statutes of Canada*, 1927, c. 215, ss. 78, 81-3, 105, and 121.

[48]*Debates, House of Commons*, 1900, col. 592; *ibid.*, 1912-13, vol. IV, cols. 6474-9; *ibid.*, 1941-2, vol. IV, p. 3399.

partment of Mines and Resources, Parliament passed other votes of supply on behalf of transportation, defence, police, postal services, health, justice, survey work, etc. Table II covers revenues and expenditures of all federal government departments in the Yukon for recent years and, in addition, shows the amount of revenues raised by the Territorial Council for local purposes.

TABLE II

Financial Year Ending March 31	Total Expenditures by Federal Government	Total Revenues by Federal Government	Yukon Council Local Revenue
1937	$576,458	$240,365	$127,795
1938	585,320	292,373	143,714
1939	573,127	351,410	154,134
1940	478,310	349,252	153,485
1941	466,422	494,236	182,034
1943			165,812

Addressing the House of Commons in March, 1937, the Yukon member estimated that the Territory had produced since 1898 at least $225 million in gold, silver, and lead production and customs duties on goods imported for consumption. Against this value to Canada the speaker placed expenditures of $11,489,883 by the Department of the Interior and an additional $20,895,649 by other federal departments, during the years 1898 to 1936. While she felt that the sum of $225 million was somewhat more than a fair return on a national expenditure of $32,385,532, it should be observed that perhaps not more than 5 per cent of the $208 million of mineral production would actually accrue to the federal treasury in royalties.[49]

Apart from the opening decade in the Yukon's history, the Territory has been singularly free from charges of maladministration. It was perhaps only natural in the very early days of a mining community far removed from the older established settlements to find levelled against the Yukon administration, or certain of its officials, charges of granting mining rights to political favourites, intervention in local elections and defalcation of accounts, as well as the

[49]The above tables and statistics are drawn from the annual Appropriation Acts in *Statutes of Canada*, 18-19 Geo. V, c. 54; *ibid.*, 23-4 Geo. V, c. 55; *ibid.*, 24-5 Geo. V, c. 23; *ibid.*, 25-6 Geo. V, c. 49; *ibid.*, 1 Edw. VIII, c. 50; *ibid.*, 1 Geo. VI, c. 45; *ibid.*, 2 Geo. VI, c. 54; *ibid.*, 7-8 Geo. VI, c. 33; *Debates, House of Commons*, 1909, vol. IV, pp. 6272-3; *ibid.*, 1915, vol. II, pp. 1580-4; *ibid.*, 1917, vol. II, pp. 1736-7; *ibid.*, First Session, 1919, vol. V, pp. 4045-6; *ibid.*, 1922, vol. II, p. 1034; *ibid.*, 1936, vol. III, p. 2782 and vol. IV, p. 3252; *ibid.*, 1937, vol. II, p. 1440; *ibid.*, 1941-2, vol. IV, p. 3397; *ibid.*, 1937, vol. II, pp. 1725-6, Mrs. Martha Black, Member for the Yukon; *Report of the Department of Mines and Resources*, 1938, p. 73; *ibid.*, 1939, p. 82; *ibid.*, 1940, p. 71; *ibid.*, 1941, p. 72; *ibid.*, 1943, p. 72. During the four years up to 1900—the heyday of Yukon mining operations—revenues totalled $4,376,673 and expenditures $3,679,290, Morang's *Annual Register of Canadian Affairs*, 1901, p. 212.

more common complaints respecting defects in the mining laws, inadequate roads, mail service and recording officials, and the enforcement of laws concerning morality, the sale of liquor, dance halls, and Sunday observance.[50] On numerous occasions during more recent years the Member of Parliament for the Yukon has paid high tribute to the officials and staff of the Department of Mines and Resources for the honest, economical, and businesslike administration of the Territory, whether under a Liberal or a Conservative government.[51]

Government of the North West Territories: 1905-44

The new Provinces of Alberta and Saskatchewan were established in 1905 and a Northwest Territories Amendment Act was passed delimiting the remaining Territories and providing for their administration. This Act provided for the appointment by the Governor-in-Council of a chief executive officer, styled the Commissioner of the North West Territories, and a Council of not more than four members to assist him in the administration. While an amendment passed in 1921 made provision for a Council of six—to safeguard the requirement of a quorum—and the appointment of a Deputy Commissioner to exercise the functions of the Commissioner during his absence, the Northwest Territories Act of 1905 and the revised statute of the following year defined the specific powers of the Commissioner-in-Council largely as they exist today.

Although the Commissioner-in-Council received the same powers to make ordinances as were on August 31, 1905, vested in the Legislative Assembly of the old North West Territories, these specifically included the following classes of subjects as are from time to time designated by the Governor-in-Council or in instructions from the Minister of Mines and Resources: direct taxation within the Territories to raise revenue for territorial or local purposes, establishment and tenure of territorial offices, appointment and payment of officers, establishment and maintenance of prisons, municipal institutions, road allowances and new highways, local licences for shops, taverns, auctioneers, etc., incorporation of companies with territorial objectives excepting railway, steamboat, canal, telegraph, and irrigation companies, solemnization of marriage, property and civil rights, administration of justice, expenditure of territorial funds and certain moneys appropriated by Parliament for the Territories, and generally all matters of a local or private nature in the

[50]J. Castell Hopkins, *The Canadian Annual Review of Public Affairs*, 1903, pp. 233-9; *ibid.*, 1904, pp. 171 and 352; *ibid.*, 1905, pp. 397-400; *ibid.*, 1907, p. 615; *Debates, House of Commons*, 1900, col. 6359; *ibid.*, 1926, vol. II, pp. 1390-3.

[51]*Debates, House of Commons*, 1938, vol. III, p. 3083; *ibid.*, 1941-2, vol. IV, p. 3399. From 1921 to the present Mr. George Black has represented the Territory in Parliament, except 1935-40 when his wife was Member for the Yukon. Mr. Black also served several terms as a member of the Yukon Council after which he was appointed Commissioner in 1912.

Territories.[52] Copies of all ordinances, of course, must be laid before Parliament, where they are subject to disallowance at any time within two years by the Governor-in-Council.

Although the pattern of Territorial government outlined above was laid down by federal enactment as early as 1905, the North West Territories were practically administered by the Royal North West Mounted Police for many years under Lieutenant-Colonel Fred White as first Commissioner. Not until 1921, when certain oil developments brought the Territories into prominence, was the first North-West Council of four members appointed to assist the Commissioner. A branch of the Department of the Interior was organized at the same time to carry out the active work of administration.[53] In June, 1921, the Council was increased to six members of which one was designated as Deputy Commissioner.

In view of the fact that the population of the North West Territories according to the 1941 census totalled only 12,028 (including 2,284 whites, 4,334 Indians, 5,404 Eskimos, and six others), scattered over a total area of 1,309,682 square miles, it is not surprising that there has been very little demand for territorial representation in the House of Commons.[54] Consequently the North West Territories Council, comprising the Commissioner, Deputy Commissioner, and five other officials of closely related federal departments, functions as the legislative body in Ottawa and serves also in an advisory capacity to the Minister of Mines and Resources on matters pertaining to the administration of the Territories.[55]

[52]*Statutes of Canada*, 4-5 Edw. VII, c. 27 (1905); *ibid.*, 11-12 Geo. V, c. 40 (1921); *Revised Statutes of Canada*, 1906, c. 62, s. 8; *ibid.*, 1927, c. 142.

[53]Department of the Interior, *The North West Territories*, 1930, p. 25; *Debates, House of Commons*, 1917, vol. II, p. 1736. Mr. W. W. Cory, Deputy Minister of the Department of the Interior, succeeded Lieutenant-Colonel White as Commissioner in 1920. Assisting Mr. Cory as members of the Council were Messrs. Gibson, Greenway, Camsell, and Colonel Perry, *Debates, House of Commons*, 1921, vol. V, p. 4113.

[54]Department of Mines and Resources, *The Northwest Territories*, 1944, p. 3; interview of Deputy-Commissioner of the North West Territories, R. A. Gibson, November, 1944. Mr. D. F. Kellner, M.P. for Edmonton East, presented a petition to the House of Commons signed by a number of residents in the Territories in 1923, asking for parliamentary representation, *Debates, House of Commons*, 1924, vol. III, p. 2994.

[55]In 1930, for example, the legislative body consisted of the Commissioner, W. W. Cory, Deputy Minister of the then Department of the Interior; Deputy Commissioner R. A. Gibson, Assistant Deputy Minister of the Department of the Interior; Dr. Charles Camsell, Deputy Minister, Department of Mines; O. S. Finnie, Director, North West Territories and Yukon Branch, Department of the Interior; H. H. Rowatt, Dominion Lands Board, Department of the Interior; Dr. D. C. Scott, Deputy Superintendent General, Department of Indian Affairs; Colonel C. Starnes, Commissioner of the R.C.M.P.; and D. L. McKeand, Secretary. In 1944 the Council was composed as follows: Commissioner Dr. Charles Camsell; Deputy Commissioner, R. A. Gibson; members of Council—A. L. Cumming, K. R. Daly, H. L. Keenleyside, H. W. McGill, S. T. Wood, and the Secretary, D. L. McKeand. *Debates, House of Commons*, 1930, vol. I, p. 742; Department of Mines and Resources, *The Northwest Territories*, 1944, p. 5.

As the first North West Territories Council was not appointed until 1921, it is but natural that a survey of its legislative functions should reveal only a few significant ordinances enacted during the succeeding decade by the Commissioner with the advice and consent of the Council. Apart from legislation respecting the administration of justice, these early ordinances deal with mortgages and sale of personal property, the conduct of billiard rooms (in which no person under eighteen years and no Treaty Indian shall be employed, play, or loiter), the care and control of dogs, the export of furs from the Territories, and the registration of births, marriages, and deaths.[56]

Of special interest is an ordinance of 1926 requiring scientists and explorers to obtain a licence from the Commissioner to enter the Territories for the purposes of practising their professions and to present the North West Territories and Yukon Branch with a statement of all scientific information secured, localities visited, routes followed, and specimens taken. Eskimo ruins are protected under an ordinance of 1930 restricting and regulating excavations and the collection of specimens of archaeological or ethnological importance to those persons receiving special permission.

The ordinances of more recent years deal with a wide range of social and economic matters pertaining to a pioneer country and reflect the diligent care with which the Territorial Council carries on its legislative function. A medical profession ordinance (1936) provides for the licensing of duly qualified medical practitioners, while another respecting chemists and druggists guarantees competency and precaution in the interests of the public (1938). A third provides for the recovery of small debts, while a fourth secures liens on the minerals or estate of a mine owner as security for payment of the mine worker (1937). A licence ordinance for all businesses, trades, and occupations requires payment of a schedule of fees by physicians, dentists, and other professions, merchants, bankers, hotel, restaurant and rooming house keepers, freighters, contractors, blacksmiths, bakers, barbers, etc. (1938). Other ordinances regulate the sale of liquor with fitting protection of Indians and Eskimos, provide workmen's compensation, inspection of boiler and pressure plants, protection against the spread of venereal diseases, and deal with the conservation of game.[57]

The Sanitary Control Ordinance of August, 1941, deserves special mention because it applies to the scattered mining, timber, petroleum, and construction camps or employees' residences in the North West Territories.[58] This ordinance safeguards the health of the populace by governing the selection of camp sites with respect to sanitation, guarding against pollution of lakes and streams

[56]*Ordinances of the Northwest Territories,* 1905-30, *passim.* When applicable, the ordinances of the old North West Territories, found in *The General Ordinances of the North West Territories in Force September 1, 1905* (Regina, 1907), are in force in the present Territories unless repealed or amended by the Territorial Council.

[57]"Ordinances of Northwest Territories," 1930-43 (mimeographed).

[58]*Ibid.,* assented to, August 27, 1941.

and the contamination of food, regulating camp drainage and living conditions in bunk and cook houses, and by making employers responsible for first-aid and emergency hospital equipment according to the size of the camp. In camps of fifteen to fifty employees, for example, the employer is required to provide for the necessary medical and surgical care of his employees and to pay the expenses incurred up to ninety days, while in camps of over fifty men he "shall contract with a legally qualified practitioner for medical aid" to his employees.

The North West Territories Council, which has held since 1939 as many as eighteen regular and numerous special sessions in a single year, also acts in an advisory capacity to the Minister of Mines and Resources on such matters of administration as the improvement of the Mackenzie River-Great Bear Lake transportation route, the provision of aircraft landing facilities, the protection of workers engaged in the mining and milling of pitchblende, the regulation of the sale of liquor, the amendment of the North-West Game Act and Regulations, the carrying out of the reindeer project, the amendment of the Northwest Territories Act, the consideration of applications for permits to carry on exploratory and scientific investigations, the regulation of mining activity especially in the Yellowknife mining district north of Great Slave Lake, the establishment of meteorological stations on Arctic islands, the provision of radio services, the formation of agricultural and nutritional surveys, the extension of educational, hospital, and medical services, the conduction of inspection tours into the Territories, the administration of law and order, and the organization of the all-important annual Eastern Arctic Patrol.[59]

The North West Territories are divided for purposes of organization and administration into three districts: Mackenzie, Keewatin, and Franklin. Mackenzie District, the portion enjoying the greatest development to date, includes that part of the Canadian mainland lying between the Yukon Territory and the 102nd meridian of longitude. Keewatin District embraces that part of the mainland, with the exception of Boothia and Melville Peninsulas, lying between Mackenzie District and Hudson Bay, together with all islands in Hudson and James Bays. Franklin District includes Boothia and Melville Peninsulas and the islands in Hudson Strait and in the Arctic Archipelago, except those adjacent to the coast of the Yukon Territory.

The Director of the Lands, Parks, and Forests Branch of the Department of Mines and Resources, who serves also as Deputy Commissioner of the North West Territories, is responsible for the administration of the various acts, ordinances, and regulations pertaining to this vast Northland. To facilitate departmental administration there is a Superintendent for the Mackenzie

[59]*Annual Report of the Department of the Interior*, 1936, p. 31; *Report of the Department of Mines and Resources*, 1939, p. 70; *ibid.*, 1941, p. 64; *ibid.*, 1943, pp. 62-3.

District and one for the Eastern Arctic. In addition, a number of outside departmental agents serve in various capacities. For example, the agent of the Mackenzie District public administrator acts also as agent of Dominion lands, superintendent of Wood Buffalo National Park, crown timber agent, mining recorder, stipendiary magistrate, and marriage commissioner. His office is at Fort Smith, where the sheriff of the Territories is likewise stationed. A medical officer at Aklavik serves as department agent for the Lower Mackenzie and Western Arctic, while the main mining recorder, stationed at Yellowknife, acts as agent of Dominion lands and crown timber for the Yellowknife mining district. Moreover, a member of the Royal Canadian Mounted Police at Port Radium serves as sub-mining recorder. Sub-mining recorders have also been appointed at Fort Simpson, Norman, Coppermine, Aklavik and Edmonton, while government medical officers at eight or more scattered points in the Territories often assume varied administrative duties.[60]

Perhaps the most important field of Territorial administration is that of enforcing law and order in accord with the common law of England and the acts of the Canadian Parliament, in so far as they are applicable to the North West Territories and have not been repealed or amended, and the local ordinances of the Territorial Council. The Northwest Territories Act of 1905 and its amendments provide a relatively simplified judicial machinery in keeping with the small and scattered population. Five stipendiary magistrates, appointed by the Governor-in-Council, exercise the same powers and functions as a judge of the former Supreme Court of the North West Territories (disestablished in 1905), while the superior courts of the provinces adjoining the Territories exercise in civil matters the same jurisdiction respecting persons, property, suits, and proceedings in the Territories as they possess within their own territorial limits.[61] The stipendiary magistrates try in a summary manner such charges as minor theft, unlawful wounding and certain types of assault, and other charges with the intervention of a jury unless the accused elects otherwise.

The Governor-in-Council may also appoint Justices of the Peace having in large measure the jurisdiction and powers of a magistrate. As there are no permanent courts in the North West Territories, all commissioned officers of the Royal Canadian Mounted Police at strategic points serve as Justices of the Peace. Detachments of the Police at the more important settlements and at remote and widely scattered posts in the Eastern Arctic enforce law and order as well as carry out other local administrative duties by means of winter

[60]Department of Mines and Resources, *The Northwest Territories*, 1944, p. 5; *Report of the Department of Mines and Resources*, 1939, p. 70; *ibid.*, 1943, p. 63. The Director of the Lands, Parks, and Forests Branch is Mr. R. A. Gibson.

[61]*Statutes of Canada*, 4-5 Edw. VII, c. 27, ss. 8-9 (1905); *ibid.*, 7-8 Edw. VII, c. 49, s. 2 (1908); *ibid.*, 4 Geo. VI, c. 36, s. 1 (1940).

3

and summer patrols which keep them in close touch with the native and white population throughout the vast area.[62]

The two major fields of industry falling within the administrative jurisdiction of the Territorial authorities are the fur trade and mining, the latter surpassing the former in production value only as late as 1939. While the Hudson's Bay Company controls most of the trade along the Mackenzie and other northern Canadian waterways, a number of independent traders operate also. In addition, the native population follows trapping as its chief occupation.

A number of native game preserves have been established in the North West Territories to assist in maintaining the basic industry of the native population. Trapping within these preserves is confined to Indians, Eskimos, and half-breeds living the life of natives, in addition to such white trappers as were operating in the areas prior to their reservation. Beavers, muskrats, musk-oxen and buffalo, as well as other game species are protected in the Thelon and Twin Islands Game Sanctuaries and the Wood Buffalo Park. Natives and half-breeds born in the Territories do not require licences, while only British subjects who held licences on May 3, 1938, and the children of fourteen years of age whose British parents have resided there for the past four years may receive licences to hunt and trap. Although there is no tax on furs used in the Territories, an amendment to the Northwest Territories Act, which came into effect on January 1, 1929, levies an export tax upon "furs to be shipped or carried from the Territories to any other part of Canada or to any other country."[63]

The Geological Survey Division of the Bureau of Geology and Topography, Department of Mines and Resources, has aided greatly in the development of mining in the North West Territories, whose mineral production (exclusive of pitchblende products) to the end of 1945 is valued at more than $22 million. Moreover, officials of the Department of Mines, at Ottawa and in the Territories, have assumed steadily increasing administrative responsibilities with the opening of new districts to mineral production and mining settlement. The development of the production of oil at Fort Norman (since 1920), of pitchblende including radium and uranium at Labine Point on the east side of Great Bear Lake (since 1930), of gold and silver in the vicinity of Yellowknife on the north shore of Great Slave Lake (since 1935), and the investigation of other mineral deposits such as lead, nickel, zinc, copper, tungsten, and coal, has meant an increase in mining and other administrative

[62]Department of Mines and Resources, *An Outline of the Canadian Eastern Arctic*, 1944, p. 34; *Report of the Department of Mines and Resources*, 1943, p. 64; *Royal Canadian Mounted Police Quarterly* (April, 1945, p. 274).

[63]Department of Mines and Resources, *The Northwest Territories*, 1944, pp. 20-1; *Statutes of Canada*, 17 Geo. V, c. 64, ss. 1-2 (1927). During the year ending June 30, 1943, the North West Territories harvested furs valued at $3,165,107.

officials at these new communities. The recording of mining claims, the issuing of miner's licences, and the enforcement of regulations respecting quartz and placer mining comprise the essential duties of the outside administrative staff of the Department.[64]

The Department of Mines and Resources also administers the lands of the North West Territories under the Dominion Lands Act. Aside from mineral-bearing lands, practically the only lands disposed of are lots in the various settlements acquired for residential, missionary, fur trading, and transportation company purposes. Although no land is available for homestead purposes, surveyed lands may be purchased for agricultural purposes. In addition, temporary use of certain lands may be had under licence of occupation, while other vacant Crown Lands may be leased under the hay and grazing regulations. Moreover, educational, religious, and charitable institutions may cut fuel-wood under free permits, although timber regulations require other parties to pay annual dues.

The Department of Agriculture has also undertaken some soil and horticultural survey work in the Mackenzie District of the North West Territories. However, more extensive study will be necessary before an adequate report of the agricultural possibilities of the region may be expected.[65]

The general welfare, health, and education of the 12,000 Indians, Eskimos, and indigent white and half-breed population in the North West Territories are also included among the numerous and varied responsibilities of the Department of Mines and Resources, which maintains officials for these purposes in the principal settlements of the Mackenzie District and at isolated points in the Eastern Arctic.[66] All medical doctors in the Territories, except those employed by the mining and petroleum companies, are full-time employees of the Department of National Health and Welfare, but serve as medical health officers under the Public Health Ordinance, for the enforcement of the sanitation and health regulations in their districts of the North West Territories. The Canadian government has assisted in the construction of some of

[64]Department of Mines and Resources, *The Northwest Territories*, 1944, pp. 31-7; *Report of the Department of Mines and Resources*, 1939, pp. 78 ff. Copies of all mining regulations may be obtained from the Mining Recorders at Fort Smith and Yellowknife or from the Bureau of Northwest Territories and Yukon Affairs of the above Department, Ottawa.

[65]Department of Mines and Resources, *The Northwest Territories*, 1944, pp. 51 and 44. See studies on settlement by Professors Griffith Taylor and C. A. Dawson, in Parts ii, iii and xi. The Department of Agriculture carried out experimental work in horticulture at Yellowknife during 1945.

[66]As Dr. Andrew Moore and Dr. G. F. Wherrett have made detailed studies of education and health services in the North West Territories (Parts ix and viii), the present writer has concerned himself here with merely pointing out the administrative responsibilities of the federal government officials. It might be noted that on November 1, 1945, the administration of medical care and hospitalization of Indians, including Eskimos, was transferred to the Department of National Health and Welfare.

the nine mission hospitals operated by the Church of England and the Roman Catholic Church and pays the missions $2.50 per diem for each patient receiving treatment. The Department of National Health and Welfare furnishes medical supplies to mission hospitals, and also serves as a consulting agency in matters of public health, nutrition, and sanitation. Moreover, a qualified medical officer accompanies the annual Eastern Arctic patrol to examine the natives at all ports of call, while extensive patrols carry health provisions to outlying areas when conditions permit.[67]

The Department of Mines and Resources, through its Lands, Parks, and Forests Branch and its Indian Affairs Branch, makes grants in support of education for white, native, and half-breed children in the North West Territories. Apart from two public schools at Fort Smith and Yellowknife and the arrangement for secondary education through correspondence courses offered by the provincial authorities of Alberta and Ontario, the provision of education in the Territories rests with the Church of England and Roman Catholic missions, which operate day and residential schools at such centres as Aklavik, Fort Resolution, Fort Providence, Fort Smith, Fort Simpson, and Hay River. Owing to the nomadic tendencies of the Eskimo in the Eastern Arctic, the mission day schools in certain outlying areas function for comparatively short periods each year. While the school ordinances and regulations of the old North West Territories have never been amended since 1905 and are presumably legally applicable today, many of their provisions are not in active operation owing to the small population and the sparseness of settlement.[68]

In addition to the limited health and educational services, the Department of Mines and Resources administers a general welfare programme which includes the provision of supplies and equipment when game and fur-bearing animals are scarce, relief rations for the aged and incapacitated natives, the establishment of game preserves for the exclusive use of Indians and Eskimos, and the development of the reindeer industry near the Mackenzie River delta.

The reindeer industry was established in the above reserved area of the North West Territories in March, 1935, when a herd of 2,370 semi-domesticated reindeer was delivered from north-western Alaska, following the study by a Royal Commission of the possibilities of such an industry (1922) and investigations by Canadian authorities of suitable grazing areas.

[67]Department of Mines and Resources, *The Northwest Territories*, 1944, pp. 6-7; *Report of the Department of Mines and Resources*, 1939, p. 71. Payments to hospitals in 1939 totalled $23,042.50, representing 9,217 days' treatment. See Department of the Interior, *Canada's Eastern Arctic*, 1934, pp. 55-8, for a brief survey of missions, schools, hospitals, and relief of destitution in the vast Arctic region among four-fifths of Canada's Eskimos and a few hundred white residents.

[68]Department of Mines and Resources, *The Northwest Territories*, 1944, p. 7; *Report of the Department of Mines and Resources*, 1943, p. 64; *ibid.*, 1941, p. 65; *ibid.*, 1939, p. 71; *Debates, House of Commons*, 1906, vol. III, p. 5880; *ibid.*, 1929, vol. III, p. 3641.

The North West Territories administration maintains supervision over the annual round-up of the main herd (numbering 6,000 head in the summer of 1944) at corrals on the reserve, the slaughtering of surplus animals, the distribution of the meat to the mission hospitals and residential schools or for relief and other purposes, the development of small herds under native management, and the training of young Eskimo herders with a view to the industry ultimately becoming largely a native one.[69]

Another field of federal administration and service, one of paramount importance, embraces the exploratory and scientific investigations of the Survey Bureau of the Department of Mines and Resources carried on in co-operation with other departments of the Canadian government interested in the North West Territories. Commencing in 1884 and becoming more frequent after the First Great War, Canadian government expeditions into the Eastern Arctic have taken place annually since 1922. While the earlier expeditions were devoted largely to the extension of geographical knowledge and the establishment of Canada's claim to sovereignty over the Arctic islands adjoining her mainland, more recently they have comprised topographical, meteorological, geological, mineralogical, biological, botanical, parasitological, medical, social, and economic investigations which have added greatly to our knowledge of the far North.

While Major L. T. Burwash, for example, has conducted important expeditions into the North during the years 1925-6, 1928-9, and 1930 under the general instructions of Mr. O. S. Finnie, then Director of the North West Territories and Yukon Branch of the Department of the Interior, and while Drs. Charles Camsell and H. W. McGill and Messrs. R. A. Gibson and A. L. Cumming, officials of the North West Territories Administration, have made inspection trips into various settlements and mining regions of the Territories (for example, in 1936 and 1939), the Canadian government relies mainly upon its numerous field forces and its annual Eastern Arctic Patrol to carry on the important work of scientific research in the many and varied fields.

Each summer the R.M.S. *Nascopie*, a vessel specially constructed for service in the Arctic and operated by the Hudson's Bay Company, sails from Montreal or some Canadian Atlantic port on its mission of inspection, investigation, and administration. Used by the Canadian government for its annual Eastern Arctic Patrol of Royal Canadian Mounted Police posts, post offices, radio and meteorological stations, trading posts, medical centres, and missions, it transports government officials, administrative officers, scientists, doctors, police, other personnel, mail, and supplies to northern Quebec, our Arctic mainland, and the islands in Hudson Strait and Bay and in the Arctic Archipelago. In addition to carrying out the scientific investigations mentioned

[69]Department of Mines and Resources, *The Northwest Territories*, 1944, pp. 22-3; *Debates, House of Commons*, 1938, vol. III, p. 3075.

above, the Patrol enables the appropriate officials to study and improve matters of administration affecting living conditions of the native population as regards health, hospitalization, education, food, clothing, fuel, and means of livelihood.[70]

Other subjects of administration in the North West Territories include the construction and improvement of various means of transportation and communication. While a discussion of these highly important public services is outside the scope of this particular study, it seems appropriate to observe that the provision of truck and winter tractor roads, airports, landing fields, seaplane bases, passenger, mail and express services, air transport, and radio communications at the various pioneer settlements and between strategic points in the Canadian Northland, are the responsibilities of the federal Departments of Mines and Resources, Transport, Post Office, and National Defence working in close co-operation.[71]

This survey of government and administration would not be complete without some reference to the first local self-governing municipal body established in the North West Territories since it was reorganized in 1905. Under authority of the local Administrative District Ordinance, the Commissioner-in-Council of the North West Territories on October 1, 1939, established the Yellowknife Administrative District on the north arm of Great Slave Lake embracing an area of slightly more than thirty-eight square miles. The local Trustee Board, which commenced to function in this busy mining community on January 1, 1940, consists of seven members—three of whom are elected by the citizens and four, including the chairman, appointed by the Commissioner. In addition, there is an elected school board of three members in charge of the local school district which employs a teacher to carry on the educational programme in accord with the Alberta curriculum. The Trustee Board of the Yellowknife Administrative District may pass by-laws governing the raising of local revenues by taxation on real and personal property and by poll-tax, the prevention of cruelty to animals, relief of the poor, the appointment of health officers and the protection of public

[70]Department of Mines and Resources, *The Northwest Territories*, 1944, p. 9, and *An Outline of the Canadian Eastern Arctic*, 1944, p. 34; *Report of the Department of Mines and Resources*, 1939, p. 70; *ibid.*, 1943, p. 70; *Debates, House of Commons*, 1941-2, vol. IV, p. 3399; Department of the Interior, *Canada's Western Arctic*, 1931, pp. 11 and 53, and *Canada's Eastern Arctic*, 1934, pp. 39-41; *Royal Canadian Mounted Police Quarterly* (April, 1945, p. 273-4). Two remarkable voyages were recently made by the R.C.M.P. patrol vessel *St. Roch* while carrying out its duties in Arctic waters; during 1940-2 it traversed the legendary North-West Passage from west to east, and in 1944 completed the historic east-to-west passage in a single season.

[71]*Report of the Department of Mines and Resources*, 1939, pp. 71-2, 80-1; *ibid.*, 1943, pp. 71-3; *Debates, House of Commons*, 1938, vol. III, p. 2884. See H. W. Hewetson's study on transportation in the North West Territories, Part VII; also the concluding section of this paper.

health, the appointment of local officials including a secretary-treasurer, the construction and maintenance of roads, streets, sidewalks, sewers, etc., the regulation of traffic, the establishment of a fire department, the support of schools, and other purely local affairs. Moreover, the local Trustee Board levies and collects the licence fees required by the Ordinance governing businesses, callings, trades, and occupations which provide an important part of the general fund of the District.[72]

Although no reliable statistical summaries of the cost of government and administration of the North West Territories are available for the forty-year period since their reorganization in 1905, a sampling of the major items of expenditure during a typical year or two may serve to illustrate the relative significance of some of the problems confronting the federal authorities. Salaries and expenses connected with the general administration of the Territories, including the erection and maintenance of buildings, Eskimo affairs, the reindeer industry, schools, hospitals, roads, investigation and development of natural resources, relief of the destitute, the administration of the Northwest Game Act, Wood Buffalo Park, game preserves and sanctuaries, etc., range from $430,000 for the fiscal year ending March 31, 1929, to $266,655 for the year 1941-2. Occasionally the vote for Arctic exploration and administration alone amounts to $190,000, while the cost of maintenance and operation of the radio services of the Territories totals from $199,425, to $318,900 in a single year. In 1930 and again in 1931 the government voted $100,000 for the purchase, herding, and maintenance of the reindeer herd in the North West Territories. The annual Eastern Arctic patrol of the *Nascopie* usually costs from $23,000 to $27,000. In addition to these items, a very considerable portion of the annual votes by Parliament for Indian affairs, Royal Canadian Mounted Police, postal services, and topographical and geological surveys is expended in the North West Territories.[73]

The virtual impossibility of making an equitable division of many of the federal departmental expenditures between the Territories and the remainder of Canada renders any discussion of administrative expenditures wholly inadequate. The general expenditures of the Department of Mines and Resources alone for administrative purposes in the North West Territories and summaries of its revenues for recent fiscal years, however, are given in the following table:

[72]*Report of the Department of Mines and Resources*, 1943, pp. 69-70; see "Ordinances of the Northwest Territories," 1939 and 1940 (mimeographed), for the provisions of the Local Administrative District Ordinance. This Ordinance was amended in June, 1945 to provide for the increase in membership of the Trustee Board from five to seven.

[73]*Debates, House of Commons*, 1931, vol. III, p. 3358; *ibid.*, 1932, vol. II, pp. 1724-5; *ibid.*, 1936, vol. IV, p. 3231; *ibid.*, 1937, vol. III, p. 2884; *ibid.*, 1939, vol. IV, p. 4644; *ibid.*, 1941-2, vol. IV, p. 3399; *ibid.*, 1928, vol. III, p. 3637. See also items in the annual Appropriation Acts, published in the *Statutes of Canada* for various years.

Year	Expenditure	Revenue
1937-38	$267,557.47	$110,744.15
1938-39	283,776.11	197,992.28
1939-40	292,028.88	150,479.40
1940-41	293,935.19	150,095.74

In addition, there was in 1940-1 a special expenditure of $26,501.64, and a credit balance of $37,570.82 from liquor profits and fines.[74]

THE WAR AND POST-WAR DEVELOPMENT OF THE CANADIAN NORTHLAND

The World War of 1939-45 has been largely responsible for bringing the polar regions of Canada into world prominence. Urgent military necessity has marshalled the required pioneering spirit, engineering skill, and financial resources to complete such enormous undertakings as the Northwest Staging Route of airports, the Alaska Military Highway, the Canol pipeline, the Catel telephone system, and numerous other Arctic airway projects, all of which place Canada in a commanding position with respect to a large volume of the future air commerce over the short transpolar routes between our own continent and the principal centres of Europe and Asia. Of special importance in developing aerial transportation facilities with Alaska, the Soviet Union, and Britain was the construction of large landing fields in the Mackenzie District at Fort Smith, Fort Resolution, Hay River, Yellowknife, Fort Providence, Fort Simpson, Wrigley, and Norman Wells, and under joint defence auspices along the Northeast Staging Route on Southampton and Baffin Islands and in Labrador, Newfoundland, and southern Greenland.

The historic Alaska Highway, which follows the Northwest Staging Route from Dawson Creek, British Columbia, to the western boundary of Yukon Territory and on to Fairbanks, Alaska, was constructed in 1942-3 following an exchange of notes between the governments of Canada and the United States. Under the terms of agreement, the United States assumed the cost of construction and maintenance until the termination of the war and for six months thereafter unless Canada preferred to assume its maintenance at an earlier date, while the Canadian government provided rights of way, timber and gravel free of charge, waived import duties, sales taxes and licence fees, and facilitated the free admission of labour and supplies from the United States. At the close of the war the 1,259 miles of the road running through Canadian territory will become an integral part of the Canadian highway

[74]*Report of the Department of Mines and Resources*, 1938, 1939, 1940, and 1941, at pp. 8-10. Mr. R. A. Gibson, Director of the Lands, Parks, and Forests Branch of the Department of Mines and Resources informed the writer that it is almost impossible to compile reliable statistical information on revenues and expenditures in the Territories because of the destruction of many old records and the changes made in the way these records were kept from time to time.

system with safeguards against the imposition of any discriminatory conditions respecting the use of the road as between Canadian and United States civilian traffic.

Likewise, under an exchange of notes between the two governments in 1942-3, the United States assumed the costs of the Canol project as a joint defence measure, while Canada undertook to facilitate its construction by measures respecting rights of way, duties, personnel, etc., similar to those mentioned above. The project involved: (1) a drilling programme in the vicinity of Norman Wells, North West Territories, designed to increase oil production for the use of the armed forces in Canada and Alaska and along the Alaska Highway; (2) the construction of a pipeline with a capacity of 3,000 barrels daily from Norman Wells to Whitehorse, Yukon Territory; (3) the erection of an oil refinery at Whitehorse; and (4) the erection of oil storage facilities at Prince Rupert and the construction of a gasoline pipeline for immediate fuel purposes from Skagway, Alaska, to Whitehorse. While the title of the right of way remains with Canada, the United States retains ownership of the pipeline and refineries until the close of the war when they will be offered for sale, with the Canadian government having prior right of purchase. Failing a satisfactory sale, their disposition will be referred to the Permanent Joint Board of Defence.[75]

The post-war future of these defence undertakings is among the major decisions of policy confronting the Canadian government. Also of vital significance to the future development of our Northland will be the extent to which the federal authorities are prepared to provide greatly increased financial appropriations, scientific investigations, permanent Arctic research centres, and highly skilled personnel for the purpose of studying Territorial problems of agriculture, mineralogy, transportation, settlement, social services, wild life, etc., of drafting policies calculated to meet these peculiar problems, and, finally, of supervising their implementation in the best interests of both our northern citizens and the nation as a whole. While the Department of Mines and Resources, in co-operation with the other federal departments, has undoubtedly accomplished a great deal in the Territories with the limited funds at its disposal, its leading officials, who are cognizant of the challenge confronting them, would be the first to admit that financial stringency is the principal reason for the delays of the past ten or fifteen years in instituting more progressive and far-reaching administrative programmes in the Northland.

With a view to the early launching of such programmes, survey parties of the Department of Mines and Resources have recently been studying wild life, soil, forests, horticulture, geology, botany, oil resources, health, education, etc., in various sections of the Yukon and North West Territories. Moreover,

[75]*Ibid.*, 1943, pp. 67, 72-3; Department of Mines and Resources, *The Northwest Territories*, 1944, pp. 8-9 and 35-6; *Debates, House of Commons*, May 5, 1944, pp. 2721-5.

administrative acumen respecting the requirements of native life in the northern environment is being displayed in the development of the reindeer industry, which has as its objective the provision of a convenient and dependable source of food, clothing, and transport for the Eskimo population. "As the natives learn to depend more and more on the herds of reindeer for subsistence they will become independent of fluctuations in the supply of game and the price of furs, and thus achieve a more stable economic life than is possible under ordinary conditions which govern their nomadic life along the Arctic Coast of Canada."[76]

The immediate post-war period will doubtless witness some significant changes in the mode of government and administration of our northern territories. Three or four courses are within the realm of possibility. (1) The Western Provinces might be extended northward to embrace neighbouring territory. (2) A new northern province might be formed to include Yukon Territory and Mackenzie District. (3) Mackenzie District might be united with Yukon Territory in order that the former may enjoy parliamentary representation at Ottawa. (4) One overall Northland development department of the federal government might conceivably be formed.

On frequent occasions during the last forty years rumours of the pending annexation of the Yukon to British Columbia have spread across the country. Mr. R. G. Macpherson, member for Vancouver City, argued at length in the House of Commons as early as June 7, 1905, in favour of uniting the Yukon to his Province. Both, he reminded the House, had the same kind of resources and people and required similar laws. British Columbia had been carrying on mining for fifty years and had solved many of the problems still awaiting solution in the Yukon. The people of his province had faith in the Yukon and realized that increased prosperity of the Territory would enhance that of the coast cities.[77] On this occasion, the Yukon Member, Dr. A. Thompson, strongly protested against such annexation, which he termed "an ignominious end to our territorial career," while Sir Wilfrid Laurier stated that his government had "no intention of marrying the Yukon to British Columbia." The question of whether the Yukon should be joined to the Pacific Coast Province or given separate provincial status was one, he believed, that could safely be left for future consideration.[78]

The question of the Yukon's annexation to British Columbia arose again in 1914, 1920, 1924, and 1938. A mass meeting of Dawson citizens, on March 3, 1914, vigorously protested such a fate, while Prime Minister Meighen declared in the House of Commons on June 8, 1920, that the matter was not under immediate consideration. The recent simplification of government

[76]Department of Mines and Resources, *The Northwest Territories*, 1944, p. 23.
[77]*Debates, House of Commons*, 1905, vol. IV, cols. 7068-9.
[78]*Ibid.*, cols. 7061 and 7080.

machinery had greatly reduced the cost of Yukon administration, thereby removing one of the major reasons for the frequent revival of the question.[79]

While the press reported rumours to the effect that the federal government in 1924 was making overtures to the government of British Columbia with a view to the latter taking over the administration of the Yukon, the Honourable Charles Stewart (Minister of the Interior) had not heard of it.[80] By 1938, however, discussions with British Columbia respecting its extension into northern territory had reached such proportions as to cause the tabling of correspondence in the House of Commons on February 28 and March 10.[81]

During the same year reports were also current of an agitation in parts of northern Alberta and northern British Columbia in favour of the formation of a new province out of certain portions of these two Provinces and a part of the North West Territories. It was stated that petitions had been forwarded to the government and resolutions passed by various boards of trade advocating such a project.[82]

That interest in the northern extension of the Western Provinces has not subsided is evident from the desire of the Alberta government to have the matter placed on the agenda of the 1945 Dominion-Provincial Conference. Should the subject come under discussion at the Conference, it may be assumed that the governments of the other Western Provinces will likewise advocate extension into the North West Territories which have recently become more accessible.

Whatever new division of territory may be arranged for administrative purposes in the future, it would seem advisable that, as far as the Yukon is concerned, the rights, peculiar sentiments and attachments of its population should be respected. While the federal government doubtless possesses the power to determine the fate of the Yukon Territory as it sees fit, the people of the frontier community should be given a voice in the negotiations.

Although the United States Department of the Interior has recently declared itself in favour of statehood as the only form of self-government appropriate to the existing circumstances in Alaska, development in the Yukon has hardly reached the stage where provincial status seems immediately advisable. Improved communications and the post-war prospect of greatly increased mining activity in the Yukon Territory and Mackenzie District appear to justify an early expansion of the Yukon Council administration to embrace the latter District, which should thereafter enjoy both local and federal representation. As for the more eastern portion of the Canadian Arctic, the present North West Territories Council at Ottawa which maintains

[79]*Ibid.*, 1920, vol. IV, p. 3282.
[80]*Ibid.*, 1924, vol. II, pp. 1107-8.
[81]*Ibid.*, 1938, vol. III, pp. 3074 and 3081-3.
[82]*Ibid.*, pp. 3074-5.

an intimate liaison with all other federal departments of governments, will suffice to institute the necessary progressive administrative programmes. Each of these departments possesses an organization of scientific services which can be made readily available in the interests of the Territories.

Whatever modifications in local administrative machinery the immediate post-war future may bring to our northern territories, it appears desirable that Canada and the United States should co-operate as far as possible in working out their development programmes for the Canadian North-West and neighbouring Alaska as a natural corollary of the co-operative defence enterprises which the two nations carried out during the war. Indeed, the establishment of the North Pacific Planning Project, envisaged in the announcement of January 23, 1943, by the Joint Economic Committees of Canada and the United States, may be considered a first step in this direction. While the United States section of this international committee engaged in the study of economic conditions in Alaska, Yukon, northern British Columbia, northern Alberta, and the Mackenzie District, withdrew in June, 1944, the Canadian section continued its studies through the various government departments concerned with the administration and development of this portion of Canada. Many field and office investigations have already been carried out and departmental reports published.[83]

Moreover, Canada's close war-time co-operation with Russia and the geographical propinquity of the Canadian Northland with the Soviet Union across the Arctic, Alaska, and the North Pacific make it imperative that the two northern neighbours work out a post-war programme of close collaboration along scientific and commercial lines. The two peoples have many problems common to the future development of their respective Northlands which offer means for an increasing body of shared experiences and contacts through which mutual tolerance, understanding and goodwill may flourish not only in their own interests but also in the interests of the peace of the world. Indeed, the Canadian government would do well to sponsor an international conference with both the United States and the U.S.S.R. concerning their common Arctic affairs and thereby achieve a major step in the realization of Canada's avowed mission—which geography, history, tradition, and science have given her—of reconciling divergent interests and developing mutual respect and friendship among the United States, the Soviet Union, and the nations of the British Commonwealth.[84]

[83]Reference to the current work of the North Pacific Planning Project is based on a statement by R. K. Odell, Assistant Canadian Director of the said Project.

[84]*Debates, House of Commons*, 1944, p. 4747. According to a press despatch from Edmonton, Alberta, dated July 8, 1944, mentioned in the House of Commons on July 10, 1944, the then Vice-President Henry Wallace advocated, in an interview in that city, an international conference of Russia, the United States, and Canada to deal with Arctic affairs. Prime Minister Mackenzie King stated that "the suggestion deserves consideration."

Hence, the time appears ripe for the Canadian government to give high priority in its post-war development programme to our Northland, no longer an inaccessible ice-bound waste, but rather a vast, almost "untapped reservoir of the earth's riches, easily and comfortably habitable with the aid of modern engineering, transport, and communications,"[85] a strategic position at the aerial crossroads of the world, a doorway to the best possible relations with Russia, and a potent agent of international peace and goodwill.

[85]V. Stefansson, *The Arctic in Fact and Fable* (Foreign Policy Association, New York, 1945).

Part Two

GRIFFITH TAYLOR

A Mackenzie Domesday: 1944

INTRODUCTION

LET us start by comparing the Mackenzie Corridor with that great Canadian highway the St. Lawrence. In the sixteenth century the latter offered the obvious means of entry into the new land of Canada. The pioneers could not have realized the cluster of large towns and cities which was to arise along the great waterway; but most of them were sure that the St. Lawrence would always be the main surface route whereby the resources of eastern and east-central Canada would be reached and exploited. Hence all detailed accounts of the geography of this area in the early days are of special interest, since in general the route is still as important as ever.

It seems to the writer that we of the twentieth century can consider the Mackenzie Corridor in somewhat the same light as the pioneers did the St. Lawrence. There is not much in the way of settlement in the north-west region at present; perhaps the total, including Indians and Eskimo, is less than seven thousand settlers. But of one thing we may be sure, and that is that in the next century the population will increase largely, and that the chief centres of settlement and supply will be much where the pioneer folk built their dwellings.

One of the chief purposes of this study is to put on record in a somewhat uniform manner the main characteristics of all the famous posts along the Mackenzie River, and, in the following chapter, along the Yukon River, and this for two reasons. Canadians of today will welcome a detailed account of the way of life of the pioneers in geographical language; while the writer hopes that this somewhat hasty survey will be a sort of jumping-off place for similar surveys made, say, every fifty years in the future. Many of the posts are sited at the most strategic points, such as where the main tributaries join the Mackenzie. For instance, there is no doubt that the settlement at Fort Smith, at the head of navigation, has a situation which recalls that of Montreal; and hence there will be an important centre in this position as long as river navigation endures. So also Resolution, Hay River, Norman, and Arctic Red are almost certain to remain the centres of their respective portions of the Mackenzie Basin, since they also command the basins of the tributary rivers which enter the main stream at these points.

4

Some sites may be changed in view of later technical advances.   There is something to be said for Reindeer Reserve as a better site for collecting the resources of the Mackenzie Delta than Aklavik.   The new port of Tuktoyak-tuk (Port Brabant) illustrates some of the reasons for starting a new settle-ment in Arctic Canada.   The oil wells of Bosworth Creek (at Norman Wells) have introduced an entirely new factor into the town sites of the north, as will be discussed later; and the same may be said of the other mineral dis-coveries of the North-West.

In some small degree this preliminary survey resembles the Domesday Book compiled for most of England in 1086.   The two volumes of the latter, still preserved in the Public Record Office in London, are of chief interest to the student as giving us a picture of the kind of settlement which obtained in England at that date.   In the present survey the main features are the de-tailed plans of about thirty settlements in the Mackenzie and Yukon Basins, which the writer hopes will picture more accurately than has been attempted before the actual conditions in 1944.   If we had a similar study of the St. Lawrence by a geographer, say in the year 1700, it would be of great value in all studies of the early days of Canadian settlement.

The General Environment.   Structure is the fundamental factor in the geography of any region.   In the survey under consideration which deals with the basins of the Mackenzie and Yukon Rivers in the north-west of the Dominion, this is as true as elsewhere.   The structural units of Canada are three in number: the great Canadian Shield, the broad geosyncline or downfold, and the series of "young mountains" which form the western quarter of the Dominion.   The present study is concerned with the northern portion of the downfold, together with the adjacent longitudinal valleys which lie immediately to the west of the northern end of the downfold.   The Mac-kenzie and its main tributaries drain the downfold, while the Yukon valley in the Territory of the same name, drains the most important of the northern longitudinal valleys among the young mountains of the Rockies.

The general course of the rivers and of the main mountain ranges in the north-west of Canada—what may be termed the "grain" of the country—runs from north-west to south-east (Fig. 1).   Many other features of the landscape seem to show this direction—as, for instance, the line of great lakes from Ontario north-west to Great Bear Lake.   It seems likely that this "grain" results from pressure exerted on the crust by the two resistant areas to east and west, which we call the Canadian Shield and the Pacific Shield.   These structural units are not mere academic correlations, as may be shown by comparing the Great Portage at Fort Smith with the obstructions across the St. Lawrence at the Thousand Islands.   Both are due to the same cause, a local prolongation of the resistant rocks of the great Canadian Shield which bars the course of a great river.

Three of the great lakes are very notable features of the landscape in the region under survey. They are Lakes Athabaska, Great Slave, and Great Bear. It seems not unreasonable to explain these lakes in terms of the margin of the great Shield. They occur where the hard edges (cuestas) of the super-

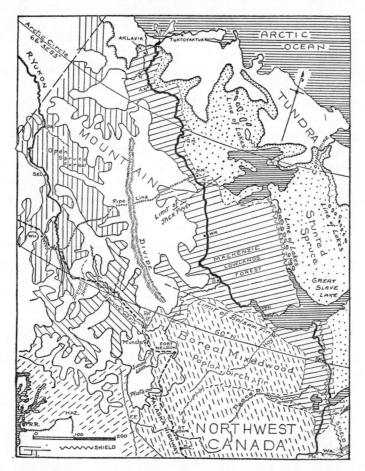

Fig. 1. North-West Canada showing the structure, communications, etc., in the regions traversed. The forest divisions are based on W. E. D. Halliday. Blank areas are mountains or tundra. The Alaska Highway is inserted. F.—F. approximate limits of frozen ground.

imposed younger rocks to the west hold back the drainage of the undulating surface of the great Shield. Georgian Bay, blocked on the west by the cuestas of the Bruce Peninsula and of Manitoulin, offers a very close parallel.

The world has just passed through a long period of mountain-building, owing (as suggested) to the compression of the weaker parts of the earth's crust between resistant areas such as the Canadian and Pacific Shields. Though the tougher rocks of the Canadian Shield did not rise into sharp folds, it seems likely that they were warped into broad undulations with the same general direction (north-west to south-east) noticed elsewhere.   Perhaps this explains the parallel courses of the Mackenzie River and of the two lines of lakes to the east (Fig. 1).   One of these links Great Bear Lake to Great Slave Lake; while still further to the east is a similar depression occupied by lakes linking the Coppermine River to the Thelon River.   The best known is the "Rocky Mountain Trench" through Finlay Forks (F.F. in Fig. 1).

However, the outstanding characteristic of most of the Mackenzie survey is the absence of marked topographic features in the vicinity of the great river.   Not until we reach the more northern portion of the Mackenzie are there any mountains near the river; but it is worth noting that the chief of these neighbouring ranges, such as the Norman Range and the Carcajou Range near Norman Wells as well as the Caribou Hills near the Reindeer Depot, are aligned along the same dominant direction.   The writer noted many topographic details on his long thousand-mile journey along the Slave-Mackenzie system, and these will be referred to in their place.   But it was impossible to go far from the steamer along much of the river, for the passengers were never sure of the length of stay, and we were usually only given a quarter of an hour's warning of the boat's departure.

Generalizing somewhat, the main geological formations encountered comprise Devonian or allied rocks from some forty miles north of McMurray as far as the Blackwater River, fifty miles north of Wrigley (wr. in Fig. 1). From this latter point to the beginning of the Great Delta alternating belts of Devonian and Cretaceous rocks are encountered, each perhaps about fifty miles wide.   There is naturally a tendency for rapids to develop as the river passes from the hard Devonian to the softer Cretaceous rocks, or where a bar of the older rocks has not yet been cut down to the general grade (Fig. 16).

Just below Arctic Red the delta lands begin, and these extend northward for nearly two degrees of latitude (68° to 70°), though it is hard to determine where the delta deposits end and the tumbled heaps of moraine, with their innumerable oval pools, begin.   Here in the delta the river breaks into numerous distributaries, with three main channels, the West, Middle, and East Branches. Aklavik is on the Western Branch, but Reindeer Reserve and Tuktoyaktuk are on or near the Eastern Branch, so that the steamer traversed many miles of tortuous link channels to get to the East Channel from Aklavik.

The Climatic Factor in the North-West.   With meteorological stations confined largely to the river or to a few of the mines to the east, there is not much chance of preparing reliable climatic maps.   However, since much of the Mackenzie Basin is relatively flat, it seems likely that climatic lines based on data observed near the river will not depart very greatly from the truth.

The writer has endeavoured to draw a map showing the advent of spring, of the type which he published some years ago for southern Ontario (Fig. 2). In this case the daily temperature of 42° F. is chosen as indicating the arrival of spring.   For instance in Toronto this temperature is the average for April 15, whereas it reaches Windsor on April 6, and Algonquin Park, far to the north, on April 26.   Trees are now beginning to show leaves, and many plants are growing freely, since 42° F. is about the temperature when the plant cell "wakes up" and chemical combination (photosynthesis) is initiated.   On the days cited this process has, of course, gone on for about half of the twenty-four hours.

The resulting map (Fig. 2) is quite interesting, and is I think accurate enough for the purpose required in the vicinity of the Mackenzie River and

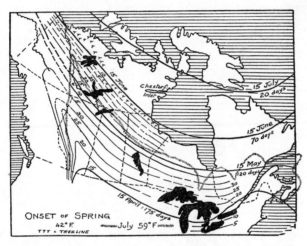

FIG. 2. The onset of spring is indicated by the day on which an average of 42° F. is first recorded. Note that Norman Wells (N.) has spring weather as soon as Gaspé. The length of the warm period is also noted. The tree-line (T.—T.) and the July isotherm of 59° F. are charted.

the northern great lakes. We see that spring (as defined) comes to Norman Wells (north of 63° N.) as soon as it does to Gaspé in latitude 49° N., on the shores of the Atlantic.   In both cases the first day to record an average of 42° F. is May 15.   Of course the phenomenon merely expresses the usual attributes of a *continental* climate (i.e., a hot summer for the latitude).   But the essential element of the climate in the Mackenzie Basin is the length of the growing season, and the relative values are given pretty well by these isopleths.

In addition to finding the date at which the temperature line reaches an average daily figure of 42° F., I ascertained the similar dates when 42° F. is reached on the return of the sun to the south in the fall. The interval between the two dates at a place (in spring and autumn) represents the best part of the growing season. Plotting the relation of the date of the "onset of spring" and the length of this growing period, one found, as one would expect, that there was a fairly good "straight-line" relation between them. The equation to this curve is $X = 113 - 0.565\ Y$; where X is the number of days after April 1 (to the day with 42° F.); and Y is the number of days between the

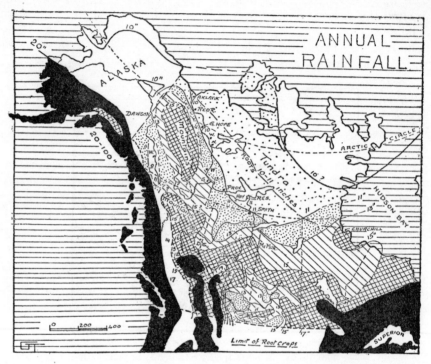

Fig. 3. A tentative map of the rainfall in North-West Canada. The 11-inch isohyet is fairly accurate, but the 15-inch isohyet is only a rough estimate. (Over 20 inches, black.) The probable limit of root crops is indicated.

spring day with 42° F. and the autumn day with 42° F. We find that Aklavik has about ninety days of warm weather (as defined), and so has a season long enough for many northern crops. Of course this formula takes no account of the variability of the temperature from year to year which is rather considerable; nor of unseasonable frosts which are a real danger in much of the Mackenzie valley. We can summarize the summer climate of the Mackenzie area as being very like that of Newfoundland in its temperatures (as we may see by comparing these places on Fig. 2), though the rainfall is far lighter in the northern area (Fig. 3).

No official map has been prepared to show the precipitation of this region, so far as I am aware. The large Atlas by Brooks and Connor does not indicate any isohyet (rain-line) between the 10 and 20 inch lines, and since all our areas have rainfalls between these limits there is no data of much value to us on the maps. However in Fig. 3 the writer has collected such data as is available (by the kindness of the Meteorological Office), and has plotted the figures in the west-central portion of the Dominion. In the south he relied on the maps published in W. A. Mackintosh's fine study *Prairie Settlement: The Geographical Setting*.[1] This map in Fig. 3 is only tentative; but it is of considerable value, since the data are fairly numerous along the Mackenzie and Yukon valleys. Between the two rivers I have suggested that there is higher precipitation, because all this region is rather elevated, but the isohyet charted is only an estimate.

In Fig. 3 the isohyets for 11 inches and for 13 inches are probably fairly accurate. Since Aklavik and Good Hope have only about 10 inches of precipitation it is difficult to believe that the 10 inch isohyet—shown on the map some five hundred miles to the east of these places—can be accurate, though it has been inserted on many maps about this position. However the area involved having this low rainfall is nearly all tundra, and has very little in the way of crop possibilities for the most part. Still, valuable mines may turn up in this area—most of which consists of the ancient rocks of the Shield—so that it behoves us to gain as accurate an idea as possible of the main climatic elements.

In the most complete study of the whole region, which is one of the very useful memoirs issued by the Department of Mines and Resources and is entitled *Canada's Western Northland*,[2] there is a very valuable map on page 74 which gives the northern limits to which various crops are likely to reach. The "northern limit of root crops" from this map is inserted as a broken line in Fig. 3. It runs from Aklavik to Churchill in the south-east, and perhaps represents a somewhat optimistic belief in the northern spread of agriculture in the Dominion. However, the reader is invited to notice the vast interval between Dawson Creek (D.C. on Fig. 3) and this line which runs close to the boundary between the conifer forest and the tundra. It would suggest that we have a belt of (admittedly poor) sub-polar croplands over four hundred miles wide which has not been exploited yet.

Summer Temperatures in the North-West. As a climatologist, the writer was prepared to meet with a complete absence of anything approaching Arctic weather during his summer journey to latitude 70° north; but the number of really warm days, when it was too hot to be comfortable, was somewhat surprising. Only on one day, June 22, and at the southernmost station of Fort Smith, did he experience a cold bleak day. Dr. J. Patterson, Director, Dominion Meteorological Services, Toronto, has made available the actual temperature data quoted in the following paragraphs.

[1] Toronto, 1934.   [2] Ottawa, 1937.

On June 20 to 22 an Arctic airmass was moving south along the Mackenzie valley. A low-pressure system developed in the vicinity of Fort Smith, helping to produce bleak weather and cold rainy conditions. The maximum on June 22 was only 52°, which was much lower than on any other day I spent in the North-West. The minimum was 32° on June 23, which was also the lowest minimum. When we reached Norman Wells on July 11, I noted the oppressive heat in my diary, and I find that the maximum on that day at the Wells was 82° F. A week later when we were leaving Aklavik—120 miles north of the Arctic Circle—my diary has the laconic note "Hot in bed, only a sheet." So that I was not surprised later to find that the official reading at Aklavik showed a maximum of 82° on that day also.

Another interesting feature of the weather in summer is the great range in daily temperature. For instance at Simpson on July 6 the maximum was 75°, but the minimum fell nearly to freezing point, giving a range of 39°. At McMurray, a day or two before I arrived there, there was a similar drop from 79° F. to 35° F. These changes are, of course, due to the chilling in the interior of a continent at night when the cloud "blanket" is absent.

Natural Vegetation. Every geographer knows that the map of the natural vegetation is of great value in determining the resources of a pioneer region. Often the distribution of the common trees can be fairly accurately determined long before the isohyets or soil classes can be plotted; partly for the reason that every settler has a fair idea of the common trees, whereas long training is necessary before the soils can be accurately charted, while somewhat expensive equipment is needed before the precipitation-lines can be placed with any accuracy on the map. Hence the map published by W. E. D. Halliday in *Forest Service Bulletin*[3] is of special importance.

The writer was much struck by the fact that there seemed to be little change in the character of the forest in the long journey of a thousand miles from Fort McMurray to Aklavik; and this is borne out by Mr. Halliday's map (Fig. 1). He charts the forests along the Mackenzie over this long distance as all belonging to his B 23 class. This forms part of his Boreal Forest Region, which he divides into fourteen sections, one of which is the *Mackenzie Lowlands* section.

The prevailing forest cover appears to be coniferous, with white spruce the major dominant, forming pure associations. Extensive fires have however favoured the admixture of aspen, balsam poplar, balm of Gilead, and Alaska white birch with this species, and the occurrence of jack pine associations on the lighter soils. On the better-drained alluvial soils such as old river banks, well developed stands of balsam poplar are very characteristic, and the poorer drained sites support numerous shallow black spruce and tamarack swamps, and large areas of wild hay meadows and willow scrub. Records would indicate exceptionally good growth for the majority of the species, where the drainage is good, and this condition continues even down to the Arctic Circle.

---

[3]No. 89, Ottawa, 1937.

The writer was unable to see anything of the country away from the river bank and its immediate vicinity. Probably here as elsewhere the soil was better drained near the river cut-banks, and degenerated somewhat into muskeg swamps as one moved a mile or so inland. This seemed to be the case in the hinterland near Norman Wells where the writer made several short excursions into the forests. One of the great problems here, as everywhere in the cold croplands of the future, is the heavy cost of draining adequately these swampy areas. In many cases it is beyond the power of the local settler to cut long enough drains to carry off the surplus water from his lands. Possibly the fact that most of the Mackenzie valley has a precipitation between 10 and 14 inches will mean that this problem is not so difficult here as in the wetter Ontario clay belt.

The writer had anticipated that the trees would diminish in size quite regularly as the latitude changed. One of the most interesting features of the survey was that it extended from 55° N. (near Lac La Biche) to Tuktoyaktuk close to latitude 70° N. In almost any other part of the world this would have meant a considerable change of environment, but this was not the case in North-West Canada. The sole really cold uncomfortable day, as stated, was experienced in the far south at Fort Smith on June 22. The four days I stayed at Tuktoyaktuk towards the end of July—when the midnight sun was clearly visible even at that late date—were much warmer. Only at one spot (on latitude 64° N.) was a snow drift observed on the river bank, and there was no ice visible in the Polar Sea; though the "ice blink," owing to reflection from the pack ice, indicated that it lay not many miles to the north of our ship, then nearly at 70° N.

The writer made notes of the diameters of the spruce trees about 2 feet above the ground at a number of stations. Thus at Providence (lat. 61° N.) they were about 25 inches in diameter in places, while at Fort Smith far to the south I saw none quite so large. A few miles north of the circle at Gillies River we measured a spruce about 5 feet from the ground with a girth of 58 inches which gives a diameter here of 18½ inches. There were many stumps of white spruce along the river bank at Aklavik (68° 16′ N.) which indicated that the largest trees had reached a diameter of about 20 inches, though those still standing seemed more usually to have diameters up to 16 inches.

To an Antarctic traveller, who knows that not a blade of grass or a flowering plant grows south of the Antarctic circle, the sight of a pile of spruce logs (probably a hundred yards long) of 20 inches or less in diameter, gathered for ships' fuel many miles north of the circle, was something never to be forgotten. It was not till we reached Reindeer Reserve (68° 45′) that large bare patches began to appear on the hills. Here the spruce quite suddenly seemed to dwindle to about 6 inches in diameter. Within a few miles it had given place to the tundra or barren grounds, which is universal in the vicinity of Tuktuk.

The writer is unfortunately no botanist, but the many varied flowers which grow in the woods along the rivers of the North-West were an unexpected sight. For instance at Hay River (lat. 60° 50′) Labrador tea with its close clusters of white flowers was everywhere, purple bugloss, green and purple paintbrush, and yellow cinquefoil were very abundant. At Gillies River in latitude 67° N., I made a special collection of all the flowers I could find in a walk through the spruce woods. Among them were a purple pea, shepherdia, a purple daisy, wild currant, a pink wild rose every yard or so, mooseberry, yarrow, dogwood, and yellow cinquefoil. A small white calla lily grew plentifully on the edge of the large pond at Arctic Red (67° 25′ N.), and the purple fireweed covered the whole slope behind the pool. The pink rose bushes were very plentiful along the river-front at Aklavik. The flora of the tundra was especially interesting since it was the first I had seen. (There is, of course, no tundra in the Antarctic.) A fellow passenger was able to name the plants for me. They are briefly described later in this memoir.

THE MACKENZIE ENVIRONMENT

The Twin Settlements of McMurray and Waterways. The real North-West may be said to begin at Waterways. Here is the end of steel; here begins the long steamer journey to the Arctic Ocean; here naturally has grown up one of the large airports in the North-West. To a student of the development of Canadian cities it is interesting to find, some three hundred miles north of closely settled Canada, far from the farmlands and close-set little towns of the prairies, not one but *two* well-defined town nuclei within only three miles of each other. As usual this is a question of site and function, and the resulting settlements are based on a complex mixture of physical and human controls.

Peter Pond reached the junction of the Athabaska and Clearwater Rivers in 1778, by way of Methye Portage on the upper Clearwater. A fort had been built in 1770, and as is often the case this fur-trading centre has been moved around and its name changed on several occasions. However the first buildings were erected close to the junction of the two rivers; so that McMurray is more than a century older than Waterways, which only dates from the arrival of the railway there in 1925.

The character of the topography is shown in the sketch given in Fig. 4. The rivers have cut down about 250 feet into the surface of an undulating plain or low plateau whose general elevation is about 1,250 feet above sea level. The valleys are rather broad and flat-floored, but in the case of the Clearwater the modern river seems to be somewhat of a "misfit," for it meanders on this flat floor. Probably the flat floors date back to the last glacial period, while the meandering stream represents the lessened drainage of these drier times.

Two small streams of considerable interest enter the two rivers. Just above the early huts at McMurray there enters Horse River, and it is in the flat floor of this valley that the main "quarries" have been made into the rich tar sands. A small settlement of some twenty houses together with several large extraction-plant buildings, constitutes the new settlement known as Abasand. A good road over a very steep hill links it with McMurray, but the alternative paths to the north were flooded, or otherwise impassable, when I visited the works. Recent research on the character of these deposits shows that they occur in separate lenticular pockets, so that it is quite difficult to estimate the total area of the deposit. The black sands differ greatly in their tar contents, and the process of extraction is quite difficult. For these and other reasons those concerned believe that the early estimates of the total value of the tar sands were too optimistic.

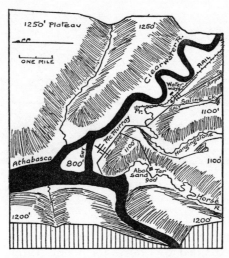

Fig. 4. Block diagram of the vicinity of McMurray, showing Waterways, Prairie (PR.), and the salt and tar-sand deposits. Looking east.

A smaller stream enters the Clearwater near Waterways, known as Saline Creek. Wells drilled in the vicinity show that there is a large supply of salt under the western margin of Waterways, and this has led to the erection of a large chemical plant employing about fifty men. A few hundred yards to the north-east is a small fish-packing plant; so that this corner of Alberta is on the way to becoming an industrial area.

When the writer visited McMurray in 1936 the airport was in the Sny (i.e., shallow branch) just north-east of McMurray. Three companies were sending out ten planes to the mining camps in the great Shield to the north.

The airway offices were mounted on runners, so that they could be dragged away from the river in the fortnight of floods in the spring. The same flooding occurred in autumn, as the northern rivers froze and held up the drainage of the river from the south. But for the last few years all the air traffic has centred at the new airport, which has been cut out of the forest on the plateau some eight miles to the south-east of Waterways. This transition from a river or lake airport to a land airport is a very common one in the rapid evolution of traffic in the North-West.

Between Waterways and McMurray is yet a third settlement known as Prairie; which in 1936 consisted of three lanes—round three sides of a square—in the vicinity of a large farm. Here were a field of oats, two large houses, and about ten small huts with a small saw mill, etc., on the bank of the Clearwater. Several herds of cows grazed in the open meadows where the oxen of

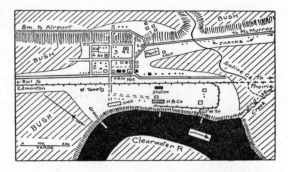

Fig. 5. A sketch survey of Waterways looking south-west. New blocks are 1—4. Dots are shacks.

the early fur traders had fed and given the district its name. In 1942 the railway had been extended to Prairie for a mile through the poplar jungle (Fig. 4). Several small steamers and barges lay in the river, and acres of ground in the vicinity were covered with the military stores of the United States Engineers. This was one of their main depots for goods going to the Canol oil fields far to the north. Unfortunately no one was allowed to photograph, sketch, or survey in the vicinity of these military depots, so I was unable to ascertain the details of the growth of this little settlement.

Since Waterways is usually the first place reached on a journey to the North-West it may be considered first. We see here illustrated in Fig. 5 several of the river terraces which are so common a feature of the Mackenzie and its tributaries. The "cut-bank" of the Clearwater is about 12 feet high, and the railway has been brought round in a loop so as to serve the large sheds of the Hudson's Bay and Northern Transportation Companies, which are just at the edge of the cut-bank. Several of the offices and a few small residence shacks have been built in or close to this rail loop, without any obvious regard for planning.

The main road leads west from Waterways to McMurray, while in the last few years another good road leads up the second river-terrace towards the airport in the south-west. This terrace is about 150 feet above the river, and about one-third of a mile back from it. As is so often the case with pioneer towns in Canada, there is no communication by road with the outside world. Railways or rivers, or of late years, airways, precede the building of anything beyond a rough bush track or "winter road" to the settled areas; and this is true of Waterways and McMurray.

In 1936 there was no school or church in Waterways, and only two stores. Today there are five or six stores, two churches, and a good school. The development of the salt plant and the opening of the large airport has stimulated settlement. Some of the men working at Abasand live at Waterways; and of course the American "invasion" at nearby Prairie helped to develop the little settlement. The most striking change was that the "town-plan" had changed from *strassendorf* (strung along one street) to "grid"; for in the intervening eight years the four blocks numbered 1-4 in Fig. 5 have been developed. These contain the new buildings already referred to, and perhaps twenty small houses. Other settlers have climbed the hill and built houses at the spot labelled "5," while some much larger houses (of the Hb type) crown the terrace near "6." There are also about a dozen new shacks in the forest clearings cut out along the main road to McMurray.

The writer some years ago put forward a scheme for the classification of towns according to stages of their evolution. He has used this with some success in a number of papers dealing with the cities and towns of Canada; and the series discussed in the present memoir is an interesting one, concerned almost wholly with the very beginnings of what must in some cases develop into important towns. The essential table is as follows; and most of the examples fall into the "infantile" division. Indeed in a number of cases we might say that they were "sub-infantile."

CLASSES OF TOWNS*

Sub-infantile towns...	Few buildings, arranged haphazard along one indefinite lane or street.
Infantile (In.).......	Haphazard distribution of buildings, several streets, no factories.
Juvenile (Ju.)........	Differentiation into zones of houses and shops starts.
Adolescent (Ad.).....	Scattered factories, no definite zones of "Ha" houses.
Early Mature (Er.)...	Residence zones fairly defined, no segregated factories.
Mature (Ma.)........	Four zones of houses. Separate commercial and industrial areas.
Late Mature (La.)....	Indications of advance to modern town planning.
Senile (Se.)..........	Large areas of town abandoned, remainder stagnant.

Annals of the Association of American Geographers, 1942.

The position of Waterways in these classes can be described as "late infantile," for there are two factories, though there is no differentiation of the zones of houses, so that the better-class residences (Ha and Hb) are separated from the poorer houses (Hc and Hd). The town has clearly changed in the last few years from the "one street" to the "grid" type of plan; though to the writer the "grid" is rather a convenience to the real-estate vendor, than an advantage to the citizen of the future!

McMurray though a larger town than Waterways has not progressed so rapidly in the last few years (Fig. 6). Since my former survey in 1936 there has been a decline at the west end near the Athabaska River, where a number of rather large houses have been torn down. However, there have been some elements of growth, such as the building of the fine brick hospital behind the Catholic church, and of the separate Catholic school in the eastern extension of the town.

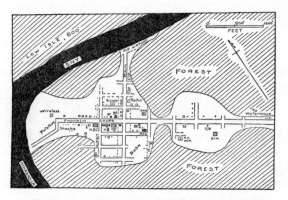

Fig. 6. A sketch survey of McMurray (57°N.) at rail-end, Alberta. (H. is hall, s. is shed.) Dots are shacks.

The main shopping street is naturally the road leading directly to Waterways and the railway station some three miles away. It is called Franklin Street, while the road named Main Street only leads to the old airport on the Sny, and is of no great importance. The town contains six fairly complete blocks, of which the one to the east is of recent date, with half a dozen small houses thereon. A somewhat unusual feature in these pioneer towns is the fact that the schools have been built in a clearing somewhat remote from the town proper, perhaps on account of the cheaper land here. I was informed that the railway might have been brought to McMurray if the land-owners had not placed rather high prices on their lots.

The half dozen shops are of a better class than those in Waterways, as is also the case with the Hudson's Bay store and the hotel. Here also is the local centre of the Mounted Police and the radio station. There is a bank, and opposite it is the office of the Canadian Pacific Airlines. As stated it is a much more important religious and educational centre than Waterways. There is a fairly well-defined Indian quarter at the north-west end of the main street, and nearby is a small Japanese group which is responsible for several acres of potatoes. Formerly most of the fur-buying occurred in Mc-Murray, but I understand that much of this is being transferred to railhead. It is obvious that Waterways, where the chief "break of bulk" occurs in the large aggregate of cargoes going north by steamer, is in an advantageous position for future progress, especially as the tar sands—of which much is hoped in the future—are about equally accessible from both centres.

As regards classification perhaps McMurray may be described as "juve-nile," since there is a definite concentration of the shops along two of the blocks in the main (Franklin) street. It has no factories, but those in Water-ways have only recently become of importance; and in most other respects the pattern of McMurray indicates a later stage in town evolution. There are three Indian reserves in the region, each some thirty miles away, and the Indian population in the shacks in the west of the town is always changing. There are about forty children attending the Catholic school and twice as many at the older school. Many of these are Indians or half-breeds.

Wheat and oats grow satisfactorily in the districts, but tomatoes must be protected from frost. Domestic roses will flower if some extra care is taken, and potatoes are plentiful. There has been some export north to the oil wells. There are about 100 houses served with electric light from the local plant, and the total permanent population is about 250. It is much greater in summer when the Indians come in from the reservation. The permanent population of Waterways is about 200.

Portage Settlements at Fitzgerald and Fort Smith. There are two small settlements in the 210 miles between McMurray and Fort Smith, i.e., Mackay and Chipewyan, but I saw nothing of them. From the plane we had a glimpse of Lake Athabaska and Lake St. Clair, but heavy clouds spoiled the view the whole journey. As explained earlier the Mackenzie River cuts through a sixteen-mile bar of granite below Fitzgerald, which is really a westerly pro-jection of the Canadian Shield. The river falls 109 feet, mainly at five separate rapids, in its course from Fitzgerald to Fort Smith. Dr. Trevor Lloyd in his valuable paper "The Mackenzie Waterway"[4] states that the early voyageur was able to run all but one of these, but it is quite impossible with modern cargo boats.

At Fitzgerald the main wharf is situated on the west bank just above the bold granite bluff which bounds the south side of the little settlement. Close by are the neat buildings of the Hudson's Bay Company. From this point two good roads were built many years ago for the transfer of cargo to Fort

[4]*Geographical Review*, New York, vol. XXXIII, July, 1943.

Smith. At the halfway station were some meadows, which served to support the horses and oxen used by the men engaged on the portage. Today all transport is done by motor trucks, some being of great size, so that it is not impossible to carry small steamers over this route. When the Americans became interested in the Norman oil field they improved the more westerly road. The two are connected (like a ladder) with numerous cross lanes, and have been in use since 1931 and 1934 respectively.

A view looking south from the granite crags (Fig. 7) shows a clearing in the spruce forest, which is roughly triangular, with each side about one-third of a mile in length. A small creek runs across the northern end of the clearing

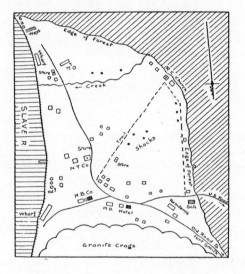

Fig. 7. A sketch survey of Fitzgerald, looking south. The clearing is about 400 yards wide.

with a dozen rough Indian shacks near its banks. Where it leaves the forest is the site of the Catholic church and mission house. There is a hotel at Fitzgerald, which is most unusual in these small settlements along the river. In addition to the Hudson's Bay Company store there are two other large sheds belonging to the Northern Transportation Company and Marine Operators, but they seem to be doing very little business. A small store and a café bordered the shore road near the creek outlet. Two small stores are near the centre of the settlement.

The completion of the great pipeline from Canol to Whitehorse has led to a considerable diminution of the trade through Fitzgerald. In fact the steamers are doing a good deal of business in bringing south some of the valuable machinery used in opening up Canol, etc. Many scows and some of these heavy machines were lying at the south end of the river bank. Several rather larger houses have been built near the school at the north-west end of the settlement, where the roads leave for Fort Smith.

There would seem to be no regular plan apparent in Fitzgerald, but it is a little unusual since the triangular clearing is not a mere strip along the river, as we shall see in most of the other river stations. In fact three minor roads branch off from the original route, so that we see the beginnings of a street plan. I was told that there were about twelve white families there, while in

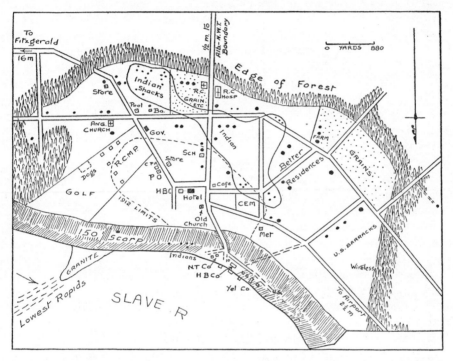

FIG. 8. A sketch survey of Fort Smith, showing the limits of the town in 1944 and in 1912. Looking south. Black dots are houses.

the summer about 150 Indians and half-breeds make Fitzgerald their head-quarters. Two Mounted Police were stationed there at the time of my very brief visit. I was able to make some sketches and run a rapid traverse, but the sketch map is less reliable than others obtained where I had more time. The settlement falls into the "infantile" class in my classification.

I am indebted to Mr. Frank Milne (Hudson's Bay Company) for further details about this interesting settlement. It was known as "Smith's Landing" until 1915, but was then named "Fitzgerald" from a police officer who lost his life in the Arctic. The region has been declining in population, especially since 1918 when an influenza epidemic carried off many of the Indian tribes who lived there. Today they spend most of the winter in the bush, but readily find employment in stevedoring on the wharves in summer. The first boat usually arrives about the middle of May, and navigation closes about October 15.

There are two farms in the district and a small amount of feed is raised locally. A good hay meadow occurs three miles from town. There is a small government school with 23 pupils, and Mr. Milne gives the present population as 127 Indians and 63 whites and half-breeds.

Fort Smith may be described as the capital of the North West Territories, though it lies on the extreme border of the latter. The line of latitude 60° N. runs a few hundred yards south of the little town, and Fitzgerald is some fifteen miles within Alberta. The reason for founding Fort Smith is still quite apparent for just above the wharves a broad belt of granite crosses the river, and the rapids can be seen from where the boats tie up (Fig. 8). Here in the early days the canoes were landed on the west bank, and here a small Catholic mission was established. The first church was built on the top of the upper cut-bank, which here forms a high sandy scarp reaching 150 feet above the river. The town is built on this level terrace or ancient flood-plain above the river. Between the scarp and the river is a built up terrace about 150 yards wide where the large sheds of the transportation companies have been erected (Fig. 8).

The old portage road now winds rather irregularly through the little town from the south-east corner obliquely across to the scarp, and then down a deep cut in the sandy bluff to the former Indian halting place. Most of the chief buildings of the town are still on or close to this road. Thus the centre of the town is the rather large hotel, which is the property of the Hudson's Bay Company and is next door to their store. Two private stores are situated on this road as well as the government office, post office, pool room, Airlines office, and the very large Mounted Police Reserve.

The Catholic church has been transferred about a mile inland to a large reserve, which also contains several mission buildings, barns, etc., as well as a large three-storey hospital. Most of the Indian huts and tents were at the time of my visit clustered in the vicinity of the Catholic mission, as is clear from the map. A few of their tents were canvas tepees, most however were ridge tents. The cemetery is near the old church just above the high sandy scarp. Until 1912 the settlement clustered round the hotel, as shown by the broken line in Fig. 8, but it has grown extensively in the last thirty years.

The second main road in Fort Smith runs parallel to the river front, but about one mile therefrom, following the curve of the river. Four or five cross streets link this second road to the river, including one which runs due south from the old church, and so reaches the Alberta boundary in about half a mile (Fig. 8). The largest building, the Catholic hospital, is at the intersection of the south road and the second main road. The Anglican church is a pretty painted wooden building where the second main road intersects the old portage road. The rectory is a pleasant wooden residence nearby. A half-dozen better residences (Hb class) are to be found mostly in the south-west quarter of the town in the region so labelled (Fig. 8).

A good many crops are grown in the vicinity of Fort Smith, especially by the French Fathers at the Catholic mission. Many acres of oats and wheat were to be seen at the farm on the western margin of Fort Smith, which was owned, I was informed, by the firm running the transport over the portage route. The local barber (Ba.) grew so many raspberries and strawberries in his plot behind the government offices that he was able to supply many of his friends. He had all the usual vegetables growing readily in this garden, while tomatoes with a little extra care flourished in the Catholic mission.

At the north-west end of the town were many new buildings erected since the recent development of American interest in our North-West. Here were United States barracks, and nearby were wireless and meteorological stations. I was unable to incorporate these in my survey for reasons stated earlier. Four groups of buildings were clustered along the water front; the largest being the capacious distributing shed of the Hudson's Bay Company. The Northern Transportation Company, the Yellowknife Transport Company, and the United States Government Supply Depot also had offices near the river, as shown on the map.

The Hudson's Bay Company has about a dozen boats on the Mackenzie River and its tributaries, of which the *Distributor* is the largest. This boat makes two or three round trips to the Arctic Ocean, depending on the character of the season. During the winter it is hauled up over heavy runways on to the shore about twelve miles north of Fort Smith. Owing to various delays the first journey north in 1944 did not start till late on June 24. We reached Providence on July 1, Norman Wells late on July 8, and crossed the Circle (lat. 66° 32' 53" N.) about 2 A.M. on July 13. Aklavik was reached about 7 A.M. on July 17, and Tuktoyaktuk about 9 A.M. on July 22. I returned in the boat to Norman Wells, where we arrived late on July 31.

The boat is a stern wheeler of 875 tons, and is about 200 feet long. It has a draught of 4 feet only, and carries a crew of thirty-two. The tubular boiler is supported on the flat bottom of the boat, with the two single-cylinder engines on the ordinary deck level. There are passenger cabins with two saloons, etc., on the upper deck, an officers' deck above this, and the chart room still higher. Hence there is a lot of top hamper which favours drifting, and this determines the navigation in lakes and ocean. The boat is unable to cross wide open spaces of water unless the weather is dead calm, so that we were frequently held up for one or two days until the not very obvious winds had completely died down. Four or five barges are lashed to the front of the steamer with steel cables, and pushed ahead in deep water on the river. But in the case of the rapids, which partially block navigation in three or four places below Fort Smith, we could only take one barge forward at a time. This partly explains why it took thirty days to travel 1,300 miles; or an average speed of about forty-three miles in the twenty-four hours. On my return I flew from Norman Wells to Fort Nelson—with several stops—in four hours. This was over 500 miles, i.e., about sixty times as rapidly!

The Great Slave Lake: Res-delta, Hay River. There is little in the way of scenery on the Slave River between Fort Smith and the Great Slave Lake. The shores are formed of river silt, usually with banks about 10-20 feet above the river. A low scrub of willow covers the flat banks for a quarter mile or so, with a broad fringe of poplar between the willows and the main forest of spruce. Occasionally patches of glacial gravel rise above the silts, as for instance at the Burnt Islands just west of the outlet of the Slave River. At the outlet near Fort Resolution there is a new depot which is called Res-delta, for obvious reasons. Our boat did not call at Fort Resolution, which is about three miles to the south of the main outlet in the delta. At Res-delta were a number of small boats and scows brought down from Fort Smith, whose cargoes were to be taken across the big lake to the Yellowknife gold-field by larger boats, which could face the occasional rough weather.

There was only one small Indian hut (built of logs) amid the ten-foot willows at Res-delta. The soil was swampy, and was covered with horsetails (*Equisetum*) below the willow scrub. The *Distributor* picked up a load of lumber here, and was much delayed because the sharp bends in the delta channel were too narrow for us to push all the barges at once. Moreover, we had to wait for some time for perfectly calm weather to traverse the hundred miles of open water (along the south-west shore of the big lake) which lay between us and Hay River. Later we had to shelter for a day or two at Burnt Islands, some twenty miles west of Res-delta. We tied up alongside the cut-bank at Hay River about 11 P.M. on June 28.

Hay River is one of the more important posts along the river, and is particularly interesting from the number of Indians (around 150) who live there. As the inset in Fig. 9 shows, the settlement is at the outlet of the river on the east bank, on a sort of blunt promontory. The Great Slave Lake is not clearly visible from the houses, but lies only half a mile through the bush in the rear. A clearing has been cut to the lake, forming part of a winter road over the frozen lake to Providence about 70 miles further west, and Yellowknife 150 miles to the north.

When the swampy surface of the forest is frozen during the cold months of the year, it is possible to drive tractors from the little railway town of Grimshaw (near Peace River) to Hay River settlement and Providence. This winter road is shown on the inset in Fig. 9. The airfield has been cleared in one of the larger islands at the mouth of the Hay River a few miles south-west of the post.

The Hay River post is one of the typical "sub-infantile" settlements along the Mackenzie. The Hudson's Bay store lies immediately above the landing-place, which is merely a gang-plank leading to a cut in the low scarp of the river terrace on which the houses have been built. Along the top of the cut-bank (or terrace) runs the sole road, which is merely a dirt track, but laid out according to the surveyed plan charting the lots in the settlement. One might perhaps compare these strung-out settlements to the "*strassendorfen*" of the German urban geographers.

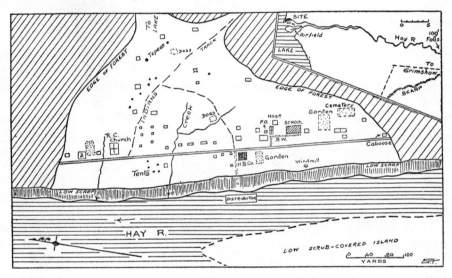

Fig. 9. A sketch survey of Hay River Settlement (61° N.), looking east. Inset is a map of lower Hay River.

At this post there are churches belonging to both Catholics and Anglicans, while the latter have a huge boarding school (three storeys high and 38 yards long) and a small hospital of eight beds. It is sad to state that the Anglican school and church have been abandoned, for a time at least, though one sister carries on the valued hospital work. The Catholic church and mission house are at the north end of the settlement, and the brothers cultivate a promising garden nearby. There is a tiny post office close to the church, and a board-walk (B.W.) links the Anglican buildings, thus removing the settlement from the lowest class of pioneer towns. The gardens contained 5-foot delphiniums, many flowering Iceland poppies, while lilac trees were coming into bloom. Grasshoppers were a grave menace to the vegetable garden, where cabbage plants were 3 inches high at the time. Tomatoes grow to good size when planted (from boxes) in the open, but the fruit needs to ripen indoors after it has been harvested.

The clearing in the forest extended some distance back from the river as the map shows, and most of the Indian huts were set back from the road along a track which extended to the south-east into the bush. Their canoes were dragged up on the shore below the cut-bank, and nearby was the power launch of the Resolution doctor, who was engaged in distributing the annual "treaty money" to the Indians. A number of the Indians lived in tents, which are shown by black dots in Fig. 9. Most of these tents were of the European pattern, but there were half-a-dozen of the old tepee type. Scattered around the settlement were about two hundred Indian dogs, all of whom are tethered or confined in log "corrals" by order of the R.C.M.P. They have even at times attacked women and children, and so are not allowed freedom.

At the back of the clearing an unusually energetic Indian was clearing and burning the muskeg to make a garden. Here the top layer was mostly a sort of peat, which was at times used to make shelter walls for the dogs. It was also burnt within a rough fenced enclosure so that the smudge would keep mosquitoes from the horses, who much appreciated the smoke. Alongside the Indian huts were the drying racks, 10 feet high or so, on which split fish were hanging. This is the normal food of the dogs, and Hay River is renowned for the abundance of fish in the vicinity. The Indians use gill-nets and catch whitefish, pickerel, and inconnu. In one tepee an Indian was smoking fish, while a bone knife for flensing skins was still observed to be in use.

There is a small farm in the vicinity where potatoes ripen by mid August, which is a month later than on the Liard River to the west. Oats are cut as green feed for the farmer's horses, as he has no ready means of threshing it. There is generally a heavy frost at Hay River by September 20. In the clearing cut to the lake, there were plenty of flowers, such as Labrador tea, bugloss, cinquefoil, and Indian paintbrush. All along the sandy shores of the lake were innumerable trunks of trees stranded there after being torn down from the river banks. There were fifteen white folk living in the Hay River settlement in 1944.

Settlements near 61° N.; Providence, Browning's Farm, and Simpson. Various large islands block a good deal of the channel of the river just to the east of Fort Providence, so that the current runs swiftly at about seven knots, and there are some rather sharp bends. Consequently we had to leave some of the scows behind on our first journey to the post, the steamer going back to bring them on a second trip. The post is on the north bank, and its general situation is clear from the inset in Fig. 10.

The cut-bank or scarp is considerably higher here than at Hay River, and shows an interesting topographic feature at its north-west end. This is an ancient "oxbow," or former channel of the river, which is about 20 feet higher than the present river level. The rounded valley of the oxbow seems to have determined the site of the landing place, as shown in Fig. 10. Here again we have, as is natural, the main road running along the top of the cut-bank about 30 feet above the river. But there are two minor "lanes" running between the lots, which show an advance on the "town-plan" of Hay River.

The Catholic buildings are closest to the landing-place, and comprise the church, a huge three-storey school, and various other buildings including a large barn. Several acres of potatoes, oats, and wheat surround the Catholic centre, and are clearly charted in Fig. 10. The Hudson's Bay store, residence,

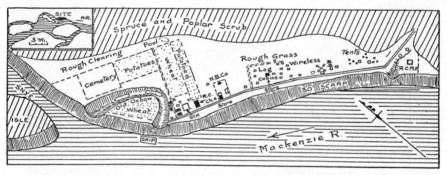

Fig. 10. A sketch survey of Fort Providence, looking north-east. The settlement is about one mile long. Inset map shows site and airport.

and outhouses are, as usual, surrounded by a neat fence. They are rather old,[5] but have the striking white walls and red roofs that add much to the appearance of these posts. They occupy the next "block" in the settlement. To the east is a cluster of small huts largely occupied by Indians and surrounding a small private store. The wireless towers and their offices follow; and after a group of Indian tents we find the Mounted Police office and residences in a fenced enclosure at the east end of the post. Here a road which leads to the new airport turns into the bush.

There are thirty-nine white folk at Fort Providence, for the Catholic mission here comprises no less than four priests and a dozen sisters. There are five whites at the airport, four at the wireless station, five at the store, and two police permanently at their station. Three white trappers have this as their headquarters, and the small store is owned by a Syrian. The Indians number 376. There are many Indian children at the large boarding school,

[5]They were rebuilt in the autumn of 1944.

for whom two toboggan slides built of logs stand out prominently near the old church. The latter is a pretty little wooden building with four rather quaint Gothic arched windows along each side. It is now used for secular purposes, being replaced by a large steepled church with dark red shingled roof. The large school is covered with sheet iron plates. There is no Anglican church at this settlement.

The wheat was about 14 inches high on July 1, and was already in full ear. The dry spring characteristic of this region is not favourable for grain, but

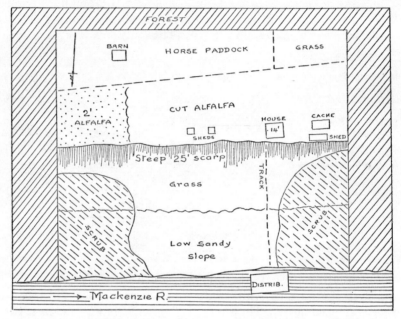

Fig. 11. A sketch survey of Browning's Farm, looking south. The farm is about sixty miles west of Providence, and is 220 yards wide.

fair rains fall in the summer. They sow seed in the last two weeks of May, and reap about the beginning of September. Potatoes can be dug by August 20, but the crop is usually taken up in the last two weeks of September. The French priests have several cows, which are kept in the barn till about April 25. They stay out in the open till early in October. There are fair natural meadows about five miles away. The settlement as a whole may be described as in an "early infantile" stage.

From Providence the river swings to the south-west and west, so that our next main stop, at Fort Simpson, is not much north of Providence. However, about half way, near where the Trout River enters in latitude 61° 15′, there is a very interesting primitive settlement called Browning's Farm. Here we had to stop—as was usual every two or three days—to take on board the cord-wood logs which form the fuel of the steamer.

Browning's Farm is a clearing about 200 yards square in the spruce forest, but of this area only a small field, about 100 × 240 yards, is devoted to grass and alfalfa. About half the clearing consists of the sandy beach and the steep grassy scarp (Fig. 11). The farmer has several acres of potatoes about four miles away in the forest, which I did not see. His alfalfa was a dense crop about 2 feet high, much of which had already been cut once. Several cows and horses were feeding in the grassy paddock near the barn. His house was

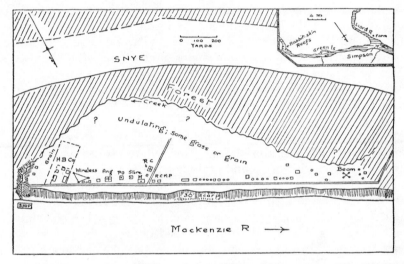

Fig. 12. A sketch survey of Fort Simpson, looking south. The scale is approximate only. Inset are the reefs and the junction with Liard River.

a neat log cabin with an attic in the ridge roof. Several small sheds bordered the house, as well as a cache elevated on tall posts after the Indian fashion. I made a full survey of this farm, because I was unable to see how the land differed from any other section of the same area for miles along the river. The nearest market for his products is about sixty miles at either Providence or Fort Simpson. In empty Australia the infrequent settlers live where there is a sufficient supply of water, for elsewhere no settlement is possible. In empty Canada the chances of widespread settlement—even if it be not much above subsistence level—seem much more promising. Soil surveys will no doubt enable those in authority to pick out the most worthwhile portions of these wide croplands of the future.[6]

[6]See Part VI on northern agriculture by William Dickson.

Just above Simpson are the Rabbit-skin rapids (inset, Fig. 12), where the floor of the river seems to be paved with huge boulders, leaving only a narrow winding passage; first near the west bank, then through a gap, and then along the east bank of the wide river. Hereabouts the current runs about eight knots, the general speed being about four. A few miles to the west are the Green Island rapids with somewhat similar features. These are charted in the inset in Fig. 12. The river is here in places only about one-third of a mile wide, though at Fort Simpson it expands to two miles wide after receiving the Liard River.

The situation of Fort Simpson on the north side of a small island in the river is clearly shown in the inset in Fig. 12. A clearing about a mile long has been made on the shore of the island, which has a cut-bank about 30 feet high. A small creek drains the islet, and its gully in the cut-bank has been used for the track up to the town level. No doubt similar small topographic details explain the position of the nuclei of many large towns. The Hudson's Bay buildings are adjacent to this gully. The wireless station with its three towers lies just west, while other radio towers sending out the "beam" to guide the planes have been erected at the extreme west end of the post.

There are Anglican and Catholic churches at Simpson, though there is no resident Anglican minister. The Catholics have a three-storey hospital built of wood and covered with iron plates. Their church is behind in a small side lane leading to extensive grass and grain fields (over fifty acres) in the undulating country behind the settlement. Between the churches are the post office and a neat private store, the latter being the airlines office also. The Mounted Police station is quite a large one, with five police resident here.

Some score of small houses front the road between the police offices and the beam towers. Most of these are log cabins, but one or two are two-storey frame cottages. Here dwell about fifteen families of Indians, who go off trapping in the season, and do stevedoring, interpreting, and odd jobs during the summer. There are several unusually large houses at the north-west end, in one of which lives the chief medical officer of this part of the river. The Catholic mission comprises four priests and eight sisters; while the radio work employs nine men, four of whom are married. The official population figures for the whole district in 1941 are: whites, 76; Indians, 378. In the settlement itself there live about forty-five white residents, the other white settlers are mostly trappers who have isolated cabins on the adjacent rivers.

The postmaster at Simpson had some acres of oats, which were nearly ready for harvest thus early in July, though they usually cut the oats towards the end of August. Barley grows well, and is used largely for poultry feed, though oats provides better straw for the horses. Tomatoes can be planted out about May 25 and usually do well. Corn, however, only rarely produces good cobs; say once in ten years. Sugar beets and potatoes are grown on a fairly extensive scale by the Catholic mission. The latter have several cows, but there is a tendency to replace horses by tractors. Over fifty acres have been sown with brome grass to improve the fodder. There is an isolated farm about four miles up the Liard River (see inset).

Some sixty miles south of Wrigley the boat stopped at Willow River for the usual fuelling operations. Here the cut-bank was composed of granite and schist boulders, in place of the almost universal river-silt. These boulders were probably of glacial origin, since the rocks in the vicinity seemed to be mostly Devonian sedimentaries. Opposite Wrigley there are bold cliffs of steeply dipping sediments, which rise about 1,200 feet above the river, which is here 315 feet above sea level. Large spruces were growing in the cracks in the rocks on the cliff face.

Wrigley is a very small settlement, containing only six whites, and the houses straggle along the top of a 25-foot scarp as shown in Fig. 13. It was

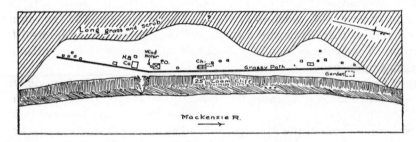

FIG. 13. A sketch survey of Wrigley (62°N.), looking west. The settlement is half a mile long.

founded in 1877 at a site 25 miles upstream from the present fort, and was moved in 1904 to its present site. It clearly represents the earliest stage of a river post, for the faint track through the long grass can hardly be termed a road. Some day, however, this may well become the "front street" of a fair-sized town, for there is no other settlement in the three hundred miles between Fort Simpson and Fort Norman.

There is only one imposing building in Wrigley, the post office and radio station, a two-and-a-half-storey frame house painted white. It is supplied with a prominent wind-motor propellor used to charge batteries for trans-mitting radio messages. Some distance along the cut-bank to the north is a pretty little Catholic church, built of sawn planks with a shingle roof. It has a little belfry and a porch at the south end, but is only occasionally opened for service. Somewhat isolated at the north end are four log cabins, with a few elevated "caches" and some tents. Here many of the Indians of the post spend the summer, and there are altogether about seventy-seven Indians in the immediate district. There is a similar cluster of Indian shacks at the south end of the settlement. The jungle of grass, raspberry canes, willow, and poplar, presses close on the settlement in midsummer, and almost impedes the path at the north end of the post.

There were two small gardens at Wrigley, in which I noted (on July 6) peas 8 inches high, lettuce 2 inches, onions 7 inches, and maize 3 inches. The Hudson's Bay store was naturally small, consisting of only one room surrounded by shelves. On one wall were displayed various reliable goods, such as rolls of cloth, gay blouses, and sweaters. On the rear wall was the tool department, with files, carborundum hones, sandals, and kerosene lamps. On the north wall were groceries in tins behind the main counter; while a small drug supply flanked the door. In this latter corner were liniment, Eno's salts, cod liver oil, and spectacles. Such seemed to be representative of the basic needs supplied by civilization to the residents and Indians around Wrigley.

The chief interest in this sketch survey is that it charts a settlement about forty years old, which has not yet advanced beyond the "sub-infantile" stage. Indeed there is hardly a road, and the church is only intermittent in function. The juxtaposition of a modern wind-motor with the Indian shacks is worth emphasizing.

Fort Norman, Norman Wells, and the Oilfields. (Lat. 65° N.) As we were crossing latitude 64° N. near the Blackwater River, there was a cry of "Glaciers on the port bow"! Here was a snow drift (about twenty yards long) on the sloping shore of the Mackenzie; and as noted elsewhere, I saw no other low-lying snow in my whole journey. We spent some hours loading wood near Saline River, where some of the spruce had a diameter of two feet. Many martin swallows occupied holes in the cut-bank, and here the heavy muskeg layer, whose support of silts had washed away, overhung the river bank like a great heavy curtain, often with large spruce trees just ready to topple into the river below.

Fort Norman is almost on latitude 65° N., while Norman Wells is 50 miles to the north-west. The former is rather picturesquely placed on the narrow promontory between the Mackenzie and its large tributary the Great Bear River, which here enters from the huge lake of that name (Fig. 14). About five miles upstream on the north bank, and dominating the scene, is Bear Rock (1,550 feet) which towers 1,300 feet above the river. It seems to be built of hard Devonian deposits, though the river above and below Norman flows through softer Cretaceous formations. As a result the river is wider and winds in meanders in the Cretaceous, especially near latitudes 64° 30' and 65° 30' N.

Fort Norman shows a definite topography, for here are two benches or terraces, both used as sites for houses (Fig. 14). The lower bench is about

20 feet above the river, and carries the little Anglican church, many Indian huts, and at the west end a store and the post office. The upper bench is about 40 feet higher; and here are the police station, the large wireless station, the Hudson's Bay buildings, the Catholic church, and a large hospital at the east end. Poplar forest as usual shuts in the settlement to the rear, and here the land slopes down to a large slough.

The houses as usual are mostly one-storey log cabins in the case of the Indians, while frame houses are used by the white settlers. However, the two residences of the religious groups are two-storey buildings. The Anglican mission has been abandoned, and a member of the large Signals staff is living

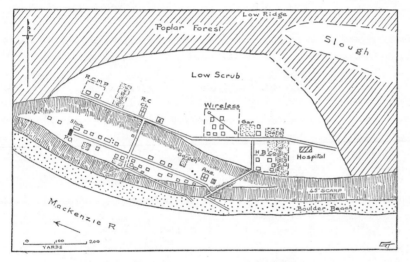

Fig. 14. A sketch survey of Fort Norman, looking north. Gardens are dotted.

there at present. The hospital is a fine building of three storeys, with red roof and white walls. Alongside is one of the new wind-motor towers, which are beginning to spread through the North-West. There are about twenty whites including half a dozen women at Norman, and some of the houses have central heating, based on oil sent down from the wells.

As the sketch map shows, there are a number of gardens in the post. The crops and conditions of growth do not vary much as we journey north. As mentioned earlier the July temperatures along the Mackenzie from Hay River north to Good Hope vary between 59° F. and 62° F., while the temperature in the same month in latitude 45° N. at Saint John (New Brunswick) is 61° F.; and about the same at Schreiber, White River and Franz—all near latitude 49° N. (Note the isotherm for 59° F. for July shown on Fig. 2.)

Crop conditions are much the same as we have observed hitherto. Tomatoes serve as a test crop in this region. They are transplanted in the open
(but under glass) at the end of May. They grow to full size, but need to be
ripened, after harvest, indoors. Celery grows well to 30 inches; while a
special bantam variety of maize shows promise. There are plenty of cabbages,
lettuce, and similar vegetables.   Five acres of potatoes are grown in the vicinity, and slough grass is cut and brought by boat for the use of a couple of
horses at the post. The latter are used in collecting wood for fuel, etc. Of
considerable interest is the seam of coal about five miles up the river. This
lignite has been burning ever since Mackenzie explored the river in 1789. It
is a poor quality coal and occurs in a capping of Tertiary deposits just south
of Fort Norman. It has not been found worth transport to date.

At Norman Wells the Mackenzie valley is about 25 miles wide. The
drainage is poorly developed and there is much muskeg. In this region the
permanent frost is found to extend about 100 feet beneath the surface, and in
the muskeg area the surface thaws to a depth of only a foot beneath
the moss covering. Like all the other river settlements, Norman Wells is
strung out along the river bank, in this case for about two miles. There is a
rather broad sloping beach below a cut-bank about 40 feet high, but the silts
from Bosworth Creek at the north-west end have built out a perceptible delta.
There is a large airport flanked by a dozen or more buildings about a mile to
the south-east of the settlement. Planes linking the oil wells to Edmonton
or to Whitehorse fly into this airport practically every day.[7]

There are four well-defined sections to the town. At the south-east end
is the residential quarter surrounding the hotel. The latter is an imposing
wooden building of two-and-a-half storeys, which is controlled by an American
army officer. This section also contains the post office, commissary, main
mess building, and many of the women's tent-houses. Duckboard sidewalks link the buildings, for the dirt roads become deep in mud when it
rains. A hospital, recreation hall and the radio station are to be found in
this quarter also. A fine clump of poplars has been preserved in front of the
hotel, and some small gardens contain a few flowers. There is no church,
though service is held in the hall occasionally. No children are allowed in the
settlement, and the seventy women are all employees of the various oil units.
The total population is about five hundred.

The next section farther to the north-west is where the engineers live,
and where their machine shops and stores have been erected. A further area
in the rear of the settlement is used to store many other of the engineer's
supplies. Very noticeable around the place were the huge bull-dozers and
carry-alls. A boiler mounted in a caboose on runners was used to supply live
steam, wherever it was necessary to sink posts through the frozen ground. It

[7]See Part IV by E. L. Bruce for a detailed analysis of the Norman Wells oil development.

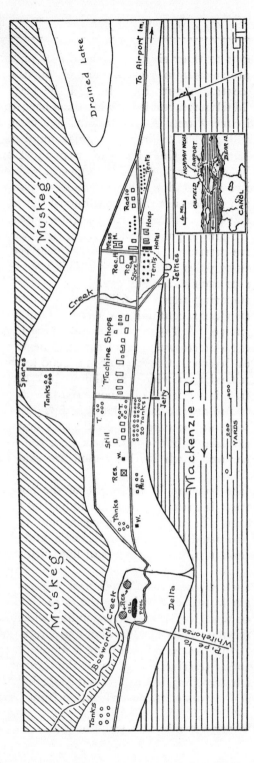

Fig. 15. A sketch survey of Norman Wells, looking north at 65°20′ N. Note the four divisions in the settlement. In the inset map Canol and the oval oilfield are indicated. (w. is a well.)

takes about half an hour to thaw six feet. All surface pipes for conveying water about the area are encased in wooden channels filled with sawdust.

The third section centres about the wells and the large still. In this section is the original Mackinnon residence which has been there since 1920 and is close to the discovery well. A few Indians live close by, and they are maintaining a small garden. There are great numbers of oil tanks, mostly painted with aluminium. One cluster of twenty just by the river is a very prominent sight from boat or plane. The large still is about 25 feet high, and breaks the oil into various grades. Other cylinders separate the gas from the liquid, and some of the gas is burning continuously in large flares down on the beach. Here there is a portable jetty made of steel pipes, used in loading oil on to barges, etc. It can be pulled ashore when the river freezes, and so it is not damaged by ice pressure. The main wharf near the hotel is simply silt piled above bundles of poles and branches. This type of wharf is often much damaged by the ice each spring and fall.

The wells are not imposing after the drilling rig is removed. One sees a black hole about 5 feet square, containing a sort of stand-pipe with a large valve and a pressure gauge. A 1½-inch horizontal pipe leads the oil to a neighbouring tank. At the north-west end of the settlement the road crosses the rather deep gully of Bosworth Creek; and in a bend in the latter are the two largest tanks on the field, from which the oil flows to Whitehorse 600 miles away. Below these tanks is a pool of oil, about 150 feet long, held up by a rough bank of muskeg; and nearby the 4-inch pipe dips into the river, which is over 4 miles wide here, and so carries the oil on its first stage to Canol. We made a visit to Bear Island, but found rather poor soil with a growth of medium spruce. Poplar and birch in this region are said to indicate the better soils.

It is difficult to place Norman Wells in one of the normal classes of a pioneer settlement, since it is essentially only an industrial camp. No doubt if the oil supplies continue for many years a permanent town will develop, but in the absence of the usual houses, shops, schools, and churches, as well as the Hudson's Bay buildings, it is quite out of line with the other pioneer towns at present.

Good Hope, the Ramparts, and the Rapids near latitude 66° N. About thirty miles downstream from Norman Wells the hard Devonian rocks give place to soft Cretaceous deposits with a corresponding widening of the river. Thereafter there are alternate belts of Devonian and Cretaceous rocks, each around ten miles wide. In this next section there is more scenery and variety than in any other portion of the river. Just below the Carcajou River are the Sans Sault rapids, which according to Camsell and Malcolm[8] (1921) offer the most important obstruction to steamboat navigation from Great Slave Lake

[8]*Geological Survey Bulletin on Mackenzie River* (Ottawa, 1921).

to the sea. "In high water the rapid is drowned out, but in low water the fall is increased and becomes a more serious obstruction. The usual canoe route is down the western channel, where the fall is more gradual than on the east side." We spent a morning taking the barges through the broken water of the rapids one at a time. As it was high water there was no appearance of a perceptible drop in the river level.

The salient features in the very remarkable thirty miles north of the Ramparts rapids are charted in Fig. 16. About ten miles above Good Hope

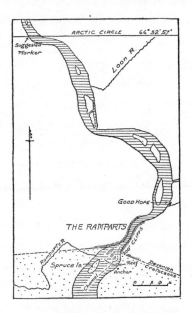

Fig. 16. The Mackenzie River near Good Hope, showing the rapids at the Ramparts, and the position of the Arctic Circle.

the river is three miles wide with rather low shores. The boat swings round to the north-east and an apparently unbroken line of vertical cliffs seems to run right across the river. This is the hard outcrop of the Devonian rocks, and a difficult reef must be crossed before the narrow outlet to the north is attained. The passage through the Ramparts is only about 500 yards wide, and the almost vertical cliffs at the sides increase from a height of 125 feet to about 250 feet at the lower end. This narrow passage is about 7 miles long, and there is nothing else like it in the whole river. The winding channel used by the steamer south of the gorge is indicated in the chart, and a good deal of the reef is visible just about water level. At very low water there is a total drop of about 20 feet, and on occasion steamers have been held for as much as 28 days trying to ascend the river. At times a strong cable has been fastened to an anchor on the shore, and the steamer hauls itself up. When we went through at high water there was little difficulty.

We arrived at Good Hope about 6 P.M. on July 12. The post is perched on the east bank of a long narrow promontory, where Jackfish Creek enters the main river (Fig. 17). The cut-bank is over 40 feet high, and all the settlers, including over 150 Indians, were collected on the top of the bank to welcome the steamer. Beyond Norman Wells there is very little transport except an occasional plane, so that ours was the first large influx of passengers and goods for the year. The North West Company founded a fort of this name near here (67° 27′) in 1805, but in 1823 it was moved north to near Thunder River and thence to an island near the present site, which was occupied in 1836.

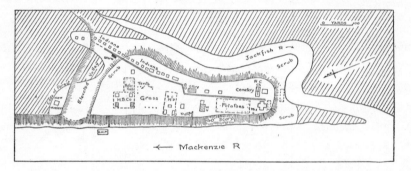

Fig. 17. A sketch survey of Fort Good Hope (looking east) at 66° N. Dotted areas are gardens.

There is more "scenery" at this post and the next (Arctic Red) than in the remainder of the river settlements. The steep scarp (Fig. 17) is surmounted by two simple tramways, up which cars laden with cargo are hauled. Jackfish Creek cuts off the back of the settlement, and lies at the foot of a slope nearly as steep as the scarp to the main river. At the northern end there is a fairly well-defined high-level valley, which probably marks a former outlet of Jackfish Creek. The white population is fourteen, but 337 Indians make Good Hope their headquarters.

The whole settlement is less than half a mile long, but it contains two stores besides the usual Hudson's Bay store. The main buildings crown the crest of the cut-bank as shown in Fig. 17. The Hudson's Bay offices are immediately above the landing place. Across a grassy field is the enclosure containing the police offices, where there are usually two police in residence. Then a large garden devoted to potatoes borders the Catholic lands, which lie on the tip of the promontory in the extreme south of the post. Here they have a relatively large church with an imposing mission house alongside. One of the priests takes a great interest in agriculture, and was quite proud of his little gasolene-driven plough.

Good Hope is famous in Canada, for here have been recorded the lowest minimum temperatures. In December, 1910, the thermometer fell to −79° F. However, the July average is 60° F. (much the same as the coast of New Brunswick), with temperatures near 54° F. in mid June and mid August. With such a summer the cold winter does not affect the growth of many useful vegetables. For instance, in the various gardens at the post, the peas were 14 inches high, and were flowering freely. Cabbages looked very vigorous with leaves 8 by 6 inches. Tomatoes do not do very well, nor do cucumbers.

The Hudson's Bay manager in 1943 grew 125 lbs. of turnips, 130 lbs. of beets, over 100 cabbages, 380 lbs. of carrots, unlimited peas and lettuce, as well as beans, onions, radishes, spinach, etc. There was of course no reason to grow large amounts with such a small population to cater for.

A somewhat unusual feature was the close-set row of Indian houses on the east side of the "main road." There were over twenty of these, mostly log cabins of course, including two stores owned by a Syrian and an Indian respectively. A number of the Indians were living in tents at the time of our visit, and these were erected in the grassy space in the centre of the post. A new wireless station was being erected at the north end of the settlement in the poplar scrub across the high-level valley mentioned earlier. Here some half a dozen men were employed.

The sad feature about Good Hope was that 80 per cent of the Indians have tuberculosis in greater or lesser degree. In the last two years there were 43 deaths and only 22 births among these Hare Indians. I noted that the ages of those who died from tuberculosis in the years 1942 and 1943 were somewhat as follows:— 76, 71, 51, 46, 35, 32, 31, 25, 25, 22, 21, 19, 15, 12, 10, 10, 8, 6, 6, 6, 6, 5, 4, 4, 3, 2, 2, 2, 2, 1, 1, 1, 1. This is a sad history, for only two of these folk had reached the allotted span of life. It seems almost impossible to get the Indians to take ordinary sanitary precautions in the face of disease, and the number of doctors in the region is entirely too small.[9]

The Indian tents were almost all of the pattern of the white folk, and mostly had board floors. A sheet-iron stove was usual, with the chimney projecting through the canvas roof. I saw no chairs, though iron bedsteads were present in some. Only a few Indian families live at the post during the winter. Their dogs were mostly tethered on the steep bank behind the settlement. Their food consisted of two whitefish (each about 22 inches long) per day. A few dogs were provided with kennels, but most lay in the open fastened by a chain to stout posts. Good Hope is to be classed as a typical "sub-infantile" type of settlement.

[9]See Part VIII by Dr. G. J. Wherrett.

NORTH OF THE ARCTIC CIRCLE

Gillies River, Arctic Red, and Fort McPherson. Twenty miles north of Good Hope the Mackenzie crosses the Arctic Circle (latitude 66° 32′ 57″ N.). Locally there seemed to be a good deal of doubt exactly where this interesting spot actually occurs, and so it is indicated fairly accurately in Fig. 16. Since in the not distant future many tourists will make this journey, it seems advisable that a permanent marker or monument be erected on the west bank of the river, where it will be readily visible from the steamer travelling north.

The *Distributor* on her first voyage in 1944 crossed the Circle about 2 A.M. on July 13. It seemed a very interesting event to the writer, who had not

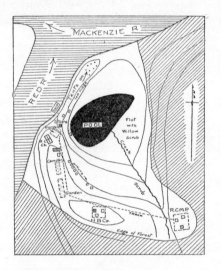

FIG. 18. A sketch survey of Arctic Red River, looking north. The pool is about 200 yards long. The form-lines are about 20 feet apart in elevation.

previously been north of 62° N., and so he was glad to have the opportunity to walk some miles along the banks in the vicinity of Gillies River (66° 43′ N.), where we stopped to fuel the boat. South of the Antarctic Circle nothing grows but an occasional patch of moss on a sunny dark rock. Here, well north of the Arctic Circle, we found three rows of logs each 8 feet high and 4 feet wide, and amounting in all to 200 cords. Many of the logs were close to 2 feet in diameter, and all were cut in the immediate vicinity of the landing, and hauled by caterpillar to the shore.

Near the banks there was a fairly dense willow scrub, but the spruce came close to the river in most places. I made a collection of the chief plants, among which were alder, wild currant, mooseberry, purple fireweed, yellow cinquefoil, purple paintbrush, yarrow, shepherdia, purple pea, and a purple daisy. Many of the spruce trees were disfigured with huge spherical bulges in the stem, which swelled the trunk to twice the usual dimensions. We stayed at Gillies River until 2 A.M. of July 14.

For a considerable portion of its course the Mackenzie flows to the west across Cretaceous beds. Here the banks were long, high, and straight, rising to 200 feet in many places. Nowhere have I seen such regular triangular "facets" along sloping cliffs, separated by shallow gullies. I counted 77 of these "facets" in a distance of 2½ miles, but I am unable to explain their regularity.

Near Thunder River much of the wide river is quite shallow, so that the boat has to skirt the southern shore for some miles. Near here remarkable

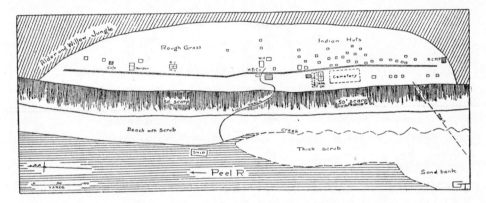

FIG. 19. A sketch survey of Fort McPherson (67°30′ N.), looking east.

mud avalanches were seen, carrying large amounts of silty material down the steep slopes of the facets. Sage-brush was abundant on these fairly steep shaley slopes. Just above Arctic Red the river curves round almost in a horseshoe at a place called the Lower Ramparts. The river is here only about half a mile wide, but there is no "rapid," and the current is about 5 miles an hour. The slopes are in the form of "facets" at the Narrows, and the beds seem to be nearly horizontal. The facets rise steeply from the river to a height of about 300 feet.

Arctic Red River post is situated at the mouth of the Arctic Red River on the east bank, just south of its junction with the Mackenzie. It has the most picturesque situation of all the posts, for the houses extend along a high curved ridge which encloses a pretty little pool, about 200 yards long, some 25 feet above the river level. Calla (arum) lilies, with large green leaves and white bract-shaped flowers, border this pool. There is a swampy area back of the pool, and the south-east slope is a blaze of purple fireweed in July.

The general arrangement of the post can be gathered from the sketch survey in Fig. 18. A novel feature is the distance away from the river of the Hudson's Bay buildings and of the R.C.M.P. post; both of which are on the hill, the latter half a mile from the water's edge. The most commanding position is that of the Catholic church on the end of the promontory nearly 100 feet above the river. The mission house and cemetery are close beside the church. There is a small store close to the landing place, with a few huts nearby. A row of small Indian huts south of the pool and a larger group between the church and Hudson's Bay Company complete the settlement.

There are only half a dozen white folk at the post, including two priests and two police. About three families of Indians live here, but there are about 218 Indians in the vicinity who make this post their headquarters and visit it during the summer. Many of their tents were erected on the shingle bank west of the pool. The small gardens were interesting owing to the latitude of 67° 30′ N. The one shown in the sketch survey just below the church, contained cabbages with leaves 11 inches long, lettuce 6 inches long, potatoes 24 inches high, but not yet in flower, peas 20 inches high and already in flower. This was on July 14, so that there was still a period of about six weeks before the growing period ended. We had some of the lettuce at lunch that day. In a small greenhouse by the garden, which had been warmed by a stove earlier in the year, tomatoes were in flower and two feet high. Other gardens had been made along the top of the ridge, which were given chiefly to the growth of potatoes. The spruce trees in the vicinity were about 15 or 16 inches in diameter.

Early on the morning after leaving Arctic Red River we were steaming up the tributary Peel River to reach the post at McPherson, which lies in the same latitude as Arctic Red, but some 32 miles to the west. John Bell had explored Peel River in 1839, and in 1840 he established Fort McPherson. In 1842-6 Bell explored the area to the west and found a practicable route up the Rat River, over the divide to the Porcupine River, and so down to the Yukon River, on which Fort Selkirk was built in 1848 (Fig. 20).

Fort McPherson agrees well with the general pattern of the river settlements, since it is strung out along the cut-bank for about half a mile (Fig. 19). The scarp is, however, rather high, and at the base are two lower terraces, so that the houses must be about 80 feet above the Peel River. The steamer berthed alongside a muddy shelf covered with a scrub of willows. A diagonal track up the scarp is used by a caterpillar tractor, which hauls the goods up to the large warehouse of the Hudson's Bay Company. A newer and larger store is being erected by the company. An unusual feature at this post is that the Anglicans have a church and mission; while the Catholics are only just commencing, in a small mission house, to make contacts with the numerous Indians. There is no Catholic priest in residence. A new police post for

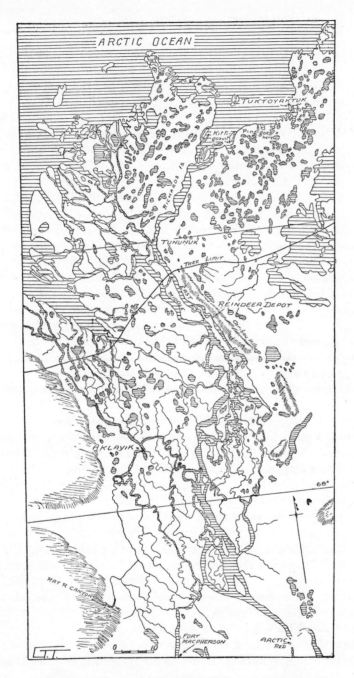

FIG. 20. The topography of the Delta of the Mackenzie, showing the undulating glacial country north of Reindeer Depot. (From the official chart.)

summer occupation is being built at the extreme south end of the settlement, and the total white population is only half a dozen. About three hundred Loucheux Indians make this their headquarters, and the Indian huts are very numerous behind the Anglican church as the sketch map (Fig. 19) demonstrates. At the north end there is a small café. In the garden near the church delphiniums, nasturtiums, and aquilegia were flowering. Peas were 24 inches high, but not yet flowering. Cabbages, lettuce, carrots and beans were similar to those at Good Hope.

The Delta of the Mackenzie: Aklavik and Tuktoyaktuk. Twenty miles north of Arctic Red we reach the head of the great Mackenzie delta (Fig. 20). This seems to be unlike other deltas observed by the writer, since the problem of deposition by a large river is complicated by the vast deposition of glacial material along the northern coasts as apparent at Tuktoyaktuk (or Tuktuk). The southern and western parts of the delta therefore show the usual branching distributaries of a large river entering the ocean. But the north-eastern portion has a much more undulating surface; and is further diversified by the unusual *ping-goes* or "mud craters," many of which were visible on the shores near Tuktuk. In this north-eastern section, judging by the area around Tuktoyaktuk, the elevation is considerably greater than in the delta proper. The most characteristic features are the innumerable lakes, more or less oval, and about one to two miles long. Tununuk, at the southern tip of Richards Island, seems to mark the boundary between the Mackenzie delta and the "lakeland" area.

Strictly speaking therefore, the delta of the Mackenzie fills a long wide gulf, about 125 miles long and 50 miles wide. It is fairly definitely bounded by the Caribou hills on the east side, which rise steeply for about 500 feet behind Reindeer Depot. Still wider highlands come close to the delta on the west. The Rat River has cut a deep gorge through the fault-scarp of the Richardson mountains, as is indicated in Fig. 20.

Half way down the delta there are three fairly well-defined channels, as well as the innumerable anastomosing branches of other small distributaries. The main channel seems to keep mainly to the east side of the "infilled gulf." Near Reindeer Depot it splits into an east and a middle channel, of which the former has the major opening to the Arctic Ocean. Near Tununuk it turns to the north-east and seems to follow a slight downwarp in the lakeland area. Its shores, within the treeless lands of the tundra, have a different topography from that of the delta proper, as can be seen from Fig. 20.

The west channel seems to be a continuation of the meandering Peel River, whose channel links with an important arm of the Mackenzie at Aklavik. The west channel enters the ocean west of meridian 136°, and no main channel opens into the well-marked bay shown in Fig. 20. It is to be noted that these delta islands alter in shape rather rapidly, and the last surveys (1943) differ a good deal from those issued previously. If the explanation given herewith that the "lakeland area" north and north-east of Tununuk does not result from river deposition, then the Mackenzie has not built a conventional triangular delta out into the sea, as has happened in the case of the classical delta of the Nile. The river has probably been filling the northern end of one of the dominant north-west to south-east depressions (drowned by the sea) mentioned in the first section of this study.

"The banks are low, built of alluvial material, and forested with spruce and willows. Northward the banks gradually diminish in height, and the forest growth decreases and gradually disappears. The depth of the eastern channel is not less than 5 feet anywhere throughout its length. The great lakes along the Mackenzie collect much of the normal silt, so that the delta is only slowly being built into the sea. They also regulate the flow of the river, and according to McConnell the average discharge is about 500,000 cubic feet per second."[10]

En route from Fort McPherson to Aklavik the boat stopped to collect fuel from the forest in the delta. Here the trees were of about 16 inch diameter, and grew upon a dark loamy sand. The banks in latitude 68° N. rose about twenty feet above the river. We tramped some distance into the forest, and were greatly annoyed by the immense numbers of mosquitoes. We landed at Aklavik at 7.30 A.M. on July 17. This settlement of Aklavik (pronounced *A-klàv-ik*) is the metropolis of the north, for there are about 170 white folk, 213 Indians and 377 Eskimo in the district. It marks the southern limit of the Eskimo in this area.

Aklavik became a small fur-trading post in 1912. In 1923 the police moved their station from Herschel Island, about 150 miles to the north-west, to this spot in the middle of the delta. The Hudson's Bay Company soon made it their centre since there was a far better supply of fuel and timber.

The temperatures at Aklavik are often high in July. From July 17 to July 27 in 1944 the maximum temperatures each day were as follows: 69°, 75°, 82°, 76°, 76°, 57°, 62°, 58°, 67°, 65°, 60°. As stated, the average July temperature in east Gaspé is about the same (i.e. 57° F.) as at Aklavik; so that there is nothing Arctic about the climate in summer, though the place is 122 miles north of the Arctic Circle. It must be remembered also that in latitude 68° N. there are over eighteen hours of daylight for the four warmer months. Of course in January Aklavik's average is −19° F., while at Gaspé it is +11° F.; a difference of 30° F. in favour of Gaspé.

On our arrival the residents were waiting on top of the 15 foot cut-bank, and it was not easy to distinguish Indians from Eskimo. Today the men have all adopted the garb of the white folk, though they usually wear a huge fur collar on their parkas. However the native women, whether Indian or Eskimo, all wear long Mother Hubbard dresses with a flounce and a border of fur. The taller figures make a rather impressive appearance in this garb.

[10]Camsell and Malcolm, *Geological Survey Bulletin on Mackenzie River.*

There is an old wooden wharf opposite the Hudson's Bay store at Aklavik, which suffers at times from ice pressure (Fig. 21). On the low cut-bank right in the roadway a wooden scow was being built. A young calf, part of Dr. Livingstone's famous herd, was eating the grass in his private garden just back of the wharf. I walked half a mile to the west along the river bank, passing the Catholic "quarter," and reached the field of oats and the large clearing with a barn, where these "polar" cattle are grazed normally.

Aklavik has been built where the Peel channel joins the west channel of the Mackenzie, i.e., about 40 miles north of the mouth of the Peel River. Originally the post was erected in 1912 on the south bank of the dis-

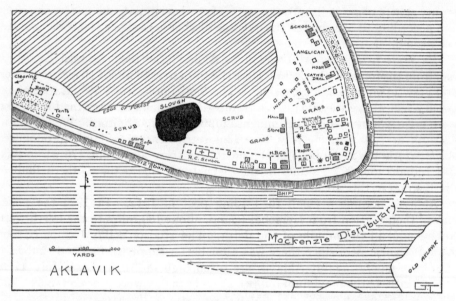

Fig. 21. A sketch survey of Aklavik, looking to the north. The figures refer to storeys.

tributary, here about 300 yards wide; but it was transferred to the north bank about 1920. It occupies a rounded promontory jutting to the south-east, and the main road borders the shore in the form of a crescent. Two other roads near the point help to form a square, and lead to the grassy clearing at the back of the settlement where a dozen or more Indian shacks are built.

The little post office is at the corner, with the radio station on the west and the police station on the north. Then in the north-east quarter of the town is the large Anglican community, much the most impressive of any such group in the whole North-West. Along this part of the river front a reserve has been left about 50 yards wide. Much of this has been ploughed in 1944, and sown with oats. This probably will not ripen, but will be cut for cattle food in late September. Behind the large radio station there is a community hall and a large private store. There is also a smaller store on the point near the post office, and yet another (with a café), between the Catholic school and the Livingstone barn. In the rear of the Catholic school is a pool or slough about 150 yards across.

Though Aklavik is not large compared with Igarka (with 15,000 inhabitants in 1937)—which the Russians have built in a similar latitude on the Yenesei River—yet it has some impressive buildings. For instance the Anglican cathedral consists of a nave with a well-proportioned square tower at the north-east corner. It is a frame building painted light yellow, as are all the buildings in the Anglican quarter. The remarkable altar picture— about 8 feet wide—represents the Wise Men presenting gifts. The various figures in the painting, which was executed by an Australian artist, are clothed in the garb of polar Canada.

To the south of the cathedral is the two-storey house occupied by the clergyman; while to the north is the large two-storey hospital, built with two wings projecting in front of the central portion of the building. Further to the north is another neat two-storey dwelling where the senior teacher lives. Then comes the large boarding school of a somewhat similar style to the hospital. Here about 50 Indian children and 50 Eskimo children live a large part of the year. They go home for the summer vacation, and we carried six Eskimo children to Tuktuk within a few days. There were several white teachers at the school.

The Catholic buildings in the west of the settlement were of a similar character, but the school was larger, comprising three storeys. A portion of this building is used as a church. There is also a Catholic hospital and a large house for the priests, of whom there are half a dozen, as well as a number of sisters. The number of children in the school was about the same as in the Anglican community. Anchored in the stream was an auxiliary yacht which belonged to the Catholic mission.

From the point of future settlement the presence of a dairy herd here is of much interest. The cows live in the barn until the end of May, when they come out and graze in the vicinity. The newly cleared spruce forest seems to produce mainly *Equisetum* (horse-tails) at first, but the grass in the older clearings among the houses and behind the settlement seems much more attractive to the cattle. There is some native grass near Aklavik which is cut and used as hay. Early in June the new grass has grown large enough to be useful. The oats is sown at the end of June, while vegetable seeds are sown two or three weeks earlier. Lettuce and radishes can be used about July 7. Towards the end of August frost is expected; and potatoes are dug early in September, while the grain is cut towards the end of this month.

About mid-October the cattle go back to winter in the barn. Dr. Living-stone distributes the milk in the usual sealed bottles, whose caps bear a printed label "Polar Sea Dairy Farm."

Aklavik has been described as the metropolis of the far north. Its possession of a cathedral, the seat of the Bishop of the Arctic, would, according to some definitions, entitle it to be classed as a "city"! But a reference to the classes described earlier in this memoir, places it among the *"infantile"* type of settlements. It has the beginnings of a town plan, in the shape of the square of streets back of the promontory. However the shops are scattered, there are no factories, and there is no definite separation of better and poorer houses among the white settlers. The Indian area is, however, as usual somewhat segregated from that occupied by the Europeans. Most of the latter live in one-storey frame houses, but there are a few of two storeys, while others are mere log cabins. As noted, the religious houses are quite superior.

The boat left Aklavik at midnight, and steamed to the east along the rather narrow western channel shown in Fig. 20 so as to reach the main channel about 8 A.M. on July 19. By 4 P.M. we were off the Reindeer Depot, where it was necessary to obtain a permit to pass through the Reindeer Reserve. The depot is very prettily sited below a cleft in the range of Caribou hills. We are now approaching the northern edge of the Taiga, and the upper parts of the hills are bare, though spruce still grows thick in the gullies. There are about a dozen houses at the depot, including several two-storey, painted, residences. Plenty of trees have been left in the settlement, and it seems a much better site for a town than does Aklavik, though I had no time to go ashore and make a survey. In the hilly country back of the depot graze the reindeer brought across by Lapps from Alaska to the Mackenzie delta. The drive of over three thousand deer occupied five years, and only concluded in March, 1935. The animals are grazed on Richards Island in the summer, and moved back to the mainland in the fall (Fig. 20). Eskimo youths are serving as apprentice reindeer-herders.

Some ten miles north of Reindeer Depot there is the greatest change in the environment on the whole journey. Here is the well-marked northern limit of the Taiga or coniferous forest (Fig. 20). The spruce forest ends relatively abruptly, and as Richards Island came into view we saw the last clumps of spruce left behind. The low muddy islands in the channel were, however, clothed with dwarf willow, cotton grass, etc., though broad mud-banks showed that some of the land had only recently been formed.

Next morning we were in the Arctic Ocean, east of Richards Island. Along the shore to the east were numerous mounds, like small volcanoes, apparently about 100 feet high. These are the *ping-goes* of the Eskimo. They seem to be mud mounds but have not been examined, I understand, by a geologist. (There was no specimen close enough to Tuktuk for me to visit it, for here as elsewhere it was necessary to keep within a mile or so of the boat, for she left as soon as the weather became at all favourable.) After reading a description by A. E. Porsild,[11] I believe that they are due to the final freezing (and expansion) of the *centre* of a mud-filled lake after a specially hot summer. They closely resemble the "apple-pie mounds" which I describe in my Antarctic book *Physiography of Macmurdo Sound*.[12] We were held up near Kittigazuit (which we did not visit) the whole of July 20 and 21, waiting for a perfect calm, so that the boat could traverse the 20 miles of open ocean which

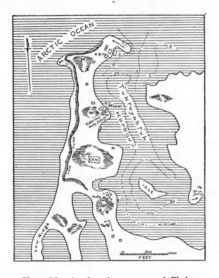

Fig. 22. A sketch survey of Tukto-yaktuk (Tuktuk), the ocean port, at 69°30′ N. (Depths from the official chart.)

separated us from the sheltered port of Tuktuk. We reached the latter at 9.30 A.M. on July 22.

Tuktoyaktuk (Tuktuk or Tuk) has only been opened as a port for a few years, and this was the second voyage made there by the *Distributor*. It was started as a convenient meeting-place for the river and ocean steamers and schooners. The river boats, as explained, are too flat-bottomed to venture far into the ocean, while the ocean boats have too deep a draught to tackle most of the channels of the delta. As mentioned earlier, the topography of the lakeland area north and east of Tununuk, consists of alternating lakes and

[11]*Geographic Review*, New York, Jan., 1938.
[12]London, 1922, p. 123.

rounded hillocks, the latter rising some 50 to 100 feet above the sea. These hillocks are quite different from the *ping-goes*, which have fairly steep sides like miniature volcanoes, whereas the hillocks are more like *drumlins*, though they do not show any marked common axial direction.

The sea has drowned many of the small depressions, giving rise to the much embayed coasts seen near Tuktuk in Fig. 20. Indeed the harbour at Tuktuk is but the protection afforded by a cluster of such hillocks, which are grouped into several islands and promontories as appears in the chart. The topography in the vicinity of the little port is shown in the map in Fig. 22 which represents a pace-and-compass survey made during our six days' stay. It was checked by the naval chart, which has only recently been completed for this area.

A long narrow promontory runs almost due north for about a mile; and shuts off a similar-shaped elongated harbour to the east, between the promontory and an island also marked by the characteristic hillocks. There is about 12 feet of water at the narrow mouth of the harbour, which deepens to 20 feet to the south. There are really two settlements at Tuktuk, for a small ship repair yard has been developed about two miles to the south-east of the main settlement, and here several small coastal schooners were drawn up on shore for needed repairs. At this ship-yard there was a small stream, from which the settlers at the mouth of the harbour received their water supply by boat as needed. This is obviously a considerable disadvantage to the future of Tuktuk.

There is of course no resemblance between this "hillock and lake" topography and the flat cut-banks and river terraces on which the settlements on the Mackenzie River have been built. The hillocks near Tuktuk were about 50 feet high, and seemed regularly arranged about 1,000 feet apart, but this may only be a local characteristic, since I did not see anything of the rest of the country. Glacial deposition, together with some elevation of the sea floor, rather than delta deposition, seems best to explain the topography of this lakeland.

There was considerable evidence of ocean erosion in the form of gravel-spits at the west side of the entrance, and again at the "heel" of the foot-shaped promontory. Moreover the exposed western coast of the promontory was cut into a continuous cliff, about 15 or 20 feet high, where the waves in storms had eaten into the promontory. The whole surface was covered with a close tundra vegetation, in which very little moss or lichen was present. Dwarf willows were abundant, and grew up to three feet high in the gullies. Some dwarf birch about six inches high was also common. Large patches of flowering lupin were abundant, also a sort of Shasta daisy, betony, and smaller patches of buttercups, shinleaf, and a few Dryas. Primulas, fireweed, Labrador tea, and cranberries with many sedges and grasses made up the rest of the cover. Near the "heel" of the promontory were beds of peat about four feet thick, exposed in the low cliff mentioned previously. This peat was in an early stage of formation, and had made little progress towards lignite.

The new Hudson's Bay store was a neat building as usual, with a residence and several sheds surrounding it. The manager was accompanied by his wife and small daughter, and apart from two Catholic priests they were the sole white residents. There was no church building; but an interesting enclosed altar could be unveiled in the main room of the French mission house, and the room then serves as a small chapel. There were about a dozen Eskimo families living at Tuktuk, some in huts near the mission, others about half a mile to the south. There were a number of small sailing boats with auxiliary engines drawn up on the beaches of the little bays. These belonged to the Eskimo, who went out catching the white whales, seals, and fish in the ocean to the north. In summer there was, of course, no vestige of snow or ice on the land, but it was interesting to see again the "ice blink" far to the north, which was familiar to me in the Antarctic. This was a sort of silvery glare due to reflection from the pack ice, which indicated that the latter was present about thirty miles to the north of Tuktuk.

In addition to the Eskimo huts, some of which, near the mission, consisted of several rooms, there were a number of tents, especially near the "toe" and "heel" of the promontory, and at the south end of the district. The sledge dogs were tethered near these tents, and several of the sledges were lying on the shingle. They were quite different from those used by the Indians farther south, being built of an open framework or deck a foot above the runners, while two sloping supports carry a cross handle at the rear. Racks for drying fish or the flesh of the white whale were much in evidence, and skins of the latter were pegged out to dry on the ground. At the end of the "toe," one of the harpoon floats—made from the bladder of some animal—was lying alongside some masses of whale-flesh. We were interested in the harpoons, with movable barbs—whose use was demonstrated by some of the whalers when they brought in the white whales. Several Eskimo graves were visited just west of the European cemetery on the hill. They consisted of a shallow hole in which the bodies were laid. These were covered with logs of wood, and left to the mercy of the wind and rain. Most of the skulls seemed to have been "collected."

One of the most interesting features was the little garden maintained by the wife of the manager so far north as 69° 27′ N. In one small patch of cultivation she had radishes, but only 1 inch high, since it had been a very cold spring. She counts on getting lettuce and spinach, and occasionally a cabbage or two. But there is a big change in the possibilities of growing crops to the north of Aklavik, as indeed the natural vegetation would indicate. There is of course permanently frozen soil only a foot below the surface, even in summer, but the conditions vary a good deal with the nature of the soil. On the Yenesei the northern limit of open crop-lands is placed at Potavpo in latitude 68° 30′, about the same as Aklavik; so that there is not much hope of agriculture at Tuktuk. The settlement is clearly in the "sub-infantile" stage.

Part Three

GRIFFITH TAYLOR

A Yukon Domesday: 1944

The Yukon Basin from Whitehorse to Dawson City

WHITEHORSE has a position on the Lewes-Yukon River system which is analogous to that of Fort Smith; i.e., it is at the south end of the navigable portion of a huge river, and hence a town has inevitably grown up at this site. The Whitehorse Rapids lie about a mile above the town and were not a complete obstacle to traffic, since in the early days many scows and rafts floated down them *en route* to the Klondike gold-field.

The history of Whitehorse falls into two parts. The first is linked with the traffic crossing from the sea by the railway to its terminus at Whitehorse, where cargo was trans-shipped to steamer or winter road. The second phase began about March, 1942, when the first American engineers arrived. Three great enterprises resulted from the war with Japan. First, a very large airport was built on the high, flat terrace behind Whitehorse; second, depots for use in connection with the Alaska Highway were placed here; third, Whitehorse became the terminus of the six-hundred mile pipeline from Norman Wells, and a large refinery was built here to process the oil. As a result the population of Whitehorse has grown almost as rapidly as did that of Dawson in the gold-rush of 1897-8. Since the latter town has declined greatly, the two towns offer very interesting contrasts in urban development.

The topography in the vicinity of Whitehorse can be understood by reference to the outline map shown in Fig. 1. This is based on a map distributed to tourists, and is really necessary to enable them to find their way about the extremely spread-out plan of modern Whitehorse. Below the rapids which appear at the extreme left of the map, the river expands into a small lake about half a mile long. This "lake" washes the foot of the remarkable bench (or terrace) of white clay, which rises some 200 feet behind the town. The airport has been constructed on the flat ground above this scarp, and the Alcan (or Alaska) Highway runs along the western edge of the airport. The White Pass Railway runs at the foot of the clay scarp, about 20 feet above the river. It suffers a good deal from small landslides which drop down the face of the clay scarp.

The modern town is built on the flat lower terrace or bench about 20 feet above the river, and this terrace expands to a width of over half a mile about a mile below the rapids (Fig. 2). Here a conventional plan of some eight roads at right angles to the river bank, crossed by seven roads parallel to the river, has been laid down. This portion of the town is all that I was able to survey, since

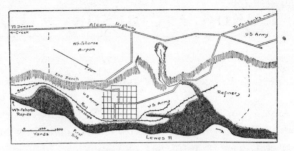

Fig. 1. The vicinity of Whitehorse—from a map
distributed to the public.

the other three or four recent sections of the town were under military surveillance, and no sketching or photography was permitted near them. These are labelled "U.S. Army" or "Refinery" or "Airport" in Fig. 1. Two main roads

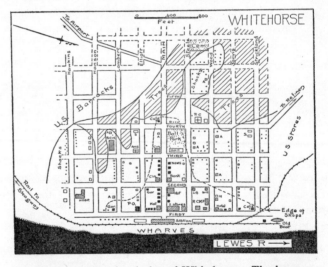

Fig. 2. A functional plan of Whitehorse. The important buildings are ruled; the shops are black; the better houses are marked A; shacks are shown by dots.

have been cut up the steep scarp as shown. One leads to the airport, and the other, after about three miles, reaches the headquarters of the army on the Alaska Highway.

The normal white population of Whitehorse is about 500, but the influx of Americans and other folk connected with the new developments mentioned above, has given it a temporary population of 8,000. This is largely accommodated in barracks and tents in the areas labelled "U.S. Army" in Fig. 1. Many of these temporary frame buildings have been erected in the southern corner of the town-plan, as may be seen by reference to Fig. 2, where the arrangement of the houses, shops, etc., is given in detail.

First Street lies about 200 feet away from the river bank, and the intervening strip carries the railway line, and the station, as well as a number of offices and warehouses. At the south end of the warehouses are a number of shacks, shown by dots in Fig. 2. At the northern end of this strip along the river is a row of old steamboats, pulled up on the shore and gradually falling to pieces. The central street at right angles to the river is Main Street; and most of the shops are to be found on this artery, or along the west side of First Street. As is often the case, the business portion of the town occupies a triangle based on the two main streets. The post office, like many of the main shops, is a two-storey building, and is situated just south of the station. The largest stores front the station on First Street, while the leading hotel is a fine establishment of three storeys on Main and Second. Here also is the bank, while two theatres face the latter. There is a ball park with a large recreation hall at the apex of the "triangle" on Fourth Street. To the north-west of the station is the government block, containing the large police headquarters, the signals depot, and the liquor store. Two smaller hotels are situated on First Street.

A list of the smaller shops in this northern centre should be of interest. Along First Street are (from north to south), a café, tailor, telegraph office, drugstore, bakery, airlines, and garage. On the south side of Main Street are an electrician, realtor, jeweller, barber, and café; and on the north side, butcher, café, bowls, and tailor. The hospital is an imposing building of three storeys in the south-east of the town, and two blocks to the east is the large school. Nearby is the interesting "Log Church" (Anglican), which is over forty years old. The Catholic church is on Fourth Street, the main cross road leading to the north.

A glance at the map shows that a large portion of the original "checkerboard" of streets is still covered with scrub, especially in the west of the town. Near the cemetery are a number of shacks built by squatters, who pay no rent. As stated, the barracks of the Americans occupy what was formerly empty land in the southwest. In the sketch map I have tried to show the largest houses by the label "A." These are much scattered, though mostly in the north-west near the Catholic church. The smaller houses and rather rough shacks are mixed together, though, as might be expected, the poorer houses border the town on the whole. The town of Whitehorse shows a definite segregation of the business section, and since there are now many factories at the refinery, but no definite zones of better-class houses, we may say that it belongs to the "adolescent" class of small towns.

As earlier stated, Whitehorse is the southern end of navigation on the Lewes-Yukon Rivers. The sternwheel steamers anchor alongside the railway line at Whitehorse, and then steam south a few hundred feet to turn in the river just above the station, a ticklish job with very little room to spare at each end. We left at 6.30 p.m. on August 3 for Dawson City and Klondike. Cargo is carried in the holds and on the deck, and they often push barges along as on the Mackenzie.

The scenery along the river is often most picturesque, and very different from that on the Mackenzie (Fig. 3). The river flows into Lake Laberge about sixteen miles below Whitehorse. The lake is about three miles wide, with blunt

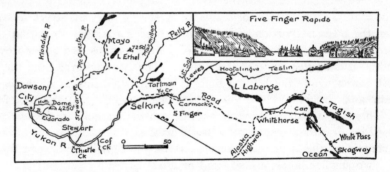

Fig. 3. Sketch map of Lewes-Yukon River from Whitehorse to Dawson City. Inset is a sketch of the rock-bar at Five Finger Rapids. The White-Pass Yukon Railway to the ocean at Skagway is charted also.

pyramid peaks of gray rock rising about 2,000 feet above lake level (2,100 feet). The steamer skirts the eastern shore, and the lake is quite shallow in places. A small settlement of ten houses is situated on the eastern shore. The Teslin River flows into the Lewes from the east at Hootalinqua, and here there is an abandoned police station, a few houses, and an old decaying steamer pulled up on shore. Quite unlike the views along the Mackenzie, were the steep, hilly, and at times mountainous, sides of the river valley. A series of terraces is present in places, reminding one of the characteristic features of the glacial valleys in central British Columbia. Fourteen miles below Big Salmon there are cut-banks formed of white varve clays 20 feet above the river, while some 500 feet higher there appear relics of another bench or terrace. Near Little Salmon there are similar terraces at about 20, 80, and 200 feet above the river. Just to the east of Carmacks the 45-foot scarp shows a very interesting geological section. At the base is about 15 feet of yellowish rubble covered by a foot or two of yellow varve clay. Above this is more coarse yellow debris, and a well-defined layer of about 2 feet of hard gravel. Above this again, is the top layer of 10 feet of white varve clay, in which are many nest-burrows cut by swallows.

The adits of several coal-mines are visible near Carmacks, one being on the east bank and several a little to the north on the west bank. We did not stop at Carmacks, where the overland trail from Whitehorse reaches the river. There was a population of thirty-two here in 1927, but it has fallen to half that figure today. Half a dozen houses, including two of two storeys, were clustered on top of the 12-foot bank. Behind was a wooded slope rising about 150 feet to another flat ridge. Among the trees on the slopes were four more log cabins.

The most scenic spot in the Yukon or Mackenzie basins, in the writer's opinion, is found at the Five Finger Rapids, which are about sixteen miles north of Carmacks (see inset in Fig. 3). Here the big river is barred by a wall of conglomerate, from 20 to 30 feet high, in which five narrow channels have been cut by the rapid waters. Only one of these is wide and deep enough for the steamer to pass through; and since the current is very swift here, the whole traverse is a matter of a minute or two. (On the return journey the steamer at times literally winds its way upstream along a chain fastened to the shore.) Such a wall-like barrier is not uncommon in a small river, but I know of no other similar obstruction, just like the concrete piers of a ruined bridge, on any river as large as the Lewes. About eight miles downstream is Yukon Crossing, where the good road to Dawson ends. But a trail on the east side of the river links the Crossing to Selkirk, Mayo, the Eldorado diggings, and Dawson.

Fort Selkirk is about the largest settlement between Whitehorse and Dawson City. The steamer stopped here for only ten minutes; so that I was unable to do more than make a panorama sketch of the settlement, which is strung out along the top of a 10-foot bank, much like those on the Mackenzie River. The fort dates back for a hundred years, but there are less than a dozen whites living there. There is the usual cluster of frame houses, painted white with the red roofs, which marks the Hudson's Bay centre. Taylor and Drury—a rival firm in the Yukon—have a fair-sized store at Selkirk also. At the west (lower) end of the village are two steepled churches; and there are about a score of other houses, mostly log cabins, which complete the settlement. The white population comprises three folk at the Hudson's Bay store, three at the two Missions, two at the telegraph station, and two at the other store. The number of Indians varies from ten to a hundred according to the season. According to our "Town Classification," Fort Selkirk is "sub-infantile" though a hundred years old.

Below Selkirk, where the large river Pelly enters from the east, the main river changes its name from Lewes to Yukon. The river is now about a mile wide on the average, though it varies in this respect a good deal. The velocity is about four or five miles an hour, and the steamer proceeds at about ten knots in general on its downstream course. (It is of course much slower on the return trip against the current.) At Coffee Creek were half a dozen houses on a flat, and here the steamer was stopped in response to a flag, waved from the bank by a pioneer woman clad in blue denim trousers. Near Thistle Creek there was time to inspect a most interesting garden cultivated by Mr. Israels. He has several fine horses engaged in hauling cordwood for the steamers. Many salmon are caught in the vicinity, and wolves and caribou are relatively abundant. On his verandah in tins were flowering fuchsias and geraniums, which were unexpected so near the Arctic Circle. The garden beds were filled with huge poppies and dahlias. Turnips, parsnips, cabbage, onions, potatoes, soybeans, raspberries, and strawberries were all flourishing in latitude 63° N. Delphiniums 5 feet high were growing wild through the bush nearby. The steamer reached Dawson City about 10 P.M. on August 5.

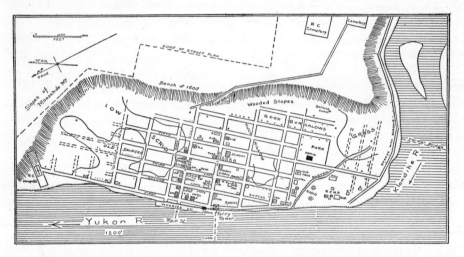

Fig. 4. Functional plan of the dwindling town of Dawson City, Klondike.

Dawson City and the Klondike Gold-field. Dawson City is built on a flat about 20 feet above the Yukon River, at a height of 1,200 feet above sea-level. Just to the east, immediately behind the town, rises Moosehide Mountain, which is 3,270 feet high. The most prominent feature in the landscape is the hollow made in the side of Moosehide, where a great landslide occurred in the past; and the large Catholic Hospital is built at the foot of the slide. The area upon which the town is built rises slightly to the east to the base of a very well-marked bench, with a flat surface at 1,600 feet. The wide "braided valley" of the Klondike River enters the Yukon just to the south of the town, and is about one quarter of a mile wide at the junction (Fig. 4). There is a long promontory of gravel to the south of the junction, and below this are a few houses which remain from the once much larger settlement of Klondike City. The low bridge across the Klondike River has been washed away.

The Yukon River is half a mile wide at Dawson, where the stream is narrower than usual. A high bluff rises over 1,000 feet directly above the water on the west side of the river, and a steel cable extends from its slopes to an 80-foot tower in Dawson. A ferry boat swings from this cable, and is carried to and fro across the river by the action of the swift current. There are only a few small houses on the west side of the Yukon. About a mile above the gravel terraces at the junction of the two rivers, the Klondike Valley broadens considerably to a flat plain a mile wide. This extends east as far as the airport (seven miles), where Hunker Creek joins the Klondike River (Fig. 3). Above Hunker Creek the Klondike plain becomes even broader, being two miles wide in places.

The most famous valley in the world for alluvial gold lies just to the south of Dawson, and is called Bonanza Creek. Its main tributary, about nine miles south of Dawson, is Eldorado Creek, which rises in the granite mass of the Dome (4,250 feet), but about six miles to the west of the highest point. Hunker Creek and a few valleys south of the Dome were also found to contain much alluvial gold. No veins, from which this alluvial was derived, have been found on the Dome, so that probably the original gold veins have been removed by erosion.

The boom time was in 1898, when there were about 30,000 people in the Klondike diggings. Today there are practically no diggers, and the gold-mining consists exclusively in dredging by means of a dozen of the largest dredges known. These are slowly working over the acres of tailings and alluvial, which remain in the valleys as the result of the labours of previous miners. During the war only three dredges were in use, each employing about seventy men in the dredging or in connexion with repairs, transport, and the camps. Some of the men live in Dawson, others in the local camps (each of about six houses) scattered near where the gold is being won.

Dawson City is the capital of the Yukon Territory, and is a more imposing settlement than any of the others described in this survey. But one of its most interesting features is that it represents a town whose best days have long passed away; and though it is by no means stagnant now, yet the streets of empty shops and the numerous abandoned cabins recall the more flourishing days of the Klondike boom. It was of special interest to find out how the abandoned portions were distributed with regard to the still thriving centre of the town.

In the original town-plan the main street (King Street) led to the east from the wharf to the 1,600-foot bench at the back of the town (Fig. 4). Three other parallel streets were laid out to the south, at about 500-foot intervals. Bordering this "grid" are two streets (Church and York) at half this interval. The cross streets (parallel to the Yukon River) are at 150-foot intervals, and are labelled First, Second, etc., as one proceeds inland. This "street grid" was carried far to the east, so that it climbed up the 400-foot scarp, and extended some distance above the 1,600-foot bench to the cemeteries. But there were never any large houses on the high bench, and now hardly any cabins are occupied amid the thick second growth, which covers the bench and the steep scarp below.

Today the centre of the town, as always, is close to the wharf at the lower end of King Street. There are several warehouses along the river here, as well as a large and imposing bank. The main hotel is also on First Street close to the river, and a large department store (partly one storey) is at the corner of King Street. The second hotel is on King Street opposite the old post office. There are four abandoned hotels in Second and Third Street, which date back to the palmy days of forty years ago. Many of the shops in King Street are built of brick, which is most unusual in the far north-west. There are four other stores on King Street, and one or two in other streets, but most of the shops in Second and Third seem to be empty or used mainly for storage. The mining companies have a good building on King, and here are some other shops and a dance hall, with a cinema at the west end.

The most imposing building is that which accommodates the administration, and the post office. This is placed nearly a mile away from the wharf in a little park in the south of the town. There is a large area near here occupied by the offices of the Mounted Police; but the huge three-storey building is abandoned, and the officers use a small frame house nearby. In this section of the town, near a long slough or pond, are two churches built by the Anglicans and Presbyterians, but the latter is no longer in use. The Catholic Church is on King Street. The public school is on Queen Street, and is a large two-storey frame building with an iron roof. There are four teachers and about 130 pupils. Nearby are a Masonic Hall, theatre hall, rink, and government liquor store.

The private houses are shown in Fig. 3, either as small circles for the pretty bungalow houses, or by dots for the less attractive shacks. There is a tendency for the better houses to collect on the slope east of the town, and behind the park. The shacks are mostly in the rather scrubby lowland in the north of the town, or in similar rather swampy land in the south near the two churches. A great deal of the street "grid" seems to be overgrown by willow scrub as indicated on the sketch map, and I was not able to ascertain if this had once contained cabins. It is of course the practice in these pioneer areas to remove cabins and houses bodily to other sites as required, since all lumber and labour is expensive in the north. Along the river road, which runs up Klondike River to Bonanza and the airport, are a number of small houses and shacks where flourishing vegetable gardens were a notable feature in the town. One or two of the private flower gardens in the better area behind the park were full of a multitude of flowers. Some of the delphiniums were 10 feet high, and I have never seen finer poppies or better turf anywhere.

Frozen ground is much in evidence at Dawson, and the current opinion is that the town "is built over a glacier." This is based on the fact that several feet of clear ice may be met with a foot or so below the surface in places. But such lenses of clear ice are common in high latitudes, and do not mean that an ancient *continuous* glacier has been covered with soil at Dawson or elsewhere. After cultivation the soil often sinks over such melted ice, and a small pond in the park was a level lawn a dozen years ago. All attempts to level this by adding soil, moss, sawdust, etc., seem to be unavailing.

One of the "shows" of Dawson is the series of glasshouses where great numbers of tomatoes are grown and ripened. The crop is sent by boat to the large population at Whitehorse. Celery was nearly 3 feet high at the time of my visit. A large dairy herd is grazed on many acres of grass near the airport, and milk is regularly delivered from this herd. Much brome grass has been planted in the native meadows; but the spread of motor tractors has done away with many of the horses, and so led to a decrease in farming. Wheat has been grown, ripened, and ground into flour, at Swede Creek a few miles south of Dawson.

I was able to make a rapid traverse of Bonanza and Eldorado Creeks, a journey of about fifteen miles. Here where thousands of miners were living around 1900 there is now only a cluster of about six houses at Grand Forks. Owing to the second growth, and to the removal of timbers, etc., there is hardly a vestige today of the teeming population which once occupied these valleys. Dawson City with its widespread "grid," its shopping centre, and segregation of the better residences falls into the "adolescent" class of city evolution.

WHITEHORSE TO PEACE RIVER; THE ALASKA HIGHWAY

I returned from Dawson City to Whitehorse by plane via Mayo. We left Dawson City by car in which we drove a dozen miles to the east to the airport in the flat floor of Hunker Creek. We passed the small settlement of Bear Creek, where there are about a dozen houses, which was once the scene of a flourishing alluvial gold-field. Near the airport Achille Fournier has a hundred-acre farm. We left the airport at 6.15 P.M. and reached Mayo (about a hundred miles away) in fifty minutes. Below the plane was the undulating plateau of this part of Yukon, in which the Hunker, McQuesten, and Stewart Rivers have cut rather deep flat-floored valleys (Fig. 3).

The flight from Mayo to Whitehorse was much the most scenic of all. We took off at 7.35 P.M. and traversed the two hundred miles by 8.55 P.M. Thus the return journey from Dawson City took about three and a half hours, instead of six days as it would have done on the steamer! Ten minutes after leaving Mayo we were flying south over Ethel Lake, an expanse of water running about twenty miles in an east-west direction (Fig. 3). Then we crossed the McArthur Mountains, whose summits rose to 7,000 feet. Along the rounded ridges were numerous large patches of snow. Ten minutes later striking "armchair valleys" (or cirques) appeared on the slopes of the Macmillan Range. The Pelly River wound in wide meanders on the flat floor of its valley. We flew just to the east of Lake Tatlmain, and crossed over a residual plateau, with steep valleys notching its margin, just before we reached Lewes River. Another ten minutes brought us to Lake Laberge, whose thirty-five miles was traversed in about a quarter of an hour. We reached Whitehorse at 8.55 P.M. on August 8.

I was allowed to traverse the Alaska Highway, which is closed to civilians, in a military autobus. Some geographical notes on this famous highway, so early in its history, may be of interest. The vehicle in use was a large Greyhound bus holding about thirty passengers, though only fourteen made the journey with me. There were two drivers, who drove for about three hours at a time, day and night. We started from Whitehorse on August 9. For several miles we passed areas covered with stores and machinery gathered during the build-

Fig. 5. Chief topographic features on the Alaska Highway from Whitehorse to Dawson Creek. The contours, etc., are only approximate. Inset is Lake Muncho.

ing of the road, and at ten miles reached a military post, where we were halted and all the passengers and their papers were examined. The 4-inch pipe, which carried the oil from Norman Wells, lay on the ground alongside the road as far as the north end of Teslin Lake (2,250 feet). For a time we coasted a small lake (Marsh Lake, 2,147 feet); but after eighty miles we stopped for a midnight meal at one of the large maintenance camps near Teslin Lake. It was now quite dark, and I was unable to take notes until about 4.30 A.M., when we were near the Continental Divide at a height of over 3,000 feet. On each side was undulating plateau-like country at about 5,500-foot level. To the north were the Cassiar Mountains (Fig. 5).

The road ascended Swift Creek by easy grades from about 2,500 feet to the Divide near Summit Lake, where the Rancheria River (RAN. in Fig. 5) rises; and then followed down this river for some fifty miles. There was a maintenance camp with fourteen huts near this highest point on the Divide. About a mile to the south were cirques in a rather high peak which rose to about 6,100 feet. Most of the rounded granite bosses rose well above the tree line. Near the lower

Rancheria Bridge was another maintenance camp twenty miles east of the other. From here we climbed up to a plateau about 3,000 feet which occupied the angle between the Rancheria and the main Liard River. This plateau was covered with thin spruce (7 inches in diameter) and poplar. We dropped down to the large Liard River, which is crossed by a steel truss bridge some 273 miles from White- horse. Here the spruce was of much larger diameter, some trees being 18 inches across. A fair amount of lodgepole pine was present here, but only a few per cent in comparison with the spruce. The main halt for breakfast was at the maintenance camp at Watson Lake, about eight miles south-east of the airport (where I had halted on my flight to Whitehorse).

Hereabouts the Alaska Highway crosses the famous "Rocky Mountain Trench," which is another example of those N.W.-S.E. depressions discussed in the previous chapter. It is a shallow fold-depression which extends from Idaho to the Kechika Valley in this district (Fig. 5). It may extend north by the Frances, Pelly, and Yukon Rivers as far as Alaska.

Twelve miles beyond Lower Watson Lake is a bridge over the Hyland River. On the west side of the river the Hudson's Bay Company has erected a fine pair of buildings with the usual red roofs. We traversed loamy country with spruce of about 11 inches in diameter. Here white spruce is more abundant, but in the higher plateau areas to the east H. M. Raup has noted the greater im- portance of black spruce.[1] Pine and poplar were relatively more abundant on the lower flats. Much the same type of country was seen all the way to Coal River, where the road runs close to the Whirlpool Canyon at the junction with the Liard River.

The highway now follows the north bank of the Liard River for thirty miles, often running below steep slopes of 1,000 feet. Just near the big bridge over the Liard is the famous Hot Spring (Fig. 5), which lies about half a mile north of the road at 422 miles from Whitehorse. We halted here for an hour, and had a pleasant bathe in water around 150°F., smelling strongly of sulphur. Several enclosed bathing sheds have been erected; and it is stated that special plants grow close to the springs owing to the mild winter temperatures.

Some twenty miles from the Hot Spring the scenery along the highway becomes quite mountainous. The road rises considerably as it proceeds south near Trout River. In places it traverses a deep valley bounded by slopes some 2,000 feet high. Gray walls of granite devoid of trees seem to bar our passage as we approach Lake Muncho (2,700 feet). There is a cluster of a dozen houses at the north end of this lovely alpine lake. From the range to the east open a number of parallel valleys, which are sketched in the inset in Fig. 5. Each shows evidence of past glacial action, and is marked by a large "fan delta." The road is now jammed between the lake and the steep slopes; and so rises and dips over

[1]*Geographical Review*, Jan., 1945.

these almost coalescing fans. About 3 P.M. we reached the large camp at the southern end of Lake Muncho, and here halted for lunch. Our journey to Dawson Creek was half over.

To the north-east of Muncho Lake appeared a veritable Matterhorn, a peak rising to 8,000 feet; while a row of pyramid mountains fringed the road on the north. As we approached Toad River we seemed to be heading right into these high mountains; and in places, signs warned that rock-falls threatened the road. We traversed an imposing canyon on our approach to Racing River, and some of the cliff faces show extremely interesting contortions in the strata. The road reaches its highest elevation (4,200 feet) hereabouts. There are some picturesque cirques in the mountain slopes to the north-east. Near the bend of the Tetsa River is a large military camp, and to the south are curious pinnacles of soft rock of the "hoodoo" type.

The mountains to the east were crowned with projecting knobs of curious shape, resembling a box, a football, and the Duke of Wellington's profile. Some fifty miles west of Fort Nelson we climbed up to the top of a ridge; and then dropped fairly steadily to Steamboat Creek. Near Kledo Creek is a saw-mill, and both the spruce and black poplar timber were of much larger size than heretofore. We reached the very large road maintenance camp at Fort Nelson about 8.30 P.M. The bus proceeded on during the night, and soon climbed to the highest lengthy portion of the road, where it attains a height of 4,100 feet. Here, as the map in Fig. 5 shows, it is crossing a portion of the main plateau of the Rocky Mountains. In this area the plateau is much dissected, but lies at a level of 5,000 or 6,000 feet, with rounded bosses rising somewhat higher.

Early next morning we dropped gradually down from 4,000 feet to the plains around the Peace River near Fort St. John. About five miles from the latter town we saw the first farms on the northern edge of the Peace River block. We reached the first hotel on the Alaska Highway, about 7.00 A.M. on August 11. After spending some hours on a survey of the little town, and visiting Mr. Hadland's demonstration farm, I drove on a distance of fifty miles to Dawson Creek. We crossed the lengthy and expensive Peace River Bridge a few miles south of Fort St. John. Here the Peace River flows in a narrow valley eroded in the floor of a wide flat, about a mile and a half across. This flat is very fertile soil, and is about 400 feet below the general level (around 2,500 feet) of the prairie; and all of it seems to be converted into flourishing farms. Between the river and Dawson Creek there was not much farming at first visible from the road. About half way we passed a few shacks and some humble farms, and then the road dropped into the Kiskatinaw Valley, where it descends below the 2,000-foot level for almost the first time on the whole journey. Near Sweetwater were some fine fields of grain, which were being reaped as we passed. More expanses of poor poplar scrub intervened, but about seven miles from Dawson Creek we entered the completely cleared lands which surround this important section of the Peace River block. I reached the southern terminus of the Alaska Highway at noon on August 11.

The Settlements of Fort Nelson, Fort St. John, and Dawson Creek. Fort Nelson was founded on a tributary of the Liard of the same name as long ago as 1800. The Indians destroyed the post in 1825, and it was re-established in 1865, so that it has had a long and varied history. The general position can be seen in Fig. 5, and today there are three separate settlements in the district. The original fur-trading post is on the east bank of the river, near its junction with the Muskwa. Three miles to the west is the large airport, and three miles still further west is the large maintenance camp associated with the building of the

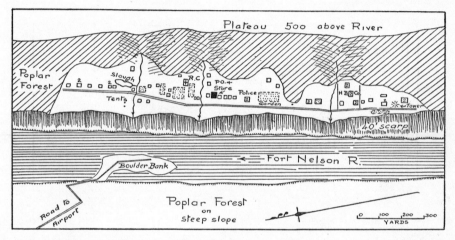

Fig. 6. Sketch survey of right bank of river at Fort Nelson, looking to east. Dotted areas are gardens; 2, 2, means two-storey.

highway. This separation of the functions of a region is rather characteristic of these new settlements, as we have seen at Whitehorse and Norman Wells.

From the central airport, where the writer landed late on August 2, it was quite a long and varied walk to the old settlement. The airport is on a flattish, thickly forested, plain, into which the Muskwa and Fort Nelson Rivers have cut deep wide valleys several hundred feet below the general level. The road zigzags down to the river passing a small sawmill, operating on the 20-30-inch spruces and poplars. It was necessary to wait on a bank of boulders in the stream for some time, until some resident on the far bank would come over in a boat and transport us across the wide river. As Fig. 6 shows, the old settlement is extended along the top of a 40-foot cut-bank for a distance of a mile. There is not much level land, for the slopes rise rather rapidly to the plateau-level, some 400 or 500 feet above the river.

A wind-motor tower is at the south end, with several two-storey houses nearby. Then comes the Hudson's Bay land, with a store, residence, and several sheds. The Mounted Police have an office here, and there is an independent store, with a café and pool-room, about the centre of the settlement. The rough lane crosses a muddy creek, and then we reach the Catholic lands with several patches of garden. The little church is a plain frame building with a porch, set back some distance from the road, and is distinguished by a huge black poplar in the foreground. At the north end of the post were nine shacks inhabited by

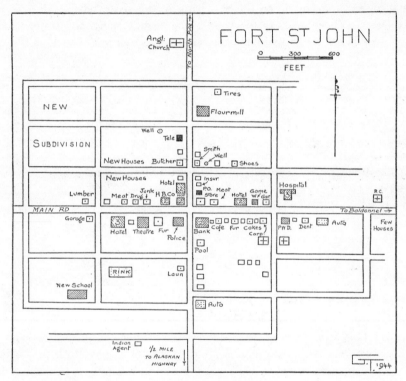

Fig. 7. Sketch survey of Fort St. John. Main buildings are black or ruled; shops have a single dot, churches a cross.

several white trappers and a number of Indians. Fur prices have improved greatly in 1944; and I was informed that a marten fur would only bring $15.00 about eight years ago, but is now worth $100, while beaver fur has risen from $10.00 to $34.00. Potatoes, cabbages, turnips, etc., do splendidly, but maize cobs and tomatoes do not ripen out of doors. Floods of unusual severity damaged the gardens in the summer of 1943. About a dozen whites live at this settlement, which is of the "sub-infantile" class. It was not permissible to make a survey of the airport, where there were said to be 750 men employed.

During my visit to Fort St. John I was greatly helped by Mr. Hadland of the local "Illustration Farm." Much of the following information is derived from him, as also are some of the data on the sketch map. The first Fort St. John was built in 1805, some distance south of the present settlement, near Pine River. It was moved in 1873, in 1885, and again to the present site in 1925. In 1928 there were three government offices in the young town, as well as the new Hudson's Bay post. The first log hotel was just being built, but most of the private residents lived in tents. The Anglican Church was erected in 1930, and the hospital and flour mill about 1933. The development of the airway to Alaska, with a very important airport about four miles to the east of St. John, together with the construction of the Alaska Highway, which runs diagonally across the southwest corner of the town, have all greatly increased the growth of the town in the last two or three years. This is clearly indicated by the sketch survey presented in Fig. 7.

The town plan is the conventional grid, based on the original township survey. In fact at the cross roads four townships meet, their boundaries being the two main roads shown in the plan. The country is almost level, and there seems no obvious reason for choosing this particular crossing of boundaries as the site of a town. The chief shops are to be found on the west-east road between the bank and the main hotel. There are two other hotels, a theatre, and a police post in the shopping centre. Three butchers, two fur dealers, several cafés, and a drug store about complete the list. Further away are the large hospital, the new school, a rink, two auto camps, two garages, and a flour mill. As usual the churches—of which there are four—are on the borders of the little town. I believe that a number of new houses have been added in the summer of 1944 after I visited the town. These have grown up chiefly in the north-west. With its well-developed street-grid, and the presence of a factory or two, this settlement may be placed in the "juvenile" class.

There are a few farms as much as forty miles north of Fort St. John. The selection of a farm-site depends on the character of the soil, which varies a good deal more hereabouts than south near Peace River. Near Baldonnell much seems to be gray soil covered by poplar or willow forest. Mr. Hadland had various types of grain on his farm, the wheat being of the spring wheat type, which is sown about the third week in April. The harvest occurs between August 10 and September 10, depending largely on whether the soil is warmed early or late in the spring. Hogs are an important product in parts of the district. Potatoes are planted in the middle of May, and some early potatoes may be dug early in August. Oats, alfalfa, and flax are other crops grown in the St. John region. It is difficult to obtain an adequate water supply, and large reservoirs are scooped out of clay soil, which collect water after the winter if there has been a good snowfall. Otherwise water is apt to run short for stock and house. Two good

8

wells have been sunk recently in the town itself. In 1941 there were 170 residents in Fort St. John, but this figure has much increased lately.

The last town considered in this survey of settlement in 1944 is Dawson Creek, where the Alaska Highway reaches the connected Dominion railways. The little farming centre (as is the case at Whitehorse) has been surrounded by the temporary barracks and warehouses of the American Army, for here material for the highway was transferred from rail to road. I was not able to make any survey of the new sections, which however did not impinge on the older settlement to the extent that they did in Whitehorse. The west-east streets are numbered from the north, so that the road next to the railway is First Street

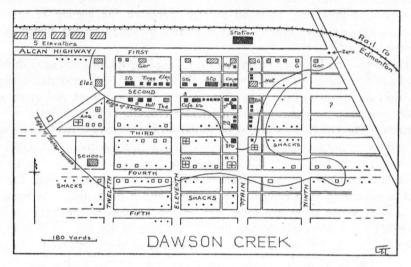

Fig. 8. A functional plan of Dawson Creek—where the Alaska Highway reaches the railway. Shops are black; main buildings are ruled; shacks are shown by dots.

(Fig. 8). This has the honour of being the first section of the great highway, and a post in the middle of the road at its east end is labelled Zero, and from here distances are measured to Fairbanks, Alaska.

In 1917 the railway was extended to Grande Prairie (about eighty miles to the south-east) and reached Dawson Creek in 1930. Farming in the Peace River block of British Columbia started about 1917, and by 1921 was scattered northwards as far as Fort St. John. The town of Dawson Creek is therefore about twenty years old, and in 1941 the population was 518.

The most prominent features of the town are the five wheat elevators on the highway at the north-west corner. These show that we are in the midst of a thriving wheat-producing area, and have left the real pioneer lands behind us to the north. The street plan is the normal grid, with the streets oriented with regard to the true North. The functional plan resembles that of Whitehorse much more than that of Fort St. John. The town has grown entirely to the south of the railway, so that the main streets resemble a T rather than a +. First Street is adjacent to the railway, and contains warehouses and garages, but no shops. These are found chiefly on Second Street, though a number are also on Main (or Tenth) Street at right angles to the former. It is unusual in a street-grid to name the cross-streets "Ninth," "Eleventh," and "Twelfth," as has been done in Dawson Creek.

The shopping area forms a sort of "T," as is usual in an asymmetric plan. Surrounding this is a zone of better-class houses, and here are the five churches and the large school (Fig. 8). Then on the margins are a great number of small houses and shacks, some of which no doubt are only temporary, and have arisen in the last year or so, since construction began on the highway. The two hotels are in the blocks next to the station in Main Street, as also are the bank and post office. There are three department stores, five restaurants, and six other general stores. Drugs, drapery, shoes, and beauty parlours are each represented by one or two shops. As in the case of St. John and other farm centres, there are many shops compared with the residents in the town, for their customers come mainly from the numerous farms in the district.

Some General Conclusions

The geographer believes that the natural vegetation is the best indicator of the possibilities of a new region. It is therefore of great importance to remember that the type of vegetation is uniform in character from latitude 57° at McMurray to latitude 68° at Aklavik. What has been done at the southern end in the way of agriculture can be done in the Far North. In general, conditions resemble those of the tip of Gaspé or the west of Newfoundland, and bear no real resemblance to the environment in the far north of Quebec Province or Labrador; though the latter are in the same (or lower) latitudes as the region under consideration.

Of the score of settlements examined in some detail few have more than about seven hundred inhabitants. In all cases it is easy to see how the population responds to the natural environment. A complete sequence of "small-town" development in a pioneer region can be based on this survey, though the writer has only given general results in this preliminary paper. Turning to the native population, the training of the Indians and Eskimos should have more stress laid on hygiene and on the adequate exploitation of their environment. The government realizes this, but not all the missions, so far as the writer's rapid survey indicated.

As regards scientific surveys, the extension of soil surveys by the governments is to be highly commended. This is the key to future profitable settlement.

We must find out which are the *best* districts, and direct all Canadian pioneers to such places. The writer has had twenty years' experience in preliminary survey work of this sort in "Empty Australia," and is firm in the belief that "Empty Canada" has far better prospects. There is no first-class land left perhaps, but there is an unlimited area which will grow potatoes and meadow hay, which some day may be of great value. The more rugged country of the Yukon is not so promising as the Mackenzie Basin. An enterprising government would send

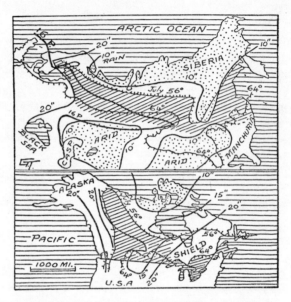

Fig. 9. The environments of Canada and the U.S.S.R. are much the same—as these climatic maps show. The undeveloped parts of Canada are ruled like similar areas in the U.S.S.R. Note limit of sixteen people to square mile in the U.S.S.R. (shown by 16 P.).

trained geographers, climatologists, and related scientists to study what has been done in exactly similar environments in Sweden, Finland, northern Russia, and northern Siberia. They are several decades ahead of Canada (owing to their greater population and resources), and we can benefit from their mistakes as well as from their successes. The similar environments are charted in Fig. 9.[2]

The place of mining and of tourism deserves some mention. Mines, in a pioneer region, perform three functions as regards settlement. The winning of valuable metals, coal, or oil, from the earth obviously brings a good deal of ready

[2]For a lengthy discussion, see the writer's "Parallels in Soviet and Canadian Settlement" (six maps) (*International Journal*, vol. I, no. 2, spring, 1946, 144-58).

money into the district. It also helps materially to make the particular region known, as for instance the Eldorado Radium Mine on Great Bear Lake. But the chief function, perhaps, is to provide a small centre which is a ready market for such crops as the country may be able to produce. It is not realized by many readers that a country like pioneer Canada can produce unlimited tons of potatoes, whose value is considerable *on the farm,* but the cost of transport to large centres of population is quite prohibitive at present. We must in a sense wait for the population to grow towards the Mackenzie Basin before many of its potential crops can be properly utilized.

The splendid road called the Alaska Highway brings up the question of the possibility of important tourist traffic. I do not see clearly what is to justify keeping this in running order after the military necessity has passed away. The scanty population was and can be served by small river boats up the Liard, Dease, and other tributaries. The new airways will be kept going doubtless, and will serve for the carriage of passengers and small merchandise. The roads may long have deteriorated before the local place-to-place traffic makes much use of them. Yet it might be possible to attract a large tourist traffic if there were a regular airline from Aklavik to Dawson City. Thus a "tourist triangle," including a voyage down the Mackenzie, and the above flight, and then a voyage up the scenic Yukon, and a long motor-bus ride south-east along the Alaska Highway, could be arranged. Some day this will be done.

The writer is grateful to those concerned for the opportunity to study the pioneer belt in this interesting transition stage of development. He wishes that he could convince the Dominion authorities of the value of a geographic training for a number of their "cadets." This is done on a large scale in England to help officers going to administer out-of-the-way portions of the Empire. In Sydney University I had six cadets a year in my Department for this purpose. It will be seen from these surveys that some settlements have not grown perceptibly in the last forty years. This condition is sure to change greatly in the next decade, owing to the spread of flying, of the search for minerals, and of the realization of the position of Arctic Canada on the air-routes to the Far East.

Part Four

E. L. BRUCE

Mineral Industry of the North-West

INTRODUCTION

General Statement. Even though the journey from Edmonton to Coronation Gulf now requires less than a day of effortless travel, one must still marvel at the accomplishments of the explorers of more than a century ago—Hearne, Mackenzie, Franklin and his associates who first traced on the map of Canada the rivers and lakes of the far North. Franklin's explorations were purely geographic in purpose; Mackenzie was an officer of the North West Company and Hearne of the Hudson's Bay Company and so their journeys were undertaken, probably in part, to extend the trade of these companies. In particular, those of Hearne were intended to fulfil the undertaking of his company to prosecute the exploration of the lands granted to it. The fact that tools and weapons of copper had been obtained in barter from the Arctic coast by the natives of the Hudson Bay region (no doubt) determined the goal of Hearne's expeditions and was a factor in the decision that they should be undertaken. In later times, the knowledge of these copper occurrences led to the geological examination of the Arctic coast by the southern party of the Canadian Arctic expedition 1913-18. Following the publication of its report much of the northern part of the North West Territories was withdrawn from prospecting. At that time this seemed hardly necessary since the inaccessibility of the region made it impossible for most prospectors to reach the reserved part. The adoption of the aeroplane by prospecting companies, however, changed the whole conception of distances and made it easy to reach any place in the North quickly and easily and, moreover, made it possible to furnish parties with supplies wherever they might be.

Acknowledgments. The following summary is an attempt to set down impressions as to the possibility of the development of important mineral industries in the North West Territories. It is based on a brief visit made possible by a grant from the Canadian Social Science Research Council. The writer is indebted to officials of the various mining companies operating in different parts of the Territories for much information and especially to Mr. Gilbert LaBine of the Eldorado Mining and Refining Company and to Mr. E. J. Bolger, E. J. Walli, and other officials of the Eldorado mine. By their

111

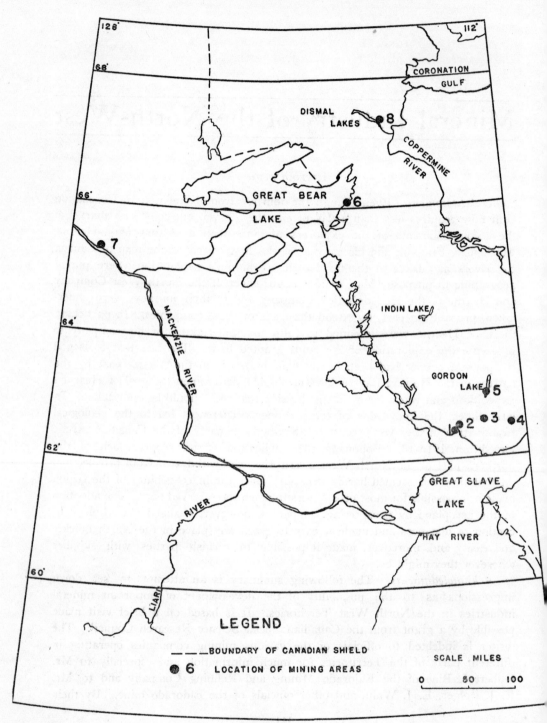

128°

112°

68°

CORONATION
GULF

DISMAL
LAKES ●8

COPPERMINE
RIVER

66°

GREAT BEAR ●6

LAKE

●7

INDIN LAKE

64°

MACKENZIE RIVER

GORDON
LAKE ●5

●2 ●3 ●4

62°

GREAT SLAVE

LAKE

RIVER

HAY RIVER

60°

LIARD

LEGEND

---- BOUNDARY OF CANADIAN SHIELD

●6 LOCATION OF MINING AREAS

SCALE MILES

0   50   100

Figure I.

assistance a much wider acquaintance with the area around Great Bear Lake was obtained than would otherwise have been possible.

The voluminous literature, dealing with mineral deposits in the North West Territories, has been freely drawn upon. In addition much information has been obtained from discussions with officials of the Geological Survey of Canada and with geologists of the various mining companies operating in the region. To all of these the writer wishes to express his thanks. He was especially fortunate in being able to visit parts of the Yellowknife area under the guidance of Dr. A. W. Jolliffe, whose work forms the basis of a great deal of the geological information about large parts of the area.

History of Mining Development. The discovery of oil in 1920 in the valley of the Mackenzie River, fifty miles north of Fort Norman was the first definite proof of the existence of any mineral deposit of major importance in the North West Territories. That discovery was an important factor in the stimulation of prospecting both for oil in the Palaeozoic and Cretaceous rocks in which oil occurrences might be expected, and for metalliferous deposits in the ancient rocks of the Canadian Shield lying to the east. A small refinery was built in 1932 to supply diesel oil, gasoline, and fuel oil, especially for the development of the pitchblende deposits of the Great Bear Lake area. In 1941 the sales of products from the Norman wells were 80,000 gallons of aviation gasoline, 112,000 gallons of motor fuel and 230,000 gallons of fuel oil.[1] This production was not the result of war demands. The Canol pipeline was not commenced until 1942.

As the older and more easily accessible areas of the Canadian Shield became more thoroughly prospected, and as the aeroplane gave easy access to distant regions, prospecting of far-away parts of it increased at a remarkable rate during the years following the First Great War. During the years 1928-9 several mining companies carried exploration to the shores of Great Bear Lake and even into the Barren Lands beyond it, but without any great success. In 1930, Gilbert LaBine made the discovery of silver and pitchblende on the east shore of Great Bear Lake that inaugurated the prospecting and mining activity in the region that has continued to the present. His discovery was by no means a matter of accident. LaBine had had experience in the Cobalt, Ontario camp and he and his party spent part of the 1929 field season in the north-eastern part of Great Bear Lake looking for the occurrences of rocks stained with Cobalt bloom, mentioned by Bell.[2]

During the trip out by aeroplane in the fall of 1929, LaBine noted an area of gossan on what is now known as LaBine Point. Returning in the spring of

[1] G. S. Hume, *Petroleum Geology of Canada* (Canada Geological Survey, Economic Geology series, no. 1944), p. 57.
[2] J. Mackintosh Bell, *Summary Report for the Year 1900: Annual Report, 1900* (Canada Geological Survey), p. 102A.

1930, he found cobalt bloom along the face of a cliff. That and the occurrence of diabase, so similar to the geological conditions at Cobalt, led him to examine the locality with some care. Native silver was found with the same assemblage

TABLE I

ANNUAL PRODUCTION OF CON, RYCON AND NEGUS MINES, NORTH WEST TERRITORIES, 1938-44

	Gold oz.	Silver oz.
*Con Mine		
1938	6,798	1,256
1939	33,633	7,944
1940	30,430	6,884
1941	40,912 (¶)	9,837 (¶)
1942	40,034	11,250
1943 (§)	20,357	4,551
1944	....	....
†Rycon Mine		
1938	....	....
1939	1,511	359
1940	3,365	761
1941 (‡)	....	....
1942	2,031	577
1943 (§)	2,620	584
1944	....	....
Negus Mines Ltd.		
1938	....	....
1939	15,995	3,613
1940	21,075	4,378
1941	18,349	3,676
1942	19,637	3,884
1943	19,080	4,791
1944 (**)	20,723	5,420

*Prepared in the Mining, Metallurgical and Chemical Branch, Dominion Bureau of Statistics, Ottawa, August 28, 1945.

†The Con and Rycon mines are subsidiaries of the Consolidated Mining and Smelting Company.

(‡) Not reported separately; included with Con production for 1941.

(¶) Includes Rycon.

(§) Milling ceased September 11, 1943.

(**) Milling ceased October 18, 1944.

of minerals that had become so well known to all prospectors from Cobalt. But, along with the pink cobalt bloom, there was gossan with orange and red colours, and, with the silver, a black mineral that does not occur at Cobalt. In his report on the silver deposits of Cobalt, Miller included a description of the silver-cobalt deposits of Schneeberg, Annaberg, and Joachimsthal, stressing the similarity of the Ontario and German deposits but noting the fact that the uranium minerals present in the latter are lacking in the former.[3] LaBine recognized the black mineral in the Great Bear Lake vein as pitchblende, the absence of which in the Cobalt ores had seemed remarkable.

The development of the deposits required time and much perseverance since they were situated in so inaccessible a region. A plant and staff had to be obtained to extract the radium from them and a market for the radium found in the face of competition from the strongly established Belgian monopoly. In spite of all these difficulties the Great Bear Lake deposits became one of the world's two main sources of radium and uranium.

From 1934 to 1939 the Eldorado mine produced minerals valued at $7,639,754. It was idle for a period in 1941-2 and was taken over by a crown company in 1944. No record of the value of the output since 1939 is available.

The Eldorado ore contains considerable native silver but pitchblende is the chief valuable mineral and the only one now being saved. The ore is concentrated by means of jigs in a mill on the property and the concentrates shipped across the lake, down Great Bear River, and up the Mackenzie to Waterways. Thence it goes by rail to the refinery at Port Hope, Ontario. Tailings are being impounded in a small lake immediately north of the mill.

The Bear Radium and Exploration Company, between 1934 and mid-summer 1939, mined from their property at Contact Lake, nine miles east of the Eldorado mine, 10,079 tons of ore from which were produced concentrates containing 348,250 ounces of silver and 6,933 pounds of U_3O_8.

The Eldorado mine now (1945) employs about 200 men. Most of them are housed in roomy and comfortable bunk houses in one of which there are a library and recreation rooms. A medical doctor is resident at the mine and furnishes medical services not only to the employees but to the few Indians in the vicinity of the mine and even to the residents of Coppermine in emergencies. There is a small but well-equipped hospital at the mine.

In 1934 gold was discovered in the area north of Great Slave Lake. The Con mine, situated on the west shore of Yellowknife Bay, began production in 1938, and the neighbouring Rycon and Negus mines followed in 1939. The production of these three mines is shown in the accompanying table. The value is more than 12½ million. Active and extensive development was carried on at many other properties and by 1941 three other mines were in production. At the Thompson-Lundmark mine, thirty miles east-northeast of Yellowknife, two inclined shafts were sunk, one on the original discovery, the Kim vein, the

[3]W. G. Miller, "Cobalt-Nickel Arsenides and Silver," (*Ontario Bureau of Mines Annual Report*, vol. xix, pt. II, 1913, p. 213).

other on the Fraser vein discovered in 1939. Both shafts reached depths of more than 300 feet before work was discontinued. A mining plant was installed, a shaft sunk to a depth of 380 feet and considerable work done on two levels at the Camlaren mine on Gordon Lake, fifty miles north-east of Yellowknife. A mining plant was installed at the Ptarmigan mine four miles east of the north end of Yellowknife Bay, a shaft 336 feet deep was sunk, and several hundred feet of lateral work done in addition to considerable diamond drilling. A mining plant was also installed at the Ruth mine, thirty miles north of Francois Bay, fifty-five miles directly east of Yellowknife.

Work ceased on all the non-producing properties during the first years of the war and has not yet been resumed on most of them. Lack of labour and supplies led to the closing of the International Tungsten and Ptarmigan mines in 1942, and the Thompson-Lundmark, Con, and Rycon mines in 1943. The Negus closed in October, 1944, and resumed milling in July, 1945. In 1944 bodies of gold ore apparently larger than any previously known to exist in the Yellowknife area were found on the claims of the Giant Yellowknife Company. This gave a new stimulus to the search for gold. Prospecting was particularly active during the summer of 1945, especially in the vicinity of Indin (Wray) Lake, north-east of Yellowknife, where gold-bearing quartz veins had been discovered as early as 1939.

Since the cost of equipping, transporting, and maintaining even small parties in this field is quite beyond the means of the average individual prospector, most of the prospecting and development has been carried on by strong and well-established mining and exploration companies. During the war years the Geological Survey carried on active search for strategic minerals, notably those of tungsten and tantalum, and, since the Eldorado Company has been taken over by the government, its prospectors and some parties of the Geological Survey have carried on an intensive search for deposits of uranium materials. Individuals are not prevented from prospecting for the latter but should they find a deposit it would at once become the property of the crown. There have been no proposals, from any quarter, that prospecting for any other minerals or operation of mines producing the ordinary metals should be taken over by the state.

TOPOGRAPHY

The North West Territories include parts of two major topographic and geologic provinces. The north-eastern part, lying east of a line running through Fort Smith, Slave River, north-west arm of Great Slave Lake, southern bay of McTavish arm of Great Bear Lake, and thence northerly to the Arctic, is part of the Canadian Shield and is underlaid by the typical heterogeneous assemblages of metamorphic and igneous rocks that are characteristic of the Shield. South-west of that line, the surface consolidated rocks are Palaeozoic and Cretaceous sediments.

Viewed from the air, the Canadian Shield part appears as a network of innumerable lakes of all sizes. Near Great Slave Lake the area gives an impression of flatness but, actually, the country is rugged although the differences of elevation are probably less than 1,000 feet. Northward toward Great Bear Lake the relief becomes greater; the east shore of that lake is extremely rugged, resembling the north shore of Lake Superior. Hills rise abruptly as much as 1,100 feet above the Lake and narrow fiord-like bays extend far inland. A short distance north of Great Bear Lake, in the basin of the Coppermine River, the country becomes flatter. The most detailed description of that area is that of Sandberg.

No high mountains exist in the area here considered, which extends from Dismal Lake eastward to a few miles beyond the 116th Meridian, and trends northward approximately following this meridian from 67th parallel to the mouth of Coppermine River.

The Copper Mountains, by which term the high land trending east southeast from Dismal Lake to Coppermine River and beyond, is designated, are formed by a series of basalt ridges with the same general trend as the range, and occupy a belt about fifteen miles wide. Towards the south they terminate abruptly in a nearly straight line, for miles, dropping with a perpendicular wall to the broad valley of slight relief adjoining the mountains to the south. The mountains attain only an elevation of 1,200 to 1,500 feet, presenting the appearance of a plateau, interrupted by a number of mutilated ridges, facing south with perpendicular cliffs of varying height, and sloping gently towards north.

The Coppermine River, traversing the valley, with a northerly course to the south of the mountain, enters the Copper Mountains about five miles below Kendall River. Striking the hard basaltic rock it curves eastward and assumes a course practically parallel with the trend of the basalt ridges for a distance of 20 miles, before it cuts its way through the ridges with a curve toward northwest and finally emerges with a northerly course on the plain to which the Copper Mountains slope towards north. In its passage through the double curve the river has cut deep, and in some places has made a narrow valley through the mountain. A number of small creeks flow at right angles into the river and drain the mountains through narrow, constricted gulches in many places dividing the hills in detached blocks. From the valley the mountains rise by steps in the nature of terraces to the summit. The highest altitude is attained by three adjoining peaks at the point, where the river begins its eastward course. The bottom of the valley in many places is occupied by low ridges and small hills consisting of clay and gravel of glacial origin. On the northwest course of the river, where the valley is quite broad, these clay and gravel deposits extend about a mile from the river on the south shore forming a typical miniature glacial landscape. A good growth of spruce is sustained from this soil, especially along the north shore of the east course and on both sides of the northwest course of the river.

To the north of Copper Mountains, the country presents the character of a plain with slight relief, traversed with narrow basalt ridges of the same general trend as the Copper Mountains. Only the first and last of these ridges attain an elevation of about 400 feet. Through this plain the river has cut a channel about 100 feet deep with perpendicular sides of sandstone, alternating in some places with shelving clay banks. Where the river cuts through the basalt ridges the channel becomes tortuous and constricted to about 50 yards and less from its average width of about 300 yards.[4]

---

[4]James Douglas, "The Copper Bearing Traps of the Coppermine River" (*Transactions of the Canadian Institute of Mining and Metallurgy*, vol. XVI, 1913, pp. 83-114).

Within their valleys the larger rivers such as the Coppermine, the Dease, and the Kendall have well defined channels in which the streams have a braided character. They differ from those of the Canadian Shield which are merely lake basins only slightly below the general level and connected by short rapid river stretches down which the overflow from each lake spills into the next lower one. On the Coppermine rapids occur where there are accumulations of boulder or where, as at Bloody Falls, the stream breaks across a diabase dyke.

The south-western division of the North West Territories lies mainly in the valley of the Mackenzie River and is underlaid for the most part by flat-lying rocks. North of Wrigley the valley is constricted between the Franklin Mountains to the east and the Mackenzie Mountains to the west. At Fort Norman the valley is twenty-five miles wide. About fifteen miles below Arctic Red River, the valley broadens into the lake-dotted delta of the Mackenzie with its labyrinth of distributory channels. The delta extends about ninety miles along the Arctic coast. In some places the north-eastern margin of the younger rocks is marked by an easterly facing scarp from a few feet to as much as 250 feet in height. Elsewhere a low, drift-covered belt several miles wide lies along the contact between the Pre-Cambrian and the later rocks.

GENERAL GEOLOGY

The rocks of the part of the Territories within the Canadian Shield have been studied in some detail in those areas where mineral deposits have been found. The great extent of the region, the occurrence of great areas of granite which surround the widely separated remnants of pre-granite rocks, and the high degree of metamorphism that some of the older rocks have undergone, make any general correlation impossible for the present at least. In most areas two or more series of ancient, highly disturbed volcanics and sediments have been found, but whether or not those of any two areas can be considered to be of the same age there is no means of knowing. Tentatively, the high metamorphosed types, intruded by granite, are called Archaean or early Pre-Cambrian.

Erosion has cut deeply into these ancient rocks, exposing the masses of granite and granodiorite that formed the cores of the early mountains. Upon the surface so developed, sediments were deposited and lavas poured out. But again it is impossible to say whether all these younger rocks belong to a single period or represent two or more. All of them have been only slightly disturbed so that dips are low, but all the Pre-Cambrian rocks have suffered severe faulting. Some of the faults are of great magnitude, traceable for dozens of miles and with horizontal displacements of several miles. Most of them are steep. No doubt they are of several ages but all seem to be late Pre-Cambrian since some of the latest of them are occupied by diabase dykes; others by giant quartz veins which have replaced their walls so that widths of 1,000 feet or more of quartz occur in some of them.

The flat lying or gently dipping rocks of the Coppermine series occupy an area along the lower part of the Coppermine River from a point about fifty miles up the river, to its mouth, and the Arctic coast for about eighty miles east and west of the mouth of the Coppermine River. The lower part of the series is mainly amygdaloidal basalt, the upper, sandstone and shale. The tilted basaltic flows form escarpments with broad open valleys between them. The lavas form the prominent elevated area known as the Coppermine Mountains. In most places consolidated rocks are concealed by ridges of gravel.

The rocks covering the Pre-Cambrian westward and forming the surface consolidated rocks of the western division of the North West Territories, range in age from Cambrian to Cretaceous. Palaeozoic sediments, the exact ages of which have not been accurately determined, outcrop around the west end of Great Slave Lake and along a chain of lakes extending northward from Great Slave Lake to McTavish arm of Great Bear Lake. Cambrian, Ordovician, Silurian, and Devonian strata have been recognized along the Mackenzie River between Fort Norman and Great Slave Lake. Middle and lower Cambrian rocks occur in the Franklin Mountains east of the Mackenzie. Ordovician rocks have been found along the west shore of the north arm of Great Slave Lake and drilling for oil north of Norman Wells has shown the presence of about 2,000 feet of salt or salty shales overlying fossiliferous Cambrian shales. In places no Cambrian rocks are present and rocks of Ordovician age rest directly on the Pre-Cambrian. Silurian rocks containing dolomite and limestone, with beds of gypsum and anhydrite, occur along the Slave, Mackenzie, and Great Bear Rivers and along the west shore of Great Bear Lake. Most of the rocks near the west end of Great Slave Lake and thence down the Mackenzie to a point below Norman Wells are Middle Devonian limestones and shales of Upper Devonian age. Cretaceous sandstones and shales, with some beds of lignite, rest on an extensive erosion surface truncating Devonian and older formations. Near the mouth of Great Bear River, Tertiary beds, probably Eocene in age, consisting of only partly consolidated sands, clay, gravel, and lignite, rest on Cretaceous and older rocks.

For the greater part of the area the Palaeozoic and Mesozoic rocks are flat lying but, in the Franklin Mountains, the Palaeozoic beds are folded and faulted. In the Mackenzie Mountains nearly undisturbed Tertiary beds overlie folded Cretaceous and older rocks.

MINERAL DEPOSITS

General Statement. Minerals of economic importance have been found in several places in the North West Territories. At Yellowknife Bay on the north shore of Great Slave Lake, gold deposits occur in the rocks of the Yellowknife series of early Pre-Cambrian age. At Great Bear Lake, silver-uranium deposits are in the Echo Bay series, also early Pre-Cambrian in age. North-east of

9

Great Slave Lake tantalum deposits have been found in granites intrusive into the early Pre-Cambrian rocks. Copper minerals occur north of the Dismal Lakes in basalts of the Coppermine series, and from early times native copper in small amounts has been obtained from the Arctic slope and from the Arctic islands. Zinc-lead deposits, probably too low grade to be of economic value under present conditions, occur in the Palaeozoic rocks south-east of Great Slave Lake. Enormous thicknesses of salt have been found in the Palaeozoic rocks near Norman Wells and oil is being produced in sufficient quantity for the local demand from the same locality.

Yellowknife Area. In the Yellowknife area six mines, the Con, Rycon, the Negus, International Tungsten, Thompson-Lundmark, and Ptarmigan have produced gold; the Negus after a period of inactivity is once again in production. At the Giant Yellowknife active development looking to early production is under way and at the Thompson-Lundmark small bodies of ore have been outlined.

The Con, Rycon, and Negus mines lie near the west shore of Yellowknife Bay about a mile south of the town of Yellowknife. The Giant Yellowknife claims are west of West Bay, an indentation of the west shore of Yellowknife Bay which occurs about a mile north-west of the town of Yellowknife.

The Negus mine two miles south of Yellowknife can be reached by a fair motor road. The rocks in the vicinity of the mine are andesites of the Yellowknife group of early Pre-Cambrian age. Altered diabase or gabbro dykes cut the lavas and these in turn are cut by a few narrow aplite dykes. The great West Bay fault trending slightly west of north lies about 2,000 feet east of the Negus ore bodies, beneath Yellowknife Bay. The relative horizontal displacement along it is about three miles, with the rocks east of it being displaced to the north as compared with those on the west side.

The ore bodies of the Negus property are lenticular masses of quartz lying in shear zones in altered andesite, gabbro, and diabase. The shear zones trend slightly west of north and dip 55° west. In places they are as much as 27 feet wide but the average width is 5 feet. Some can be traced for more than 400 feet. The bodies of quartz in the shear zones are as much as 12 feet wide. In addition, there are numerous lenses of quartz only a few feet long and a few feet thick lying parallel to the main shear. Practically all of the gold is in the quartz, but not all the quartz contains gold enough to form ore. The chief metallic minerals are sphalerite, chalcopyrite, arsenopyrite, and gold; there are a large number of rarer species including some tellurides.

Most of the ore is mined by ordinary shrinkage methods, but, in some veins, containing high gold content, the rock is removed along one side of the vein which is then blasted down onto canvas. During the period of operation of the mine about 69 tons of ore were mined daily. From this about 10 tons of waste were sorted. Up to mid-summer 1939 the average gold and silver value of the ore sent to the mill was $31.64 per ton. Operating costs exclusive of head office, pre-production costs, depreciation, and taxation were $17.15 per ton milled.[5]

The Con and Rycon mines, operated by the Consolidated Mining and Smelting Company, lie along the shore of Yellowknife Bay immediately north of the Negus mine. The rocks exposed on these properties are similar to those of the Negus. The ore occurs in a north-south shear zone in ellipsoidal and massive lavas. Parts of the zone have been replaced by quartz and ferruginous carbonate. These are the ore shoots. Metallic minerals occur in these replacement bodies in small quantities, but considerable variety. Pyrite and arsenopyrite are the most common. Gold is only rarely visible.

In August, 1939, 110 tons of ore were milled per day; the gold content was 1 ounce per ton. Milling was discontinued in September, 1943 but development work continued. The most extensive workings are on the 950-foot level; the bottom level is at 1,250 feet.

The Giant Yellowknife claims are on the west shore of Yellowknife Bay about one and a half miles north of Yellowknife. The rocks are greenstones and tuffaceous sediments similar in every respect to those at the Con and Negus mines but lying on the east side of the West Bay fault. It has been suggested that the Giant area and its veins actually are the eastern part of the Con-Negus zone, displaced by the West Bay fault. Most of the ore zones of the Giant lie in a marked north-south valley deeply buried beneath swamp deposits.

North-south trending shear zones roughly parallel to the West Bay fault contain numerous quartz veinlets. The shear zones are broken by cross faults which displace the ore bodies, in places causing overlap so that the ore lenses are double. The attitude and character of these cross faults will probably not be definitely determined until mining operations expose them. Not all of the shears contain ore nor are all parts of any one shear of ore grade. The East zone is believed to have a length of more than 600 feet with an average width of 37½ feet and an average gold content of 0.43 ounces uncut or 0.37 ounces cut. The A.S.D. zone lying farther north has a length of 370 feet, a width of 33½ feet, and a grade of 0.266 ounces uncut or 0.208 ounces cut. A northern extension of this is 700 feet long, 64½ feet wide, and has an average estimated gold content of 0.43 ounces per ton. In addition there are the south zones lying near the west fault, the Brock veins, the Ole shear in the northern part of the property. From the Brock veins, 74 tons of ore were extracted prior to 1939 and sent to Trail, B.C. for treatment. The recovery was 647 ounces of gold and 45 ounces of silver with a total value of $10,000 or $24.34 per ton.

[5]C. S. Lord, *Mineral Industry of the Northwest Territories* (Canada, Geological Survey Memoir 230), p. 117.

The mineral assemblage of the Giant ore is simple. It consists of fine-grained quartz, pyrite, and some arsenopyrite replacing the sheared andesite. Where there is any considerable quantity of arsenopyrite, the quartz is bluish gray owing to the finely divided particles of the metallic mineral. A little stibnite has been found.

So far, excepting for the inclined prospect shaft on the Brock vein, and a second shaft farther north, work on the Giant Yellowknife deposits has been confined to surface work and diamond drilling. The surface buildings were being added to rapidly in the summer of 1945, and a three-compartment shaft was sunk during the following winter to expose the main east zone at depth.

Great Bear Lake Area. The rocks along the east shore of Great Bear belong to a series of highly altered sediments and volcanics known as the Echo Bay series. These are intruded by diabase and by granite. The rocks of the Echo Bay group comprise porphyries, probably both lavas and intrusive masses, banded chert, argillite, quartzite, limestone, conglomerate, and some tuff. The Cameron Bay group of conglomerate, sandstone, tuff, and argillite may be younger than the Echo Bay group.

The Eldorado mine is situated on Labine Point on the east shore of Great Bear Lake.

The Eldorado ore bodies occur in three shear zones with roughly east-west trends, but converging easterly, which cut highly altered sediments and feldspar porphyries, probably lavas, of the Echo Bay group. The shears are probably later than the granite since one of them transects a dyke of aplite. The zones vary in width from mere cracks to widths of as much as 30 feet. Six feet may be considered to be the average. In places the walls of the shears are sharp and the shear zones are bounded by seams of gouge. Elsewhere there is a gradation from sheared to massive rocks. Many of the zones branch. Within the shear zones there are ore shoots consisting of one or more lenses of pitchblende lying parallel to the walls of the shear. Some lenses of solid pitchblende nearly 2 feet in width and 40 feet or more in length have been found, but most of them are much smaller. Metallic minerals make up not more than 5 per cent of the ore shoots. Pitchblende and chalcopyrite are the most abundant, but dozens of other species occur in greater or less quantities.

The ore is concentrated by jigs and tables. The concentrates are packed in canvas bags and shipped by boat across Great Bear Lake down the Bear River, taken across a 8-mile portage around the most rapid and shallowest part of the river, thence by barge up the Mackenzie River to Waterways. Before the ore was requisitioned for military purposes it was shipped to Port Hope, Ontario, for the preparation of radium salts. Active prospecting, using the Geiger counter, an instrument which registers the rate of emission of emanations from radio-active bodies, is being carried on both by the Eldorado Company and by parties of the Geological Survey of Canada. Some discoveries have been made in the region extending south-east from Great Bear, possibly as far as Lake Athabaska. What the future of these deposits will be is a matter of speculation only. The extremely rugged nature of the country inland from the east side of Great Bear Lake will make the cost of development and exploitation of any deposits in that region extremely high. Nevertheless their unique character and the fact that costs need not be a controlling factor, may mean an industry of some importance provided that commercial uses for the atomic energy of U235 are developed.

The Arctic Slope. Native copper occurs in the rocks of the Coppermine series; weapons and utensils made from it were articles of commerce among the primitive peoples along the coast from early times. Occasionally a large mass of the metal is found in the glacial debris. During the summer of 1945, a mass weighing 75 pounds, presumably from one of the islands, was brought to Coppermine and was taken to Yellowknife. The similarity of the rocks to those with which native copper occurs on Keweenaw Point, Lake Superior, has led to search for similar deposits in them.[6] O'Neill pointed out that although native copper is widespread in the basalts of the Coppermine series, most of it is in very thin films. He ascribes the lack of large deposits to the fact that at Coppermine the rocks are not much disturbed, whereas on Keweenaw Point they have been folded, dip steeply, and have suffered faulting which permitted the introduction of considerable quantities of copper-bearing solutions derived from some deep zone.

In 1931 fissure veins and replacement deposits with quartz and considerable quantities of chalcocite and bornite were found in basalts north of the Dismal Lakes about forty-five miles south of the mouth of the Coppermine River. Parties sent out by the American Metals Company were investigating that area during the summer of 1945.

Valley of the Mackenzie River. The oil at Norman occurs in a coral reef of Devonian age. The reef is sufficiently porous to form a fair reservoir and the shales by which it is surrounded are impervious enough to retain the oil in the reef rock. The area of the field is limited and no other pool has been discovered yet. The Imperial Oil Company is, however, carrying out an intensive examination of a large part of the lower part of the valley of the Mackenzie and it is not impossible that other pools may yet be found.

During drilling for oil, tremendous thicknesses of salt were found. Beds with more or less salt in them extend from underlying Cambrian shales upward for 2,000 feet. Possibly they correspond, at least in a general way, to the 200 feet of salt at Waterways, where salt is being produced.

[6] J. J. O'Neill, *Geological Report, Canadian Arctic Expedition* (Canada Geological Survey, summary report, 1916), p. 333.

Lead and zinc sulphides occur in the Presque Isle dolomite of middle Devonian age, on the south-west shore of Great Slave Lake about thirty miles south-west of Fort Resolution. The beds of dolomite seem to form a low dome. Solution by ground water has developed sink hole topography. Carbonates, pyrite, galena, and sphalerite have been deposited along joints and in certain beds along the crests of small anticlines. A considerable amount of surface work and some drilling were done on these deposits some years ago but without proving the existence of any ore body of commercial size and grade.

ECONOMIC FACTORS AFFECTING MINING DEVELOPMENT

The development of a mining industry and the size of the industry depend first upon the geologic factors—the size and mineral content of the ore body, and, secondly, upon the economic factors that control the cost of operation. The value of the ore is fixed for each tonnage available; costs are to some degree controllable. Costs depend upon availability and efficiency of labour, transportation, supplies of material, power, etc., and, to a very important degree, upon the taxation policy of the government.

Costs at Yellowknife

General Statement. The following table gives the pre-production and operating costs during the periods of operation of the Con and Negus mines.

TABLE II

	Pre-production costs	Milling rate 1938-9 (tons per day)	Operating costs	Gold content of ore milled
Con mine	$1,100,000	110	$13.43	0.82 oz.
Negus mine	579,171.67	60	17.15	0.90

In both mines the pre-production costs will be considerably increased by the amount spent in development carried on from 1943 when no ore was being milled.

The projected capital expenditures at the Giant Yellowknife are as follows:

Shaft	$691,000
Underground drilling	$100,000
New surface plant	$350,000
Other expenses	$ 90,000
	$1,231,000

The future of the Yellowknife area will probably be measurable by the degree of success that these four mines, the Con, Rycon, Negus, and Giant

Yellowknife achieve. The grade and size of their ore bodies are doubtless equal to those of any others that will be found and they are situated in the most favourable location. Assuming an average cost for them of $15.00 per ton, a grade of 0.3 ounce/ton at least would be necessary to cover operating costs, taxes, etc., and even that would leave little to repay pre-production costs and supply any dividend return on investment. Thus it becomes evident that deposits situated at any great distance from Great Slave Lake would prove to be unworkable unless of unusually high grade. Even in those mines at the lake, the costs are so high that large quantities of material that would be of ore grade in Porcupine or Kirkland Lake must be lost.

Transportation. High transportation costs are at the root of practically all other high costs. From Edmonton to Waterways, freight is carried by the Alberta Northern Railway, which is still classed as a road under construction, and on which, therefore, rates are somewhat higher than normal. From Waterways barges carry freight down the Athabaska and Slave Rivers and across Great Slave Lake. En route goods must be taken across the sixteen-mile portage from Fitzgerald to Fort Smith. Formerly most of the boats on the Mackenzie used wood and much time was lost in loading fuel. Diesel engines have now almost entirely replaced the wood burning ones. The greatest drawback to navigation on the Mackenzie is the shortness of the season. During the winter, freight to Yellowknife is brought by way of Grimshaw on the Peace River branch, from which place a winter road leads to Hay River on the south side of Great Slave Lake, a distance of 400 miles. Usually men, mail, and a considerable amount of perishable goods are transported by air. Passenger rates from Edmonton to Yellowknife in the summer of 1945 were $110 one way, to which must be added the 15 per cent tax. All transportation is, of course, interrupted for several weeks during the freeze-up in the fall and the break-up in the spring, except at the places where airfields are constructed. An all-weather road is being built from Grimshaw to Hay River but it will not obviate the two periods of traffic interruption. Moreover, in the summer there will be additional trans-shipment necessary from tractor to barges at Hay River.

Labour. There is no supply of local labour. Few Indians now live in the Yellowknife area and they are not of much use for underground work. All miners must be brought in from outside. Hence labour costs and turnover are high, especially as men must be flown both ways and many do not wish to stay longer than the year usually stipulated as the minimum period for free passage both ways. The 15 per cent tax alone on aeroplane fares is said to cost the Negus mine 15 cents per ton of ore treated.

Food. Practically all food except fish must be imported. Vegetables can be grown where there is soil, but soil occurs only in small pockets. Some small gardens are grown but, with two exceptions, all of those at Yellowknife are cultivated by way of recreation. There seems no possibility of local production, even of the hardiest of vegetables, meeting any considerable part of the needs of a community the present size of Yellowknife and the mines adjacent to it.

It is possible that agricultural settlement of some areas south of Great Slave Lake, for example the valley of the Hay River, might in time supply some food for the Yellowknife mining areas, but it seems doubtful if any such agricultural development could furnish a very large part of the food needed for mining communities the size of those of Northern Ontario or Northern Quebec.

At the Yellowknife mines the cost of food per man per day is about $2.55. Of this amount $1.00 is usually charged against the man's wages; the remaining $1.55 is carried as part of the mine's labour costs.

Fuel and Power. All of the mines now use diesel engines to supply power. The oil for these is brought up the Mackenzie River from Norman Wells during the short navigation season. Large storage facilities are necessary. The cost of freight in 1944 was $20.00 per ton. That rate meant a loss to the transportation company and is to be raised to $30.00 per ton. The shipping season is short and there is practically no return cargo. There could probably be some reduction in cost if specially designed tank barges were used, but that would mean a large capital expenditure. It has been suggested that oil be brought from McMurray, thus giving a down stream haul for the loaded barges. It would, however, require a pipeline at Fitzgerald and involve delay in loading.

Timber. North of Great Slave the forest growth is scanty and the trees small. South of the lake and in the delta of the Slave River, mine timber sufficient for present needs in the Yellowknife area can be obtained. The timber, however, is not entirely satisfactory and probably would not be worth transporting to any great distance from the shores of Great Slave Lake.

Economic Conditions at Great Bear

The difficult conditions that obtain at Yellowknife are still more acute at Great Bear. Being near the Arctic Circle, the length of the winter nights introduces adverse health conditions. All the men at the Eldorado mine receive violet ray treatments daily during the winter and vitamin pills are available to all men eating in the general dining-room. Lack of proper rest during the continuous light of the summer months is perhaps as serious as lack of sunshine during the winter period. Transportation costs, both for fresh food and for men, is a serious item in costs. One way fare from Edmonton to Port Radium by C.P.A. plane is $175. As the Eldorado Company operates its own planes, cost to the Company may be somewhat less. During the long winter the lake forms a good landing area for planes equipped with skis; during the short summer, pontoon-equipped planes are used. Landing on the lake offers considerable difficulty at times since even gentle winds produce waves of considerable size in the open lake. Hence it is often necessary to land in the fiords that indent the east coast. Since these are narrow and commonly have walls that rise steeply for nearly 1,000 feet, landing a loaded plane in bad weather is somewhat hazardous. The rugged nature of the country would make it difficult to find a level area of sufficient size for a landing field.

Oil for fuel and for diesel power is obtained from Norman Wells. Transportation costs are high since barges must be pushed upstream from Norman Wells to Fort Norman and thence up Great Bear River to the foot of the rapids. It is transferred by truck across a road some eight miles in length and loaded into scows for the further journey up a river almost as rapid as that around which the road leads, but with depth enough to allow shallow draft barges and tugs to operate. From the head of the rapids to Great Bear Lake takes eleven hours upstream and less than three hours downstream. At the lake, freight must once more be trans-shipped to other and larger barges to make the crossing of the lake. Added to these difficulties there is of course the shortness of the season of water navigation; ordinarily it is about two months. During the winter, freight can be brought across the lake by tractor train and the government is now constructing an all weather road from the foot of the rapids to Great Bear Lake.

Even though Great Bear Lake lies close to the borders of the barren lands there are some stands of fair-sized spruce on the south side of the lake. From these the Eldorado mine is able to obtain mine timbers; timber for the new shaft-house also can probably be obtained from there.

The original workings were made underground. A tunnel carried into the side of the hill furnished entrance to the shaft with the hoist room and shops, etc., occupying excavations adjacent to the tunnel.

Economic Conditions on the Arctic Slope

Copper deposits occurring in the Coppermine basin would have to be of exceptional grade to be workable. Transportation northward to the coast would not be difficult, but concentrates would have to be taken along the coast westward during a short season of navigation either through Bering Strait or to the Mackenzie River. The long haul upstream by the latter route would be entirely too costly to be borne by any base metals ore. Transportation by way of Bering Strait is even less feasible. Chipman and Cox state that most of those most familiar with navigation along the Arctic coast agree that ships could pass through the straits and reach the Coppermine but that they could not return the same season.[7] The only alternative is transportation by air,

[7] K. Chipman and J. Cox, *Report of the Canadian Arctic Expedition, 1913-1918*, vol. XI, pt. B, p. 34.

which seems out of the question. In any case, the excessive costs of transportation, both of concentrates from any mine in that area and of supplies being brought in, would limit production to a very small tonnage of exceptionally high grade material. In other words, any mining industry that might possibly ever be established would be so small and so short lived that it would add very little to the commercial life of the region.

Summary

So far as can be judged at present, the mineral resources that may be considered of possible economic importance in the North West Territories are: (1) Those of unusual character, such as the pitchblende deposits of Great Bear Lake and the tantalite pegmatites north-east of Yellowknife; the commercial value of the latter has not yet been proved; (2) Gold deposits of the Yellowknife area; (3) Possible deposits of copper minerals in the Coppermine River basin and on the Arctic islands; and (4) Oil at Norman Wells and possibly in other parts of the Mackenzie River valley, and deposits of other kinds that will be of value only as the gold, pitchblende, etc., are exploited.

Mining costs in all parts of the Territories are high and labour will always be difficult to get and keep. The great distance of the Yellowknife area from centres of population and the severity of the climate introduce difficulties that probably can never be completely overcome. High costs will severely handicap the mineral industry of the region and will restrict the quantity of mineral products that can be mined.

Inadequate transportation is the most serious handicap under which a mining industry in any part of the Territories must operate and is the most important factor in producing high costs. The Mackenzie River furnishes transportation facilities for the western part of the region but the season of navigation is extremely short. Construction of a railway even to Yellowknife would be extremely difficult and costly, not only on account of distance but because Great Slave Lake and the Slave River delta interpose barriers to a direct southward line. The truck road under construction from Grimshaw on the Peace River line to Hay River on the south side of Great Slave Lake offers the only alternative to a railway, but cost of transportation by trucks will be high. Moreover, loads will have to be transferred to boats at Hay River and traffic will be interrupted during considerable periods at freeze-up and break-up.

Power offers little difficulty. There are two possible sites for development, that at Lockhart River and that in the Snare River basin.

Until the Great Bear Lake area and the Coppermine River basin are shown to have important deposits, other than those of uranium minerals, transportation by way of the Mackenzie River, Great Bear River, and the road being built to overcome the worst of the rapids on it will probably be all that will be possible, and may be adequate since cost is not so vital a factor in the case of these rare minerals as it is in the exploitation of deposits of gold or of base metals.

Obtaining labour and technical personnel will continue to present serious problems since it is imperative that men should not be expected nor allowed to work for too long periods in this northern region. Holidays will be expensive and in some way they should be chargeable, in part at least, to the operating expenses of the mine.

Unless a prosperous mining industry can be developed, the main product of the North West Territories will continue to be furs, as it has been in the past. Neither the forest nor the soil can support a primary industry of any considerable importance. It may be that the lakes may furnish some fish, but transportation would again be a serious handicap to any large-scale production. Some assistance is necessary to foster the present small mining industry, to prolong the life of the mines developed, and to increase to a maximum the total output of minerals from them. On the other hand the amount of public money that should be spent in furnishing facilities for and giving assistance to an industry that is based on wasting assets and that therefore must in the end be temporary is a matter for very careful consideration. The problem is rendered the more difficult in that no industry can be visualized that can make use of facilities installed for the mines after the ore bodies are exhausted.

It would seem, however, that governmental assistance would be justified to the following extent: (1) Completion of a good all weather road as projected from Grimshaw to Hay River; (2) Building of roads from Great Slave Lake northward as rapidly as new mineral deposits of promise are discovered; (3) Improvement of navigation on the Mackenzie River; (4) Adjustment of freight rates on the railways north from Edmonton; (5) Immediate removal of the luxury tax on aeroplane fares in the Territories; (6) Adjustment of the income tax for those employed in the region so that cost of living bonuses will not be taxable and will not operate to increase the tax rate; (7) Removal of taxes on mine machinery and supplies for properties in the North West Territories and revision of all other taxes now collected from mines operating in the region.

REFERENCES

CAMSELL, C. and MALCOLM, W. *The Mackenzie River basin,* Canada Geological Survey, 1921, Mem. 108.

DOUGLAS, JAMES. "Copper-bearing traps of the Coppermine River," Transactions of the Canadian Mining Institute, 1913, vol. 16, pp. 83-101. Contains a report on the geology by Dr. August Sandberg. Sandberg's report is also quoted verbatim in O'Neill's *Report of the Canadian Arctic Expedition,* 1913-1918, vol. XI.

DUNCAN, GORDON G. "Exploration in the Coppermine River area, Northwest Territories," Canadian Institute of Mining and Metallurgy, Bull. no. 227, Mar., 1931.

FRANKLIN, JOHN. *Narrative of the journey to the shores of the polar sea in the years 1819, 20, 21 and 22 with an appendix on various subjects relating to science and natural history,* London, 1823.

GILBERT, G. "Copper on the Coppermine River, N.W.T." Economic Geology, 1931, pp. 96-108.

HEARNE, SAMUEL. *A journey from Prince of Wales' fort, in Hudson's Bay, to the northern ocean, undertaken by order of the Hudson's Bay Company for the discovery of copper mines, a northwest passage, etc., in the years 1769-1770, 1771 and 1772,* Dublin, 1796.

HENDERSON, J. F. *Preliminary report Beaulieu River area, Northwest Territories,* Canada Geological Survey, Paper 39-1, 1939.

————————and JOLLIFFE, A. W. "Relation of gold deposits to structure, Yellowknife and Gordon Lake areas, Northwest Territories," Transactions of the Canadian Institute of Mining and Metallurgy, 1939, vol. 42, pp. 314-36.

HUME, G. S. "Petroleum geology of Canada," Canada Geological Survey, Economic Geology Series, no. 14, 1944.

ISBISTER, A. K. "On the geology of the Hudson's Bay territories and of portions of the Arctic and northwestern regions of America; with a coloured geological map," Quarterly Journal of the Geological Society, London, 1855, vol. II, pp. 497-520.

JOLLIFFE, A. W. "Mineral possibilities of the Northwest Territories," Transactions of the Canadian Institute of Mining and Metallurgy, 1938, vol. 40, pp. 663-77.

———————— *Rare element minerals in pegmatites, Yellowknife-Beaulieu area, Northwest Territories,* Canada Geological Survey, Paper 44-12, 1944.

———————— *Yellowknife Bay—Prosperous Lake area, Northwest Territories,* Canada Geological Survey, Paper 38-21, 1938.

———————— *Yellowknife River area, Northwest Territories,* Canada Geological Survey, Paper 36-5, 1936.

LORD, C. S. *Mineral Industry of the Northwest Territories,* Canada Geological Survey, Mem. 230, 1941.

NORRIE, J. P. "Prospecting and exploration of Dominion Explorers, Limited, in the Great Bear Lake-Coppermine River area," Canadian Institute of Mining and Metallurgy, Bull. no. 227, Mar., 1931.

O'NEILL, J. J. "Geological Reports, Canadian Arctic expedition, 1915," Canada Geological Survey, Sum. Rept., 1915, 236-41, 1916; 1916, 331-4, 1917.

———————— "Notes on the occurrence of native copper in Arctic Canada," Canadian Institute of Mining and Metallurgy, Bull. no. 59, 1917, 180-6.

———————— *Report of the Canadian Arctic Expedition,* vol. XI, Geology and Geography, 1924.

STEWART, J. S. "Petroleum possibilities in Mackenzie River valley," Transactions of the Canadian Institute of Mining and Metallurgy, 1944, vol. 47, pp. 152-71.

TYRRELL, J. B. "The Coppermine country," Transactions of the Canadian Mining Institute, 1912, vol. 15, pp. 508-34.

Part Five

M. J. and J. L. ROBINSON

Fur Production in the North-West*†‡

GREAT changes have taken place in the fur trade since the early days when it dominated all other pursuits and inspired the exploration which opened to colonization the vast country which is now Canada. The early exploratory history of the Canadian North-West is primarily concerned with the movements of adventurers who penetrated farther and farther northward to tap the sources of furs. The Hudson's Bay Company, formed in 1670, was at first content to establish trading-posts on Hudson and James Bays and encourage the Indians to bring their furs down the rivers to the coast. The trade of the St. Lawrence Valley and Great Lakes region was in the hands of the French *voyageurs* who were pressing to the westward.[1]

After 1763 the rivalry between the two groups became very keen. Scotch traders began competing with the French from Montreal and expanded into the North-West. The Hudson's Bay Company, finding that its furs were being diverted to the south, countered by also sending parties inland. Cumberland House, 230 miles from the mouth of the Saskatchewan River, was established in 1774 and became the distributing and collecting centre for the Company's interior trade. In 1784 the Montreal merchants combined to form the North West Company, and during the latter part of the eighteenth century fur traders pushed to the Arctic and Pacific Oceans. In order to retain the trade of the new fur areas both companies established a network of northern posts and serviced them with large canoe brigades.

The North West Company was first to enter the Mackenzie Valley. Following Alexander Mackenzie's historic trip to the Arctic, it mapped out fur areas and established posts at Fort Chipewyan (1789), entrance to Mackenzie River (1790), Lac la Martre (1793), eighty miles west of Great Slave Lake on Mackenzie River (1796), Great Bear Lake (1799 and again in 1804), Fort

*Written in the Bureau of Northwest Territories and Yukon Affairs, Lands, Parks and Forests Branch, Department of Mines and Resources, Ottawa.

†The authors wish to acknowledge the assistance of officers of the Wildlife Division of the Lands, Parks, and Forests Branch, and the Fur Trade Department of the Hudson's Bay Company.

‡Reprinted in this volume by permission of the *Canadian Geographical Journal.*
[1]A. S. Morton, *A History of the Canadian West to 1870-71* (Toronto, 1939).

Simpson (1804), Fort Good Hope (1805), and Fort Liard (1805).[2] For the first time traders were in continuous contact with northern Indians and encouraged them to bring furs directly to their posts.

The Hudson's Bay Company attempted to match the expansion of its southern rival and established posts on Slave River, twenty-five miles south of Great Slave Lake (1803), and on Moose Island in Great Slave Lake (1804). In 1806, however, the Company found that it could not meet the competition and withdrew from Athabaska District. A reorganization of the Company in 1810-11 resulted in renewed expeditions into the North-West. Utilizing its short river supply route to Hudson Bay, the "Honourable Company" was able to regain its share of the fur catch. Finally, in 1821, the two competing companies amalgamated under the name of the Hudson's Bay Company and there followed a more orderly expansion.[3]

During the first half of the nineteenth century the Hudson's Bay Company had a monopoly of the trade of this large area of Canada in which fur was the only known resource. Throughout the period the post factors of the Company maintained various regulations aimed at conservation of many of the fur species and imposed definite restrictions which prevented overtrapping of others. In 1825 Indians were discouraged from hunting beaver during the summer, and in 1830 the catch for certain districts was restricted to the average for preceding years. In 1839 only large muskrat were accepted, and at some posts certain furs were refused over a period until their numbers increased locally. The rule of the Hudson's Bay Company ended in 1869 when Rupert's Land, comprising the vast woodlands and tundra of Northern Canada, was bought from the Company by the newly-federated government of Canada.

Fur-laden ships had been passing through Hudson Strait for 250 years before the first trading-post was established in that area.[4] Beginning in 1909 at Wolstenholme, on the north-west corner of Ungava District (now Quebec), the Hudson's Bay Company started to tap the Eastern Arctic fur resources. White fox is the only economic fur-bearer living in the Arctic tundra area, but catches were good and a market was available, enabling the Company to increase the number of its posts and encourage more of the Eskimo inhabitants to become trappers. Revillon Frères, a French-Canadian trading company, established posts in the Eastern Arctic during the nineteen-twenties, but was bought out by the Hudson's Bay Company in 1936.

Posts were opened along the coasts of Hudson Strait and northward in Baffin Island: Lake Harbour (1911), Cape Dorset (1913), Stupart's Bay (1914), Frobisher Bay (1914), Pangnirtung (1921), Pond Inlet (1921),

[2]H. A. Innis, *The Fur Trade in Canada* (New Haven, 1930).

[3]D. Mackay, *The Honourable Company* (Toronto, 1938).

[4]J. W. Anderson, "Trading North of Hudson Bay" (*The Beaver*, Dec., 1939).

River Clyde (1923), Arctic Bay (1926 and again in 1936), and Fort Ross (1937). The ice-breaker *Nascopie* was built by the Hudson's Bay Company in 1912 to bring annual supplies to these isolated posts, and the sturdy ship has continued to service this ever increasing trade up to the present.

Throughout the years when settlement was spreading across Canada the North West Territories remained a vast fur preserve which annually produced a large fur catch for the scattered native population. These pelts were turned in at the trading-stores for more and more of white-man's goods until the native life became almost completely centred around trapping. As population spread

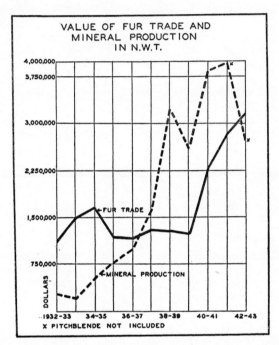

northward, exploitation of the fur resources of this frontier area increased. Independent fur traders entered the field, but few were able to compete successfully with the efficient organization and widespread service of the Hudson's Bay Company. Competition for furs meant that overtrapping was encouraged and little was done to protect the fur-bearers. This situation was encouraged unfortunately by the false assumption that such vast areas with a sparse population could not be depleted.

The number of white trappers increased rapidly during and after the years of the Klondike gold-rush, when some of the gold-seekers remained in the Territory. A further influx came during World War I when fur prices rose steeply, and another increase, after 1920, followed the collapse of the oil

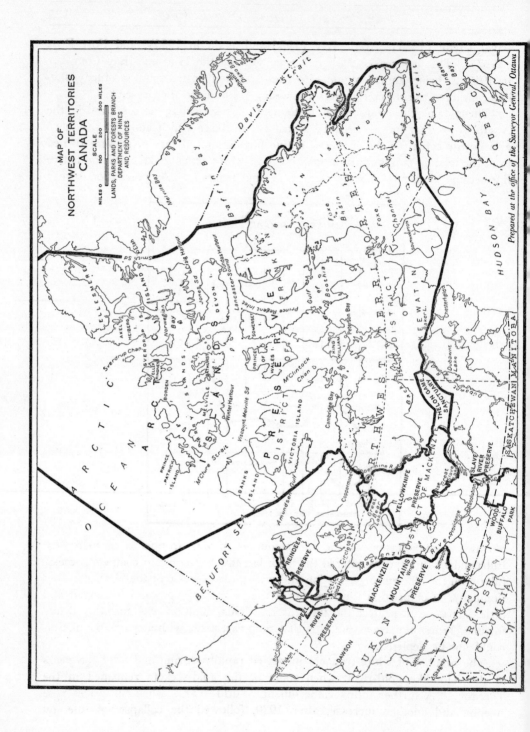

MAP OF
NORTHWEST TERRITORIES
CANADA

SCALE
MILES 0 100 200 300 MILES

LANDS, PARKS AND FORESTS BRANCH
DEPARTMENT OF MINES
AND RESOURCES

Prepared at the office of the Surveyor General, Ottawa

"boom" at Norman Wells. The intensive trapping of the two decades (1900-20) was one of the chief factors in reducing the numbers of certain Mackenzie District fur-bearers.

When the present North West Territories administration was organized in 1921, conservation regulations were immediately instituted to protect the declining fur-bearing animal population. The North West Territories Game Regulations,[5] which have been evolved over the years, are concerned with two vital factors: (1) the welfare of the native population, and (2) the economical harvesting of the fur crop. The former is reflected in the regulation which limits the number of white trappers to resident British subjects who held licences on May 3, 1938, and have continued to live in the Territories. Newcomers are not allowed to trap in the Territories. Such restrictions recognize that the welfare of the Indians and Eskimo now depends on trapping and provide protection from excessive white competition. The natives have been further assisted by the setting aside of several large preserves in which only native-born Indians, Eskimo, or half-breeds living the lives of natives are permitted to hunt or trap. No trading-post can be opened without permission from the administration and approval of its location. This centre then serves the natives for either food or relief in times of stress.

The second aim of the regulations, the economical harvesting of the fur crop, is more difficult to attain,[6] and depends largely upon having an accurate picture of the number of animals being trapped regionally within the Territories. Measures have been instituted towards this end: (1) declaring open and close seasons upon the trapping of most animals; (2) fixing a maximum bag for certain fur-bearers; (3) creating preserves and sanctuaries in which no one is permitted to hunt or trap (e.g., Thelon Game Sanctuary), and others in which only those who hunted or trapped before the creation of the preserve are granted permits (e.g., Wood Buffalo Park, Mackenzie Mountains Preserve).[7]

The administration keeps abreast of fur and game conditions by co-ordinating information supplied by various organizations in the area.[8] Each trader reports

[5]Administration of the Act comes under the Minister of Mines and Resources, who is advised by the Northwest Territories Council. Direct supervision is the responsibility of the Bureau of Northwest Territories and Yukon Affairs, while enforcement is carried out by the R.C.M.P., who are *ex officio* Game Officers. A booklet containing game regulations may be obtained from the Bureau of Northwest Territories and Yukon Affairs, Department of Mines and Resources, Ottawa.

[6]C. Camsell, "Natural Resources and their Conservation" (*Canadian Geographical Journal*, July, 1942).

[7]*The Northwest Territories: Administration, Resources and Development*, Bureau of Northwest Territories and Yukon Affairs, Dept. of Mines and Resources (Ottawa, 1944).

[8]This information has also been assembled by the Bureau of Animal Population, Oxford University, and parts of it were published in a series of annual articles in the *Journal of Animal Ecology*, Cambridge, England. "Canadian Arctic Wildlife Enquiry, 1935 to 1942," by D. Chitty.

the total number of furs of all kinds which are turned in at his store, and a record is maintained of the Fur Export Tax paid on each pelt. Similarly, the R.C.M.P. fill in "Native Game and Fur Returns" from information supplied by individual natives. The police officers further assist by submitting periodic reports on general game and fur conditions within their areas.[9] Every two years a wildlife conference is held in Ottawa with representatives of the provinces attending to exchange facts and opinions concerning wildlife management.[10] Information of this nature has been assembled here to present not only a picture of fur production in the North West Territories, but also a more detailed study of fur catches within smaller regions of this extensive area.

PRESENT FUR TRADE

By virtue of its geographic and climatic environment, Canada is destined to continue playing an important role in the fur trade of the world, provided that

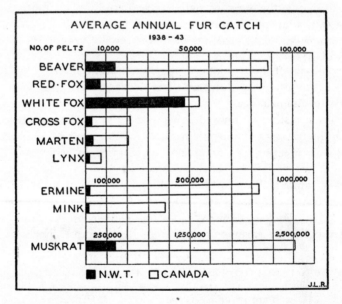

adequate supervision is exercised. Although the relative value of the fur trade is decreasing as Canada becomes more industrialized, the absolute value of fur production has remained generally constant during the past twenty years, averaging about $15 million annually. As more and more of our country became set-

[9]W. H. Nevin, "Policing in the Arctic" (*The Beaver,* Sept., 1945).

[10]R. M. Anderson, "The Distribution, Abundance and Economic Importance of the Game and Fur-Bearing Mammals of Western North America" (*Proceedings of the 5th Pacific Science Congress,* 1934).

tled, the trend was to bring the furs closer to the market by fur-farming. Fur farms, producing chiefly silver foxes and mink, have contributed about 30 per cent of the value of Canadian production over the past ten years.

The North West Territories contain some of the best fur environment of Canada, producing pelts of prime value. Since their area comprises more than one-third of the Dominion, and much of this great region is economically suitable only for the production of fur, the importance of North West Territories fur to the total trade of Canada is considerable. In total value, the fur catch of the Territories has continually constituted about one-tenth of the value of the Canadian catch during the past two decades. In total number of pelts, the Dominion-wide harvests have increased in the past ten years from about 4 million annually to over 7 million while those of the Territories have increased from about 200,000 to 500,000 pelts. The accompanying chart illustrates the average annual catch of various North West Territories fur-bearers during five years (1938-43) as compared with the same averages for all of Canada. The relative importance of white fox, beaver, and muskrat is clearly evident.

Until 1920 the fur trade was virtually the only industry of the Territories. In that year oil was struck below Fort Norman and the attention of prospectors was directed northward. It was not until the discoveries of radium in 1930 and gold at Yellowknife in 1934 that mining began to displace the fur trade as the region's chief industry. Because of the geographic character of the country, however, and the dependence of the native population upon the fur trade, the latter industry will remain fundamental in the economy of this area.

White trappers are not numerous in the North West Territories. Although the number of trapping licences issued each year remains between 500 and 550, the actual number of active trappers is much smaller. Most of the present-day trappers are old-time residents of the Territories.[11] Nearly all of them live in the Mackenzie Valley, chiefly around Fort Smith, Simpson, and Aklavik. Only a few trap in southern Keewatin District and none in the Arctic Islands (Franklin District). The following table shows that about 20 per cent of the furs traded are caught by white trappers, and this percentage has remained fairly constant over the past decade.

AVERAGE PERCENTAGE OF EACH FUR-BEARER TAKEN BY WHITE TRAPPERS

	1932-35	1940-43
Red Fox	39	42
Lynx	29	23
Mink	22	23
Muskrat	15	20
Ermine	25	20
Beaver	12	19
Marten	15	10

[11]M. Lubbock, "Canada's Fur Trade Today" (*The Polar Record*, Jan., 1939).

Trapping is the chief source of income of the Mackenzie District Indians, but they still depend upon wild game for a large part of their food.[12] Summer fishing usually provides enough fish to keep families and dogs alive, and larger autumn catches are dried or salted to be used during the early winter. Fresh meat is obtained during the winter from moose or the wandering herds of caribou. Trapping begins in November when there is enough snow on the ground for travelling. A group of families usually camps together, living either in tents banked with boughs or in log cabins. The men visit their trap-lines periodically to bring in fur, while the women and children remain around the central camp. Occasional trips are made to the nearest trading-store to exchange winter furs for food and supplies, and nearly all natives come to the settlements for the religious

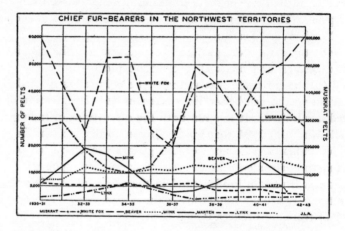

CHIEF FUR-BEARERS IN THE NORTHWEST TERRITORIES

holidays of Christmas and Easter. Most families own log cabins in the white settlements and spend one or two months there during the summer.

The present fur trade of the North West Territories is still predominantly in the hands of the Hudson's Bay Company, which has forty-one trading-stores in the Territories and an additional nine in Arctic Quebec.[13] Of the remaining 103 traders, most are individuals, and no other organization has more than three stores. In total numbers of pelts, the muskrat is the leading fur animal of the region, followed by white fox, beaver, ermine, red and cross fox, mink, marten, and lynx. Since most of Keewatin and all of Franklin District are north of the tree-line, nearly all the fur-bearers, excepting white fox, are caught in Mackenzie District. It is to the latter district that most of the following material refers.

The accompanying graphs (on which only the leading five regions and one of the lowest are shown) illustrate the numbers of various fur-bearers caught

[12]G. Pendleton, "Life in the Mackenzie Valley" (*The Beaver*, March, 1943).
[13]The Company has over 200 trading-posts in Canada.

within certain districts during the period 1932 to 1943. They show which areas
are the chief producers of certain types of fur, and also mark the cyclic variations
in numbers caught. Biologists believe that nearly all fur-bearers fluctuate in
numbers over a period of years; e.g., four-year cycle for white fox, and ten-year
cycle for lynx.[14] The graphs show regionally the actual numerical variations
produced by these biological phenomena, but even their significance must be
interpreted with caution.

The charts illustrate the numbers of furs traded at the stores, and, although
these figures should approximate to a percentage of the number of animals in the
wild, such factors as good or bad hunting seasons, availability of food, ambition
of the natives, climatic cycles, forest fires, current fur prices, conservation mea-

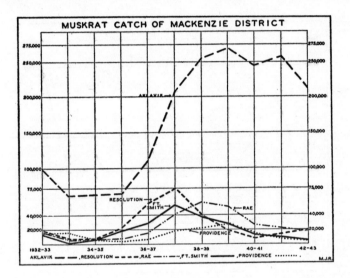

sures, new trading posts, and other human disturbances must be considered
before arrival at definite scientific conclusions. Despite these difficulties, trends
and fluctuations can be seen, and the information is important in planning future
conservation measures.

Muskrat. About 300,000 muskrat, representing one-seventh of the Canadian
muskrat catch, come from the North West Territories, and at present 75 per cent
of this total is obtained in the Mackenzie River delta. There nature has created
an exceptional habitat for these small fur-bearers. The Mackenzie River breaks
up into a great number of rivers, streams and cut-off channels, and among them
lie innumerable lakes of all sizes. Muskrat food is plentiful in the delta and,
despite an annual harvest which now exceeds a quarter-million pelts, no decrease
in numbers is evident. The delta has consistently been the best muskrat area

[14]E. J. Seton, *The Arctic Prairies* (Toronto, 1911).

in the Territories, its percentage of the total Territories catch having steadily increased from 50 per cent in 1933 to 75 per cent in 1943.[15]

Muskrat are caught by being trapped, either in their houses in the ice or in burrows along the stream banks, and by being shot in the water after the ice breaks up. Equipped with a light "ratting" canoe and a .22 rifle, a native can move rapidly from one stream or lake to another and shoot from 100 to 200 "rats" in a night.

Smaller numbers of muskrat are traded at nearly all the Mackenzie Valley posts, since lowland, lakes and swamps are typical of the district. The most important of the lesser areas are Slave River delta (15,000 to 75,000 annually) and the lake country north-west of Fort Rae.

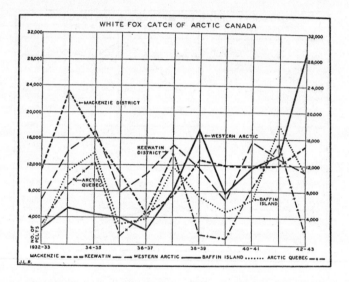

White Fox. Nearly all (an average of 87 per cent) of the Canadian white (Arctic) fox catch comes from the North West Territories, the remainder being caught in Arctic Quebec. Ranching attempts in southern districts, as well as in the Arctic, have not been successful. The white fox is one of the few economic resources of the Canadian Arctic and the only product which the Eskimo inhabitants can trade for white man's food, utensils, and equipment. Because there is a definite short-period cyclic variation in numbers of white foxes, a factor of real instability exists in Eskimo economy.[16]

[15]A. E. Porsild, "Mammals of the Mackenzie Delta" (*The Canadian Field-Naturalist*, Jan., 1945).

[16]J. L. Robinson, *An Outline of the Canadian Eastern Arctic: its Geography, Peoples and Problems*, Bureau of Northwest Territories and Yukon Affairs, Department of Mines and Resources (Ottawa, 1944).

The variation is one of abundance every four years, with a particularly low year occurring between the peaks.[17] For example, the take in the Lake Harbour area, Baffin Island, dropped from a peak of over 4,000 pelts in 1941-2 to less than 200 in 1943-4. The accompanying graph shows that the four-year cycle in white fox numbers is fairly definite in the Eastern Arctic regions, but is less regular in the Western Arctic and Mackenzie District.

In Mackenzie District the white fox catch comes chiefly from two areas, both north of the tree-line. White trappers go out into the Barren Grounds east and north of Reliance, at the eastern end of Great Slave Lake, and spend the winter trapping in the area, returning to Fort Smith or northern Alberta settlements in the spring. The white fox catch at Aklavik comes largely from Banks Island, and the steady increase since 1937 is chiefly due to the rich catches resulting from a change to inland trapping by the Eskimo on the island.

The Eastern Arctic region, which includes Baffin Island, Keewatin District, and Arctic Quebec, is the leading producer of white fox pelts. Among the smaller comparative areas which are shown on the graph, Keewatin District has been a consistently good producer. The Western Arctic region, which includes the western Arctic Islands and the north coast of Mackenzie District, has returned exceptionally large catches in some years, and has increased in importance since 1937.

Beaver. The North West Territories produced about 15 per cent of the annual Canadian beaver catch during the years 1938-43, and this proportion has increased in recent years as a result of close seasons in other provinces. Despite the fact that numbers caught in the Territories have remained fairly constant (about 12,000 annually during the decade preceding 1943), it was believed that the area was being overtrapped, and conservation measures have become necessary to maintain the supply. A close season was declared in 1928 for three years in Mackenzie District, and when it was reopened in 1932 a quota of fifteen beaver per hunter was decided upon. By 1940 beaver were almost exterminated in the Mackenzie River delta, and the area was set aside as a special sanctuary in which they could not be trapped.

Current high prices of fur have resulted in further inroads into the beaver population of the southern part of Mackenzie District, necessitating a close season in the area south of Liard River and east of a line joining the Liard River and Great Bear Lake. North of this area the season has been shortened to two months (March and April), the quota reduced to ten, and shooting of beaver prohibited.

There appears to be little cyclic variation in the Mackenzie District beaver catch, as indicated by the accompanying graph; slight fluctuations in various regions depend largely on current regulations and prices. In general, the number

[17]C. Elton, *Voles, Mice and Lemming* (Oxford, 1942).

trapped and shot increased from 1939 to 1941, but since then totals have fallen off, especially at the southern posts. Catches at Fort Simpson have remained consistently high and increasing, while those from the lower Mackenzie River posts of Norman, Good Hope, and Arctic Red River have remained fairly constant (about 1,400 annually).

Beaver is one of the fur-bearers easily exterminated, and the record in the Territories, as well as in the rest of Canada, shows a tendency towards depletion. At the same time, beaver is one of the fur-bearers easiest to preserve under careful management. Successful experiments with beaver sanctuaries, such as those run by the Hudson's Bay Company on Charlton and Akimiski Islands in James

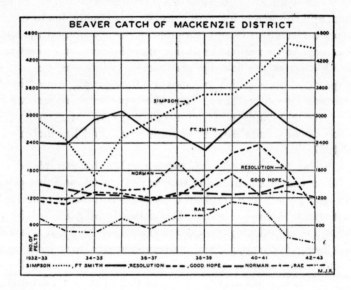

Bay, show that a harvest can be obtained without depleting the supply.[18] These projects point the way for similar steps in other parts of the Territories.

Ermine. Although the ermine (weasel) catch of the Territories ranks fourth in total numbers, its relative value is much less. The area produces only 1.5 per cent of the total Canadian annual catch. Ermine is known as an "incidental" fur at the trading-posts; i.e., very little attempt is made to trap ermine, and those turned in are usually caught in traps set for other animals. Much of the ermine catch results from the trapping activities of boys who are learning the fundamentals of their future occupation.

Regional totals fluctuate with slight peaks occurring every two or three years. A peak was reached in 1939-40, and totals have declined rapidly since then.

[18]D. E. Denmark, "Beaver Conservation by the Hudson's Bay Company" (*The Canadian Surveyor,* Jan., 1945).

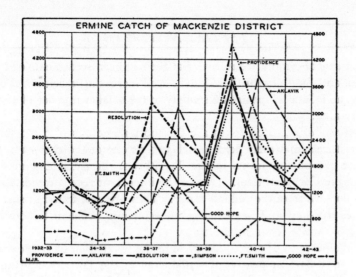

ERMINE CATCH OF MACKENZIE DISTRICT

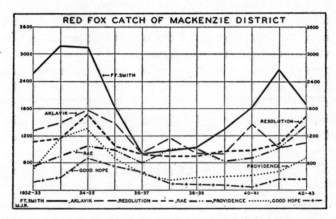

RED FOX CATCH OF MACKENZIE DISTRICT

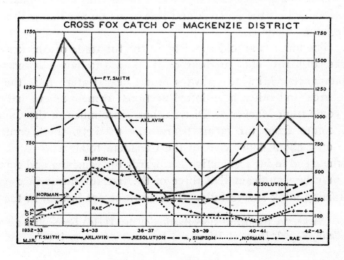

CROSS FOX CATCH OF MACKENZIE DISTRICT

Largest returns of ermine are recorded at the southern settlements of Providence, Resolution, and Smith, with the Aklavik area increasing recently. Lower totals at Norman and Good Hope are due chiefly to the smaller number of Indians trapping in the area.

Coloured Foxes. Red foxes are the most numerous of the coloured foxes in the Territories, and their pelts are classed as one of the cheaper types of fur. Since there are no fox farms in the Territories, the catch amounts to only 7 per cent of the Canadian total. One of the important recent trends has been the extension northward of the red fox range. They are now found in small numbers beyond the tree-line and are causing an economic problem by destroying the more valuable white foxes in the traps.

There appears to be a ten-year cycle in the population of red-foxes. A peak was noted in 1934-5 at nearly all settlements in the District, and another was reached in 1944. The bottom of the cycle occurred during the years of 1937-9, which were also low years for some of the other fur-bearers of the region. The Fort Smith area has always produced the largest number of red foxes, followed by the Aklavik, Resolution, and Rae regions.

Cross foxes are found in smaller numbers in the same areas, and follow the same general cycle as red foxes. One of the chief differences is the proportionately larger number of cross foxes (as compared with the number of reds) that are trapped in the Aklavik-Arctic Red River-McPherson area. The Fort Smith and Resolution areas produce the largest numbers of cross fox pelts as well as red.

The cyclic fluctuations of the fox population have long been studied by the biologists,[19] but many phases are still unexplained. Whether the cycles are due to a straight predator-prey relationship, to periodic disease epidemics, or to combinations of these and other factors, is still to be fully determined. It is particularly noticeable that the Aklavik and Rae areas do not follow the general fox cycles of the other sections.

Mink. The mink is an old stand-by in the fur trade of Mackenzie District. As in the case of many other fur-bearers, it appears to have a seven to nine-year cycle of abundance. Mink are always found near water; thus the Mackenzie River delta area and other lake-dotted sections form excellent habitats. Fine mink pelts come from Mackenzie District, but, since much of the Canadian mink production comes from fur farms nearer the markets, the Territories' catch amounts to only about 4 per cent of the Canadian total.

Since the trend in fur production is towards fur-ranching and controlled wild catches, it may be significant that three of the five fur farms in the Territories today are raising mink successfully. Two of these are located in the Mackenzie

[19]C. H. D. Clarke, "A Biological Investigation of the Thelon Game Sanctuary" (*National Museum Bulletin No. 90,* Dept. of Mines and Resources, Ottawa, 1940).

delta area south of Aklavik, and the third is on an island near Yellowknife. The mink are fed on imported meal, but their diet is supplemented by fish, which are found throughout the Territories in large numbers.

Within the last twenty years there have been three mink peaks in Mackenzie District. The first was recorded in 1923-4 and totals were higher (21,000) than in the next peak of 1932-3 (18,000). The second peak was not reached until a year later at some of the settlements, and was not evident until 1934-5 at Simpson, Norman, and Good Hope. The third peak of 1940-1 also varied regionally within the District over a period of three years. As is the case with many of the fur species which are being actively trapped, it is noticeable that succeeding peaks

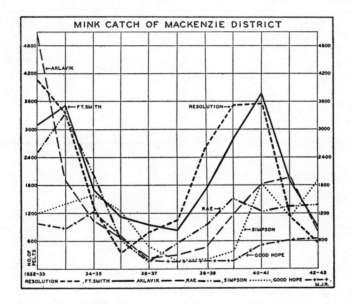

MINK CATCH OF MACKENZIE DISTRICT

tend to be lower than previous ones. Careful attention will be given to the expected mink peak of 1948 to determine if the total mink population of the District is actually declining, or if the smaller catches are due to the low-water period of recent years.

In good years the Slave River delta area, tributary to the posts at Resolution and Rocher River, has had the largest mink catch, but, strangely, has had one of the lowest in poor years. Mink numbers have been more consistent around Fort Smith, but the Aklavik and Rae areas failed to reach the peaks in 1940-2 which were recorded in 1932-3.

Marten. Mackenzie District was once the best marten country in Canada. In the period 1851-6 the average annual marten total exceeded 30,000 pelts, and some sections produced numbers greater than the present take of the whole

Dominion.[20] Excessive trapping soon decimated this valuable fur-bearer, and
by 1930 the average annual catch of Mackenzie District was only about
5,000 pelts. In 1936 the marten season was shortened one month, and in 1940 a
quota system of two animals south and twenty north of the Mackenzie-Liard
Rivers limited each trapper's catch. As there was no apparent improvement in
the following years, a close season was declared in 1943 which is to remain in
effect until marten recover their status. Since the District was producing about
18 per cent of the Canadian catch, closing the season reduced the income of
Indians and whites, but fortunately this has been balanced by increased prices for
other furs.

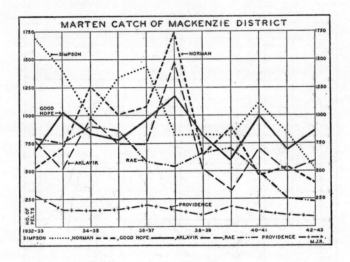

Marten live in the high forested valleys of the South Nahanni and Peel
Rivers in the Mackenzie Mountains and also in the lowland swamps north of
Great Bear Lake. Since the closing of the season in Mackenzie District, Indians
from Arctic Red River and Fort McPherson have been able to go into the Peel
Valley of Yukon Territory and bring out valuable catches of marten. In recent
years the marten population has been too low to show any cyclic fluctuation,
but the graph does illustrate the rapid decline of marten at Simpson, Norman,
and Rae, and the relative increase at Good Hope and Arctic Red River. The
Resolution-Providence area, along the south shore of Great Slave Lake, has
had few marten in the past decade.

Lynx. The Canadian lynx catch is comparatively small (about 7,000 pelts
annually), and about 22 per cent came from the Territories during 1938-43. It

[20]C. H. D. Clarke, "Status and Distribution of Certain Mammals and Birds in the Mackenzie River and Western Arctic area in 1942 and 1943" (*The Canadian Field-Naturalist*,
May, 1944).

has been fairly well established that lynx have a ten-year cycle of abundance, which is correlated with the cyclic abundance of rabbits.[21] The Mackenzie lynx peak occurred in 1934-5 and, although complete totals have not yet been tabulated, it was expected that 1944-5 would also see an increased catch.

The Simpson-Providence area is the only section where lynx are caught in comparatively large numbers. The Arctic Red River-McPherson area had a good catch in 1934-5, but has done poorly since. During the period of scarcity catches were low at all settlements except Simpson. Rae and Resolution have continually been poor areas for lynx.

Other Fur-Bearers. In addition to the chief fur-bearers described above, there are others that are caught in smaller numbers in the Territories. Coloured

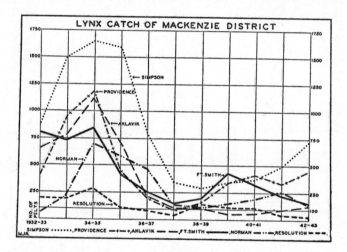

foxes include from 200 to 400 silver foxes annually, trapped chiefly in the southern part of Mackenzie District, and about ten to twenty black foxes. Blue foxes (a colour phase of the white fox) are found in the same Arctic areas as white foxes at a ratio of about 1 per cent. About 300 otter are trapped annually, coming chiefly from Fort Smith and Rae. The fisher is one of the most valuable of Canadian fur-bearers, and, although a few hundred are trapped annually in northern British Columbia, thirty-six has been the highest number caught in any one year in the Territories since 1932. Skunks are found occasionally in traps, and from fifty to a hundred are turned in each year to the posts. From 500 to 1,000 wolves are shot or trapped annually, and, although their fur value is not high, they are killed whenever possible. Wolves and, in the Barren Grounds, wolverines prove the nemesis of trappers, for each year they destroy valuable fur in the traps.

[21]C. Elton and M. Nicholson, "The Ten-Year Cycle in Numbers of Lynx in Canada" (*Journal of Animal Ecology,* Nov., 1942).

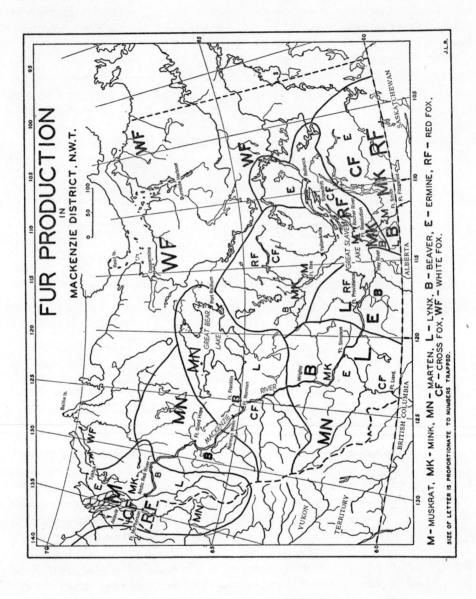

FUR PRODUCTION

IN

MACKENZIE DISTRICT, N.W.T.

M – MUSKRAT, MK – MINK, MN – MARTEN, L – LYNX, B – BEAVER, E – ERMINE, RF – RED FOX,
CF – CROSS FOX, WF – WHITE FOX.

SIZE OF LETTER IS PROPORTIONATE TO NUMBERS TRAPPED.

J.L.R.

CONCLUSION

In breaking down the Territories' fur catch into regions, one is able to see where the various centres of animal population are located. Some areas are important because they produce the largest percentage of certain furs, while others are important for the general high numbers of a variety of furs. The accompanying map illustrates the regions tributary to the posts which were used on the graphs, and the chief fur-bearers of each region. In order to obtain some idea of the densities of mammal populations, one should correlate the number of pelts caught in each area with the number of trappers. (See map of Indian population.)

The following table rates the importance of each region in the production of pelts of eight chief fur-bearers of Mackenzie District. It readily shows the significance of Simpson as a fine-fur area, since this section, which includes

LEADING FUR AREAS OF MACKENZIE DISTRICT

Place	Beaver	Marten	Lynx	Mink	Muskrat	Red Fox	Cross Fox	Ermine	Ind. pop.
Fort Smith	2	6	3	2	4	1	1	2	290
Resolution	3	7	8	1	3	3	3	2	584
Providence	6	8	2	6	5	5	7	1	523
Rae	8	5	6	4	2	4	4	6	918
Simpson	1	1	1	5	7	6	6	3	657
Norman	4	3	4	7	8	7	5	7	374
Good Hope	5	2	7	8	6	8	8	8	337
Aklavik	7	4	5	3	1	2	2	4	639

the posts of Liard and Wrigley, ranks first in the production of beaver, marten, and lynx, the more valuable furs. This importance is mirrored by the fact that there are fifteen to twenty traders in the Simpson area and twelve active white trappers. In total numbers of all furs, Fort Smith ranks highest, recording fairly large numbers of all species excepting marten. This area, which includes the northern part of Wood Buffalo Park, produces the greatest number of coloured foxes and rates second in beaver and mink. The Resolution area, which includes the trading-posts at Rocher River and Snowdrift, is also one of the leading general fur areas, ranking among the first three producers for all furs excepting marten and lynx.

In total annual value of fur production, the Aklavik-Fort McPherson-Arctic Red River area is by far the most valuable section of the North West Territories. During the period 1938-43 the average annual catch had a value of over $500,000. Two chief fur-bearers, muskrat and white fox, constituted 85 per cent of this value. The remaining centres, listed in the following table, have annual catches valued at from $100,000 to $200,000, and usually the value of one particular fur-bearer is about 40 per cent of the total. In the Resolution area, for example, the white fox catch from east of Reliance has been the most valuable. At Fort Smith beaver constituted 36 per cent of the average annual value, while at Simpson 55 per cent of the total value consisted of beaver pelts. Similarly, at Providence, Norman, and Good Hope beaver comprised 36 per cent of the annual fur value, but muskrat was the most valuable fur-bearer at Rae.

AVERAGE ANNUAL VALUE OF FUR PRODUCTION—1938-43

Aklavik	$505,000
Resolution	198,000
Fort Smith	190,000
Simpson	175,000
Rae	140,000
Good Hope	90,000
Norman	90,000
Providence	87,000

The general picture of fur production in the North West Territories shows that there are periods of fluctuation in the numbers of various fur-bearers.[22] The years 1933-5 were generally good fur years, while the period 1936-9 resulted in poor catches. From 1940 to 1944 catches were again quite high, but whether this was due to the very high prices paid for furs during the war years, or simply to a period of fur abundance, can be determined only over a longer period.

The successive peaks for most species have gradually become lower and lower in the Territories. It was apparent that even this sparsely-settled fur area could not withstand intensive trapping, and regulations were instituted to curtail overtrapping.[23] Fur catches are now more controlled, but the depletion of certain stocks means that conservation and restocking steps are necessary to build up the area to its former position as a fur-producer. Before such measures can be instituted, further research work and study are necessary to determine more closely the actual status and numbers of fur-bearers in the Territories.

In order to maintain fur production in the Territories, the Administration is introducing an improved system of forest fire protection and preparing a programme of conservation education for the natives. The establishment of fur farms is being encouraged as a means of stabilizing production. Plans under consideration for future wild-life management include the improving of certain areas (by methods similar to those employed in 1938 in Wood Buffalo Park

[22]L. Butler, "Fur Cycles and Conservation" (*Transactions of the 7th North American Wildlife Conference, 1942*).

[23]C. G. Hewitt, *The Conservation of the Wild Life of Canada* (New York, 1921).

with the construction of dams and earth-fills to maintain water levels), special supervision of productive areas like the Mackenzie Delta, and the introduction of registered trap-lines to prevent overtrapping.

The North West Territories provide a natural environment excellently suited for fur production—a resource which utilizes large areas of apparently

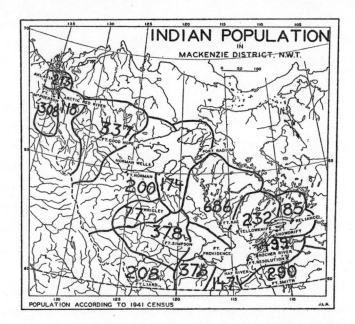

useless country. In the current inventories of resources of our vast Canadian North-West, the fur-bearing animals must have proper attention in order to maintain their position in the total Canadian economy. The fur trade of the Territories has seen many changes, but it is not a spent force nor in danger of extinction if wise management prevails. Because of its importance to the natives and the permanent white population, one can feel confident that fur will remain one of the most valuable exports of the Territories.

Part Six

WILLIAM DICKSON

Northern Agriculture[1]

FOR many years an important proportion of the food requirements for the northern regions of Canada has been imported at relatively high cost from "outside." This applies particularly to such protective foods as fruits, milk, butter, eggs, etc., of which consumption has been necessarily restricted. Local production of such food has been severely limited by disadvantages of soil and climate and by the prevalence of occupations, hunting, trapping, trading, and mining, which conflict with agricultural employment.

Several factors in recent years, however, have stimulated increasing interest and enquiry into the agricultural possibilities of northern Canada. There has been an increase in the total food requirements owing to the influx of population, bringing dietary habits acquired in regions of adequate agricultural production, in connection with such developments as the Alaska Highway, the Norman oil wells, the Yellowknife gold mines and the expansion of various government services. Growing evidence of nutritional disorders, especially among native races, has drawn attention to a need for a greater consumption of foods which could be secured from gardens or small farms. Then there is the aspect of scientific enquiry, partly related to problems of northern agriculture as such, and partly complementary to agricultural research in southern regions.

This growing interest, incidentally, derives some stimulation from the reported exploitation of Arctic agricultural resources by the U.S.S.R., and has a bearing on questions of circum-polar defence.

The purpose of this article is to present a brief review of some of the information now available on conditions affecting agriculture in the northern regions of Canada, and to suggest some possible lines of future development. A definite southern boundary to "northern Canada" being difficult to locate, the fifty-seventh parallel of latitude is selected for this purpose, with references to more southerly points as conditions may warrant. North of this arbitrary

[1]Agricultural research and extension work in the North West Territories and the Yukon is co-ordinated through an Inter-departmental Committee on Northern Agriculture, of which Dr. E. S. Archibald, Director, Experimental Farms Service, and Mr. R. A. Gibson, Deputy-Commissioner of the North West Territories, are joint Chairmen. It is on the authority of this Committee that the above article is presented.

boundary attention will be directed mainly to the Mackenzie Basin, more briefly to the Yukon and northern British Columbia, and merely in passing to the Laurentian Shield.

AGRICULTURE IN THE MACKENZIE BASIN

The Mackenzie River flows in a north-westerly direction through north-western Canada, draining to the Arctic a watershed of about 700,000 square miles. The greater portion of this basin lies on the northern extension of the Central Plain which is one of the major physiographic features of the North American continent, occupying in Canada the relatively undisturbed sedimentary geological region between the western mountain ranges and the Pre-Cambrian Laurentian Shield. Quite appreciable areas west of the main ranges of the Rockies and on the western edge of the Shield, however, are also drained by the Mackenzie. The southern edge of this vast drainage basin occurs at about the latitude of Edmonton, and extends north for over 1,000 miles, with climatic conditions ranging from temperate through sub-Arctic to Arctic conditions. Both in agricultural practice and possibilities there is a corresponding range from the highly fertile farmlands of the upper Peace River to treeless tundra on the Arctic coast with permanently frozen subsoil. The region therefore presents an almost ideal gradation of conditions for research in northern agriculture.

Physiography of the Mackenzie Basin. The main physiographic divisions of the Mackenzie Basin are the Rocky and Mackenzie Mountains which form a somewhat abrupt boundary on the west, the Pre-Cambrian peneplane of the Laurentian Shield on the east, and the intervening northward extension of the Great Central Plain of North America, underlain by relatively undisturbed sedimentary rocks. The more southerly portion of the plain region within the basin is occupied by the Alberta Plateau, extending slightly north of the sixtieth parallel of latitude, north of which occur the less elevated Mackenzie Lowlands.

The Alberta Plateau occupies all of northern Alberta excepting the lowlands around the western end of Lake Athabaska and the Slave valley, all of British Columbia east of the Rockies, and extends some distance into the North West Territories where its northern boundary is sharply marked by an escarpment south of the upper Mackenzie and Great Slave Lake. The elevation of this Plateau ranges from slightly over 1,000 feet in the north and west to over 2,000 feet near the Rockies. Its surface has been described as "a gently rolling plain, rather poorly drained, and characterized by morainic ridges, outwash plains and glacio-lacustrine deposits." Superimposed on this plain are a number of isolated hill masses, of which the more important are the Caribou Mountains (3,500 feet) lying south of the western arm of Great Slave Lake, and the Birch Mountains (2,300 feet) south-west of Lake Athabaska. Other hill masses include the Buffalo Head Hills south of Fort Vermilion, the High Hills and

Watt Mountain (2,500 feet) west of Fort Vermilion, and the Clear Hills (3,500 feet) north of upper Peace on the Alberta-British Columbia boundary.

The principal members of the Mackenzie River system on the Alberta Plateau are: the Athabaska, running from the Rockies eastward above Edmonton and then north to Lake Athabaska; the Peace, with sources beyond the Rockies, flowing roughly east then north and then north-west to join the Slave just below Lake Athabaska, the Fort Nelson and Pettitot Rivers which drain the north-western portion of the Plateau to the Liard, and the Hay River draining the north-western corner of Alberta into Great Slave Lake. In their upper reaches the Peace and Athabaska Rivers, with many of their tributaries, flow through deeply trenched valleys. Many of the smaller streams, however, are somewhat sluggish, much of the Plateau being covered with marsh, muskeg, and lakes. Well drained areas occur to some extent along the deeper river valleys, especially on the upper Peace.

The Mackenzie Lowlands extend north-west from the Alberta Plateau for a distance of some 800 miles with an average width of about 200 miles. Low land along the valley of the Slave and around Lake Athabaska represents a southern extension of this region. Average elevations are considerably lower than on the Plateau, much of the area being under 700 feet and generally under 1,000 feet. Aside from the Mackenzie Mountains, the principal hills of this region are the Horn Mountains (2,600 feet) north of the Mackenzie near Fort Providence, the Norman Range and Franklin Mountains west of Great Bear Lake, and the Richardson Mountains west of the delta. A low range of hills east of the delta is shown on some maps as the Reindeer Mountains, but is not indicated on other maps.

Within this region the principal members of the Mackenzie River system include the Slave, Great Slave Lake, the Mackenzie proper, the Liard, Great Bear Lake and Bear River, Peel River, and the delta. The Slave, flowing northward from Lake Athabaska, follows the western edge of the Shield for part of its course and in its lower reaches winds through an alluvial plain. Great Slave Lake (elevation 500 feet) extends east into the Shield and west into the Lowlands, with a northern arm which follows the edge of the Shield. The Liard, with sources in the mountains of the southern Yukon and northern British Columbia, drains the north-eastern part of the Alberta Plateau, as already noted, and enters the Mackenzie at Fort Simpson. About halfway from Great Slave Lake to the Arctic Ocean, Great Bear Lake extends well into the Lowlands on the west and the Shield on the east, and is drained by Great Bear River into the Mackenzie at Fort Norman. West of the lower Mackenzie the Peel River drains a broad valley in the Mackenzie Mountains, the "Peel Plateau," to flow north to the delta. Finally the Mackenzie enters the Beaufort Sea through a delta of alluvial deposits, which forms an intricate maze of waterways. Extensive deltas are also formed where the Athabaska enters Lake Athabaska and where the Slave enters Great Slave Lake.

Through most of its extent the surface of the Lowlands region is swampy and ill-drained, with extensive muskegs broken by sand or gravel ridges. Well-drained areas seem to be confined to the higher banks of the main rivers.

Along its eastern boundary, the Lowlands region makes contact with the Laurentian Shield on a line running up the east side of the Slave valley from Lake Athabaska to about the middle of Great Slave Lake, and thence to about the middle of Great Bear Lake. East of this line the terrain is characteristic of the Laurentian Shield, being a region of lakes and exposures of Pre-Cambrian rocks and with few soil deposits. The general elevation of the Shield in this region is about 1,500 to 1,700 feet, and while no distinct hill masses are reported, the topography is hummocky and broken.

Climate of the Mackenzie Basin. Climate is the chief limiting factor in the development of agriculture in the Mackenzie Basin. The Mackenzie climate is characterized by cold winters, short, moderately warm summers, and light precipitation. Certain selected data on temperature and precipitation for representative points in the Mackenzie Basin are presented in Table I, together with comparative data for Ottawa.

An important characteristic of temperature conditions in the Mackenzie Basin is a generally north-westerly trend of summer isotherms, especially during the summer months. Thus the mean summer (June, July, and August) temperatures at Fort Smith and Fort Good Hope, separated by over 6° of latitude, are almost the same, 56.9° and 56.5° respectively. For this reason summers along the lower Mackenzie are considerably warmer than would be the case if the isotherms exhibited an east to west trend.

In northern latitudes the low average summer temperatures and short growing season are compensated by relatively long hours of sunlight. At Fort Norman, for instance, there are over 2,300 hours of daylight during the summer months from May to August inclusive as compared with 1,980 hours at Beaverlodge, and 1,840 hours at Ottawa. One effect of the long hours of summer daylight in the northern Mackenzie is to promote vegetable production.

One of the hazards affecting agriculture in the Mackenzie Basin is the high frequency of summer frosts. This is indicated by the short average frost-free period (see Table I), based on the frequency of temperatures of 32.5° Fahrenheit or lower. Throughout the Basin this average period is less than 100 days, in some locations considerably less, as compared with 148 days at Ottawa. Actually, throughout the Mackenzie Lowlands frost may be expected in each of the summer months.

In common with more southerly parts of the Central Plains, the average precipitation throughout the Mackenzie Basin is light, about one-half to one-third

TABLE I

SELECTED DATA ON TEMPERATURE AND PRECIPITATION AT REPRESENTATIVE POINTS IN THE MACKENZIE RIVER BASIN AND AT OTTAWA, ONTARIO

Location	Latitude N.	Elevation above Sea-Level	Years in Record	Mean Temperature (F.) June to August	Mean Temperature (F.) December to February	Mean Temperature (F.) Annual	Average Frost-free Period	Mean Precipitation May to August	Mean Precipitation Year
		feet		°	°	°	days	inches	inches
Aklavik, N.W.T.	68° 14'	25	12	51.5	− 17.2	15.2	64.9	4.12	10.28
Fort McPherson, N.W.T.	67° 26'	150	30	54.9	− 19.5	16.1	70.2	4.82	10.06
Fort Good Hope, N.W.T.	66° 15'	214	30	56.5	− 21.0	17.0	52.3	4.93	10.63
Fort Norman, N.W.T.	64° 54'	300	30	55.9	− 15.7	19.5	44.4	6.45	11.22
Fort Simpson, N.W.T.	61° 52'	415	41	58.3	− 13.7	23.8	84.1	6.31	12.96
Fort Resolution, N.W.T.	61° 10'	515	23	55.6	− 11.8	23.2	92.9	4.75	11.90
Hay River, N.W.T.	60° 51'	529	45	55.4	− 10.7	23.7	87.1	5.31	11.77
Fort Smith, N.W.T.	60° 00'	680	25	56.9	− 11.2	25.0	56.1	6.72	13.01
Fort Nelson, B.C.	58° 50'	1230	5	59.8	− 4.7	30.9	…	6.16	13.91
Fort Chipewyan, Alta.	58° 43'	714	43	58.4	− 6.7	26.9	73.6	5.99	12.55
Fort McMurray, Alta.	56° 44'	829	37	58.6	− 3.9	29.9	65.9	9.06	17.71
Fort Vermilion, Alta.	58° 23'	950	33	58.1	− 6.9	27.6	68.3	6.56	11.90
Beaverlodge, Alta.	55° 10'	2484	27	57.8	11.2	35.6	91.3	7.72	17.55
Ottawa, Ont.	45° 24'	260	53	66.6	13.9	41.6	148.0	12.80	34.24

Data by courtesy of the Meteorological Service of Canada.

of the Ottawa precipitation. Despite a probable low evaporation-precipitation ratio and some degree of sub-irrigation from frozen subsoils, summer droughts are experienced in northern districts.

Soils. Soil conditions are determined by climate, geology, topography, age, and vegetation, and are capable of being markedly modified by the works of men. In various localities one or more of these factors may be dominant. In the Mackenzie Basin the influence of climate is exhibited in a gradation of zonal soil types ranging from fertile, black grasslands on the upper Peace River, through grey wooded soils to the treeless tundra where plant growth and soil formation is inhibited by a permanently frozen subsoil. Geology is the dominant factor on the Laurentian Shield, with its great expanse of crystalline rock, resistant to soil forming processes. Geological processes have been involved in the deposition of soil materials, in such forms as morainic ridges, lacustrine plains, river benches, river flats, alluvial plains, and deltas. The influence of topography is mainly evident in drainage conditions, good agricultural soils being found only where drainage is relatively unimpeded. All of these factors influence the type of vegetation in any locality which, in turn, exerts a profound influence on the soil in which it grows.

Information on the nature, distribution, and extent of various types of soil in the Mackenzie Basin is rather scanty, few scientific investigations of soil conditions having been made, nowhere comparable to the comprehensive soil surveys which have covered large areas in the agricultural regions farther south. For most of the Mackenzie Basin, soil conditions must be inferred from the known topographic, climatic, and geological conditions, and from the somewhat superficial observations of travellers.

Land classification surveys along the southern fringe of the Mackenzie Basin in Alberta were made during the years 1929 and 1930 by the Soils Department of the University of Alberta. Most of the areas covered lie outside of the region being considered in this article, but a broad band along the middle Peace River around and above Fort Vermilion, does lie within the region under consideration. No further definite soils investigations were undertaken in the Mackenzie Basin until the years 1943 to 1945 inclusive, when Dr. A. Leahey of the Dominion Experimental Farms made exploratory soil surveys along the Alaska Highway, the Liard River, and along the water route from Waterways, Alta., to Aklavik on the Mackenzie delta. The following description of soil conditions includes quotations from Dr. Leahey's preliminary reports.

Incomparably the best farming land in the Basin is found around the upper Peace River of Alberta and in the adjacent Peace River block of British Columbia, generally referred to as the "Peace River Country." Being located on the higher levels of the Alberta Plateau (2,000 to 2,600 feet), and deeply dissected by the upper Peace and its tributaries, the area is well drained. Soils vary from the black grassland to the grey-bush type and are generally fertile. Extensive settlement has taken place in the Peace River district, mostly south of the Clear Hills, and an agricultural economy has been developed which is typical of the more settled regions of the prairies to the south. The technical needs of agriculture in this region are served in part by the Dominion Experimental Station at Beaverlodge, Alta., which has been in operation since 1915. The bulk of settlement in the Peace River Country lies south of latitude 57° North, and is mentioned here only in passing.

Elsewhere throughout the Mackenzie Basin, good agricultural lands are found at scattered locations, mostly on lacustrine and alluvial deposits such as river flats and flood terraces, and generally in the western areas of the Alberta Plateau. The best of these lands, already under partial development, are located on the west side of the Peace River as far north and including the Fort Vermilion district. Other known areas on the Plateau occur along the Alaska Highway east of the Rockies, notably in the Fort Nelson area, and around the Hay Lakes north-west of Fort Vermilion. On the Mackenzie Lowlands, lands which might be used for agriculture, but with some climatic disadvantages as compared with the Plateau areas mentioned above, are located in the alluvial valley of the Slave, along the southern shore of Great Slave Lake, in the valley of the Liard and in the Fort Simpson area. In this connection the following observations of Dr. A. Leahey on soil conditions in the Mackenzie Basin north of latitude 60° are pertinent.

"From the viewpoint of physiography and age there are two important divisions in soils [of the Mackenzie Basin] that can be made; namely the upland or mature soils of the region and the lowland or recent soils.

"Cutting across the two broad divisions mentioned above is the effect of climate on vegetation, soils and land. Observations on the nature of these features on the uplands led to the conclusion that in a broad way the region could be divided into at least three distinct zones. These are:

Zone A. The Northern Plains Zone: This zone lies south of a line drawn from the south side of the Slave River delta to Camsell Bend.

Zone B. The Sub-Arctic Zone: This zone lies north of Zone A and extends to about north latitude 68°.

Zone C. The Arctic Zone: This zone lies to the north of Zone B. Aklavik lies within this zone.

"While this zonation was based on the physical features of the lands adjoining the river valleys it may be of interest to note that existing climatic data show that the mean annual temperature in Zone A is above 23°F., in Zone B between 18° and 20°F., and in Zone C about 15° or less.

"The dominating factor which has created differences between the vegetation and soils in zones A and the other two zones has been the general absence of frozen subsoils in the Northern Plains zone and the almost universal presence of frozen subsoils in the Sub-Arctic and Arctic zones. The effect of permanently frozen subsoils has been twofold.

1. Frozen subsoils have greatly retarded or prevented any leaching of the soils.

2. Frozen subsoils have prevented any drainage through the soils. Hence the amount of poorly drained land is much greater where the subsoils are frozen. Since poorly drained areas almost always become muskegs or swamps in all the region the percentage of muskegs and swamps is much greater where the subsoils are frozen, that is under similar topographic conditions.

"1. *River Bottom Lands.* The effect of differences of climate on these lands is not particularly noticeable. There are some differences in natural vegetation, and muskegs are more prevalent in Zones B and C where frozen subsoils occur than in Zone A. Owing to their youth, however, there is little difference between these soils in the three different zones.

"The great bulk of these soils are of intermediate texture, ranging from fine sandy loams to silt loams. Generally there is very little difference in appearance or chemical composition between the surface layer and the sub-surface layers, except that the texture usually becomes coarser with depth. This latter characteristic does make some of these soils somewhat droughty. In colour the river bottom soils vary from a brownish grey to a dark grey. Both surface and subsoils are usually fairly well supplied with organic matter. The surface soils are neutral to alkaline in reaction and the subsoils are always alkaline owing to the presence of carbonate of lime. Generally they are fertile soils, and are easy to cultivate. On account of their nature and location they are the most important group of possible agricultural soils in the Mackenzie district.

"The river bottom lands are heavily wooded except for occurrences of open sloughs and flats. These open areas vary in size from a few square rods to several hundred acres. Spruce, Willow and Alder are dominant trees on these lands from Waterways to the Arctic. Black Poplar is plentiful in zone A but becomes scarcer toward the north, although small groves are to be found on the delta near the ocean. Aspen poplar is common in some locations in Zone A but is scarce in Zone B and is not present in Zone C. The tree growth on these lands is more luxuriant than on the adjacent uplands.

"2. *The Uplands.* The uplands, except for open swamps are entirely wooded in Regions A and B. In Region C, the uplands are open and I presume they would be considered as tundra. Between Regions A and B, the effect of frozen subsoil has been most marked. In both regions spruce, alder and willow are abundant, but aspen poplar which is a dominant tree in Zone A is of minor occurrence in Zone B while birch occupies the reverse position; pine is a common tree in Zone A but is scarce in Zone B. Tree growth is considerably better in Zone A. In Zone B the trees are of a distinctly scrubby nature.

"Muskegs are abundant in Region A, but generally only occupy depressional areas whereas in Zone B, they cover the greater portion of the country, occurring not only in depressional areas but also on all land that has not got good external drainage. Actually at first sight muskegs appear to cover nearly all the upland in Region B as a muskeg type of vegetation covers even the ridges. However, on such locations the moss cover is usually quite thin and the land should not be classified as muskeg.

"Insofar as soils are concerned the typical well drained upland soil in Region A is the leached grey wooded soil that is the prevailing type found in the wooded areas of the Prairie Provinces. In Region B the grey wooded soil does not occur. Here the upland soils are immature and show very little signs of profile development. Between the wooded upland soil of the northern part of Region B and the tundra soil of Region C, no difference was observed.

"The upland soils of course vary in their nature within each region depending on their geological origin. Hence we may find alluvial soils, lacustrine soils, and glacial till soils, varying in texture from sands to clays in each region. However, for present purposes I will confine my remarks to those upland soils that are at present or likely will be used for agricultural purposes.

"1. *Upper River Terraces.* These are river laid soils which have not been flooded for a long time. With one important exception, such soils range in texture from sands to loams. While these soils are low in organic matter they are and can be made into fairly good garden soils where the texture is not too sandy. Soil fertility is more of a problem on such soils than on the lower river terrace soils. However, for certain garden crops they may be even superior to the lower river terrace soils.

"2. *Heavy glacial till soils.* These soils are fairly stone free, glacial till soils occurring in Region B. The mineral soil is low in organic matter and is apt to have a rather undesirable physical condition. However, where some of the overlying peat, usually a few inches thick, is incorporated with the mineral soil both the fertility and handling qualities are improved. These heavy glacial till soils are the usual upland type adjacent to the river in the northern part of Zone B and in Zone C.

"In discussing the agricultural possibilities and problems of the area under consideration I would like first to mention what I consider is the agricultural significance of the previously mentioned zones.

"*Zone A.* This is the warmest region and for that reason it is the area most likely to suffer from drought, despite the fact that it receives slightly more total precipitation than the other areas. Here, except on the higher locations agriculture could likely be practised away from the rivers and other bodies of water if suitable soil could be found.

"*Zone B.* Successful agriculture can likely be only practised in the river valleys and on the uplands immediately adjacent to the rivers."

"*Region C.* Successful agriculture can likely be only practised in the river valleys, which as far as the area covered in this report is concerned means the delta of the Mackenzie River.

"While in 1945 the best gardens were seen in Region B, I am of the opinion that the number of different crops that can be grown becomes smaller from Region A to C.

"Insofar as garden crops are concerned past experience shows that if suitable crops are chosen good results may be expected in most years. On the river lowlands generally other factors rather than lack of soil fertility determines the yield of crops. On the uplands the use of fertilizers may be desirable and even necessary in places. Such fertilizers should carry a high content of nitrogen.

"Apart from soils the chief limiting factors in crop production appear to be: (*a*) drought—particularly in Region A; (*b*) short growing season; (*c*) insects. None of these in the area where agriculture is likely to be practised are insurmountable problems.

"Insofar as general agriculture is concerned I cannot see much possible development except to a limited extent in Region A. While I am not saying that general farming is not possible in Regions B and C, the nature of the country is such as to render farming difficult, costly, and generally impractical."

As regards the acreage of arable land in the Mackenzie Basin north of the fifty-seventh parallel of latitude, nothing better than a rough estimate is possible. One such estimate is 4 million acres, broken down as follows:

Fort Vermilion district	2,600,000 acres
Great Slave Lake and Slave River	200,000 "
Liard River Valley	200,000 "
Fort Nelson district	500,000 "
Mackenzie River banks	500,000 "
	4,000,000 acres

Pending further investigation the above figures should be treated with extreme reserve. Further, the wide distribution in small tracts of many soil areas detracts considerably from their settlement possibilities.

Outside of the farming districts on the upper Peace River, including the Fort Vermilion district, agriculture in the Mackenzie Basin is confined to a few small farms, and to gardens at the various settlements. According to a questionnaire survey made in 1943, there are not more than ten small farms throughout the Mackenzie Basin north of the sixtieth parallel of latitude, and it is probable that a similar pattern obtains in most of the region south of that line. Gardens seem to be more numerous, but are generally small. The only approach to commercial production is with potatoes along the upper reaches of the Mackenzie

River, total production being in the neighbourhood of about 150 tons, or the yield from about twenty to thirty acres of fairly good land.

In this connection it is interesting to note the quantity and variety of food imported into the Mackenzie region of the North West Territories. Estimates based on the above-mentioned questionnaire survey would indicate total imports of about 750 tons in 1943, including some 340 tons of flour, 80 tons of canned vegetables, 54 tons of canned meat, 50 tons of canned milk and 28 tons of butter. Imports of eggs amounted to about 50,000 dozen.[2] These imports, with some additional items, were to meet the needs of a population of 6,000 to 7,000 persons, of which the larger proportion was of native origin. A large percentage of the imports, of course, were used in the gold-mining centre at Yellowknife (population of 1,410 in 1941).

It is to be expected that the total flour requirements for the region would be met by imports, since this relatively non-perishable product can be economically secured from outside points. The question arises as to whether a greater percentage of other food products might not be produced locally, keeping in mind the possibility that the difficulties and hazards of northern agriculture might be offset by the great distances over which imports must be transported. The travel distance by rail, portage and river, from Edmonton to Fort Simpson, for instance, is over 1,100 miles, and over 1,960 miles to Aklavik. The answer, of course, lies partly in difficulties of climate and partly in occupational practices, with respect to which some historical references may be illuminating.

The early history of the Mackenzie Basin was that of the fur trading companies. In 1784 the North West Company was organized in Montreal to strengthen the competition of Canadian fur traders with the Hudson's Bay Company, with a programme which included active exploitation of the Mackenzie Basin. Previous to 1784, independent traders had operated in the Athabaska region, the original Fort Chipewyan on Lake Athabaska having been established by Peter Pond in 1778. North West Company posts were established on the south shore of Great Slave Lake in 1786, near the present site of Yellowknife in 1790, at Livingstone's Post on the Mackenzie eighty miles below Great Slave Lake in 1796, at Fort Simpson in 1804, at Fort Good Hope in 1805, and Fort Norman prior to 1810. Farther south posts were established near the present site of Edmonton in 1794 and at Fort Vermilion in 1798. The Hudson's Bay Company had no posts north of Great Slave Lake before 1821. In that year the North West Company was merged with the Hudson's Bay Company, and the latter then took over the more northern posts. Subsequently Hudson's Bay

[2]The complete table of food imports to each Mackenzie Valley settlement has been published in "Land Use Possibilities in Mackenzie District, N.W.T." (*Canadian Geographical Journal,* July, 1945, p. 47).

Company posts were established throughout the Mackenzie Basin; Fort Mc-Pherson in 1840, Fort Providence in 1868, and Aklavik in 1912.

The union of 1821 brought greater stability of employment to Hudson's Bay Company servants, and attempts were made to improve food conditions at the posts by growing vegetables and even cereals, mainly barley. In the early days all goods in the Mackenzie region were moved by waterways, with frequent laborious portages. For this reason the cost of imported foodstuffs was prohibitive as regards all but the most indispensable articles of diet. Flour was so costly that many company employees used locally grown barley gruel as a substitute for bread. By 1826 gardens were kept at all posts as far north as Fort Good Hope.

It is important to note that the selection of sites for fur-trading posts was not determined in relation to soil conditions, but on the basis of access by water routes and a reasonably adequate distribution throughout the fur territory.

Around the middle of the last century, various Roman Catholic and Anglican missions throughout the Mackenzie Basin became interested in the development of farming and gardening in connection with church schools and hospitals. At Fort Providence, for instance, a convent was established in 1867 by the Grey Nuns of Montreal, who brought in some cattle and started a farm. By 1916 over 160 acres on this farm were under field crops and about nineteen acres under vegetables and some flowers. It is likely that much of the clearing and cultivation was done by hand or by oxen since it is reported that no horses were in use north of Great Slave Lake in 1888.

Another missionary enterprise of interest in northern agriculture took place at Fort Vermilion where, in 1878, a farm was started by the local Anglican Mission with the object of avoiding the heavy cost of importing flour from the Red River settlement in Manitoba. At that time the cost per bag of flour in this district was £5 sterling. In 1879 a Mr. Shadrach Lawrence became superintendent of the mission farm. In the sequel, a son of Mr. Lawrence was to establish the Dominion Experimental Substation for agricultural investigations in the Fort Vermilion district. By 1907 over 1,200 acres of land were under cereal crops and a roller process flour mill of twenty-five barrels daily capacity was operated by the Hudson's Bay Company for the northern trade. This mill has since been dismantled, although the acreage under cultivation has increased to over 7,000 acres.

Such agricultural development as has taken place in the Mackenzie has proved sensitive to changes in methods of transportation. The introduction of steam navigation along the Athabaska and Slave from Fort McMurray to Fitzgerald in 1884, and from Fort Smith to the full length of the Mackenzie in 1887, seems to have stimulated considerable agricultural production, to the extent that cattle were introduced to some of the northern posts. A decline, however, seems to have followed the completion of the railway from Edmonton to Waterways in 1925. The acreage under cultivation on the formerly large Bruno Mission farms at Salt River near Fort Smith, and at Fort Providence, has been greatly reduced. More efficient and rapid methods of transport seem to have lowered the cost and widened the range of imported foodstuffs and correspondingly the dependence of northern traders, officials, trappers, and miners on locally grown food. Even the old dependence on game for meat has been lessened by imports of canned meat, and in Yellowknife at least, of refrigerated fresh meat from Edmonton.

Judging by past experience, therefore, it seems unlikely that agricultural production beyond the range of railways in the Mackenzie will do more than supplement with variety and freshness the food supplies that can be imported. In the first place, the cost of producing food in the north is high, land is difficult to clear, farm labour is very scarce and unreliable in the face of more lucrative occupations, and the hazards of frost, drought, and insects are discouraging. Barring an increase in population which may accompany the exploitation of northern mineral resources, and the inculcation of better dietary habits in certain sectors of the population, no great increase in northern crop production can be expected. In this respect the combined effects of custom, relative cost, and physical handicaps demand realistic appreciation.

There are, of course, some promising possibilities of development in supplying local farm produce to the relatively large population of the mining centre of Yellowknife from such areas as the lower valley of the Slave and other points on the southern shore of Great Slave Lake. Further, the proposed construction of an all-weather highway from Grimshaw to Great Slave Lake *via* the Fort Vermilion area would place the latter district, with its proved capacity for extensive mixed farming, in a position to supply the Great Slave area, including Yellowknife, with adequate supplies of meat, butter, eggs, potatoes, and vegetables.

It may be of some use at this point to present something in the nature of a check-list of points in the northern Mackenzie Basin at which farming or gardening has been conducted. The term "points" is used advisedly since outside of the Fort Vermilion and upper Peace regions, cultivation has been only in small acreages at quite widely separated settlements. The following table presents estimates of population, and number and acreages of gardens and farms at various points in the Mackenzie Basin, as secured from residents of each location by means of a questionnaire survey in 1943. Populations as given for the North West Territories were supplied by the 1941 Census; for other locations estimates only are given. Population figures refer to the districts around each location.

TABLE II

ESTIMATE OF POPULATION AND NUMBERS AND ACREAGES OF GARDENS AND FARMS
IN THE MACKENZIE RIVER BASIN NORTH OF LATITUDE 57°N., AND EAST
OF THE ROCKY MOUNTAINS

Location (Includes surrounding district)	Year First Settled	Estimated Population 1941	Gardens		Farms	
			Number	Total Acres	Number	Total Acres
Aklavik, N.W.T.	1912	757	12	4	1	4
Fort McPherson "	1840	325	10	1	0	0
Arctic Red River "	1891	129	2	2	0	0
Thunder River "	....	...	2	2	0	0
Fort Good Hope "	1836 (1805)	351	5	4	0	0
Norman Wells "	1920	} 439	Several		0	0
Fort Norman "	1810		10	4	0	0
Fort Wrigley "	1877	83	5	1	0	0
Fort Simpson "	1804	438	30	15	4	70
Fort Liard "	1800	216	8	2	0	0
Trout River "	....	16	..	..	1	5
Fort Providence "	1862	415	4	6	1	6
Hay River "	1868	161	10	8	0	0
Buffalo River "	....	3	1	1	0	0
Fort Rae "	1852	767	4	2	0	0
Yellowknife "	1935	1,410	4	5	0	0
Fort Resolution "	1800	635	10	7	1	4
Fort Smith "	1874	531	30	50	3	50
Nelson Forks, B.C.	....	52	5	2	0	0
Fort Nelson "	1800	50	12	6	0	0
Fort Vermilion, Alta.	1789	2,000	250	150	75	7,000
Keg River "	1914	145	30	15	20	1,300
Hay Lakes "	1929	300	30	10	0	0
Little Red River "	1816	300	9	3	0	0
Fort Chipewyan "	1804	850	50	20	0	0
Fort McMurray "	1808	400	100	50	0	0
TOTALS.............		10,773	633	370	106	8,439

Data from Questionnaire Survey, 1943.

Naturally, the degree of success in field or garden production at various
points has been variable, depending on soil, drainage, and other conditions, being
generally better in southern than in northern districts. In this connection the

following statement made in 1943 by the Reverend A. S. Dewdney of the Anglican Mission at Fort McPherson may be of interest as regards agriculture in northern latitudes.

. . . there can be no question that gardens and livestock and probably grain can be successfully grown here. We have not had a failure of garden stuff in our six years here. In most years produce can be sold locally at good prices, e.g., eggs at $1.00 to $1.25 a dozen. I am hoping to sell some of my eggs next winter and make part of the heavy cost of importing feed in this way. If I can get goats next year I hope to sell part of the milk. As an experiment I cut hay on rough land nearby this summer and have a little over half a ton stacked—cut with scythe, handled with a garden fork and carried home on my back. There are good meadows further away which I plan to try next year. A great deal could be done with proper equipment and little hired help. . . . One of the difficulties of developing gardening in this district is that until June 15th the natives are busy hunting muskrat and have no settled homes. In spite of this a number of them have grown small gardens. They are keen to get potatoes, cabbage, lettuce and carrots. . . . The ideal would be to have a large community garden here at the Fort, properly fenced and divided into family plots.

Agricultural research in the Mackenzie Basin has been largely confined, with the exception of the work at Beaverlodge and Fort Vermilion, to small trials with cereals, hay crops, and vegetables conducted by the Dominion Experimental Farms in co-operation with the Roman Catholic Missions at Fort Smith, Fort Resolution, and Fort Providence from 1911 to 1940, and Fort Good Hope from 1917 to 1940. These trials indicated that in suitable locations near river channels, reasonably good crops of hardy vegetables and especially potatoes could be secured in the majority of seasons. Trials were also conducted at Fort Simpson from 1941 to 1944. Unfortunately, considerations of distance prevented regular inspection of these trials and the securing of comprehensive data on results.

As has already been intimated, the experimental work in agriculture at Beaverlodge, while lying within the Mackenzie Basin, properly belongs to more southern conditions. The work at Fort Vermilion, however, may merit some reference. In the spring of 1907, Mr. F. S. Lawrence of Fort Vermilion undertook to conduct agricultural experiments in the interest of the Dominion Experimental Farms. This work has been in progress continuously to the present. From 1908 to 1933 the experiments were conducted on the farm of Mr. Robert Jones. Begun on a small scale, the work was gradually expanded to include variety tests of practically all field and garden crops known to Canadian agriculture. It was determined that cereal crops could be grown dependably, subject to occasional damage from spring and fall frosts, that forage crops generally gave high yields, and that vegetables and flowers could be grown satisfactorily. Until 1933 these experiments were conducted on river bottom land.

In 1933 charge of the Fort Vermilion Experimental Substation was assumed by Mr. F. A. Lawrence and a new area of land, more representative of the district, was purchased by the government. Results already secured on the new location confirm in general the previous findings. Incidentally, in addition to his duties at Fort Vermilion, Mr. Lawrence made periodic trips down the Mackenzie, reporting on agricultural conditions, a practice originally started by Mr. W. D. Albright, former Superintendent of the Dominion Experimental Station at Beaverlodge.[3]

Recently, beginning in 1943, the Experimental Farms have undertaken an expanded programme of experimental and demonstrational work in the northern Mackenzie Basin. The soil exploratory trips of Dr. A. Leahey along the Alaska Highway and northern waterways have already been noted. During 1943, Dr. Leahey was accompanied by Dr. A. V. Brink of the University of British Columbia, who made botanical observations along the route followed. Similar observations were made in 1944 by Mr. F. S. Nowosad of the Agrostology Division, Central Experimental Farm, Ottawa, from Fort Nelson, B.C., to Fort Liard, N.W.T., and thence down the Liard to Fort Simpson. In each case the botanical observations were correlated by soil conditions.

During the summers of 1944 and 1945, Mr. F. V. Hutton[4] of the Dominion Experimental Station at Morden, Man., travelled extensively through the northern Mackenzie Basin with the object of promoting more and better gardens in that region. The 1944 season was spent largely in fact finding and in giving personal advice on horticulture to northern residents. On the basis of his 1944 findings, in co-operation with some thirty-four residents of the principal settlements from Fort Smith to Aklavik, Mr. Hutton organized comprehensive variety trials with vegetables, and flowers, as well as fertilizer tests for the 1945 season. In addition to supervising these trials, Mr. Hutton initiated some fairly intensive experiments in growing field and garden crops on several types of soils around the Yellowknife district. In the future it is proposed to continue this work and further expand it to include an Experimental Substation for northern agriculture, possibly at Fort Simpson, together with several minor substations.

On the basis of his investigations, Mr. Hutton recommended that vegetables suitable for growing in gardens at all posts along the Mackenzie River are: broccoli, brussels sprouts, kale, cabbage, cauliflower, carrots, lettuce, turnips, spinach, swiss chard, rhubarb, rutabagas, and radish. South of Aklavik, potatoes, beets, parsnip, peas, and chives are added to the list; beans are recommended from Fort Good Hope south, and marrow, cucumber, onions, and tomatoes from Fort Simpson south. Corn and squash are not recommended north of Fort Smith.

Experiences of individual gardeners indicated that watering or even irrigation is desirable in many seasons to secure satisfactory growth of crops. In

[3]See article "Gardens of the Mackenzie," by W. D. Albright, in the *Geographical Review,* January, 1933.

[4]Now Superintendent, Dominion Experimental Station, Prince George, B.C.

fact, for many Mackenzie River locations, watering is an essential practice where fertilizer is used. Concentrated fertilizer is imported for garden crops to a limited extent, and at heavy cost.

At this point it is interesting to note that the Hudson's Bay Company has for several years encouraged gardening at its posts throughout the north to the extent of conducting competitions and awarding prizes for the better gardens. This has been done in the interests of better nutrition and morale among its post managers. From the results of this programme, considerable information on gardening, including soil-less culture and the use of small greenhouses, is being secured.

As regards greenhouses, Mr. Hutton found four of these in the Mackenzie Basin north of Fort Smith; one small commercial greenhouse at Yellowknife, and smaller "home-made" greenhouses at Fort Simpson, Fort McPherson, and Akla-vik. The chief function of these is to start seeding for transplanting. Apparent-ly no attempt has been made at winter use of greenhouses; it is probable that the cost of operation and suitable construction would be prohibitive in relation to the value of the product.

Mention may be made of the reindeer herd which is maintained by the Dominion government for the benefit of Eskimos to the east of the Mackenzie delta. The nucleus of this herd was secured in Alaska in 1929 and moved by laborious stages to its present range by 1935. It now numbers somewhat over 8,000 head, is a source of meat supply in the Aklavik district, and provides a potential means of livelihood to Eskimos along the Arctic littoral.

Agriculture in the Yukon Territory and Northern British Columbia

According to the 1941 Census there were only twenty-six farms, covering a total area of 2,781 acres, in the Yukon Territory, while in northern British Columbia west of the main range of the Rockies and north of latitude 57° north, there were only five farms with a total acreage of 1,036 acres. The total population of this entire region in 1941 was approximately 6,400 persons. A large per-centage of the food consumed, including potatoes, eggs, butter, etc., was imported.

The relative insignificance of agriculture in this region is no doubt due to major adverse factors of physiography and climate. The entire territory is broken by mountain ranges with valley floors ranging in elevation from about 1,000 feet to possibly over 3,000 feet. The more important watersheds are formed by the headwaters of the Yukon River draining the south-western area of the Yukon territory north-westward to Alaska, the Liard draining eastward through the Rockies from the south-eastern part of the Yukon Territory and adjacent areas in British Columbia; the Stikine River draining the extreme north-west of British Columbia south-westward to the Pacific; and the Finlay, flowing south along the Rocky Mountain "trough" to cut eastwards to the Peace

River through the Rockies at Finlay Forks. All of the region under consideration is separated politically from the Pacific Ocean by the southern extension of the coast of Alaska.

Climatic conditions in the region under review are generally marginal as regards cultivated crop production. Precipitation is low throughout the year, summers are cooler than in corresponding latitudes east of the mountains and the winters quite cold.

Selected data on temperature and precipitation are presented in Table III for several points in the Yukon and northern British Columbia.

Soils. The mountainous nature of the country limits soil suitable for crop production to a few valleys with glacio-lacustrine deposits, and mainly to river-flats. Dr. A. Leahey, who made an exploratory investigation of soils along the Alaska Highway to Kluane Lake and down the river route from Whitehorse to Dawson in 1943, makes the following comments on soil conditions in the region visited:

"The climate of the Yukon is dry and, as might be expected, in no place are the soils weathered deeply. Furthermore, while nearly all the soils are covered with trees, few signs of a definite leached layer so characteristic of wooded soils in northern latitudes were found. Some incipient development of the characteristic light grey A2 horizon of the podsolic soils was noted under spruce on light textured soils in a few local areas.

"The Yukon is known as a region of permanently frozen soils. However, in the southern Yukon, that is from Teslin Lake to Kluane Lake, unfrozen soils are the rule, not the exception. North from Whitehorse frozen soils become more common—first on the northern slopes, then on the level land and finally, in the Dawson and Mayo districts, even the southern slopes are apt to be frozen at a shallow depth unless they have been cleared by man or fire. West of Kluane Lake frozen soils are also the rule even on southern slopes.

"In the southern part of the Yukon the lands with sandy or intermediate soils appear quite drouthy. However, they do not appear as drouthy as one might expect considering the limited amount of rainfall received. In the central part of the Territory the almost complete coverage of spruce and the mantle of moss appears to make the country a fairly moist one although the precipitation here is only slightly higher than in the southern part.

"The surface soils of the Yukon have two prevailing colours, depending on drainage conditions. The well drained soils are distinctly reddish brown in colour, while the poorly drained and recent soils on the river floodplains are black or dark grey in colour.

"Observations indicate that all the mineral soils in the Yukon are comparatively low in organic matter. The mineral plant food is probably at a satisfactory level as most of the soils have been derived from a variety of rocks. The

TABLE III

SELECTED DATA ON TEMPERATURE AND PRECIPITATION AT POINTS
IN THE YUKON TERRITORY AND NORTHERN BRITISH COLUMBIA

Location	Latitude N.	Elevation above Sea Level	Years in Record	Mean Temperature F.				Average Frost-Free Period	Mean Precipitation		
				June to August	December to February	Annual			May to August	Year
		feet		°	°	°		days	inches	inches
Dawson, Y.T.	64° 4′	1062	41	57.0	− 15.6	22.9		73.9	5.27	12.61
Mayo, Y.T.	63° 35′	1625	12	55.7	− 11.6	24.5		66.2	5.57	11.04
Whitehorse, Y.T.	60° 43′	....	2	54.9	5.2	31.0		48.2	4.29	10.70
Carcross, Y.T.	60° 11′	2171	31	52.5	2.8	29.2		43.1	3.15	8.96
Lower Post, B.C.	59° 57′	....	5	55.7	− 4.2	27.9		...	6.72	15.52
Atlin, B.C.	59° 35′	2240	36	51.0	11.0	32.0		...	3.35	11.22
Prince George, B.C.	53° 50′	1862	29	56.0	18.0	39.0		64.9	7.41	20.81

Data by courtesy of the Meteorological Service of Canada.

reaction of the soils is satisfactory as only a few of the sandy, non-agricultural soils were decidedly acidic.

"The Yukon is essentially a hilly country broken by many mountain ranges. Therefore, agricultural soils are only apt to be found in the valleys and on the lower slopes. Again, owing to the latitude of the region, it is likely that agriculture is only possible on the lower elevations.

"The preliminary soil survey conducted in 1943 shows that west of the Rocky Mountains there are no large blocks of land fit for general agriculture. However, in so far as soils are concerned, areas of land suitable for agriculture can be found within a reasonable distance of any present settlement or any likely future settlement.

"The largest block of arable land in the Yukon lies in the Takhini-Dezadeash Valleys. In addition, this is the best land seen in the southern Yukon, that is from Selkirk south. The river flats of the Yukon have a more fertile soil and may have almost as large a total acreage. However, they occur as scattered parcels along probably 300 miles of river front. This is a serious disadvantage in building up a farming community, but it is an advantage in that some arable land is apt to occur near any development work on the Yukon River."

No definite soils investigations have been made in the northern British Columbia mountain region apart from the line of the Alaska Highway covered by Dr. Leahey. From the reports of surveyors, geologists, foresters, etc., who have penetrated this region, it is evident that there are tracts of soil of varying quality and acreage at scattered locations, mostly on bench or bottom lands along river valleys, the greatest single area reported so far being in the valley of the Finlay and Parsnip Rivers north and south of Finlay Forks.

Tentative estimates of the major acreages of arable land in this region are summarized as follows:

ESTIMATED ACREAGE OF ARABLE LANDS IN THE WESTERN YUKON AND NORTHERN BRITISH COLUMBIA WEST OF THE ROCKY MOUNTAINS

Upland Soils—Dawson (Leahey)	6,000	acres
Flats along Yukon River and its tributaries (Leahey)	60,000	"
Takhini-Dezadeash valley (Leahey)	120,000	"
Tagish and Little Atlin flats (Leahey)	8,000	"
Terraces of the Liard (Leahey)	17,000	"
Finlay-Parsnip valley	500,000	"
Other (small) areas	80,000	"
	791,000	"

Early exploitation of the fur resources of the Yukon and northern British Columbia probably began about 1800, with trading routes established up the

Liard from the Mackenzie and up the Stikine from the Pacific. Penetration of the Yukon River valley began about 1840 along a route which led from the Mackenzie *via* Fort McPherson over the height of land to the Porcupine River and thence to the Yukon. Apparently, no important settlement accompanied this stage of development.

With the discovery of gold in the Cariboo region of central British Columbia in 1858, a considerable business in packing supplies for prospectors over various routes in northern areas led to early agricultural activities of a sort, the local production of forage for pack horses, principally along the Stikine River. In some localities gardens seem to have been cultivated. It was not until the Klondike gold-rush of 1898, however, that any serious interest developed in agriculture. In the early years of the present century some farming, gardening, and horse ranching were in progress around Dawson City and at scattered points along the water route from the south. In that period the large population (over 20,000, maintained by the mining industry of the Klondike area afforded a sure market for farm and garden produce, and some quite sizable farms were developed, producing vegetables, meat, milk, butter, eggs, and forage for pack- and draught-horses.[5] No exact statistics on agriculture for the Yukon region were available before 1931, but it is known that heavy importations of food, including eggs, butter, canned milk, and vegetables continued throughout the boom period. Probably the farming development, as separate from household gardens, did not exceed by more than two or three times the twenty-seven farms listed in 1941. The decline in the population of the Yukon, from 27,219 in 1901 to 4,157 in 1921, had an adverse effect on agricultural development.

The construction of the Alaska Highway and of the oil pipeline from Norman Wells to Whitehorse reawakened interest in the agricultural possibilities of the Yukon and northern British Columbia. One of the main objects of the investigations conducted in 1943 by Dr. A. Leahey was to determine the practicability and location for agricultural experiments in the Yukon, assuming some increase in market possibilities.

As early as 1915, the Dominion Experimental Farms instituted some co-operative cropping trials in the Yukon. The following remarks on this work will indicate the nature of farming in this region.

In 1917 the Experimental Farms instituted a limited amount of experimental work on the farm of James Farr, at Swede Creek, some eight miles west of Dawson City. Work on this project began in 1918. One area of about ten acres was placed under treatment to improve the soil by means of green manure, farmyard manure, and fertilizer. Considerable difficulty was experienced in securing reasonably speedy decomposition of green manure crops owing to low

[5]See "Agriculture and Forests of Yukon Territory" (*Canadian Geographical Journal,* Aug., 1945).

temperatures and low rainfall. Best results were secured with manure, and some response was noted to fertilizers.

The need for manure on cultivated soil in this area was shown in 1925 when the yield of potatoes secured on two acres of lightly manured land was 200 bushels per acre, while only 68 bushels per acre were secured on a corresponding unmanured area.

In most years it has been possible to mature good crops of wheat, oats, and barley at Swede Creek. In a few years early frosts have made it desirable to harvest these crops as cereal hay.

As regards forage crops, timothy and alfalfa were found to be reasonably satisfactory, although the alfalfa did not produce seed. Red clover was usually winter-killed.

Experimental work at Swede Creek was discontinued in 1925.

Further trials were conducted during the years 1932, 1933, and 1934 at Carmacks, Y.T., where roots, cabbages, cauliflowers, peas, beans, potatoes, barley, oats, and fodder corn were grown. Trials with grasses, clovers, and cereals were conducted from 1936 to 1938 inclusive, at Carcross, Y.T., where summer frosts proved a serious hazard.

In 1944 the Experimental Farms formally established the Pine Creek Experimental Substation at Mile 1,019 on the Alaska Highway, about 106 miles west of Whitehorse. This substation is intended to serve two main purposes: to determine the unknown agricultural possibilities of the reasonably large area of arable land in the Takhini-Dezadeash valley in which it is located, and to serve as the centre for technical, advisory, and promotional work in agriculture and gardening for the Yukon and northern British Columbia. The initial work of clearing land for agricultural experiments and of erecting the necessary buildings was carried on in 1945 preparatory to initiating a comprehensive series of experiments in 1946. During 1945 the officer in charge of Pine Creek Substation, Mr. J. W. Abbott, made a survey of agricultural conditions in the Yukon valley, making personal contact with farmers and gardeners.

The choice of the present location for the Experimental Substation was guided by the existence of promising markets for agricultural products at Whitehorse, with railway connection to the south and river connection to the Dawson area in the north, as well as along the new Highway. Moreover, the Takhini-Dezadeash valley represents the largest known compact tract of potential farm land in the region west of the Rockies.

The Takhini-Dezadeash valley is located in the south-western Yukon on the headwaters of the Takhini River which drains eastward to the Lewes River near Whitehorse and thence north-west to the Yukon, and on the Dezadeash River which drains west and then south through the Alsek River to the Pacific. Of its characteristics as affecting agriculture, Dr. Leahey states:

"While on two drainage systems this area lies in one continuous valley from the Lewes river to the Shakwak valley, a distance of approximately 100 miles. The valley averages from three to four miles in width to the high hills and mountains on either side. The elevation of the valley floor is not known at the present moment but it probably lies between 2200 and 2400 feet above sea level. The eastern half of the valley is drained eastward into the Lewes river by the Mendenhall and Takhini rivers and the western half is drained by the Dezadeash river which flows into the Alsek river and thence to the Pacific Ocean. Numerous sizable creeks flow into these rivers from the north and the south. Generally the main rivers flow near the southern edge of the valley.

"A picture of the parent materials of the soils in this valley can best be obtained by visualizing this entire valley as being occupied in post glacial times by two lakes. Clays were deposited on the floor of these lakes while near their edges gravel and sand benches were formed. Later these lakes were drained and the present systems of drainage were established. The tributary streams brought down sands and gravels which were deposited along their courses. Erosion of the lacustrine deposits took place to some extent resulting in the redeposition of clays and silts along some of the present river flats.

"Thus today we find the main type of soil on the upland position of this valley is a clay soil free from stones and of apparent good quality, while immature clay soils may be found on some of the lower benches near the river. Along the streams and on the valley sides gravels and sands of low agricultural value are present. Then at Champagne there is a stretch of sand, partly duned, completely covering the valley floor for a distance of five to six miles. This valley has a very pleasing appearance both with regard to topography, native vegetation and soils. A brief description of each of these features is given below.

"The general topography of the valley with a few exceptions is level to gently rolling in an east-west direction with an undulating to gently rolling slope to the south. Exceptions to this general statement are the eastern end of the valley, from Stony Creek to the Lewes river which varies from gently rolling to rolling land, the sand dune area at Champagne and the level clay plain just east of Champagne which comprises approximately 15 to 20 square miles.

"Much of the valley has a park-like appearance. It is estimated that spruce either in solid stands or in clumps occupies about half the valley, while aspen, poplar, willow and open grassy areas cover the remainder. Many of these aspen trees have a stunted appearance. The eastern end of the valley carries considerable pine, but these trees only extend westward a few miles past the old ferry crossing on the Takhini river. It should be said that the aspen and willow areas could be easily cleared and most of the spruce stands could be cleared without great cost.

"The principal type of soil is the mature lacustrine clay. This probably covers about two thirds of the entire valley. This soil varies in its nature depending whether it is covered by grass or by spruce.

"The agricultural possibilities of the Takhini-Dezadeash valley are difficult to assess properly. Perhaps a better valuation can be given after the soils have been analyzed and the ecology studied. At present the writer can only advance the following points for consideration.

"The greatest factor against the area is its dry climate and the danger from late spring and early fall frosts. It is true that the valley does not appear to be as dry as at Whitehorse, the nearest meteorological station, even allowing for the difference in the texture of the soils in the two areas. Then again there may be some significance in the fact that pine only penetrates the valley for a short distance.

"The whole area is a virgin one in so far as agriculture is concerned. Gardens have been raised at Champagne, but these have been grown on sand which may receive some seepage water.

"It is worth noting that the Indians at Champagne winter out their horses. This would indicate that the native grass is self curing and that the snowfall is comparatively light."

AGRICULTURE IN NORTHERN AREAS OF THE LAURENTIAN SHIELD

Because of its adverse climate and scanty soil covering, the northern areas of the Laurentian Shield present few opportunities for gardening. However, a few enthusiasts have succeeded in producing some vegetables by various expedients, such as gathering together soil material from various points, and growing such quick-maturing vegetables as cress, radishes, etc., by utilizing soil-filled boxes and barrels for this purpose, or by improvising greenhouses. Gardens of collected soil have been reported from such points as Fort Rae, Eldorado Mine on Great Bear Lake, and even at Coppermine, well north of the tundra line. It is reported that soil has been shipped by water to such points as Chesterfield Inlet for this purpose. Improvised greenhouses have been utilized by Hudson's Bay Company agents at such Arctic posts as Cape Dorset, Sugluk, and Baker Lake, to provide some relief from the monotony of canned vegetables. Such devices, however, merely accentuate the non-agricultural nature of the region.

One possibility of producing vegetables in northern Shield localities is the use of soil-less culture, i.e., the growing of plants in sand-filled containers, fed by chemical nutrients in solution, and exposed more favourably to the summer sun's heat than would be possible at ground level. This method, which has been used with complete success at the military post at Goose Bay, Labrador, might find useful application at other northern points.

Future Possibilities

It is hoped that sufficient information has been assembled to support the following conclusions regarding the future possibilities of agriculture in the Canadian North:

(1) On the basis of past experience there are few grounds for anticipating any marked, spontaneous increase in the volume of agricultural production in northern Canada, assuming no radical changes in population. One main controlling factor, the relation of the cost of local production to the cost of importing food supplies, is likely to remain operative. Improvements in the processing of imported foods, especially as regards the preservation of vitamins, may to some extent offset a growing tendency to produce vegetables and other protective foods locally for reasons of health.

(2) The conditions implied in the foregoing statement may be modified through an abnormal increase in population stimulated on geo-political grounds by the government, or by a marked increase in the exploitation of northern mineral resources. Improvements in fur resources in the North West Territories are likely to benefit principally the native races.

(3) For any reasonable increase in food consumption in northern Canada, there would appear to be sufficient soil resources for food production in the existing pattern. The widespread distribution in relatively small tracts of such land, however, would place any general development of agricultural production for "outside" markets beyond immediate consideration.

(4) There is definite need for improvement in the technique and materials of northern agriculture. This applies particularly to better adapted varieties of forage crops, vegetables, and small fruits, the management of northern soils and the control of insect pests. Livestock and poultry production in larger settlements such as Yellowknife presents additional problems. In the far North the problem of "permafrost"—permanently frozen subsoil—has important agricultural aspects. Expanding Experimental Farm activities, as described above, are designed to cover, in some degree, these northern problems.

THE GLACIAL VALLEYS SOUTH-EAST OF LAKE MUNCHO AS SEEN
FROM THE ALASKA HIGHWAY (PART II)

TRANSITION IN INDIAN HOMES: TIPI OF CANVAS, CANVAS TENT,
LOG HOUSE (PART II)

WRIGLEY—FIFTY YEARS OLD. NOTE BIRTH OF MAIN ROAD
ON THE RIGHT (PART II)

THE RAMPARTS ON THE MACKENZIE RIVER, TWENTY-FIVE MILES
SOUTH OF THE ARCTIC CIRCLE (PART II)

LOUCHEUX INDIANS ON THE CUT-BANK AT GOOD HOPE (PART II)

THE MOST NORTHERN GARDEN IN CANADA. AT TUKTOYAKTUK—
69°26′ N. LAT. (PART II)

THE PROGRESS OF CIVILIZATION: CATHEDRAL, HOSPITAL, AND
"COLLEGE" AT AKLAVIK (122 MILES NORTH OF ARCTIC CIRCLE).
FIELD OF OATS IN FOREGROUND (PART II)

THE MIDNIGHT SUN AT COPPERMINE: THREE HOURS OF ARCTIC
"SUNSET" AND "SUNRISE" PHOTOGRAPHED AT TEN-MINUTE
INTERVALS

EAST SHORE OF GREAT BEAR LAKE NEAR THE ELDORADO MINE
(PART IV)

NEGUS, CON, AND RYCON MINES FROM THE EAST (PART IV)

BRAIDED STREAM IN DEEP VALLEY: COPPERMINE RIVER
ABOVE BLOODY FALLS (PART IV)

BLOODY FALLS, COPPERMINE RIVER (PART IV)

FAULT EXTENDING NORTH-EAST FROM HORNBY BAY,
GREAT BEAR LAKE (PART IV)

NEGUS AND CON MINES FROM THE AIR (PART IV)

CON MINE, YELLOWKNIFE (PART IV)

YELLOWKNIFE, LOOKING SOUTHWARD (PART IV)

YELLOWKNIFE, 1945 (PART IV)

GARDEN AT YELLOWKNIFE (PART IV)

PART OF SURFACE PLANT OF ELDORADO MINE. NOTE THE CLIFF
OF DIABASE ACROSS THE BAY (PART IV)

BOOM OF LOGS FOR MINE TIMBERS AT ELDORADO (PART IV)

TRANS-SHIPMENT OF FREIGHT AT OUTLET OF GREAT BEAR
LAKE (PART IV)

MACKENZIE RIVER DELTA (PART V)

MINK FARM (PART V)

MACKENZIE RIVER DELTA (PART V)

MARTEN (PART V)

TRAPPER'S CABIN NEAR FORT SIMPSON (PART V)

CROSS FOX (PART V)

TRADING-POST. WHITE TRAPPERS ARRIVE AT TRADING-POST
ON JAMES BAY. NOTE CARIBOU PARKA WORN BY
ONE OF THE MEN (PART V)

BEAVER (PART V)

FUR WAREHOUSE (PART V)

SETTING A TRAP
FOR MINK (PART V)

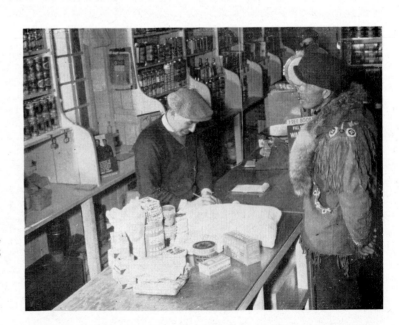

TRADING
FURS
(PART V)

SAMPLES
OF HIS
WINTER'S
CATCH
(PART V)

MUSKRAT
(PART V)

KOMATIK WITH FAN-HITCH USED BY TRAPPERS IN EASTERN
ARCTIC (PART V)

ESKIMO SCHOONERS AT HERSCHEL ISLAND (PART IX)

ESKIMO FAMILY,
AKLAVIK (PART IX)

TRAVELLING OVER FLOODED ICE IN LATE SPRING IN
CORONATION GULF AREA (PART IX)

ESKIMO SPLITTING FISH AT CORONATION GULF (PART IX)

ESKIMO EXAMINING NETS AT COPPERMINE (PART IX)

Part Seven

H. W. HEWETSON

Transportation in the North-West

FORTY-ONE per cent of the area of Canada lies outside provincial boundaries. If we include, in addition, the vast unpeopled or sparsely-settled regions of the northern parts of all but the Maritime Provinces, we reach a figure of between 75 and 80 per cent of the whole area of Canada which plays little or no part in Canadian life. The war served to bring the great Northland into the consciousness of Canadians. There is a growing realization that in this vast stretch of territory, Canada possesses something to which few nations have anything comparable. At the same time reports of new undeveloped resources in the North are coming with more and more frequency. The result is a growing feeling among Canadians that Canada's Arctic and sub-Arctic regions have too long been ignored and neglected. The hope is dawning that this great stretch of country can some day be converted into a real national asset.

It is obvious that any development which is to come in the North cannot proceed faster than transportation facilities will permit. Transportation takes on an added significance when one bears in mind the enormous distances in Canada's north country. It must be remembered that Canada's undeveloped North is three to four times the size of settled Canada.

While there will probably always be complaints about northern transportation until it reaches the standards maintained in the more advanced parts of the populous world, the northerner's present conception of adequacy falls far short of such high standards. Transportation in the North would be considered satisfactory if it met the following requirements.

First, and foremost, there must be reasonable certainty that goods will be delivered at points beyond railhead in the same year that they are shipped. Freight, with the exception of an insignificant amount moving by air, goes into the North by water. The practice is to get in during the navigation season supplies enough to last till the opening of navigation in the following year. The failure of these supplies to arrive before freeze-up may mean actual hunger before spring for the people who must winter in the North, for the white man who can "live off the country" is very rare indeed. In Yukon this test is met without trouble, but in the Mackenzie District it is a recurring source of worry. The short navigation season coupled with almost annual difficulties brought about by low water require herculean efforts on the part of northern transportation officials to get the freight through nearly every year. That they usually succeed with little or no time to spare is no reason for complacency about the situation.

Secondly, travellers in the North would like greater certainty than now exists as to the time of arrival at their destinations. It is only a very naive newcomer to the North who expects to adhere to a previously arranged time-schedule. But delays stretching into weeks are a cause of much complaint. The typical mode of passenger travel in the North today is by air. The period of delay comes in the late summer and early fall, when many thousands of summer workers wish to get "outside." The trouble is caused by a shortage of planes and weather conditions, which may ground planes for days at a time. This situation is not only irksome but also expensive for those compelled to stop over.

When the above two conditions are being satisfactorily taken care of, the northerner finds a complaint in the charges of the transportation companies. By the standards of settled Canada these are very high. But this does not mean that northern transportation companies make large profits, or any profits at all. Only one major transportation system in the North, the White Pass and Yukon Route, is dependent solely on earnings from northern transportation. The others, including the two large water carriers in the Mackenzie District, and Canadian Pacific Air Lines as well, are all subsidiaries of larger companies engaged primarily in other activities. While these subsidiary companies do not have to make profits to continue operations, it is only to be expected that an effort will be made to keep the losses as low as possible. As the demand for transportation services in the North is on the whole quite inelastic, the natural result is that rates are high. Any enforcement of lower rates would probably drive most of the existing companies out of business. Nevertheless, lower rates are essential to the development of the North. At present it is only valuable commodities, such as furs, gold, and radium-uranium ores, that can stand the high transportation charges out, although it may be noted that the silver-lead ores from the Mayo district in Yukon reached outside markets profitably in years when prices were high enough. But the North has large resources of not merely base metals but such things as fish, which will require very much lower freight rates than at present in effect if they are to be developed.

From the standpoint of development in the North, greater frequency of transportation service at many places is to be desired. While remote fur posts may be satisfactorily served at present by one or two boat visits a year,[1] any expansion of economic activities in the districts in which these places are located will require much greater frequency of service. And in framing transportation policy, it must be kept in mind that more frequent transportation service must generally precede economic development in many areas of the North. Yukon Territory receives, on the whole, much more frequent transportation than does the Mackenzie District.

[1]A year's supplies may be brought in on one trip, and a year's catch of furs taken out.

Faster ground and water transportation would have distinct benefits to the North. The only important improvements in this respect seem to lie with the construction of railways and highways. Only a few dreamers think of the former in the sparsely settled north country, but the war activities in building the Alaska Highway and various winter roads in the North have drawn attention to the possibilities of road building.

Other desiderata in transportation, such as comfort and hostess service on aeroplanes, are of very secondary importance in the North.

Many of the difficulties in northern transportation are occasioned by the weather, about which man can do little (unless atomic power can at last give him some control). Others have to do with insufficient equipment or lack of powerful-enough equipment. These can be remedied at a cost, and the question becomes one of whether the improvements justify the outlay of money or not. The attitude of northerners has changed on this matter as a result of the war. Observation of what could be accomplished and how things could be speeded up when a seemingly unlimited number of American dollars poured in, has naturally led to the feeling that the same thing could be continued if only Canadian government officials will it to be. But the Canadian North has no longer the United States Treasury on which to draw, nor is the urgency of war still present.

Because of the unprofitableness of northern transportation, it seems inevitable that the money for major improvements can come only from the Dominion government. It is perhaps worth remembering that most of our railway mileage and much of our other transportation services in Canada have been publicly subsidized rather heavily. The Canadian territories have not benefited, save to a negligible extent, by government subsidies in the past. This, of course, is no justification for granting them subsidies now. Some of the money from government transportation subsidies in the past has been spent unwisely, some of it wisely. The same will probably be true about any subsidies granted to the North. But the conclusion seems inevitable that important transportation improvements in the North will not come without government subsidies. Our present knowledge of the North, though very imperfect, would seem to suggest possibilities that were worth the gamble of a reasonably large sum of money.

Two courses are apparently open. We can wait until the needs of such booming districts as Yellowknife force transportation improvements to be made, or we can effect the improvements ahead of development in order to hasten it. We have adopted the latter policy many times in the past, again sometimes wisely and sometimes very unwisely. We should profit by our mistakes of the past and not undertake grandiose schemes without a more thorough investigation of the possibilities than has frequently been the case. Possibly immediate policy should look towards providing Yellowknife with reasonably adequate transportation before looking elsewhere, although perhaps the problems of Eldorado are more serious and pressing. However, should the main transportation difficulties of known productive areas be ever reasonably solved, a policy might reasonably be instituted of making moderate improvements in transportation in likely districts in anticipation of actual development. Whether the North has "real" possibilities or is essentially a "frozen waste," it seems inevitable at the present time that it will get more and more government assistance.

As an alternative to subsidies to existing northern transportation companies, the government could take over the operation of all the services itself. As the losses in operation would presumably continue, the necessity of making up these deficits would in effect be equivalent to a subsidy paid by the Canadian taxpayer.

YUKON TERRITORY

There is a widespread opinion that Yukon is a district with a past but no future. Perhaps the older sourdoughs of the Territory contribute to this feeling in their attitude of suspicion and resentment towards government improvements. The country seems to suit them as it now exists and they are afraid that any developments in transportation might bring in a number of unwelcome new-comers. In the heyday of the Klondike gold-rush of 1898 estimates of the population of Dawson range from 30,000 to as high as 60,000. Undoubtedly there was a much larger number of people who never succeeded in reaching the gold-fields. The firstcomers staked the richest and most easily worked claims. The latecomers naturally began to drift away again. Moreover, the gold that could be obtained by the relatively crude methods of the individual miner began to play out. Machine methods became necessary and this brought in big companies. By 1908 Yukon Consolidated Gold Corporation, Ltd., had acquired the assets of virtually all the companies that had begun operations, and controlled practically all the mining claims along the Klondike River and its creeks.[2] Yukon Consolidated has been operating profitably ever since. During the recent war only three of their eleven dredges were working, but this was attributable to the man-power shortage, not to a lack of gold. The *known* gold reserves are conservatively estimated in excess of $100 million. The Klondike area will be an important gold producer for many years to come, but this industry alone cannot support the population of its early days.

Dawson City, because it was built on too extensive a scale in its youth, presents a picture of decay today with its many unoccupied buildings and homes. However, an examination of the facts will reveal that the decline in population ended about thirty years ago. Since that time the population has about held its own, until a drain on its male inhabitants set in during the war. Dawson's early size, though contributing to the impression of decline, has been responsible for bringing to the district many of the amenities of civilized life which other-

[2]The claims not controlled by Yukon Consolidated are nearly all on high ground where lack of water prevents their being worked.

wise would probably not be present in a place so remote from the settled world. Telephones and electric light have been in operation since the turn of the century. Two banks still operate branches, a former daily paper continues to publish three times a week, a high school from which students matriculate into the University of British Columbia is still in operation, and several hotels, a number of large stores, a modern hospital, and a public library still operate. And, as an indication that all Dawson's facilities do not date from the early days, there is a motion picture theatre open daily.

It may be noted, too, that the Klondike district, besides gold, has the most developed agricultural area in the North. Besides farms, there are a number of greenhouses within the city itself. Of course, the markets are strictly local.

It is worth while pointing out that the Klondike district is the only example in the North of area-settlement as opposed to point-settlement. There are five post offices[3] in operation in a stretch of fifty-two miles. Also down the Yukon River from Dawson is the post office of Forty Mile, about that distance away.

Elsewhere in central Yukon, the Mayo district should be mentioned. The town of Mayo is situated on the Stewart River southeast of Dawson, and owed its prosperity to the silver-lead mines about forty miles north at Keno. The town was flourishing enough in its prosperous days to have a branch of the Bank of Montreal. But it proved a war casualty in 1941 when the mines were forced to close. At present Mayo exists largely as a fur-trading centre. But it is a district which may be expected to revive.

The war brought more than 40,000 people to southern Yukon in the vicinity of Whitehorse. These consisted largely of United States army personnel, construction workers on the Alaska Highway, pipeline, and refinery, and the persons who moved to Whitehorse to cater to the needs and amusements of this large influx of newcomers. The oil refinery at Whitehorse has now been closed down, and with it went much of the hopes for Whitehorse's future. While some copper mining was carried on in the vicinity of Whitehorse until about fifteen years ago, the essential reason for the town's existence was as a transfer point between rail and water transportation. However, the town has all the facilities of a place much larger than its pre-war population of less than a thousand, and its heavy influx of short-time visitors left the town with more than it had had hitherto. For instance, it now has a telephone system built from equipment formerly in use in Mayo.

Yukon's fourth town, Carcross, about forty miles south of Whitehorse and on the railway may be mentioned. This place, while the headquarters of a small airway, owes much of its prosperity to the tourist business occasioned by the scenic beauties of the long lakes in the vicinity stretching over the British Columbia border.

[3]Dawson, Glacier Creek, Granville, Paris and Radford.

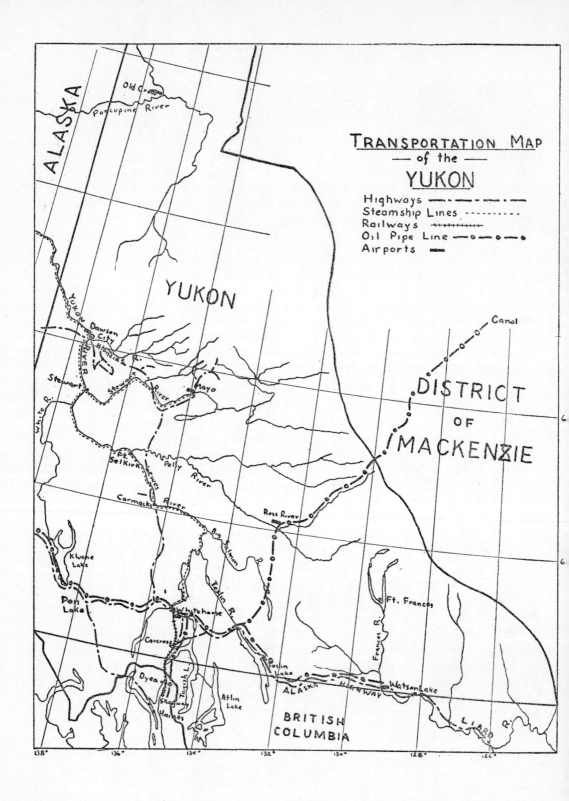

Along the river between Whitehorse and Dawson, furs have constituted the principal economic activity with trading posts operating at Carmacks, Fort Selkirk, and Stewart River. However, the coal deposits near Carmacks appear to be large. Coal has been mined here for a long period, although not continuously, but its market has never been more than local.

Yukon still has large "blank" spaces which are imperfectly known, although mineral finds have been reported at various places many times. The Yukon River leaves the territory nearer the British Columbia border than the Arctic coast, and the whole of this large region to the north contains only one fixed settlement, that at Old Crow on the Porcupine River. The eastern part of the territory has produced premium furs, but many districts have been "trapped out" and at present only two "permanent" trading posts are in operation in this district, Ross River and Fort Frances. The Canol pipeline and road (now abandoned) cut across this region. Lastly, the whole of southern Yukon except within the vicinity of Whitehorse has been very imperfectly known. The Alaska Highway crosses this region and will presumably be the means of opening up whatever resources exist. So far, however, there have been no reports of spectacular mineral finds along the Alaska Highway.

Historic Approaches to Yukon. The first white man known to have entered the present Yukon territory was Robert Campbell of the Hudson's Bay Company in 1840. He approached Yukon by way of the Liard River, went up its tributary the Frances, and crossed over the short divide to the Pelly River. In 1843 he descended this latter river to its junction with the Yukon River.

In 1846 J. Bell, also of the Hudson's Bay Company, entered the territory in the far North to reach the Porcupine River by ascending the Peel River from the Mackenzie to Fort McPherson, thence up the Rat River, over the divide, and down the Bell River to the Porcupine.[4]

These two routes into the Yukon, while both practicable enough for canoes, both suffer the defect that the approach is from the North West Territories. Except for a few who used these routes during the Klondike gold-rush and for the Canol activity during the war, there has been very little occasion for travel between Canada's two territories.

New approaches do not seem to have been used until the earlier eighteen-seventies. From that time on, various types of water craft entered Canadian

[4]The explorations of these two men resulted in the founding of two posts. Fort Yukon was established in 1846 at the confluence of the Porcupine and the Yukon. In 1869 when it was proved that this lay in Alaska territory, the Hudson's Bay Company abandoned the post and moved up the Porcupine to Canadian territory at Rampart House. This post was also later abandoned. Fort Selkirk was established at the junction of the Pelly with the Yukon in 1849. It was burnt down by Indians in 1852 and the site deserted until the twentieth century.

territory from Alaska by way of the Yukon River. When it is noted that Yukon Territory lies over eleven hundred miles from the mouth of the Yukon River in Bering Sea and that this mouth is far from the "civilized" world, it can readily be understood that such a route can have little commercial importance.

About the same time as the first opening of the Yukon water route into the territory, entry was also made to the southern part of the territory by the famous Chilkoot Pass from Skagway.

Gold mining has been carried on in Yukon since 1881 and at a number of different places, but it was not until the rich strike of placer gold in the Klondike in 1896 that the industry attracted the attention of the outside world. Following the announcement of the strike, many thousands of would-be gold miners sought to reach the gold-fields by every approach that seemed at all possible. The majority used the Chilkoot Pass. This route follows a very steep ascent from Skagway on tide-water, over the height of land and down to Lake Bennett in Yukon Territory. There some sort of water craft would be constructed and the Lewes-Yukon River followed to Dawson. Many lost their lives in the Whitehorse rapids above Whitehorse town.

An alternative route was the Chilkat Pass. Starting from Dyea, a short distance west of Skagway, this involved a long overland journey to the Lewes River in the vicinity of Carmacks.

Others attempted to get inland from the coast by way of the Stikine and other rivers, and then proceed north overland to the Yukon waterways system.

Besides the routes from the south, a number endeavoured to reach the Klondike from both the west and the east. Several thousand made the tedious journey up the Yukon River from Bering Sea. The eastern approach was from railhead at Edmonton. From that place some attempted to reach Whitehorse by following much the same route as the present Alaska Highway. Others made for the Mackenzie River and endeavoured to reach Yukon both by the Liard and Peel Rivers.

In 1898 construction was started on a railway over the White Pass from Skagway to Whitehorse, which was completed in 1900. The White Pass parallels the Chilkoot Pass to the east. The former pass had been tried by a few gold seekers, but was not as practicable for the traveller on foot as the Chilkoot.

Ever since the opening of the railway practically all freight and, until the coming of air travel, all passengers entered Yukon by the White Pass route. Steamers, however, still run down the Yukon River into Alaska, and the Alaska Highway holds out the possibility of a side-door entrance.

Two airlines now enter Yukon from the outside. Canadian Pacific Air Lines reach Whitehorse from Fort St. John, B.C., a junction of lines from Edmonton and Vancouver. Pan-American Airways land in Whitehorse from Seattle and Juneau, and go on to Fairbanks. Canadian Pacific Air Lines also have connections with Fairbanks.

The White Pass and Yukon Route.[5] Because of a confusion which has arisen in many people's minds as a result of a multiplicity of names, it may be well to state at the outset that four existing companies, the Pacific and Arctic Railway and Navigation Company (Alaska), the British Columbia Yukon Railway Company (British Columbia), the British Yukon Railway Company (Yukon), and the British Yukon Navigation Company (Yukon) all operate as one system under the title "White Pass and Yukon Route." All these companies have common shareholders and officials, and are so unified as to have but one common bank account. This has been the situation from the beginning, the various company charters being made necessary by the different political jurisdictions through which the system operates.

The White Pass and Yukon Route is primarily British financed. Seattle is the headquarters of the American company, and Vancouver of the three Canadian companies. Skagway, Alaska, is the operational headquarters. The W. P. & Y. R. now operates all common carrier rail and water transportation in Yukon Territory.

Surveys and construction of the railway portion of the system began in 1898 and by 1900 the whole line was in operation. This consists of a narrow-gauge railway (3 feet in width) from Skagway up a 3.9 per cent grade for sixteen miles to the summit of White Pass, thence across the north-west corner of British Columbia skirting Lake Bennett, and into Yukon Territory where the railway follows an easy gradient to Whitehorse at the head of navigation on the Yukon River system. The total length is 110 miles. Carcross, Yukon, is the only intermediate place on the line with a station agent, but all trains stop over at Lake Bennett station for meals. The essential service is one mixed train in each direction per day, but during the war, freight trains were almost continuously running.

On October 1, 1942, the railway portion of the W. P. & Y. R. was leased to the American army for the duration of the war and six months thereafter. The terms of the lease called for the retention of all the railway's employees, for no diminution in the service to civilians, and for no financial obligations on the part of the W. P. & Y. R. for any improvements or additional equipment

[5]Most of the information about the W.P. & Y.R. was obtained from Mr. C. J. Rogers, President and General Manager of the system, supplemented by conversations with other employees and with officials in Yukon territory. An account of the effects of the building of the W.P. & Y.R. on the Yukon mining industry together with the essential facts of its early history can be found in H. A. Innis, *Settlement and the Mining Frontier* ("Canadian Frontiers of Settlement," ed. W. A. Mackintosh and W. L. G. Joerg, vol. IX, Toronto, 1936), chap. II.

which may be turned over to it on the termination of the lease. The American army greatly lengthened all siding, straightened the line in places, and added a great deal of new rolling stock.[6] It would seem probable that most of the new rolling stock will stay with the W. P. & Y. R., but most of the new siding will likely be torn up as being unnecessary and expensive to maintain. It thus appears that the railway will have the equipment and facilities to handle a very much larger volume of traffic than it ever was called on to handle before the war.

Operating conditions on the railway are difficult. The sixteen miles out of Skagway to the summit of White Pass require the use of five locomotives for the average train. Snow conditions in winter are also very difficult. The line has been blocked for as much as six weeks at a time, and snow plows are in continuous operation all winter.[7]

On completion of the railway to Whitehorse, the W. P. & Y. R. began at once to operate steamship services down the river and quickly achieved a monopoly as a common carrier. While the principal service operated was between Whitehorse and Dawson, the company also operated on the river the whole distance to Bering Sea until 1922. In that year a railway was completed into Fairbanks, and the United States government began operating boats between Fairbanks and Nome. In return for the W. P. & Y. R.'s agreement not to operate on this section of the river, the United States government agreed to leave the section from Nenana, Alaska,[8] into Yukon Territory to the private company. The W. P. & Y. R. operates one steamer between Dawson and Nenana, one round trip usually being made a year. This service is a great convenience to mining men and others who wish transportation across the international boundary in this region.

Two other water routes are also operated by the company. One is on the Stewart River from Mayo to the Yukon River at the post of Stewart River. Dwindling traffic from Mayo has left this service to one small gas-boat. From Carcross, steamers run up scenic Tagish Lake into British Columbia. This has always been a popular tourist trip. The sea route from Vancouver or Seattle to Skagway, the picturesque mountain scenery of the railway to Carcross, and then the lake trip have appealed to a large number of people who could not spare the time for the longer trip to the Klondike.

A number of long narrow lakes crossing the Yukon-British Columbia boundary combine their waters to form the Lewes River, which leaves the north end of Lake Tagish. Approaching Whitehorse, the river runs through Miles

---

[6]For instance, the number of locomotives was increased from ten to thirty-three.

[7]One of the reasons for building through White Pass instead of the Chilkoot is that the latter would usually be quite impassable in the winter.

[8]Nenana is on the Tanana River, a short distance up from the Yukon River. There are rail connections here to Anchorage.

Canyon and the Whitehorse Rapids which, being impassable to river boats, make Whitehorse the head of navigation. About twenty miles north of White-horse the Lewes widens into Lake Laberge, about forty miles long. Leaving the lake the water becomes very swift for the stretch known as "Thirtymile River." This bit of the river is troublesome in that boulders and other materials are carried down by the water. Both the government and the company under-take work here each summer to clear the channel. This piece of fast water ends where the Teslin River joins the Lewes.[9] Shortly afterwards the Big Salmon River helps to swell the Lewes and no serious navigation handicaps are encountered until about twenty-five miles north of Carmacks, the first permanent post north of Whitehorse. This troublesome spot is known as Five Finger Rapids, and is formed by a series of four small islands which cross the river. The difficulties of up-stream navigation here are met by the use of a submarine cable, so that the ships literally pull themselves through in going south. The junction of the Pelly River with the Lewes at Fort Selkirk marks the beginning of the Yukon River proper.[10] No further serious difficulties are encountered north of this within Canadian territory, although there are spots of swifter water known as rapids which occasion angling back and forth across the river. The White River, the only large tributary from the west, brings down a quantity of silt forming sandbars and islands, but after the Stewart River enters the Yukon the water becomes quite deep and difficulties of this sort are past.

The low-water plague of the Mackenzie River system has its counterpart on the Yukon, but the difficulties are much less serious. The chief trouble arises from the fact that the lake sources of the Lewes are all glacier fed so that high water is not reached until July or August. The various tributaries of the river, however, are snow fed and reach flood at the beginning of the navigation season and by late summer are starting to recede. To meet this difficulty, the W. P. & Y. R. constructed a dam across the Lewes River above Whitehorse to hold back the waters accumulated in the latter part of the year. This is gradually opened beginning about the first of May. This has the additional advantage of helping to drive the ice out of Lake Laberge, the principal reason for the delay in the opening of navigation in the spring.[11] Experienced Yukon River men estimate that there is always a minimum of 4 feet of water in the river.

[9]It may be noted that the Yukon waterway in Canada is generally a swift river, the minimum rate of flow anywhere being about four miles an hour.

[10]Locally, the Lewes River is also called the Yukon. The double nomenclature would seem to be needless, for though the river is much broader below Fort Selkirk, there is no change of direction where the Lewes becomes the Yukon. The Pelly comes in at right angles.

[11]Because of the fact that the W.P. & Y.R. has never been granted a monopoly of navigation on the Yukon, there is a feeling on the part of the company officials that the government should take over the responsibility and expense of the dam.

Navigation opens as a rule between May 15 and 20, but has been as late as the middle of June. The season is closed usually by the middle of October.

The Yukon steamers are stern paddle-wheelers which burn wood as fuel. The wood is loaded at frequent intervals from stocks placed along the river banks by contractors. The ships, while all more than forty years old, are of a size to accommodate over one hundred passengers apiece and are all fitted up with many conveniences for tourists. Of late years the company has shuttled two ships back and forth between Whitehorse and Dawson all summer. The down stream trip lasts about forty hours, with the return trip lasting five or six days. The result of this is that Yukon River points get very much more frequent summer service than the places in the Mackenzie District, and moreover, as only small freight loads are required to be moved at one time, the freight can be stowed on the ships themselves and barges are rarely necessary. Barges are used chiefly for moving things such as massive mining machinery which are too bulky to be placed on the ships.

Besides controlling the rail and water transportation of Yukon, from 1935 to 1942 the White Pass and Yukon Route also operated an airway between Whitehorse and Dawson. In the latter year this airline was taken over by Yukon Southern Air Transport, which in the following year was absorbed into Canadian Pacific Air Lines. The W. P. & Y. R., however, still acts as agent for the airway north from Whitehorse.

The White Pass and Yukon Route has remained solvent since 1900 without government assistance. A number of years showed losses on operations, but during its whole life it has been able to return its investors an average of about 1 per cent a year.

But the economic situation of the system is difficult. There have been wide variations in the volume of business from year to year. Moreover, traffic is far from balanced in the two directions. The movement of freight has generally been almost entirely inbound. This consists chiefly of settlers' and mining supplies. Before the war from 5,000 to 7,000 tons of freight were moved annually to Dawson, and something between 1,000 and 2,000 tons moved between Dawson and Nenana. Outbound there has been little but the lead-silver ore from the Mayo district, which has been shipped in only some ten or twelve years of the W. P. & Y. R.'s existence. In some of the years that this traffic moved, it amounted by weight to more than the inbound tonnage. But Yukon's principal export, gold, is shipped out from Dawson by registered air mail, so does not benefit the company's revenues.

Passenger traffic has always been relatively heavier than on rail and water carriers in Canada as a whole, averaging about 25 per cent of the W. P. & Y. R.'s revenue. A large part of this has been tourist traffic. While the war cut off tourists from outside, a great many of the large population stationed around Whitehorse took advantage of the river service for short vacations to

Dawson.   Yukon is the only part of the Canadian North that has had any tourist business worth mentioning.   This is accounted for by picturesque scenery, modern travel and housing conveniences, and the "romance of '98."   If the last named, together with the American war-time activities, could be advertised properly, Yukon might well have a booming post-war tourist business.

The accounts of the railway and waterway sections of the W. P. & Y. R. are so interwoven that separation is virtually impossible.   The usual railway statistics are furnished annually to the government,[12] but because of joint revenues and joint costs, the accuracy of their segregation from the system as a whole is doubtful.   Moreover, the ratios of the different items to one another differ so much from similar ratios of other railways that it is very difficult to test the W. P. & Y. R. by the usual economic methods.   For instance, in 1941, the last full year's operations before the American "invasion," the proportions of the various groups of operating expenses to the total operating expenses for the W. P. & Y. R. and for all Canadian railways were:[13]

	W.P. & Y.R. (British Yukon)	All Canadian Railways
*M.W.S.	36.9%	19.9%
*M.E.	13.5	24.4
Traffic	6.1	2.6
Transportation	35.8	47.0
Miscellaneous	—	1.7
General	7.7	4.4
	100%	100%

*Maintenance of way and structure, and maintenance of equipment.

Both the individual cost items and the revenue statistics are just as much out of line.   However, it may be noted that the W. P. & Y. R.'s operating ratio for 1941 was only 64 compared to a figure of 75 for all Canadian railways. Despite this it suffered a small loss on the 1941 season.

The W. P. & Y. R. as a whole has had gross revenues between $650,000 and $1,300,000 annually.   To attain these figures, rates and fares, of course, are relatively high.   Although the inhabitants of Yukon seem to have become resigned to high transportation charges as well as prices and little vocal complaint is now heard except from newcomers, in 1909 the Board of Trade of Dawson City lodged a complaint about the rates to the Board of Railway Commissioners.[14] The Board at first ruled the rates excessive and ordered sub-

[12]The White Pass and Yukon Route's accounts appear under the title of British Yukon.

[13]Computed from *Statistics of Steam Railways of Canada for the Year ending December 31, 1941.* (Transportation and Public Utilities Branch, Dominion Bureau of Statistics, Ottawa, 1943).

[14]*Dawson Board of Trade* v. *White Pass and Yukon Railway Company,* 5/219; 6/346; 7/216; 9 C.R.C. 190; 11 C.R.C. 402; 13 C.R.C. 527.   An account of the case may be found in D. A. MacGibbon, *Railway Rates and the Canadian Railway Commission* (Boston, 1917), pp. 101 ff.

stantial reductions, but on appeal with evidence being brought forward that the railway would be forced out of existence by the lowering of the rates, the decision was reversed. This case stands as a precedent that a railway cannot be compelled to make charges so low that its investment would be lost. It may be noted that the situation would probably have been different had the W. P. & Y. R. been able to maintain the volume of traffic of its earliest days.

The Canadian Railway Freight Classification is not used. Instead, the system uses one of its own in which there are just three classes, A, B, and C with some multiples of Class C, the highest. The Class Rates, L.C.L. (per 100 pounds), from Vancouver to Whitehorse are for the three classes $3.55, $4.00, and $4.95. A negligible amount of traffic moves over the railway only between Skagway and Whitehorse. The rates here are $3.03, $3.33, and $4.24 respectively. The water rate from Whitehorse to Dawson is $1.25 per 100 pounds. However, the bulk of the traffic does not move on class rates, but on special commodity rates which are appreciably lower. Commodity rates are quoted on canned goods, coal oil, feed grain, flour, hay, condensed milk and cream, sugar, and mining machinery.

Passenger fares are approximately 10 cents per mile on the railway. On the river they are about $40.00 for the downstream journey from Whitehorse to Dawson, and about $60.00 for the upstream trip.

No sketch of the White Pass and Yukon Route would be complete without mentioning the fact that it has a peculiarly loyal set of employees, most of whom have been working for it for more than twenty years. The system treats its employees very generously, and has avoided labour troubles.

Speaking generally, it may be said that the White Pass and Yukon Route provides the settled part of Yukon with much more reliable and frequent transportation service than is experienced in any other part of the Canadian North. However, the rates are very high, being higher than those of the Mackenzie District on a ton-mile basis.[15] But in the absence of a greatly increased volume of traffic, it would not appear as though there were any means of lowering the rates save through a government subsidy in some form.

The Former Klondike Mines Railway. While at the height of the gold-rush several railway companies were chartered to build into Yukon, none of these railways ever reached the construction stage. The only other railway aside from the W. P. & Y. R. which has ever operated in Yukon was a short one wholly within the territory, the Klondike Mines Railway. This line was opened in 1906 and ran some thirty miles from Dawson to Sulphur Springs, with short branches up some of the Klondike's creeks. Dwindling traffic caused the railway to close down in 1915.

[15]The reverse is the case in air transportation.

Other Water Transportation. Many of the Yukon River's tributaries are navigable, and are used for water transportation to some extent. There are fur-trading posts up some of these rivers, and these are reached by various types of craft, chiefly gas-boats, with some barges. Low water usually causes a shut-down in operations at the end of July on the Teslin, Pelly, and Macmillan[16] Rivers, but the Stewart River season is prolonged by September rains in the Mackenzie Mountains. The White River is navigable by fair-sized craft for a considerable distance, but is now little used. In the far North, the Porcupine River flows into the Yukon, 321 miles below Dawson in Alaskan territory. Goods for Old Crow and a few Indian settlements on its banks are unloaded at Fort Yukon and proceed up the Porcupine in small boats.

Highways. Some maps of Yukon Territory show what seems to be an extensive system of highways. It is easy to get false impressions from such maps, for the great bulk of the mileage consists of winter road only. Use in summer is precluded by the absence of means of crossing the numerous streams whether by bridge or ferry. Further, while most of these roads were used regularly in the days of horse-drawn vehicles, the coming of the aeroplane made the carriage of mails by land almost unnecessary, and most of the roads have become impassable through lack of use. The distinction between "road" and "trail" in the North is rather fine, but a lot of the mileage would be better classed under the latter term than the former. The term "road" is again mis-leading, for most of them are much too rough for ordinary automobile travel.

However, before the war there were about 150 miles of usable automobile roads outside the towns. Such roads included about fifty-two miles from Dawson up the Klondike River as far as Granville with numerous side roads, thirty-five miles from Mayo to the mines at Keno Hill, forty miles from White-horse to Carcross, and the southern portion of the old Whitehorse-Dawson trail from Whitehorse as far as Carmacks.

The war brought into being the tremendous project known originally as the Alcan Highway, but later renamed the Alaska Military Highway.[17] Built by the United States army and various contractors, the road was begun in March, 1942, and was officially opened throughout its entire length on November 20 of the same year. However, most of the gravelling was done subsequently and improvements were still being made up to V-J Day. The total length of the road is about 1,523 miles, of which 1,220 are in Canada. While this highway has been cited as one of the greatest engineering accomplishments in the world, its chief claim for distinction in this field is that a road of such length should

---

[16]A tributary of the Pelly.

[17]Numerous booklet, newspaper, and magazine articles have appeared dealing with this highway, but official documents are not yet available to the public. Cost figures quoted differ widely and are at best merely guesses.

14

have been built in such a short time through an unsettled wilderness of mountains, rivers, and trees.

While this road is not of uniform quality, in general it can be said that it is wider and better surfaced than most non-paved roads in Canada. Particularly is this so in the section in the Peace River block in British Columbia, where the road is 36 feet wide. Most of the bridges and other such works have been built as permanent structures. The Peace River bridge, thirteen miles south-east of Fort St. John, must now be included with Canada's greater bridges, for it is one of the longest in the country.

The highway starts from Dawson Creek, B.C., at the end of steel of the Northern Alberta Railways in the Peace River block. The road runs north-west, touching Fort St. John and Fort Nelson in British Columbia, and enters Yukon near Watson Lake. From here it crosses Yukon Territory through Whitehorse and finally terminates at Fairbanks, Alaska. There is a branch from Tagish to Carcross, which has caused the abandonment of the former Whitehorse-Carcross road. Another branch was built from the highway near Kluane Lake in south-west Yukon to tidewater at Haines, Alaska, but this branch has now fallen into disuse.

As yet the Alaska Highway has had only a very restricted non-military use. Its chief civilian uses have been for local traffic between Dawson Creek and Fort St. John, local traffic again in the vicinity of Whitehorse, and the means by which Canadian Pacific Air Lines can truck gasoline, oil, and spare parts to its airports at a very much lower cost than formerly prevailed. At present the road is being turned over to the Canadian government, which has not yet announced its permanent maintenance policy. Should it fail to maintain the road, the time will almost certainly come when this will be cited as a very short-sighted policy. The road gives access to many thousand square miles of territory as yet completely undeveloped but which many persons believe can be made of use. Yet the cost of maintaining the Alaska Highway will be very high, and it is apparent that the immediate benefits in peace-time will be slight. But certainly, from the standpoint of long-range vision the Alaska Highway must not be allowed to return to the wilderness, but immediate post-war policy must remain speculative until some approximation of actual maintenance costs can be made.

Another American war-time highway project involved the building of a road from Camp Canol on the Mackenzie to Whitehorse to serve the pipeline. Only about two hundred miles of this were gravelled and usable by the ordinary automobile. However, the abandonment of the Canol project means that road-way will soon return to its original wild state.

Airways. Flying began in Yukon in the late nineteen-twenties and consisted originally of charter-bush work by various companies, chiefly Yukon Airways and Exploration, Pacific Alaska Western, and the Treadwell-Yukon Mining Company. Pan-American Airways began its Seattle-Fairbanks service about 1930 and used Whitehorse as a refuelling point. However, it was only during the latter part of the war that Pan-American began doing any revenue business in Canadian territory. Northern Airways, Ltd., began operating out of Carcross in 1931. It does charter work, and has a winter-mail contract between Carcross and Atlin and Telegraph Creek, B.C. This airway is somewhat unique in being a small one that has remained completely independent.[18]

The White Pass and Yukon Route began an air service between Whitehorse and Dawson through Mayo in 1935. Despite the employment of some of the ablest pilots in Canada, this airline was marred by a series of bad accidents. The case is sometimes cited as showing the disadvantages in the operation of an airway by railway officials. In 1938 Yukon Southern Air Transport was formed to operate between Edmonton and Vancouver and Whitehorse. Thus at last Yukon was given air service from the "outside." In 1941, Yukon Southern absorbed the W. P. & Y. R.'s airway, and began operating the service north of Whitehorse. Yukon Southern was one of the ten companies amalgamated into Canadian Pacific Air Lines in 1942.

Canadian Pacific Air Lines. Canadian Pacific Air Lines flies scheduled planes to and from Whitehorse from the "outside" six days a week. At Fort St. John, B.C., the traffic on a plane from Edmonton, and on a plane from Vancouver are consolidated into one. Beyond Fort St. John, landings are made at Fort Nelson, B.C., and Watson Lake, Y.T., before reaching Whitehorse. Service continues beyond Whitehorse to Fairbanks, Alaska. In the reverse direction, Fort St. John is again the junction point for the services to Edmonton and to Vancouver.

North from Whitehorse, C. P. A. runs two regular round trips a week to Mayo and Dawson, with landings being made at Fort Selkirk once a week.

But, as with all northern flying, the scheduled flights represent only the minimum service, unless the weather forces cancellations. Additional trips are made frequently as traffic warrants.

Largely because of the American activity on the Alaska Highway, the air route to Whitehorse consists of thoroughly modern airports with radio-range stations and all the other equipment of up-to-date airlines. This route has all the facilities to become part of an international air route to the Orient.

Aside from the airports at Whitehorse and Watson Lake, the other landing fields are scarcely out of the class of "emergency landing fields," consisting of little more than cleared-off pieces of level ground. There are four or five additional landing fields constructed for emergency purposes in Yukon which

---

[18]The resourcefulness required to keep a small airline with seven or eight employees operating successfully is perhaps suggested in the fact that Northern Airways builds many of its own air-frames in "spare time." Mr. G. T. Simmons is an able managing director.

do not have regular service. Other points can be reached by air only by float planes. It may be noted that Yukon has far fewer lakes than the Mackenzie District to serve as natural landing fields for seaplanes.

A consideration of Canadian Pacific Air Lines' northern services as a whole, together with a discussion of some of the peculiarities of northern flying, will be postponed to the section on the Mackenzie District.[19]

Other Forms of Transportation. Before the coming of the aeroplane, winter mails were carried north from railhead at Whitehorse by stage-coaches or sleighs drawn by horses. Passengers and a small amount of freight were also moved in this way. At the present time horses are very rare in Yukon, or indeed anywhere in the Canadian Territories.

The picturesque mode of travel in the North, the dog-team, seems to be on the decline in the Yukon.[20] While the typical team of seven or eight dogs can haul about a 100 pounds per dog and make from fifteen to seventy miles a day depending on the weather, the condition of the trail, and the experience of the driver, dog-teams have never been important for freight carriage as the food for dogs and driver take up too much space. The dog-team is essentially a mode of individual winter travel, and is used by all persons stationed in isolated places who have to make a number of relatively short trips in the winter. The dog sled in winter corresponds to the canoe in summer.

Caterpillar tractors have not been used extensively in Yukon. They have a use on emergency trips in winter, but the aeroplane has largely displaced them.[21]

Most of the Canol pipeline was laid in Yukon. The long line from the Mackenzie River to Whitehorse has now been abandoned, but three extensions out of Whitehorse still serve a useful purpose. One of these lines follows the railway from Whitehorse to Skagway, and is used for carrying California oils from tidewater into Yukon. Another line goes from Whitehorse to Watson Lake, and is a useful means of cutting the price of gasoline at that airport. The third pipeline runs from Whitehorse to Fairbanks.

Communications. Canadian Government Telegraphs built a line down the Yukon River in 1900, the line running from Dawson to Ashcroft, B.C., where it connected with C.P.R. Telegraphs. At present Telegraph Creek, B.C., on the Stikine River is the southern terminus of the line, messages to and from points south of here being relayed by radio. The equipment of this telegraph line is old and out-of-date,[22] but it can still handle all the business that arises satisfactorily.

[19] P. 220.

[20] For instance, Old Crow in the far North is the only R.C.M.P. post still using dogs.

[21] As the placer mining of the Klondike closes down in the winter, there is no occasion for tractor trains to carry in mining machinery when the navigation season is closed.

[22] For instance, the line consists of iron wire, not copper.

The White Pass and Yukon Route operates a telegraph line between Whitehorse and Skagway from which places messages can reach the rest of the world.

The American army constructed telegraph, teletype, and telephone lines along the Alaska Highway between Whitehorse and Edmonton. These communication systems, now handed over to the Canadian government, are not as yet operated commercially but may well be in the near future.

Similar lines were built along the Canol pipeline road, but have now been abandoned.

The only other instance of an inter-urban telephone line is that of the W. P. & Y. R. between Whitehorse and Skagway, this being for company use only.

Radio has become an important means of communication in Yukon, and radiograms may be sent to and from the outside world through the agency of the Royal Canadian Corps of Signals.

The Mackenzie District

Settlement in the Mackenzie District, in contrast to Yukon Territory, is spread over a very much larger area. Distances to be covered are much greater, and consequently the transportation problems are increased. The 1,661 miles from railhead at Waterways to Aklavik may be compared with the 460 miles from railhead at Whitehorse to Dawson. Moreover, the important mining developments of the Mackenzie District are a considerable distance east of the Mackenzie River. This gives the settlement a breadth of territory which is lacking in Yukon, and it also means that the transportation routes cannot consist of a "main line" with a few minor branches. All in all, the transportation problems of the Mackenzie District are more difficult of solution than those of Yukon.

Although Sir Alexander Mackenzie made his famous trip to the mouth of the Mackenzie River in 1789, the only economic activity of this vast region which related to the outside world until after the First World War was trapping. The fur industry, however, resulted in the establishment of a number of permanent trading posts, most of which are now of considerable age. At each of these posts is a Hudson's Bay Company store, a varying number of "Freetraders' " stores, a post office, a Royal Canadian Mounted Police station, a signals station, a mission church (sometimes two), and perhaps a mission school and a mission hospital. Those with landing fields built during the war also have a small group of airway personnel, the larger ones having Department of Transport establishments as well. The majority of these posts are located on the Mackenzie waterway from Fort Smith on the Slave River to the Beaufort Sea of the Arctic Ocean. Consequently calls can be made at the greater number of them in the course of one long trip. However, there are some fur posts which are off the main route and require special transportation service.

The value of the furs taken varies widely from year to year, but there is no discernible upward trend in the fur production of the District as a whole. Thus, unless measures are taken which will greatly increase the numbers of fur-bearing animals,[23] there seems to be little prospect of the purely fur-trading post increasing much in size. Gardens are planted around most of the posts, it is true, but the possibilities of a commercial agriculture developing would seem to depend wholly on large mining camps springing up in the vicinity of the posts,[24] for a market in the outside world in the present stage of our progress is unthinkable. The oil wells and refinery at Norman Wells are responsible for the only settlement[25] on the Mackenzie River not based on furs. But the market for the oil from here is confined to the Mackenzie District, so that Norman Wells itself is likely to find its growth controlled by the growth of the whole District. Metal mining is unlikely to develop close to the Mackenzie River.

The fur-trading posts down the Mackenzie waterway from the south are:[26] Fort Smith (1874) on the Slave River; Fort Resolution (1800); Hay River (1868), the last two being on the south shore of Great Slave Lake; Fort Providence (1862); Fort Simpson[27] (1804); Wrigley (1877); Fort Norman[27] (1810); Fort Good Hope[27] (1805); Arctic Red River (1891); Fort MacPherson (1840), on the Peel River twenty-eight miles from the Mackenzie; and Aklavik (1912). Aklavik is considered the terminus of the Mackenzie river route, but since 1936, posts along the Arctic coast and on the adjacent islands have been serviced from the Mackenzie. To accomplish this one boat a year proceeds beyond Aklavik to the newly established transport depot at Tuktoyaktuk[28] on the Arctic Ocean, where freight is transferred to the deeper draft "ocean" vessels. Marked on most maps at one of the mouths of the Mackenzie is Kittigazuit. This was a post opened in 1915, but abandoned in 1929.

Of all these places, Aklavik with its white fox, has by far the largest annual "take" in furs. The Fort Resolution-Fort Smith area in the extreme south ranks

[23]Conservation measures instituted so far have been aimed primarily at the prevention of the extinction of these animals.

[24]One such commercial farm, "Browning's Farm," has been cleared from the bush on the left bank of the Mackenzie between Fort Providence and Fort Simpson. A market is found for the produce at various posts along the river. However, this market is very limited, and there is little prospect of success in the multiplication of such farms.

[25]Apart, perhaps, from Reindeer Station, below Aklavik. This is the headquarters of the Reindeer Preserve established by the government.

[26]The date following each name refers to the year of its establishment.

[27]The three posts on the Mackenzie River established before the North West Company was merged by the Hudson's Bay Company in 1821, Simpson, Norman, and Good Hope, were established by the former Company. Simpson was originally known as Fort of the Forks, not receiving its present name until 1850. Good Hope had two shifts in location before reaching its present site in 1836.

[28]Commonly known as Tuk-tuk. The post office has named it Port Brabant, following a decision of the Geographic Board of Canada.

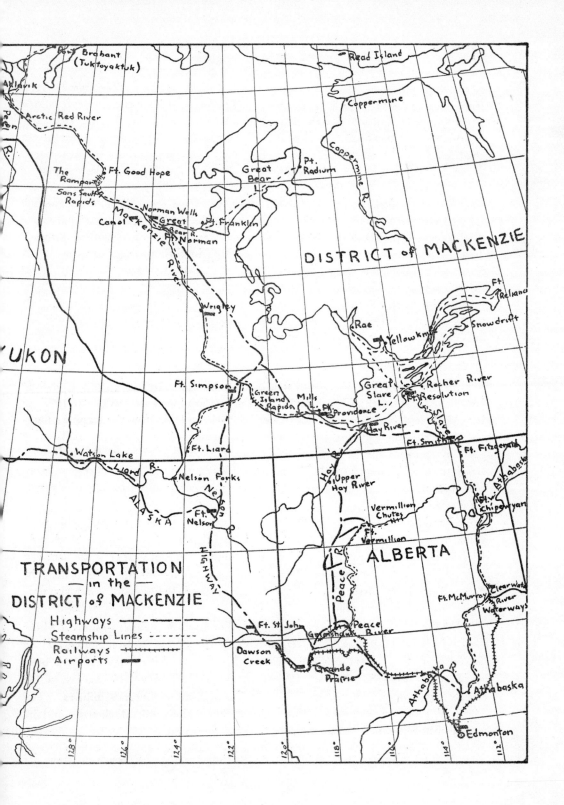

Port Brabant
(Tuktoyaktuk)

Read Island

Aklavik

Coppermine

Arctic Red River

Coppermine R.

Pt. Radium

The Ramparts
Ft. Good Hope

Great Bear L.

DISTRICT of MACKENZIE

Sans Sault Rapids

Norman Wells
Great Bear R.
Ft. Franklin
Mackenzie Canol
Ft. Norman

Ft. Reliance

Wrigley

Rae
Yellowknife
Snowdrift

YUKON

Ft. Simpson
Green Island
Mills
Rapids
Ft. Providence

Great Slave L.
Rocher River
Ft. Resolution
Slave R.

Hay River

Ft. Smith
Ft. Fitzgerald

Watson Lake
Liard R.
Ft. Liard

Nelson Forks
Nelson R.

Hay R.
Upper Hay River

Athabaska R.
Ft. Chipewyan

ALASKA

Ft. Nelson

Vermillion Chutes

Ft. Vermillion

ALBERTA

HIGHWAY

Peace R.

TRANSPORTATION
— in the —
DISTRICT of MACKENZIE

Ft. McMurray
Clearwater River
Waterways

Highways ————
Steamship Lines -------
Railways ++++++
Airports ▬

Ft. St. John
Peace River

Dawson Creek

Grande Prairie

Athabaska R.
Athabaska

Edmonton

next. Fort Simpson is the most important fur post on the middle river. Aside from furs, some of these places have possibilities as transportation centres, and Fort Smith in addition has the administrative offices for the North West Territories located within the Territories. Hay River, as the terminus of the tractor road from Grimshaw, Alberta, to Great Slave Lake and of the all-weather road at present being constructed, has the possibility of developing in importance in the transportation field. From Fort Nelson, British Columbia, on the Alaska Highway there is a through navigation route *via* the Fort Nelson River and the Liard River to the Mackenzie River at Fort Simpson. This route has already been used to reach the lower Mackenzie before navigation opened from Fort Smith.[29] Thus, Fort Simpson may take on some added importance as a transportation centre. At Fort Norman, at the mouth of Great Bear River flowing from Great Bear Lake, some freight in and out of the Eldorado region must be transferred between boats on the two rivers. So Norman may have some expansion for this reason. Fort McPherson would benefit should the route to the Porcupine River in Yukon ever come again into important use.

The "off the line" fur posts of the Mackenzie District may be placed in five groups.

At the eastern end of Great Slave Lake the Hudson's Bay Company established Fort Reliance in 1833. This was abandoned in 1835. In 1927 an R.C.M.P. detachment was stationed here, largely to look after the trappers passing through here into the barren lands. However, there are two small active posts in operation on the south side of the lake to the east of Slave River, Rocher River (Taltson River), and Snowdrift. This region is in the Pre-Cambrian country, and is of interest to prospectors with copper seeming to have the greatest possibilities.

Near the head of the North Arm of Great Slave Lake is Rae. This post, which has the largest Indian population in its vicinity of any of the Mackenzie District posts, was for a long period far removed from any other settlement but now has the largest settlement, Yellowknife, as a not too-distant neighbour. The direct route from Great Slave Lake to Great Bear Lake (with forty-six portages) passes through Rae.

On the Liard River is Fort Liard. Farther south in British Columbia where the Liard is joined by the Fort Nelson River is the post of Nelson Forks, and up the latter river is Fort Nelson. These three posts, which have always been served from Fort Simpson on the Mackenzie River, now have access to the Alaska Highway in the south. This holds out interesting possibilities. The Liard valley has a somewhat milder climate than along the Mackenzie, and its agricultural potentialities should receive some attention.

[29]The ice in Great Slave Lake delays the navigation season even though the rivers are free.

Where Great Bear Lake discharges into the river of the same name stands Fort Franklin. On all but recent maps this appears as the "site of," but the Eldorado traffic caused the reopening of the post though not on a full-year basis.

Lastly, along the Arctic coast of the Mackenzie District a number of traders have operated stores from time to time, and one of the most permanent posts has been Coppermine on Coronation Gulf. In this district there are rich deposits of copper, but copper cannot stand the expensive transportation to the outside world.

Despite the reports by several early explorers of mineral deposits at various places in the Mackenzie District, no attempt to develop mining occurred until after the First Great War. Oil was the first. While oil seepages along the Mackenzie north of Fort Norman had long been known, it was not until 1920 that any drilling was attempted. This was begun by the Northwest Company, a subsidiary of Imperial Oil, Ltd.[30] Although two wells were brought into production, the lack of a market caused them to be capped by 1925. The mining activity at the Eldorado mine on Great Bear Lake and at Yellowknife during the thirties caused a revival of operations at Norman Wells.[31] Two more wells were brought into production and a refinery, built in 1939, came into operation in 1940.

The American Canol Project, started in 1942, caused a tremendous increase in activity in the Mackenzie oil fields. Camp Canol, the base for the pipeline construction and operation, was established on the opposite (west) bank of the river. The pipeline was completed in 1944 and the refinery in Whitehorse opened at the same time, but the close of the war caused the whole project to be abandoned. However, the Canol Project served the purpose of stimulating geological exploration, so that by the end of 1944 fifty-six wells were oil producers.[32] Norman Wells is now a proven oil field.

The loss of the Whitehorse market, of course, greatly reduced production at Norman Wells but this is now on the upgrade again. The growing mining communities provide an ever-enlarging market, and moreover there is a marked tendency throughout the whole Mackenzie District to replace wood as fuel with oil. There is at present no prospect of an outside market, but with an expanding mining industry in the District it would seem as though Norman Wells has an assured and growing future.

In 1930 the important discovery of pitchblende was made at Echo Bay on the east side of Great Bear Lake. Eldorado Gold Mines, Ltd.,[33] at once began

[30]It is of interest to note that this enterprise later involved the first use of the aeroplane in the North-West Territories.

[31]The name given to the settlement about the oil field, about thirty-five miles north of Fort Norman.

[32]G. S. Hume and J. A. Link, *Canol Geological Investigations in the Mackenzie River Area* (Mines and Geology Branch, Ottawa, 1945), p. 77.

[33]Later changed to Eldorado Mining and Refining, Ltd.

to develop the property, and by 1933 had a mill at the mine and a refinery at Port Hope, Ontario, in operation. The company also operated its own water transportation. Canada very quickly became the second important producer of radium in the world. Disorganized markets occasioned by the war caused the mine to close down in 1940, but it was reopened in 1942. At the beginning of 1944 the company was expropriated by the Dominion government and turned into a Crown company. Since that time the operations have been greatly stepped-up, but a strict censorship prevailed regarding all activities at Port Radium.[34] It is now known, of course, that the government's interest was in the uranium rather than the radium. The present prospect seems to be that the Great Bear Lake mining field will continue to develop.

Port Radium has serious transportation difficulties. Not only is the water route in and out of it long and roundabout, but from sixteen to over twenty[35] handlings of the freight must be made between Port Radium and Edmonton. And Edmonton is neither the origin nor destination of Port Radium freight.

Gold was discovered near the Yellowknife River on the north side of Great Slave Lake in 1934. The settlement of Yellowknife was established, and a minor gold-rush developed. By 1942 seven mines[36] were in production, but by the end of the war owing to the increasing shortage of man-power and the difficulties in obtaining equipment and supplies, only two mines remained open. However, prospecting and diamond drilling continued over a very large area to the north, east, and south of Yellowknife. The close of the war has occasioned an influx of people on a greater scale than before. A gold fever is raging which has produced a great optimism for the future, not the least of the predictions being that Yellowknife is destined to be a greater gold-field than anything in Northern Ontario.[37] What the future will hold cannot, of course, be known, but it seems reasonably certain that this area on the edge of the Pre-Cambrian Shield is heavily mineralized.

It may be noted that the Yellowknife area contains many minerals other than gold, but that mineral is the only one valuable enough to warrant shipping to outside markets with the high transportation costs. It is of interest that tantalite has been found on the north-east shore of Great Slave Lake. This ore contains tantalum, an element for which researches of recent years have found many uses.

[34]Now the official name of the settlement about the mines and mill, formerly called Eldorado.

[35]The number varies according to the number of times the freight must be put in warehouses en route.

[36]Including one on Outpost Island in the middle of Great Slave Lake. Maps not quite up-to-date show Outpost Island as a port of call on the airways, but the property is now abandoned.

[37]It is of interest to note that at present, three branch banks are operating in Yellowknife.

The location of Yellowknife, at the centre of the north side of a very long east-west lake, creates many transportation difficulties. Any form of land transportation skirting the lake involves too long a route to be considered seriously at the present time. The rapid increase in population also has resulted in the inability to get sufficient food to the town to prevent shortages before spring.

Historical Approaches to the Mackenzie District. The Methye Portage between the Churchill River and the Clearwater River was discovered by Peter Pond in 1778. The Clearwater flows into the Athabaska River, and the latter into Lake Athabaska. From here the Slave River flows to Great Slave Lake, whose outlet, the Mackenzie River, reaches the Arctic Ocean. For over a hundred years the Methye Portage was the only route used into the Mackenzie District, the point of origin for both freight and travellers being York Factory on Hudson Bay.

In 1875, Edmonton was first reached by river-steamer along the North Saskatchewan River, and some ten years later a rough road was built from Edmonton north to Athabaska Landing[38] on the Athabaska River. Although a series of rapids on the Athabaska have to be passed before the Clearwater River is reached at Fort McMurray, this new route through Edmonton grew rapidly to one of equal importance with the Methye Portage route.

The railway from Calgary reached Edmonton in 1891, and this not only finished the steamer traffic on the North Saskatchewan, but also ended the Methye Portage route into the Mackenzie District.

A railway was built from Edmonton to Athabaska Landing in 1912, but the Athabaska River route was abandoned in 1915 when a railway reached the town of Peace River. For the next few years the Peace River was used to reach the Slave River north of Lake Athabaska. The Peace River is broader than the Athabaska and avoids the troubles occasioned by sandbars on the latter river, but between Peace River town and the Slave River, navigation is interrupted by a portage around Vermilion Chutes.

In 1921, the Clearwater River about eight miles from the Athabaska River was joined to Edmonton by rail, and at once this route ended the use of the Peace River for reaching the Mackenzie River. The railway in 1925 was extended to within about four miles of the Athabaska and the town of Waterways created. But the railway has stopped there[39] and has not yet been extended to Fort McMurray.

Ever since 1921 almost all freight has entered the Mackenzie District *via* Waterways. Because of an exceptionally low-water year in 1938, the following

[38]Now the town of Athabaska.

[39]The American army built about two more miles of rail west of Waterways in 1942 to their shipyards, named Prairie, half way between Waterways and Fort McMurray. This extension, however, is not now in use.

winter a rough tractor trail was cut through to Hay River on Great Slave Lake from Grimshaw, near Peace River town, the purpose being to get supplies into the District which had failed to get through before freeze-up. The American Canol Project brought a revival of this route for winter freighting by tractor train. During the past year, work began on the construction of an all-weather road to Hay River. Thus it is altogether possible that this entry to Great Slave Lake may come to take more and more business away from the Athabaska-Slave route.

Lastly, the Fort Nelson-Liard route to the Mackenzie River holds out some speculative possibilities, as the post of Fort Nelson is on the Alaska Highway.

Northern Alberta Railways. No railway operates in the North West Territories,[40] but the Northern Alberta Railways plays a very important part in Mackenzie District transportation. The Northern Alberta Railways is a consolidation of four railways[41] and is jointly owned by the Canadian National and Canadian Pacific Railways. There are two main lines. The longer extends north-west from Edmonton through the Peace River country to Dawson Creek, British Columbia. Here the Alaska Highway begins. On a northern fork of this Peace River line is the station of Grimshaw, from which runs the tractor road to Hay River. The other main line, the former Alberta and Great Waterways Railway, runs north-easterly from Edmonton to Waterways. Over this line is carried practically all freight destined for the Mackenzie District. On this portion of the N.A.R., unlike the rest of the railway, rates somewhat higher than the Prairie Standard Tariff are charged. This contributes to the high transportation costs of the Mackenzie District. The Northern Alberta Railways, while possessing poor roadbeds and run-down rolling stock, provides the certainty in transportation which a railway can give.

Water Transportation in the Mackenzie District.[42] Water carriers have always been the principal means of transport in the Mackenzie District. The

[40]A few railway companies have been chartered to build in the Territories, mostly before the turn of the century. The most fantastic of these was undoubtedly the Hudson's Bay and Northwest Railway (originally the Hudson's Bay and Yukon Railways and Navigation Company), chartered in 1897 (60-1 Vict., c. 46) to build from Chesterfield Inlet on Hudson Bay to a point on the Yukon or Porcupine Rivers.

[41]Edmonton, Dunvegan and British Columbia Rly. Co.; Alberta and Great Waterways Rly. Co.; Central Canada Rly. Co.; and Pembina Valley Rly. Co. The first three of these experienced great financial difficulties and came into the hands of the provincial government of Alberta in 1921 and 1926. The Pembina Valley Rly. was a provincial one from the start. The province sold out all four railways to the Canadian National and Canadian Pacific Railways jointly in 1929, when the Northern Alberta Railway Company was incorporated.

[42]Most of the information in this section was obtained in numerous interviews with officials and employees of the two major companies, and by personal observation. See also J. L. Robinson, "Water Transportation in the Canadian Northwest" (*Canadian Geographical Journal,* Nov., 1945).

aeroplane has provided the speedy means of travel so desirable over the north country's great distances, but it is not yet capable of moving bulk freight economically. Aside from mail and air express, freight is carried by air only in an emergency.

In the earliest history of the Mackenzie District, canoes were the sole water craft used, but in the eighteen-twenties these began to be replaced by York boats. The York boat was a shallow-draft, open boat about 40 feet long, and was propelled by both oars and a square sail. However, most of the upstream journey had to be made by towing the boat from the bank. York boats dominated the transportation picture for over sixty years, until the first steamer, the *Wrigley,* appeared in 1886.[43] The modern era may be said to have begun in 1908 when the Hudson's Bay Company put into operation the stern-wheeler *Mackenzie River.* This ship, with comfortable accommodation for passengers, is still in service. Since 1908 a number of other steamers and motor vessels have been added, but only one of larger size than the *Mackenzie River,* the Hudson's Bay Company's *Distributor,* built shortly after the first World War. The freight transported is all carried on barges, which are pushed by the parent ship (though sometimes towed on Great Slave Lake in rough weather). As many as five barges are pushed at once.

The Mackenzie waterway is divided into two distincts parts, known as the upper river and the lower river. The upper river route runs from railhead at Waterways, down the Athabaska River to Lake Athabaska, across the western end of the lake to Fort Chipewyan, and down the Slave River to Fitzgerald.[44] Here, a series of rapids involving a total fall of 109 feet necessitates the use of a portage road to Fort Smith, sixteen miles away. The upper river route is wholly within Alberta, the portage crossing the boundary with the North West Territories. From Waterways to Fitzgerald is 287 miles, the distance to Fort Chipewyan being 187 miles.

The lower river route goes from Fort Smith down the Slave River to Great Slave Lake. From here a very important branch crosses the lake to Yellowknife with an extension on to Rae, and a less important branch runs eastward in the lake. But the main route goes westward from the Slave River to the entrance of the Mackenzie River and continues uninterruptedly down to Tuktoyaktuk. Branches from the Mackenzie River include the Great Bear River route, which is interrupted by a portage, but then continues for the rest of

[43] The steamer *Grahame* began operating on the upper river between Forts McMurray and Fitzgerald in 1884.

[44] Originally called Smith's Landing. The post office name is *Fort* Fitzgerald, but some doubt exists as to whether this settlement is entitled to the name or not. The older fur posts, with some sort of fence to protect them against Indians, were designated "forts." The same confusion exists with respect to Rae and Wrigley. It may be noted that locally the word "fort" is seldom used of place names in the North.

the way up the river and across the full length of Great Bear Lake, and the Liard River route which continues up the Liard's tributary, the Fort Nelson River.

The distances from Fort Smith to the points along the Mackenzie River route proper are as follows. Three hundred and three miles must be added to get the distance from Waterways.

*Res-delta, near the mouth of the Slave River	177	miles
Fort Resolution	204	”
Hay River	279	”
Fort Providence	357	”
Fort Simpson	513	”
Wrigley	665	”
Fort Norman	817	”
Norman Wells	867	”
Fort Good Hope	990	”
Arctic Red River	1204	”
Fort McPherson	1258	”
Aklavik	1358	”
Tuktoyaktuk	1545	”

*Res-delta was a depot established during the war, but nothing remains to mark the location.

From Res-delta to Yellowknife is 100 miles, or 277 miles from Fort Smith. Rae is 80 miles farther. Rocher River is 227 miles from Fort Smith and Snowdrift 367 miles. Fort Liard is 200 miles up the river from Fort Simpson, Nelson Forks 274 miles, and Fort Nelson 400 miles. Up Great Bear River, small boats proceed about 45 miles from Fort Norman. Then follows an eight-mile portage, and about 45 more miles to Great Bear Lake. From here the shortest distance across the lake to Port Radium is about 200 miles, but the boats usually travel a more circuitous route.

Two other northern water routes may be mentioned, for though they do not involve transportation in the Mackenzie District, they are both operated by Mackenzie River Transport, a department of the Hudson's Bay Company, the largest water carrier in the North. The first of these routes is the one eastward along Lake Athabaska as far as Stony Rapids, 412 miles from Fort Chipewyan. When Goldfields was in operation, this was a very important route, but since the closing of that camp the route services merely two Hudson's Bay posts. However, this adds to the congestion at Waterways. The other route is on the Peace River from Peace River town to Vermilion Chutes, 350 miles. Before the coming of the railway to the Peace River country, service was operated on the Peace River as far west as Hudson's Hope, British Columbia. Also, on this river, boats were operated below the Chutes to the

Slave River. This service has now been abandoned, the one Hudson's Bay Company post[45] on this portion of the river now being reached by a portage road from Vermilion Chutes.

The upper river is the source of much greater difficulties than the lower river. There is a yarding difficulty at Waterways to begin with, and multiple barge loads have to be assembled some eight miles down from that place, the barges being taken individually from Waterways. Troubles occur all down the Athabaska River owing to shifting sandbars. Even on the early trips of the year, it is rare for any but the smallest motor boats to get through without going aground two or three times, each such event involving a delay of from one to several hours. But the greatest difficulties occur at the spot known as The Willows, on the channel now used of the Athabaska's delta into Lake Athabaska. At the end of the season the water gets very low here, in both 1944 and 1945 being little more than a foot and a half deep. As most of the feverish activity to get the freight through occurs as freeze-up is approaching, the delays here are very serious. Heroic measures have to be taken, including rushing every available boat in to help, so that their combined power may be able to push the barges ahead along the sandy bottom, towing from the shore, and partially unloading the barges. All these things mean several days' delay. The western end of Lake Athabaska is shallow, particularly when the wind is from the west, and ships may have to delay their crossing. The entrance to the Slave River[46] involves rapids, which are a source of trouble in the low-water season. In the spring the water here flows southward from the Peace River to Lake Athabaska. The remainder of the route down the Slave to Fitzgerald presents no serious difficulties to an experienced pilot.

The Willows difficulty is a very serious one. Little attempt has been made to rectify it other than by some dredging, but dredging does not seem to provide a solution to the problem. Probably only a large-scale engineering undertaking could solve the difficulty completely, but so far more speculation has been given to finding some alternative route to Great Slave Lake. However, such an alternative route would not be a water one.

A glance at the figures on the tonnage of freight moving north from Waterways will give some impression of the seriousness of the situation in the past few years. When the Mackenzie District was only a trapping country, less than a thousand tons of freight would be shipped north each season. The development of mining in the thirties caused the figure to jump to between fifteen and twenty thousand tons. In 1942 the Canol Project alone added some twenty thousand tons. After this the tonnages fell back to around twenty-five

[45]Little Red River.

[46]Known as Rivière des Rochers as far as the mouth of the Peace. This is not to be confused with Rocher River Post on Great Slave Lake.

thousand annually until 1945, when the rapid influx of people to Yellowknife caused them to start upward again. The Americans added two or three diesel boats and some barges to the river fleets, but ever since 1942 the available equipment has had to be strained to the utmost to get the freight through.

The lower river route has its difficulties too, but they are less serious than on the upper river. The Slave River from Fort Smith to Great Slave Lake is a meandering river, but as its minimum depth is about 5 feet no troubles are encountered. Storms on Great Slave Lake frequently delay ships for as much as a week, with an all-time record of nearly three weeks. Great Slave Lake, too, provides the key to the opening of the navigation season, for the ice in the rivers disappears long before it does in the lake.[47] As the ice is piled up at the entrance to the Mackenzie River for some time after the rest of the lake is clear, Yellowknife is reached each year before the points on the Mackenzie. Down the Mackenzie River itself there are four places with special navigation difficulties. The first of these is a stretch of fast water known as the Providence Rapids, a few miles above Fort Providence. This calls for expert pilotage, and the situation is made worse by the fact that buoys are not placed to mark the channel until after the first boats have gone through each year. The greater difficulties occur on the up-stream journey, where many of the boats are unable to push more than one barge at a time against the current. About seventy miles above Fort Simpson swift water begins again and continues nearly as far as the settlement. The most serious difficulty of all occurs about twelve miles from Fort Simpson at the spot known as Green Island Rapids. Here many boats and barges have been wrecked, and a large tonnage of freight has gone to the bottom of the river. One of the chief difficulties is that each year the ice shifts the large boulders on the river bed, so that a new channel has to be found each season. The other two bad spots both lie between Norman Wells and Fort Good Hope. These are the Sans Sault Rapids and the Ramparts, the latter a narrowing of the river and having the most picturesque scenery on the entire Mackenzie waterway. The serious difficulties are on up-stream journeys. In the earlier part of the season when the water is high, the Sans Sault is not troublesome but the Ramparts often involve attaching cables to the shore and pulling the boats through. On the other hand, in the low-water period at the end of the season the Ramparts can be negotiated without trouble, but the Sans Sault often becomes practically impassable.[48]

[47]The navigation season opens as a rule somewhere between June 10 and June 25. The opening is about a month earlier on the upper river. Freeze-up occurs usually in early October.

[48]These spots present the chief difficulties for experienced pilots. Inexperienced pilots are lucky to get through without a wreck, as was demonstrated by the Americans on the opening of work on the Canol Project. It has been said that only about one of every ten persons who train as pilots ever becomes successful.

Aside from the navigational hazards, waterways officials in the Mackenzie District are continually concerned about the depth of the water. This determines the loads that the barges can carry. In good years, barges can draw 4 to 4½ feet of water; though oldtimers assert that thirty years ago 5 feet was typical. In bad years such as 1938, 1944, and 1945 barges could be loaded to no more than 3 feet in the latter part of the season. A barge loaded to draw only 3 feet of water is carrying only about half the tonnage of freight of one loaded to over 4 feet.

The endeavour to keep the season open as long as possible during the past few years has resulted in many ships of the Mackenzie's fleet being frozen in during the winter at various places down the river. This causes delays in opening the season the following year, for crews have to go north to reach their ships, a rough overhauling must be done, the ship must make the long, slow trip to Fort Smith, and a more complete overhaul must be made before the ship can start again for the north with a load of freight. The Liard River route from the Alaska Highway has been used to hasten the start of these operations.

Both of the tributaries to the Mackenzie can take only small boats. The Liard River is deep enough at flood, but this occurs before navigation is open on the Mackenzie. By the time the first boat reaches Fort Simpson *via* the Mackenzie, the Liard has begun to recede, and it is shallow for the rest of the season. The Great Bear River requires small boats on each side of the portage in the middle, and a deeper draft vessel across the Lake.[49]

Two companies do most of the water carriage in the Mackenzie District. These are Mackenzie River Transport, a department of the Hudson's Bay Company, and Northern Transportation Company. The latter began as an off-shoot of Canadian Airways in 1931, was taken over by White Eagle Mines in 1934, and by Eldorado Mining and Refining in 1936. When the last-named company was expropriated by the Dominion government in January, 1944, Northern Transportation was taken over as well. Consolidated Mining and Smelting established a small fleet of its own in 1938, but in the following year this was absorbed into Mackenzie River Transport.

Some smaller water carriers also exist. The Yellowknife Transportation Company is the chief of these, and the only purely common carrier by water. This company is interested chiefly in freighting to Yellowknife, but goes elsewhere as business warrants. Dow (D'Aoust) Brothers, freetraders in the eastern part of Great Slave Lake, have the facilities for doing a small amount of water carriage. Lastly, the McInnes Products Corporation, whose primary

[49]A road was begun in 1945 running from the foot of the rapids (the western end) right through to the lake. When this is completed, the necessity for the second river boat trip with the extra freight handling involved will be eliminated.

15

business is shipping fish from Lake Athabaska[50] to American markets helps out usually in the end-of-the-season rush on the upper river.

The Hudson's Bay Company has always been interested in Mackenzie transportation to service its many trading posts, and gradually became a common carrier as well. When the *Mackenzie River,* with its cabins for passengers, was launched in 1908 the company was definitely in the transportation business. Since that time it has added three other steamships,[51] and various smaller vessels classed as motor ships, motor boats, and motor tugs. The steamships are built of wood and have stern paddle wheels. Until 1944 all of them burned wood as fuel, but the *Distributor* was converted to oil for the 1945 season. The *Mackenzie River,* which did not operate in 1945 as it was having its hull rebuilt, is also being changed to oil. The *Northern Echo,* which had been condemned by the government inspector, had to be brought back into use towards the end of the 1945 season. These four ships, while much the largest on the Mackenzie waterways, are perhaps not economical in that much of their space is devoted to passengers, a business which is passing to the airway. The smaller Mackenzie River Transport boats all use Diesel fuel, and are screw propelled. They are in the freight business exclusively.

Mackenzie River Transport operates on all the waterways mentioned above, with the exception of the Great Bear route, which is left exclusively to Northern Transportation. In addition, it operates in the Arctic Ocean from Tuktoyaktuk with the *M. V.*[52] *Fort Ross.* This company, because of its many trading posts, carries the bulk of the food and other trade goods into the Mackenzie District, and also transports mining equipment and supplies for certain companies, notably Consolidated Mining and Smelting. All in all it handles about two-thirds of the freight moving inward. South bound its chief freight consists of furs, but it has only about one-twelfth of the tonnage in this direction as it has going north.

Northern Transportation Company has no ships the size of Mackenzie River Transport's steamships, but it prides itself on the power of its two steel ships, the *Radium King* on the lower river, and the *Radium Queen* on the upper river. These have accommodation for only seven passengers each, and as the rest of Northern Transportation's fleet transport only freight, the company is very little concerned with the passenger business. The recent announcement that the government will spend a million dollars on new barges for Northern Transportation suggests that it is expected that the company will move much more freight than it has in the past. Northbound it carries all the freight for Port Radium and a great deal of that destined for various mining companies, but in

[50]In 1945 this company also began taking fish from Great Slave Lake.

[51]The *Distributor* on the lower river, and the *Athabasca River* and *Northern Echo* on the upper river. Note the spelling of "Athabasca" here.

[52]Motor vessel, a class above motor ship.

recent years has handled only a little over a quarter of all the northbound freight. However, Northern Transportation's loads are better balanced in the two directions, for besides the ores of Great Bear Lake it moves most of the oil upstream from Norman Wells. All in all it has nearly three-quarters of the southbound business, but this amounts to only about half its northbound tonnage. The fact that Northern Transportation is owned by the government has benefited its business only to the extent of the exclusive Port Radium trips.

Besides the Great Bear Route, Northern Transportation operates to Yellowknife and down the Mackenzie to Aklavik, with occasional trips as far as Reindeer Station. It does not compete on the Liard River or usually in eastern Great Slave Lake.

The rates by water on the Mackenzie are the only northern transportation rates which have been appreciably lowered during the past fifteen years. In 1930 the typical rate from Waterways to Aklavik was about $240 a ton. Now it is around $100. Competition does not seem to have had much to do with the reduction, the chief explanation seeming to lie with the much greater volume of traffic. There are minor contributing factors such as the change in management and policy of Mackenzie River Transport during the interval. The two major companies are in competition for only a very small part of the traffic, and certainly during the past few years have not had to offer rate concessions to attract business. Contracts tie up most of the business of the larger shippers with one company or the other. Until recently, rates varied greatly from shipper to shipper, and were determined on an individual contract basis. A general trend towards uniformity, however, has set in of late years, and reliance may be placed in the published rates being the actual rates charged. In 1945 the rates per 100 pounds from Waterways to important points were:

Fitzgerald	$0.75
Fort Smith	1.15
Yellowknife	1.90
Fort Simpson	3.40
Norman Wells	3.90
Aklavik	4.90

No rates are published to Port Radium.

The passenger business is of negligible importance, providing as a rule much less than 2 per cent of the total revenue. Because of the very variable duration of the long journey down the Mackenzie, charges for cabins and meals are usually separated from the transportation fare.

The Mackenzie does not hold out much possibility of tourist business. There is some appeal to jaded travellers who want to see something different, but the scenery is apt to be described as monotonous and the trip slow. Sixteen days is about the fastest time from Waterways to Aklavik, the return trip taking about twice as long. The *Distributor* normally is scheduled to make two round trips a year between Fort Smith and Aklavik, one being extended to Tuktoyaktuk. But if the season is late in opening, one trip is all that can be made the full distance.

The portage between Fitzgerald and Fort Smith consists of two closely parallel roads. The older of the two is operated by Northern Freighters, Ltd. (formerly Ryan Brothers). This company does all the hauling for Mackenzie River Transport. The second road, built in 1934, handled Northern Transportation's business, and was operated by Corser and Duncan. This road was greatly improved by the Americans. The road with Corser and Duncan's fleet of trucks was taken over by the Dominion government in 1944 along with Eldorado Mining and Refining Transportation. The charge for hauling freight between Fitzgerald and Fort Smith is $8.00 a ton.

Because of cramped quarters, Northern Transportation in 1945 moved its docks from Fort Smith eight miles down the river to its shipyard at Bell Rock. This increases the road haul from Fitzgerald to twenty-four miles.

Roads and Tractor Trains. Automobile roads in the Mackenzie District are all purely local. The two roads from Fitzgerald to Fort Smith, with one extended eight miles farther, are the longest now in use.[53] When the Great Bear River road is completed it will be some fifty-four miles long and the longest. Of the others, the only roads leaving the settlements are to the nearby airports and in the case of Yellowknife from the town to the mines which are close-in. Muskeg and the many lakes and rivers would present difficulties to highway building in the Mackenzie District, although the brush is easy to clear. However, no large highway schemes have as yet been proposed.

The low water of 1938 gave rise to an urgent need to get supplies to Yellowknife during the winter. An unimproved road ran north from Grimshaw, Alberta, for fifty or sixty miles, and continued on as a trail running northeastward to Fort Vermilion and then north-westward to Upper Hay River Post. From the last named place a trail which could be used by tractors was cut through beside the Hay River to the post of Hay River on Great Slave Lake. From here tractor trains crossed on the lake ice to Yellowknife. By 1942 this route had become practically unusable. But because of the urgency of getting the Canol supplies north without waiting for a new navigation season, the Americans once more brought this trail into use as a winter road. In addition from just south of Hay River, a winter road or trail was built to Fort Smith. In the other direction the road was extended to the Mackenzie River just below Mills Lake,[54] and continued on the other side some distance in from the river

[53]The Canol pipeline road was, of course, the longest in the Mackenzie District, but this is rapidly becoming unusable.

[54]Mills Lake is a widening of the river west of Fort Providence.

northward as far as Norman Wells. A trail of sorts had existed from Fort Nelson to Fort Simpson, and this was continued across the river to join the road leading to Norman Wells. The road north and west of Hay River was used in only one winter and is now presumably impassable. However, the route to Hay River has continued to be used.

Most of the latter lies within Alberta, but in 1945 an agreement was reached between the provincial and Dominion governments whereby the latter agreed to pay for an all-year road from Grimshaw to Hay River. A number of the contracts have already been let, and work on the road has commenced. This road should be of great significance to the Mackenzie District for it will provide an alternative means by which supplies can reach Great Slave Lake despite low water on the Athabaska River.

The tractor train now plays an important part in northern transportation. Unlike the placer mining of the Klondike which has to close when the creeks are frozen, the mines of the Mackenzie District operate throughout the year. Because of breakdowns and other unforeseen developments, some form of winter transportation is required.[55] The caterpillar tractor train has supplied the answer. Used regularly since 1938, tractor trains were very active in hauling supplies for the Canol Project, and have had a growing use ever since.

A standard tractor train[56] consists of a tractor, priced at around $10,000 pulling a number of 15-ton sleds[57] and a caboose. The crew consists of two drivers, two brakemen, and a cook. The train runs for the full twenty-four hours, and averages about fifty miles a day. Because of the difficulties in effecting repairs, an attempt is made to start each season with new tractors. The season does not begin until the ice on Great Slave Lake is at least 40 inches thick,[58] which usually occurs about the middle of January. Operations may be continued for about a hundred days. Rough ice is a continual problem, and extreme cold weather also makes for delays. Rivers are avoided if at all possible, as the ice on them varies too much in thickness. Tractor trains have to avoid all but the slightest grades.

Rates for tractor-train haulage are all matters of individual contracts. Typically, about 25 cents a ton mile is charged for lake haulage, and about 35 cents a ton mile for bush hauling.

[55]Tractor trains carry all sorts of freight, including food. But because it is an expensive means of transport, winter supplies whose need can be anticipated are usually brought in by water during the summer.

[56]This information was obtained from Mr. Harry Ingraham of Ingraham Brothers of Yellowknife, the principal tractor train operators. A company has been formed known as the Grimshaw-Yellowknife Transportation Company. This company, however, is not the sole operator of tractor trains.

[57]The record is twenty-eight.

[58]Later in the year, the ice frequently is more than 5 feet thick.

Canadian Pacific Air Lines.[59]   It is difficult to over-estimate the importance of the aeroplane to the north country, and particularly to the Mackenzie District. While Yukon Territory had its mining boom before the days of air travel, the Mackenzie District had to wait for transportation by air for all the mining development which has since taken place.   The exploratory and prospecting work necessary could scarcely have been done and continue to be done without the aeroplane.[60]   In an area of such great distances, the aeroplane alone has made possible the speedy travel so desirable and necessary in the North.   And aside from the mining industry, this means of transportation has been invaluable in doing away with much of the isolation of northern posts by providing them with frequent mail and parcel express service.

Yet, it must not be forgotten that air transportation is not the complete solution to the transportation problems of the North.   The aeroplane is likely to handle the greater part of the passenger business, the mails, and the light parcel service.   But it cannot as yet handle bulk freight except at prohibitive cost. The war showed us that aircraft could be built to carry large loads, but the factor of cost was ignored.   Costs certainly must be considered in commercial transportation.   The older water transportation must still be used to move the staple supplies into the North and the North's bulk production outside.   Moreover, air transportation as yet is not on a full twelve-months' basis to the many places in the North without landing fields for wheeled planes.   For planes equipped with floats in summer and skis in winter, there is a period of about a month in spring during break-up and another month in fall during freeze-up when operations must be suspended.   Exceptionally cold weather sometimes prevents flying altogether, or at best causes great difficulties.   In the late summer, bush fires can cause low ceilings and poor visibility which keep planes grounded for days and even weeks at a time.[61]   This latter situation occurs during the heaviest traffic period of the year, the outbound movement of late summer and early fall.   However, means of solving some of these difficulties are gradually being evolved, and it can be expected that they will have an ever-lessening importance in the future.

[59]Officials of C.P.A. were most helpful in answering questions.   While numerous writings of a journalistic sort dealing with northern flying have appeared in recent years, there does not seem to be any published work dealing with the *economic* peculiarities of northern flying as compared with air transportation in settled areas.   As with the White Pass and Yukon Route, Canadian Pacific Air Lines show sources of revenue and costs of operation which are far different from the usually expected standards for airways.

[60]Radio is entitled to some of the credit.

[61]Undoubtedly the Department of Transport safety rules are responsible for many flight cancellations.   The requirement that the weather must be suitable at both the point of departure and the point of destination is a very different thing from the "if you can see across the lake, chance taking off" rule of bush-pilot days.   Despite the fact that the early pilots had a remarkably low flying-accident rate, no one can quarrel with the D.O.T. rules.

Flying was first begun in the Mackenzie District in 1921, and by 1926 a start had been made on air-mail service. General air activity began about 1929 and gradually came into the hands of two companies, Canadian Airways, which also operated in other mining and pioneer areas in Canada, and Mackenzie Air Service. Most of the early flights were charter work, but regularly scheduled trips were gradually introduced. The two companies, both of which were coming more and more under Canadian Pacific control, were consolidated in 1941 as United Air Service, Ltd. In 1942 United became part of Canadian Pacific Air Lines. The close of the war has brought some independents into the field doing charter work out of Yellowknife. While there is certainly a field for additional air services, it is to be hoped that these newcomers will have sufficient financial backing to continue operations in an activity that has yet to show profits.

Seaplanes were used exclusively in the Mackenzie District until 1942. The many lakes and rivers of the District made these planes suitable, but airway officials realized very clearly that their cost of operation was roughly double that of wheeled planes.[62] However, the expense of building landing fields was a deterrent to change. It was not until the American activity on the Canol Project began, that wheeled-plane traffic was started in the district. The United States constructed airports at Fort McMurray, Embarras (an emergency landing-field beside the Athabaska River just south of Lake Athabaska), Fort Smith, Fort Resolution, Hay River, Fort Providence, Mills Lake, Fort Simpson, Wrigley, Norman Wells, and Canol Camp. In 1944 the Dominion government cleared a small landing-field at Yellowknife, which was enlarged in 1945 and connected by road with the town. In addition, radio beacons[63] have been installed and weather reports are given at all airports. While the Mackenzie District's airports are not up to the standard of those on the route through Whitehorse, they nevertheless make possible regular service by the larger wheeled-planes at all the points above enumerated. The remaining settlements of the Mackenzie District are still served by float-and-ski planes. Prospectors' charter trips are, of course, all done by float planes.

Regularly scheduled flights include a six-a-week service between Edmonton and Yellowknife, with weekly round trip flights between Yellowknife and Port Radium. Daily service has also been given between Edmonton and Norman Wells, some trips *via* Fort Smith and others *via* Fort Nelson and Fort Simpson. However, in the winter of 1945-6 this has been cut to a twice-a-month service. Float planes make round trips between Fort Smith and Aklavik about once a month, and Coppermine is reached from Yellowknife about four times a year.

---

[62]Taking into consideration the higher cost per unit weight, the greater consumption of fuel, the slower speed, the smaller revenue load in proportion to total weight, etc.

[63]Not radio range stations.

But, as is characteristic of northern airways, additional flights are frequently made as business warrants.

Canadian Pacific Air Lines, as has been typical of air transportation companies generally until very recent years, does not make public its accounts. Consequently, exact figures of revenues and costs may not be quoted, but a few peculiarities of C. P. A.'s operations may be noted. On the revenue side, C. P. A. makes about the same percentage of its gross earnings from its passenger business as does Trans-Canada Air Lines (nearly half), but the carriage of mails brings C. P. A. something less than a quarter of its total revenue, whereas T. C. A. has more than 40 per cent of its earnings from this source. However, C. P. A. has large earnings from express and freight (nearly 30 per cent of the whole), whereas T. C. A. gets only about 2¼ per cent of its revenue from the carriage of goods other than mail. C. P. A. also gets an appreciable revenue from chartering planes (about 5 per cent of the whole), while T. C. A. has virtually no earnings of this kind. On the other hand, T. C. A. receives a substantial revenue from services rendered for other airlines as well as incidental earnings from war contracts in its shops at Winnipeg. C. P. A. has nothing to match this. The combined domestic airlines of the United States earn about two-thirds of their revenue from passengers, one-fourth from mail, and the remaining twelfth chiefly from express.

Comparisons on the basis of operating revenue per mile flown is perhaps of more significance. Whereas, T. C. A. and the American lines during late years have averaged about $1.10 per mile flown, C. P. A.'s figure has been around 75 cents. Some of the reason for the difference is due to the large mileage flown by C. P. A. float planes, but of more importance is the seasonal nature of C. P. A.'s business. In the spring and early summer the bulk of the traffic is moving northward. Then, after a let down in mid-summer, a heavy rush southward begins which continues well on into the fall. There is a falling off in traffic in the winter. Thus, even in the seasons of strain, it is seldom possible to get capacity loads in both directions on round trip flights. This lack of balance in revenue loads in the two directions is something peculiar to northern flying and is not experienced by airlines operating in settled areas.

The two sources of revenue open to C. P. A. which are of trifling importance to other airlines are of interest. Air express in the North is even more expensive to the user than it is elsewhere, but its substantial volume is due to the much greater difference in time of delivery by air and by ground transportation, than is the case in settled districts. A certain amount of northern air express also arises from emergency reasons. But with the present cost of carrying freight by air, it is absurd to think of the aeroplane as solving the north's freight transportation problems.

Revenue from the charter service varies chiefly with prospecting activity.

The principal base is Yellowknife, from which point planes are chartered to carry prospectors and their equipment to points hundreds of miles away. There is no good substitute for the aeroplane for this purpose.

Turning to operating costs, C. P. A. compares very favourably with T. C. A. on the basis of costs per mile flown, although its figures are from 12 to 15 per cent higher than the average of the American lines. But some of the individual items are very different. C. P. A.'s costs are conspicuously high in flying operations and in aircraft maintenance. They are appreciably lower than the usual case in passenger service, traffic and sales, and advertising and publicity.

Flying operations are costly to C. P. A. chiefly because of expensive gasoline and oil. The inability to move these things to the various northern airports by rail greatly increases their cost to the airline. Sometimes they have to be flown in, which, besides being an expensive method of transportation also cuts down on the revenue weight which the planes can carry. The pipeline and the trucking on the Alaska Highway greatly improved the situation for C. P. A. on the Yukon flights, but in the Mackenzie District, despite Norman Wells, it is still difficult.

While most northern airports are equipped to do minor repair work, large maintenance depots are necessarily far apart. Regular periodic overhauls can be arranged to take place in Edmonton, but emergency work frequently requires men and spare parts to be flown long distances. Again, these things cut down on space for revenue business.

An additional expense not met with on other airlines is the necessity of building and operating staff houses for employees at northern points.

The biggest items of expense under the general heading "Passenger Service" of an airline are stewardess service, food for the passengers, and passenger liability insurance. C. P. A. is able to keep these costs below the typical ones largely by cutting down on the frills. C. P. A. also does not find it necessary to spend as much on the solicitation of business as do other airlines.

Fares and rates charged by Canadian Pacific Air Lines are higher than the usual airline rates, but this is to be expected in view of higher costs of operation. It may be noted that the present C. P. A. tariffs, aside from the 15 per cent government tax, are the same as those established during the nineteen-thirties.[64] Lower charges would be of no benefit to a company whose facilities are already strained to the limit. Higher charges, though perhaps leading to larger gross revenues,

[64]Examples of fares and rates are:

Edmonton to	One-way passenger fare (without tax)	Express rate per pound
Whitehorse	$85.00	$0.43
Yellowknife	110.00	0.50
Norman Wells	206.00	0.73

are impracticable in terms of the ill will they would create. Complaints about C. P. A. rates are frequent enough now, especially in the Mackenzie District where higher charges prevail than on the Yukon run. The difference is explained largely in terms of lower fuel and oil costs on the latter route. Residents of the Mackenzie District object more to the express rates than to the passenger fares, particularly in view of the fact that the Mackenzie District provides C. P. A. with the bulk of its express business.

The government's announcement of policy in March, 1944 to the effect that the railway companies of Canada would have to divest themselves of subsidiary airlines within a year of the end of the war, has created an uncertainty about Canadian Pacific Air Lines' future. The air transportation industry is somewhat peculiar in that investment in it has continued to grow rapidly despite regular losses on operation. While during the past three or four years, some companies have shown signs that at last the period of deficits seems to be at an end, this is certainly not true of Canadian Pacific Air Lines. Until some means can be found of bringing about substantial reductions in operating costs or radical changes in technology take place, there seems to be little prospect of operating northern flying services profitably. A new company with new equipment may not fare so badly in its initial stages while its maintenance costs are low, but inevitably it must run into regular losses. The thing that must not be allowed to happen is the suspension of service due to financial reverses. Somebody with large financial resources must be back of a northern airline to make up the losses and keep the planes in operation. The Canadian Pacific Railway Company is one such financial backer. The alternative seems to be only the Dominion government, probably through Trans-Canada Air Lines.

Communications in the Mackenzie District. The Mackenzie District has no telegraph lines. Such telephones as exist are not commercial. Typically they connect such things as a settlement with its airport. Two private telephone lines connect Fitzgerald and Fort Smith.

Rapid communication in the District is made by means of radio. Sending stations are very numerous. Formerly, many of them were operated by the Hudson's Bay Company and others, but now most of them have been taken over by the Royal Canadian Corps of Signals, which handles radiograms at rates which are not out of line with telegraph rates in the rest of the country. The Department of Transport and Canadian Pacific Air Lines also operate radio stations.

ADDENDUM

NOTE. The above was written in January, 1946. Changes in the northern transportation picture occur from time to time. Down to May, 1947, the following events of major importance have taken place: (1) By order of the Board of Transport Commissioners, the maximum rates on the Waterways branch of the Northern Alberta Railways have been reduced to the Prairie Standard Scale. (2) Mackenzie River Transport of the Hudson's Bay Company is planning to withdraw as a common carrier. The large outlays that would be required to modernize its fleet to the standard of Northern Transportation's new equipment is apparently responsible. (3) Canadian Pacific Air Lines have reduced appreciably their rates and fares. The table in foot-note 64 should now read:

Edmonton to	One-way passenger fare (without tax)	Express rate per pound
Whitehorse	$ 75.00	$0.43
Yellowknife	80.00	0.29
Norman Wells	144.20	0.73

It may be noted, also, that C. P. A.'s financial return showed a large improvement in 1946.

Part Eight

G. J. WHERRETT

Health Conditions and Services in the North-West

The Scope of the Survey. The survey was confined to Mackenzie District. The places visited were Fort Smith, Fort Resolution, Hay River, Fort Providence, Fort Simpson, Norman Wells, Fort Good Hope, Arctic Red River, Fort McPherson, Aklavik, Yellowknife, and Port Radium. Fort Norman and Rae were not visited, but information in regard to these was obtained from medical officers for these areas. All but one doctor in the area were interviewed. The hospitals and schools were visited and the authorities in charge were most co-operative in supplying information. Useful interviews were had with the clergy, R.C.M.P., R.C.C.S., Hudson's Bay Company officials, independent traders, oil and mine operators, and many other residents of the Territories. The officials of the North West Territories Council and of the Indian Affairs Branch were most helpful. It is regretted that the visit did not coincide with any treaty trips by Indian doctor agents, but it was possible to observe and examine patients in hospitals and children remaining in the schools for the summer, and many of the native population visiting the medical officers or within easy access to the centres. It was felt that a clear picture was obtained of health conditions and health services and the problems in this land of great distances.

One is filled with admiration at the courage and devotion of the missions, which have laboured for many years to bring Christianity to the area and to carry health and healing also. It is with a feeling of pride that one notes the work of the medical officers who, without adequate transportation, are attempting to give medical care to the small scattered population of an area which, including the Eastern Arctic, comprises two-fifths of the land area of Canada. The record of accomplishment is an impressive one. It is to be regretted that it is not better known to outsiders, who are apt to hear only of unsatisfactory conditions that tend to make the headlines. Some of these are bad—notably the situation in regard to tuberculosis. No one knows this better than officials of the Department of Mines and Resources, and it is to be noted that the survey was suggested in a spirit of self-criticism by the Department, which implies that it is an accepted fact that improvements are needed to bring to these people services that can approach, in some measure,

229

those which are the right of every Canadian and which white residents of the nine provinces enjoy.

This report will attempt to give a picture of conditions in the Mackenzie River district from the standpoint of health services. To do this it will include the geographical distribution of the population, health statistics, and medical and hospital services. It will try to point out the gaps in such services and give suggestions that seem to be practical as to how these services can be improved.

The Population of the North West Territories. The 1941 census gives the figures of 12,028 for this area. These were classified as 4,052 Indian, 5,404 Eskimo, and 2,284 white. There were 282 listed as half-breeds. The Indians and Eskimos are about equal as to sex distribution, but in the white population the males outnumber the females three to one. The number of white residents in the area has increased since 1941, with the oil development at Norman Wells, gold at Yellowknife, and radio-active substances at Port Radium. The Eskimos are to be found mainly in the Eastern Arctic, there being 1,582 as listed in the Western Arctic, with 3,822 elsewhere. Those do not include an additional 1,965 as listed for Ungava and northern Quebec. The actual population of the Mackenzie valley and Western Arctic areas is evidently, then, about 8,038, with whatever increase has taken place since 1941.[1]

The population of the Mackenzie area is scattered throughout the territory. The number of people living in, or adjacent to, the settlements is listed in Table I. It will be noted how widely separated these settlements are and how great is the problem of providing medical and hospital services.

TABLE I

POPULATION OF THE MACKENZIE AREA, 1941

	Total	White	Indian	Eskimo
Aklavik and district...............	757	167	213	377
Fort McPherson and district........	325	17	308	...
Arctic Red River..................	129	11	118	...
Fort Good Hope and district.......	351	14	337	...
Fort Norman and district..........	264	63	200	1
Wrigley and district...............	83	6	77	...
Fort Simpson and district..........	454	76	378	...
Fort Liard and district	216	14	202	...
Fort Providence and settlement.....	415	39	376	...
Hay River and district.............	164	16	147	1
Fort Resolution and district........	635	136	499	...
Rae and district...................	767	81	686	...
Reliance and district...............	94	9	85	...
Great Bear Lake	175	1	174	...
Fort Smith and district............	531	241	290	...

[1]These were classified as 4,052 Indians (plus 282 half-breeds), 5,404 Eskimo, and 2,284 whites (162 of whom live in the Eastern Arctic).

In addition to the centres listed in Table I there are the population centres of Norman Wells, Yellowknife, and Port Radium, where a white population has developed in connection with oil projects and mining companies, each having its own medical and hospital services.

Health Administration in the North West Territories. The health policy from the territorial standpoint is directed from Ottawa by the Commissioner,[2] through the resident doctors who are also medical officers of health, while the health of the Indians is the responsibility of the Indian Affairs Branch, as in the provinces. Ordinances are passed by Council to deal with the various problems that arise from time to time, e.g., the Sanitary Control Ordinance, the Venereal Disease Ordinance, and the Workman's Compensation Ordinance. The Vital Statistics Ordinance covers the registration of births, marriages, and deaths in the Territories. A sanitary survey was carried out in 1938 in many of the centres for the Council by officials of the Department of Pensions and National Health, and reports and recommendations were made available. This was most helpful and should be repeated as soon as possible.

It is the writer's conviction that it would be of advantage to consolidate these ordinances into a health code to cover public health in the Territories, and to be administered by a Chief Health Officer for the Territories. Frequent consultations between the Chief Health Officer and the local doctors would lead to more uniformity in measures to improve sanitation, encourage immunization, study nutrition, and develop a tuberculosis-control programme.

Morbidity and Mortality. The background for the picture of illness and death is set forth in the data supplied by the Vital Statistics Branch of the Bureau of Statistics (Table II). To those who can read between the figures, these tables set out in bold relief the particular health problems of the area. After reading that the tuberculosis rate is 415, as compared to 52.8 for the rest of Canada; diseases of the first year 99.8 as compared to 54; puerperal causes 16.2 as compared to 7.8; pneumonia 141.3 as compared to 51.8; it is with relief that one reads that most of the infectious diseases do not occur in the Territories. In the five years (1937-41) there were no deaths from measles and scarlet fever, and only one death from diphtheria. There were, however, some deaths from whooping cough and typhoid. This brighter side of the picture provides only limited comfort and carries with it a warning. Sooner or later, these diseases will make their appearance, with air transportation linking these centres with the outside, with the white population coming in as it has done during the war, and as oil and mining operations increase. While this survey was in progress this danger was emphasized by the report of an epidemic of diphtheria at Eskimo Point, with 48 deaths out of 170 cases. This shows what an epidemic can do in a native population in which no im-

[2]Now handled by the Department of National Health and Welfare.

munization measures had been carried out. There were a few cases of mumps and chickenpox at Fort Smith and Resolution, but they seem to have been confined to this area.

TABLE II

DEATH-RATES IN THE NORTH WEST TERRITORIES FROM CERTAIN SPECIFIED CAUSES
PER 100,000 POPULATION, FIVE-YEAR AVERAGE. 1937-41

(Rates computed on preliminary census figures for 1941)

Causes of death	All races	White	Indian	Eskimo
Typhoid fever†	16.6	....	*	37.0
Scarlet fever	....	....	....	....
Whooping cough	8.3	....	23.1	....
Diphtheria	*	....	....	*
Tuberculosis, all forms	415.7	43.7	761.4	314.6
Influenza	83.1	43.7	23.1	148.0
Measles	....	....	....	....
Cancer and other malignant tumours	16.6	43.7	*	18.5
Diabetes mellitus	8.3	43.7	....	....
Anaemias	*	....	....	*
Meningitis (non-meningococcal)	8.3	....	*	18.5
Intracranial lesions of vascular origin ⎫ Hemiplegia and other paralysis of ⎬ unspecified organs ⎭	8.3	....	*	*
Convulsions (under five years of age)	....	....	....	....
Diseases of the heart	41.6	87.3	46.1	18.5
Diseases of the arteries	8.3	*	....	*
Bronchitis	16.6	....	23.1	18.5
Pneumonia	141.3	*	115.4	203.6
Diarrhoea and enteritis	16.6	....	46.1	*
Appendicitis	8.3	*	....	*
Hernia, intestinal obstruction	8.3	*	....	*
Nephritis	*	....	*	*
Diseases of the prostate	....	....	....	....
Puerperal causes	16.6	....	25.1	18.5
Congenital malformations	8.3	....	*	*
Diseases peculiar to the first year of life	99.8	43.7	46.1	166.5
Senility	49.9	43.7	*	92.5
Suicides	16.6	43.7	*	18.5
Homicides	8.3	*	*	*
Other violent deaths	158.0	174.7	69.2	222.1
Other specified causes	149.7	43.7	92.3	259.1
Ill-defined or unknown causes of death	374.1	43.7	115.4	740.2
Total (exclusive of stillbirths)	1,687.7	611.4	1,453.6	2,231.6

*Less than 0.1 per 100,000 population.
†Including paratyphoid.

Venereal diseases, according to all reports, have not been a great problem in the Territories heretofore. With the coming of troops to this area, cases have been developing at Fort Smith and to a less extent in other areas. Every effort is being made to bring this problem under control. The ordinance respecting the prevention of venereal disease gives medical officers adequate authority to deal with the problem. Treatment is at public expense and is compulsory. A territory so adequately served by the R.C.M.P., and in which the residents are so law-abiding, must be the envy of health departments elsewhere in Canada.

The high rate for tuberculosis has already been mentioned; 415.7 per 100,000 for all races, as compared with 52 for Canada; 761.4 per 100,000 for Indians, which is fifteen times the rate for the white population, about the same as for Indians in the rest of Canada. It is 314.6 for the Eskimos. There is good reason to believe that these rates would be higher if figures included deaths from tuberculosis from the group listed as "ill-defined and un-specified." This is the group where there was no doctor in attendance. Doctors and others expressed the opinion that many of these were also tuberculous. These figures clearly indicate that tuberculosis is the greatest health problem in the Territories. Its incidence is probably higher in the Indian population than in this same group elsewhere in Canada. This is further borne out by reports from doctors, missions, R.C.M.P., and citizens generally throughout the area. While in the main the disease assumes the pulmonary form, there are many cases of tuberculous meningitis, and glandular and bone tuberculosis are common. There is some reason to think that this is evidence that the epidemic of tuberculosis has not been so long in operation in the Territories as in other parts of Canada, as these forms tend to become less in proportion as time goes on.

No doubt the high rates for pulmonary tuberculosis and other respiratory diseases also are influenced by climatic conditions in the Territories and the mode of life of the natives. One can imagine the close confinement, poor ventilation, and intimate contact inevitably to be found during the long winter months. It will be apparent to anyone that an open case of tuberculosis would infect all the other members of the family.

There is no denying that the rate is a terrific one and much concern is shown by all residents of the Territories. There is closer mingling of the white population and natives than in the rest of Canada, and considerable anxiety is shown on the part of white residents with children as to the possibilities of contracting tuberculosis in this highly infected environment.

The condition in the North West Territories serves to emphasize the urgency of the whole problem of the native population and tuberculosis. A vigorous programme is needed, not only to save the Indian and Eskimo from this scourge brought by the explorers, traders, and settlers, but to save the white children of today from the disease introduced by their forefathers.

One frequently hears it stated that the death-rate from tuberculosis is so great that the Indians are dying out in the Territories. While conditions are particularly bad in certain areas with a dwindling of the individual bands as at Good Hope and Rae, there has, in general, been an increase in population, as shown by the records of the Department for the individual bands from 1939 to 1943. There was an increase from 3,757 to 3,955 during these years. It must be remembered that the change in population is not accounted for by births and deaths only, as transfers, enfranchisements, etc., are included in the population in 1939 and 1942.

Medical Officers. Medical officers are stationed at Fort Smith, Fort Resolution, Fort Simpson, Fort Norman, and Aklavik. These are full-time government employees and are also Indian Agents, with the exception of those at Fort Smith and Aklavik. They are also health officers for the respective districts. They attend the natives, indigent whites, or half-breeds. They attend the white population on a fee basis. At the time of the survey, medical and hospital services were being provided by the United States Army at Norman Wells and Canol to the men working on the oil project. A doctor is also situated at Yellowknife, who is employed by the mining companies and who is also medical officer for the town, and his services are available on a part-time basis to the Department. A doctor is also employed by the Eldorado Mining and Refining at Port Radium.

There is no doubt that each and every doctor is performing invaluable services, but their districts are too large, with the transportation provided. When it is remembered that distances are often up to three hundred miles between settlements and the means of transportation are still dog teams and boats, with an occasional chartered plane, it can be realized that they are often asked to perform impossible tasks. The doctors at Fort Resolution, Fort Simpson, and Aklavik have cabin boats, which are used for inspection trips and in the course of their duties. These boats provide a relatively slow method of travel, and are now an inefficient and outmoded means of transportation of medical personnel. One of the first requirements is a plane service available to the medical staff, so that emergencies can be handled promptly and regular visits made to all settlements. Medical officers have too many administrative duties in addition to medical work. Either non-medical agents or assistants should be appointed, so that the doctors can have full time for medical duties.

It is strongly recommended that the whole service be reorganized with a full-time director in charge, with authority to carry out the programme laid down by the Department. At present, each doctor is responsible directly to Ottawa and there is lack of uniformity as to duties and health measures carried out. The director should be located at Fort Smith, be free to devote his full time to the direction of medical policy, and have transportation available, to visit all districts annually and to outline the general programme to be carried out.

The qualifications of medical officers, having in mind the specific problems of the North, should stress the following points. They should be able to provide average medical care and should have a fair knowledge of public-health practice and at least a year's experience in tuberculosis. They should be able to interpret x-ray plates and have a working knowledge of the treatment of tuberculosis, including the use of pneumothorax. Medical officers should be allowed to visit outside medical centres for refresher courses every three years to keep fully informed on medical thought and practice.

The tuberculosis problem requires special attention. There is need for a sanatorium of fifty beds at Fort Smith. The same building could also house the medical director. The local hospitals throughout the area should be used for the treatment of tuberculosis. They should serve as diagnostic centres and as a clearing house from which patients could be sent to the central institution. This will be further discussed in connection with hospital facilities. There should be a staff member who would be in charge of tuberculosis work in the Territories. He should not only direct the sanatorium, but organize early diagnosis surveys throughout the territory. Portable x-ray equipment is available, complete with its own power, which can be obtained for approximately $1,500, and which could be used throughout the year and transported, if necessary, by plane.

Hospital Services. The hospitals are mainly operated in the Territories by the missions of both the Church of England in Canada and the Roman Catholic Church. This applies to the two hospitals at Aklavik and the hospitals at Fort Simpson, Fort Resolution, Rae, and Fort Smith. In addition, there is a small nursing home (not operating at the time of the visit) with a registered nurse in charge, in connection with the school at Hay River. The Indian Affairs Branch now operates the hospital at Fort Norman.[3] A mining company owns and operates the hospital at Yellowknife, and a small hospital is to be constructed shortly by the Eldorado Mine at Port Radium.

The Government of Canada has contributed towards the construction costs of some of the mission hospitals and also pays a fixed amount per day for each native, indigent white, or half-breed receiving treatment. These hospitals have operating-room facilities. The hospitals at Fort Smith and Aklavik have x-ray equipment, but the others have not. Practically no laboratory equipment is to be found and very little laboratory work is done, except at the hospitals at Fort Smith and Resolution. The hospital at Yellowknife is as well equipped as to operating room, maternity room, x-ray and laboratory, as hospitals of similar size in other parts of Canada. As Table III shows, there is no lack of hospital beds available in the Territories.

One is amazed at the number of hospital beds which are to be found in the Mackenzie River area and appalled at what little use is made of them. In the

---

[3]Burned down in February, 1946.

Yukon and the North West Territories, the ratio of hospital beds per 1,000 population (30.1) is four times that of British Columbia, which has the highest hospital bed complement of all the provinces. But in the Territories there are, on the average, at least 150 beds, or two-thirds of the total, unoccupied every day of the year. When these hospitals were visited, they were practically empty. As an example, at Aklavik, where the two mission hospitals provide seventy-five beds, there were only five patients under treatment. It is true that it was the period of the year when the hospitals have the fewest number of patients, but a study of the records shows that only on rare occasions, such as the influenza epidemic of last year, are the beds at anything like full occupancy. One feels that there has been a lack of overall planning in the construction of these hospitals, and certainly duplication in the case of Aklavik. On the other hand, the writer feels that the missions have been sincere in

TABLE III

HOSPITAL BEDS IN THE NORTH WEST TERRITORIES*

Fort Smith (R.C. mission hospital)	43	beds
Fort Resolution " " "	26	"
Rae " " "	30	"
Fort Simpson " " "	35	"
Aklavik " " "	25	"
Aklavik (Anglican mission)	48	"
Fort Norman (Indian Affairs Branch)	10	"
Yellowknife (Consolidated Mining and Smelting Company)	16	"
Total	233	"

*There are, in addition, sick bays at Hay River and Providence in connection with the schools.

their efforts to bring hospital services to the people, and the Department has been singularly lacking in providing leadership and advice in location, construction, services rendered, and equipment.

If these were built to be used only as general hospitals, there are obviously too many beds. While we realize the difficulties of treating tuberculosis in general hospitals, some effort should be made to salvage this wastage and turn it to account in meeting the major health problem of the area, which is tuberculosis. It is a violation of all health principles to have within the community empty hospital beds, while there are open cases of tuberculosis spreading infection in the homes.

This is a challenge to the Department and to the hospitals. The Department should pay the cost without penny pinching, and the hospitals should give a service and create an atmosphere which will induce patients to accept treatment and to remain as long as necessary. It would appear that the medical staff should be increased and that grants should be made to improve hospital equipment and services. The medical officers should have full charge of the medical care, including admissions and discharges. There should be a long-term programme: (1) to educate the Indian to accept treatment; (2) to train nursing and medical personnel to care for this type of case.

One fears that it has been the policy of the Department (and this is borne out by opinions expressed in the Territories) to reduce expenditures by discouraging the admission of patients and encouraging the care of these people in their homes. It is obvious that such a policy will never solve the problem of such an infectious disease as tuberculosis. As long as a native is born, lives, and dies in an atmosphere of contagion, and with the standard of living what it is, tuberculosis will continue to wreak havoc in these areas.

Health and the Mission Schools. All the mission schools in the Territories were visited. While classes had been discontinued for the summer months, a number of the children were still in residence. The condition of the buildings and classrooms was good and health of the children in residence was excellent. There were a number of children with old quiescent tuberculous bone and gland lesions.

The school authorities reported that the health of the children improves during the school term as a general rule. On admission, there is evidence of malnutrition that improves on regular diet and routine of the school. In practically every school visited it was reported, however, that cases of tuberculosis develop during the term, resulting fatally. This brings up the question of health examination and supervision. While tuberculous infection in the school environment must be less than at home, nevertheless, every effort should be made to eliminate the possibility of open cases being present among the pupils at any time during the year, since contact is so intimate that the spread of infection must readily take place.

As a general rule, medical officers inspect the schools and treat any children who are ill. Only in the minority of instances, however, is there a regular examination of all children on admission and no x-ray surveys are carried out. In some schools, immunization and vaccination are practised; in others, not at all. One cannot stress too strongly the importance of all these procedures.

Inquiry was made as to diet, and menus submitted seemed adequate. Cod-liver oil is provided by the Department and given from September to April. Diet problems present difficulties in a country where, during the long winter months, there is little sunlight, and fresh vegetables and fruits are hard to obtain. It is essential that an adequate supply of vitamins be given at all times. Information derived from studies on nutrition that the Department has made should be utilized to work out a standard diet for all schools.

The Department should give careful study to the problems of health conditions in the schools. Health examinations, including x-ray, immunization, adequate diets, and health education, should be a routine practice in all schools. X-ray facilities are available in both hospitals in Aklavik and these should be utilized. One of the duties of a chief health officer would be the development and supervision of the school health programme.

Medical Services in Outlying Centres. This problem is undoubtedly one of the most difficult ones to solve since it is quite out of the question to supply medical services for such places as Fort Good Hope, Arctic Red River and Fort McPherson, Wrigley, Fort Providence, Hay River, and other centres at the eastern end of Great Slave Lake. There is no question, however, that these places could be given better service than at present with plane transportation available to the medical services of the region. In many instances situations arise which appear to be emergencies, entailing chartered planes and mercy flights. Some of these are emergencies, but in many instances the condition has been present for weeks and months, and it is evident that regular visits would prevent many useless emergency flights. "To save a life" is something that always appeals to the imagination, and pilots and medical men will risk their lives in bad weather, when too often the situation has existed for weeks and knowledge of conditions would forestall it.

It would be a great help and a practical step to have established first-aid posts in many of these centres, even if only for a part of the year. The nursing outpost at Hay River is a good example. Here a trained nurse and midwife have been rendering a great service to the people for many years. One would like to see more of these centres established.

More consideration should be given to training of native women in first aid and care of the sick. A start was made in this matter at Aklavik and several native girls were given instruction with this in view. It seems evident that such personnel will require more preliminary education than has been given heretofore, longer training, and some supervision in their community centres. Such a plan would require the co-operation of the schools in choosing the more promising pupils, a more carefully thought-out course of training by the hospitals, and supervision from mercy outposts and first-aid centres. Such a plan is likely to fall short of its objective without more public-health and social workers to undertake a plan of health instruction in the various community centres.

The Lack of Medical and Nursing Services. The proportion of deaths which occur without the skilled attention of either a doctor or a nurse is appalling. The figures from the Bureau of Statistics for the five years from 1937 to 1941 are shown in Table IV. It is to be noted that the greatest proportion of these is to be found among the Eskimo population, which is 84 per cent, but the figures are 48 per cent in the Indians and 37 per cent in the white population.

The question might be asked as to whether there is any provision in outlying centres for emergency medical attention. In actual fact, the natives have been trained over the years to look for help in the following order from residents of the territory. They first seek the doctor if available, failing that the R.C.M.P., then the missionaries and the traders. Where no doctor is available, the Mounted Police and others have performed gallant services in rendering the only medical attention given. They have attended every type of case from simple conditions to that of difficult labour. In paying tribute to these people, special mention should be made of the wives. Fortunate indeed are those communities where one of these happens to be a graduate nurse.

The North-West is a colourful country. Everywhere you go you see first the Hudson's Bay Company with its distinctive architecture, buildings well painted in white and red, the name and trademark well displayed. The R.C.M.P. also immediately catches the eye, with its buildings, the flag ever displayed, and the mounties in their distinctive uniform. The administration or the medical services are apt to be in the background. Trade and law are thus represented at every post. Are medical services less important? Should

TABLE IV

	Total deaths	Without doctor or nurse	
		Number	Per cent
Total population..........	1,217	840	69
White "	74	28	37
Indian "	399	192	48
Eskimo "	729	613	84

(Not stated: Deaths 15; died without a doctor or nurse—7.)

not the Department have at every post a distinctive building that would house the administration and the medical services? This may seem a small point, but one has a feeling that the respect paid to the Hudson's Bay Company and the R.C.M.P. has been increased by the touch of showmanship which they have used to good advantage throughout the years, and which others dealing with the Indian might well emulate.

It is impossible to make such a survey without being imbued with the same enthusiasm as that shown by others who have visited the North. It is a vast country, more important to Canada than many of us realize. The war has taught us something of its importance from the standpoint of defence. Post-war aviation routes may well reveal its importance in international flying. Its resources of fur, oil, fish, and minerals have only been touched. While prophecies of a huge population developing quickly can be discounted, there is every likelihood that the number of people will grow steadily and more and more white families will go into the North and will need health, welfare, and educational services—the right of every Canadian.

The people of the North are impressive. Their integrity, stability, and courage win the confidence and admiration of an outsider. Anyone who lives there—white, Indian, or Eskimo—and carries on his or her work, whether it is the government officials, the missionaries, doctors, Mounted Police, miners, trappers, or traders, is doing a tremendous work for Canada and the country owes them a debt far out of proportion to the size of the population. The cost of services which they require should never be estimated on the same basis as the same service elsewhere, even if these should cost double the equivalent services in other parts of the Dominion.

Solution of Socio-Economic Problems Important. Although this report deals only with medical services, it must be stated that health cannot be divorced from socio-economic conditions and a health programme will fail if, at the same time, efforts are not made to improve the economic status of these people. This question crops up in every discussion. Progress will be continually blocked unless the Indian's age-old habit of spending all his money as soon as he gets it can be changed, or some system devised whereby the money which he receives be spread over the twelve months of the year. If this were done, it would provide for most of his needs.

It should also be borne in mind that similar conditions and problems are to be found in other northern areas of Canada, and in fact, wherever there are Indians. These problems demand attention just as much as those of the far North. The Indian problem is on the conscience of the Canadian people until more action is taken. It is high time that the Department formulated a health policy founded on the needs of the people, rather than the meagre sum that "Treasury Board" will allow it to put in the estimates. Such a policy is an essential part of a larger programme which should be instituted and which would rehabilitate the Indian and bring him into full Canadian citizenship, as was envisaged when the first Indian policy was formulated.

RECOMMENDATIONS

In making recommendations to improve health services, I have tried to determine what is practical and can be developed on a permanent basis. Very few of them are original. They have nearly all been made by officials of the Department, both in Ottawa and from residents of the Territories. They have all been discussed with the people with whom I came in contact and there was a singular unanimity of opinion as to their urgency and necessity.

These recommendations could be put into practical operation with a moderate expenditure of public funds. The capital expense called for is the construction of a small sanatorium, which would also be used to house the administration office. It also includes the cost of a plane. The remainder of the expense involved is for increased personnel and to improve services in hospitals already built. To this must be added the cost of treating an additional number of patients.

(1) The medical services of the North West Territories should be reorganized into one service with the appointment of a full-time director,

resident in the Territories. His duties would be to formulate a health policy to be carried out in all districts.

(2) Medical services should be divorced from administration, so that medical officers will have full time for medical duties.

(3) An additional medical officer should be appointed at Rae, and possibly Coppermine. Although Fort Chipewyan is not in the Territories, the doctor at Fort Smith at present is responsible for this area. An additional medical officer is required to serve the Athabaska area in Alberta.

(4) Medical officers should possess the following minimal qualifications: (a) ability to provide general practitioner's service and to deal with surgical emergencies; (b) one year's experience in diagnosis and treatment of tuberculosis, and ability to read x-ray films and give pneumothorax treatments; (c) a general knowledge of public-health administration and practice. Medical officers should be permitted and indeed required to visit medical centres outside the Territories every three years for refresher courses to acquaint themselves with current medical and public-health practice. Medical officers in the North West Territories should be given a higher classification than officers engaged in similar work in other parts of Canada.

(5) A plane service should be made available to the medical services of the area, so that regular visits could be made to all centres and to deal with emergencies that arise. Such services should consist of a Norseman plane, experienced northern pilot and mechanic, and be based in the Territories.

(6) All hospital services should be brought up to a uniform standard, hospitals to be provided with adequate operating-room, laboratory and x-ray facilities. Medical officers should have charge of all admissions and discharges and should decide medical policy. Additional grants should be made, if necessary, to bring all hospitals up to uniform standard.

(7) A tuberculosis officer should be appointed for the area, and a sanatorium be built and operated at Fort Smith by the Department to serve as the centre for diagnosis and treatment. Clinics for early diagnosis should visit all centres annually. This could be done by staggering Indian treaty trips and utilizing portable x-ray equipment, able to generate its own power if necessary.

Hospitals should be used for treatment of tuberculosis. There are approximately 150 empty beds throughout the area that could be used for treatment, suitable cases being sent to the sanatorium. Every effort should be made to persuade the Indians to take institutional treatment and thus remove open cases from the settlements. If this fails, compulsory treatment should be instituted; but before this is resorted to, the treatment provided should be above criticism.

(8) Nursing and First Aid Centres should be introduced at points where population does not justify a resident doctor, e.g., Fort Good Hope, Arctic Red River, Fort McPherson, Fort Providence, Fort Liard, and Reliance.

(9) Medical officers should undertake regular visits to schools, to conduct annual examination, including x-ray examination, of all pupils. No active cases of tuberculosis should be permitted to remain in schools. Vaccination and immunization should be carried out. Standard diet for the schools should be outlined and uniformly provided.

(10) Dental services should be made available to the area.

(11) Nutritional studies and surveys now undertaken by the Department should be extended to the North West Territories.

Part Nine

ANDREW MOORE

Education in the Mackenzie District

THE duties assigned to the writer, as his part in the project of the Canadian Social Science Research Council for the study of the Canadian Arctic, were: (a) to visit Indian Residential and Day Schools as well as non-denominational schools for children who are not wards of the Dominion Government; (b) to survey all educational facilities and activities; (c) to make recommendations for improving educational services. In pursuing this assignment during the months of July and August, 1944, the localities were visited in the following order: (a) Fort Smith, (b) Norman Wells, (c) Arctic Red River, (d) Aklavik, (e) Fort McPherson, (f) Fort Good Hope, (g) Fort Simpson, (h) Fort Providence, (i) Hay River, (j) Fort Resolution, (k) Yellowknife, (l) Port Radium. Thanks to a very complete list of key people provided by the Department of Mines and Resources, it was possible to meet those who knew most about the matters under investigation and who, without exception, were most co-operative and anxious to provide all relevant information and all possible assistance.

Curriculum. As a result of contacts with traders, trappers, miners, engineers, oil operatives, transportation personnel, R.C.M.P., clergymen, teachers, and natives, including some of mixed blood, two extreme points of view were evident concerning the education of natives who are wards of the government.[1]

More than one old-time resident of the Mackenzie District is of the opinion that Indians are better off without any of the white man's schooling. Two criticisms of the effect on the Indian of the white man's schools as at present conducted are: (1) that the Indian boys when they return to their native bands after four or five years of such schooling are not nearly as competent as trappers or in general in their natural environment as boys who never left the bands; and (2) that the boys who attended the white man's school are neither good Indians nor good whites. Some old-timers claimed that the most unscrupulous and unreliable among the Indians were those who as boys had attended the white man's schools. Nearly everyone interviewed had a good word for the girl graduates of the white man's schools. For example, one old

---

[1] In this report they will be called "Indians," which term will include both the "Indian" and the "Non-Treaty Indian" as defined in the Indian Act (R.S.C., 1927, chap. 98, sec. 2). All other individuals having a mixture of Indian and any other blood will be referred to as being of mixed blood.

trapper confided that whenever he was forced by the weather or other emergency to remain temporarily with a band of Indians he always sought refuge with a family where the woman had gone to school.

On submitting these criticisms to members of the clergy and teachers operating Indian schools, their answers were definite and concrete. They admitted that at first an Indian boy who had spent four or five years in a residential school was not likely to be as good a trapper or as efficient in the life of an Indian generally, but they claimed that almost invariably after a year or two spent with his band he was more efficient than were boys who had not gone to school. They also remarked that a large proportion of the Indian boys who had been to school had not returned to their bands but had made good in wider spheres of activity. On request several schools provided lists of former schoolboys who have made good as trappers, as guides, on boat crews, as interpreters, etc. With respect to the second criticism the reply was that by far the greater majority of former boy-pupils lead exemplary lives but that the relatively few who go wrong receive a great deal of publicity.

Some who were consulted expressed the other view that Indian children were entitled to the same educational opportunities found elsewhere in Canada, in order that they might, in due course, assume the full responsibilities of Canadian citizens.

Under the present conditions in Mackenzie District, it seems to me that the path to follow lies between these two extremes. Whether we like it or not, white man's civilization is thrusting itself upon these natives at a rapidly increasing rate and appropriate educational measures should be adopted. It is more than likely, however, that more than one generation will be required to fit them to assume the full responsibilities of citizenship.

A middle-of-the-way curriculum is therefore desirable for the natives of Mackenzie District at the present stage of their development. This curriculum should have two main objectives. First, it should include as much of the white man's knowledge and behaviour as will assist them to enjoy a more abundant and efficient life in their own environment. Secondly, it should equip them to cope satisfactorily with the impact of the white man's civilization upon their lives not only at the present moment but also with the long-range objective of gradually enabling them to utilize as much of his civilization as will function satisfactorily in their changing world. It is essential that they become, ultimately, self-respecting and self-supporting Canadian citizens no longer under the tutelage of the government. The fundamental principle cannot be too strongly emphasized that all educational and social-improvement programmes in this area must be directed toward re-establishing the native in his own self-esteem and self-sufficiency which will in itself go a long way toward removing that attitude of superiority which some white people display toward him. The deterioration of Indian morale is emphasized by such authorities on Indian life as Dr. D. Jenness[2] and the Rev. Dr. G. H. Raley.[3] It is noticeable that the Eskimo do not have any great feeling of inferiority in dealing with the white man. In fact when the white man is among them in their own environment the reverse is true. Centuries of tutelage have robbed the Indians of their independent spirit and self-reliance. All possible measures should be taken to restore them.

No school curriculum can of itself accomplish these objectives, but at the present stage of development of these Indians the following is recommended: (*a*) reading, writing, and arithmetic on the elementary school level; (*b*) simple social studies with emphasis on citizenship, conservation, and simple business practice; (*c*) health and hygiene including modern physical education; (*d*) nature study which would assist them to understand the scientific background of much of their native woodcraft and nature lore; (*e*) an adaptation of the modern general shop courses and organization to develop fundamental manual skills and to include emphasis on motor mechanics or carpentry or mining or prospecting or navigation or agriculture or forestry or whatever would especially help them in their immediate environment; (*f*) a suitable adaptation of home-making courses for the girls; (*g*) the preservation of their native handicrafts wherever necessary; (*h*) appropriate instruction in art and music; (*i*) development of suitable extra-curricular activities in a variety of projects including Red Cross activities, dramatics, journalism, etc.; (*j*) lectures by visiting scientists, statesmen, etc. Throughout this whole curriculum the greatest possible use should be made of audio-visual aids and radio. It is understood that the Indians and mixed-bloods always show great interest in motion pictures.

It is comparatively easy to state such simple objectives and outline a curriculum designed to achieve them. It is much more difficult to establish and operate the organization and administration necessary to accomplish and maintain the desired results. First, there must be appropriate school law and regulations. Second, adequate school accommodation (buildings, grounds, equipment, etc.) must be provided. Third, an alert, fully trained, and experienced teaching staff is essential. And the greatest of these is the teaching staff. Unfortunately the teaching staffs in most of the schools in Mackenzie District are weak. There is no lack of devotion or desire to serve the Indian children, but in nearly every case they are uncertificated and not abreast of modern methods and practice. Instead of being under-qualified, teachers in the North West Territories should have special training over and above the usual requirements for recognized certification. More will be said on this point in a recommendation to be made later.

[2]D. Jenness, *Indians of Canada* (National Museum of Canada, Bulletin no. 65, Ottawa, 1932), pp. 257-9.

[3]G. H. Raley, "Canadian Indian Art and Industries" (*Journal of the Royal Society of Arts*, vol. LXXXIII, Sept., 1935, pp. 991-4).

17

Taking Education to the Native. In the past, in the North West Territories, the practice has been to bring the Indian children into the white man's settlements and buildings to receive such education as has been given them. Could not something be done to take much of such a curriculum to them in their own environment? Although the life of these Indians is nomadic to a considerable degree, there being no reservations in the North West Territories, it follows a fairly consistent pattern from year to year. During the winter months they are on their trap lines and hunting. These activities are not infrequently carried on from a central location where a group of families congregate each season especially if they are a band organized under a recognized chief. In the summer months they usually gather at well-known rendezvous locations generally where a river runs into a lake or where a smaller river runs into the Mackenzie. These spots are good fishing locations and here they catch fish for themselves and their dogs. One of the complaints most frequently heard from officials and traders is that of late years it has become too much their habit to loiter around the settlements and waste their substance in liquor and gambling. Meanwhile their families and dogs starve. Something constructive done to keep them from idling around the settlements would be all to the good. The principle of taking as much as possible of suitable white man's lore to the Indians in their native environment might be tried out. Two suggestions are made, (1) the fitting out of a "school barge," (2) the establishment of a "community centre."

In northern Ontario the school railroad car has proven very popular and successful. A member of the R.C.M.P. who had observed these school cars in operation suggested that a school barge be fitted up to visit at Indian rendezvous points on the southern shore of Great Slave Lake. There are several such points east of Fort Resolution commencing at Rocher River. Although such a school barge could only function for from three to five months in the summer, it might accomplish a great deal. Dr. J. B. MacDougall of the Ontario Department of Education, who was in charge of the school-car service in northern Ontario, states most emphatically that even a few months each year paid good dividends. The pupils were anxious to make the most of their opportunities and there were not the distractions of the older communities. A school barge or barges could serve adults as well as children. Health education, conservation programmes, modern methods of handling fish and fur products, and numerous other things that the Indians must know if they are to assume the responsibilities of citizenship could be presented, especially if motion pictures and the radio were properly utilized. In any event it would seem that this school-barge idea is worth a trial.

There are several rendezvous points where a Community Centre could be tried out, through which not only education, but also health and recreation facilities, could be made available to the natives, and where some attempt could be made to organize a more satisfactory existence for the natives, based perhaps on the development of co-operative institutions.   Salt River was suggested as one suitable point.[4]

After visiting this deserted Indian Settlement, located where the Salt River joins Slave River, the writer recommends that a thoroughly organized and well-planned community-centre project be attempted at this location. This would need to be a long-range project with adequate financial support. It would be necessary for some trained social worker, experienced with natives of this type, to visit the region to make the preliminary surveys and evolve a five, ten, or even twenty-year comprehensive plan as would be necessary to give the experiment an adequate opportunity to demonstrate its value.   This specialist, or someone suitable for the purpose, would have to be on the ground during the experiment to supervise it.   Some form of compulsion might be necessary in the initial stages and supervision and control would at first have to be in the hands of a suitable white man or men, working as much as possible through the Indian chief concerned.   In due course, natives could gradually take over the key positions with the ultimate objective of having them run it themselves to the greatest possible extent.   This would be in accordance with the long-range fundamental principle of helping these natives to become rehabilitated in their own esteem and in that of their white neighbours.   Those who know these natives well give the assurance that they

[4]The following memorandum by Mr. M. J. Dempsey, a veteran Park Warden in Wood-Buffalo Park is of interest in this connection.

"There are about thirty families of treaty Indians living at Fort Smith.   Prior to 1930 about one-half of these Indians lived regularly at Salt River Settlement about twenty miles down Slave River from Fort Smith, and the other half used to spend the first half of the summer there putting up dry fish.   They have gradually all moved to Fort Smith and established homes where they make a much poorer living than when they lived at Salt River Settlement.   The late Chief Squirrel had his permanent home at Salt River Settlement and there were two trading posts there.   Now there is no settlement and no trading posts.

"The Indians are living in Fort Smith to be able to take in as much as they can find in opportunities to get liquor and gamble.   At Fort Smith they do not have the natural recreation of the Indian and instead try to imitate the whites which is contrary to their best interests.

"At Salt River Settlement a properly established community properly supervised with a school, church, some kind of medical facilities, enforced sanitary precautions, and amortization of the fur catches to ensure that the women and children would at all times have sufficient proper food, would in a few years result in developing a feeling of thrift and self-respect in the Indians and have the effect of improving the health of the Indians generally.

"At Salt River Settlement the soil is good and the Indians could be encouraged to raise gardens which would also be of great benefit in producing a kind of food which is noticeably deficient in their diet at present.

"There are two other locations which would be very suitable and would be worth investigating.   One is at the Fox Lake Indian reserve on Peace River and one at Fond Du Lac on Lake Athabasca.   At both of these locations the chiefs are men of outstanding qualifications and are trying to improve the conditions of the Indians under them but have not the necessary authority to enforce co-operation.

have it in them to accomplish this but that they must be brought to stand on their own feet and forget the idea that the government will not see them starve.

In Aklavik it was suggested that some such project, with suitable modifications, could and should be tried out among the Eskimo. For two or three months during the summer, considerable numbers of Eskimo leave the coastal regions and rendezvous on heights of land as much as a hundred miles inland to hunt the caribou. Suitable summer buildings could be erected and a teacher and a nurse flown into one of these points for the season. The Eskimo, it was felt, would welcome such an opportunity to take advantage of suitable white man's learning and would profit greatly by even a short period each summer.

One writer on Eskimo habits states:

> Although no Eskimo camp-site may be classed as permanent or certain there are some places where the camps are used throughout the year and they usually remain in the immediate vicinity of some favorable hunting spot for several years. Although some of the families, or members of a family, may be absent from it for a time, there is usually someone there. Such camps are the closest approximation to a native village that these migratory people have . . . . Usual summer camps are generally found at the same place for several years in succession but during the summer months only. They are quite often located on off-shore islands or at the mouths of rivers . . . . A summer camp at the mouth of a river is so located as to permit fishing there in July when the fish are going out to sea, and again in September when they are running upstream to the interior lakes.[5]

It is recommended that a similar, but less elaborate Community Centre be tried out at some specially selected campsite among the Eskimo, possibly in the Coppermine area.

In the rural parts of several of the Canadian provinces are to be found specialists in agriculture who live and work among the agriculturalists in many areas. Could not selected Indian and Eskimo youths, both male and female, be given special social-service training with a view to returning to their native environment to live among and teach and counsel both the young and the adult members of their tribes and bands? This is no new recommendation; but could not an immediate start be made in trying it out on an experimental basis in at least one or two carefully selected areas? Female social workers of Indian blood living with their bands could render especially useful service.

Anyone charged with the responsibility of carrying out such experiments might secure information from study of the projects developed in Alberta under their Metis Population Betterment Act,[6] in Saskatchewan through their Northern Areas Branch,[7] and in Manitoba under their Fur Rehabilitation

---

[5] J. Lewis Robinson, "Eskimo Population in the Canadian Eastern Arctic" (*Canadian Geographical Journal*, vol. XXIX, Sept., 1934, p. 134).

[6] Revised Statutes of Alberta, 1942, chap. 329.

[7] *Saskatchewan Gazette*, vol. XL, July 15, 1944, p. 4; and the *Annual Report of the Northern Areas Branch, 1941-2* (Regina), p. 18.

Block Regulations.[8] Incorporated in the Manitoba projects is the principle of conserving the spending power of the participants by paying the returns from their furs to them on a monthly basis rather than in a lump sum.

Indian Schools. One of the terms of reference called for the inspection of Indian residential and day schools in Mackenzie District of the North West Territories. Since these schools were not in operation at the time of the visit, inspection in the full meaning of the term was not possible. No regular classes were being taught so that no observation could be made of any of these schools in normal operation. Hence, little first-hand knowledge could be obtained concerning the teaching methods, discipline, classroom management, teacher-pupil relationships, academic advancement, and the many other factors which go to make up classroom instruction. The majority of the teachers were interviewed and found to be most co-operative in explaining how they conducted their classrooms, in outlining curricula followed, in providing timetables, in submitting exercise books, in showing accommodation and equipment, and in general, supplying all information possible when the classes were not in actual operation. It must be emphasized, however, that this is not a report on an inspection of these schools within the usual meaning of this term. One simply tried to form the most accurate estimate possible based on the qualifications, experience, and personality of the teachers, the adequacy of the accommodation and equipment, and the general characteristics and background of each school.

The schools visited in order of contact were: (*a*) in Fort Smith: (i) the day school conducted under the auspices of the Roman Catholic Mission; (ii) the non-denominational day school; (*b*) in Aklavik: (i) the Anglican residential school; (ii) the Roman Catholic residential school; (*c*) in Fort Simpson the Roman Catholic day school; (*d*) in Fort Providence the Roman Catholic residential school; (*e*) in Fort Resolution the Roman Catholic residential school; (*f*) the non-denominational school in Yellowknife. Owing to shortage of personnel the Church of England day schools at Fort Mc-Pherson, Fort Simpson, and Hay River had not been in operation during the 1943-4 school year. At Hay River the nurse remaining in charge after the missionary left did what she could, but emphasized that her efforts could not qualify for the status of a school.

A somewhat detailed report on individual schools has been submitted to the Canadian Social Science Research Council. Here only the general impressions are recorded. School accommodation was much superior to that of the average rural, or small town school functioning at the same level in the Prairie Provinces. The premises were usually much cleaner and kept in a better state of repair. The heating and sanitary conditions were at least equal if not superior to such prairie schools. The library and supplementary reading material were below the prairie standards. The playground areas and equip-

[8]*Manitoba Gazette*, vol. 73, March 4, 1944, p. 156.

ment were about equal to those of the prairies. On the whole the physical
school plants, their equipment, and state of repair were above the prairie
average. From what was observed in exercise-books, time-tables, and curricula, as well as from conversations with the teachers and clergy concerned,
the general standard of instruction and the academic advancement would
seem to be considerably below that of the prairie schools.

Even without regular inspection, much information concerning academic
standards in these denominational schools could be obtained if they would
utilize the practice followed by the two non-denominational schools at Yellowknife and Fort Smith which require their pupils to take the tests provided
and marked by the Correspondence Branch of the Alberta Department of
Education. It was mentioned that the Anglican residential school at Aklavik
has such action under consideration.

The only two fully qualified teachers encountered in the denominational
schools were to be found in the Church of England residential school at
Aklavik. These held recognized first-class professional certificates from Ontario and Alberta respectively. The academic standing of the remaining
teachers ranged from Grades VIII-X. They had no recognized professional
teacher-training or provincial teachers' diplomas. One or two of these were
"out" in other parts of Canada and one was in hospital. The writer would
like, however, to take this opportunity to pay a tribute to this earnest group
of teachers who have devoted their lives to the education and welfare of the
Indian and Eskimo children of the North West Territories. Although nearly
all of them are uncertificated, the majority certainly have considerable
native ability for teaching and the children under their care are receiving
a fine service. But no matter how great one's ability for teaching may be,
one is always the better for professional training and refresher courses.

So far as school law and regulations were concerned in the North West
Territories, no one seemed to have them very much in mind. Since there has
been no professional inspection of these schools, those in charge were living up
to their own conceptions of school law and regulations not because they had
to so much as because they wished to do so. One's whole impression in this
respect was most refreshing. Nowhere did anyone in charge of, or teaching
in, these schools seem to have anything to hide. With the invigorating
candour of the North they were most anxious to disclose all the facts and seek
direction if any were available. The only official regulations seemed to be
the very brief and sketchy set to be found on the inside back cover of the
"Daily Register" supplied by the Indian Affairs Branch of the Department
of Mines and Resources which are quoted below.

INDIAN DAY SCHOOL REGULATIONS

All Indian Day Schools shall be kept open the prescribed number of days in each year.

A circular letter will be sent teachers each year, setting forth the date of opening and
closing; the number of teaching days during the academic year; and holidays allowed. It is

expected that teachers will closely adhere to the dates as set forth in this circular letter. In the event of a teacher not obtaining this circular by June 1st each year, request should be made to the Department for a copy.

Where, in the interest of the school work, such action may be desirable, the holidays allowed during the summer (two months) may, upon the recommendation of the local agent, be taken at some other time of the year; but no change is to be made without the express approval of the Branch.

The morning session shall be from 9 a.m., to 12 noon and the afternoon from 1 p.m., to 4 p.m., with a recess during each session of not less than 15 and not more than 20 minutes. There shall be no deviation from this regulation without the approval of the Branch.

Salaries of teachers will be paid monthly, on the basis of ten (10) teaching months in each school year. In the case of isolated schools in northern Communities, salaries will only be paid upon receipt of the quarterly return of attendance.

Teachers should prepare promptly, at the end of each quarter, on the form for that purpose, a return showing attendance, days taught, etc., and fill in all particulars under the various headings, as required by the form. They should send the completed return to their local Indian agent, who will transmit same to the Department. THIS IS IMPORTANT.

Summer holidays are not taken into account in payment of yearly salaries. Each school year shall begin and end on the dates mentioned in the circular above referred to and the yearly salary allowed will be paid for the period taught between those dates only, unless, as herebefore stated, special provision has been granted for a change in the holiday period.

All teachers will be required to give at least one month's notice of their intention to resign.

The 1898 Consolidated Ordinances of the North West Territories as amended up to the time of the erection of the provinces of Saskatchewan and Alberta in 1905 provide a foundation for a publicly supported school system.[9] Presumably these are still in full force and effect in the North West Territories as at present constituted but would scarcely apply to Indian schools.

The official curriculum of the Indian Affairs Branch, which also is printed on the back cover of the "Daily Register," is quoted below.

PROGRAMME OF STUDIES FOR INDIAN SCHOOLS

The PROGRAMME OF STUDIES herein prescribed shall be followed by the teacher as far as the circumstances of the school permit. Any modifications deemed necessary should be made only with the sanction of the Branch.

TEXTBOOKS   While in the case of most subjects, Provincial textbooks are used, it should be noted that the Indian Affairs Branch prescribes certain books which have been found specially suitable for Indian Schools. Particulars regarding these books may be obtained on application to the Indian Affairs Branch, Ottawa.

REQUISITIONS   When preparing requisitions for school material ask only for these texts authorized above. The Indian Affairs Branch requires you to adhere strictly to this rule. Teachers will please note the instructions on the "Requisition for School Material" form No. 413. Indian agents will supply these forms.

TEACHERS—NOTE THE FOLLOWING SUGGESTIONS

LANGUAGE   Every effort must be made to induce pupils to speak English and to teach them to understand it. Insist on English even during the supervised

[9]The Consolidated Ordinances of the North West Territories of 1898 and Amendments, chap. 75, *The School Ordinance*, 1901, chap. 29.

play. Failure in this means wasted efforts. (In some schools in Quebec, where French is the classroom language, the word "French" should be substituted in the above instruction where the word "English" appears).

READING

Do not hear the children read, teach them to read. Do not use the phonic method to teach beginners unless it is for children with serious disabilities. Remember reading is a basic skill. Great care should be taken to teach it properly. The primary division members should be grouped and regrouped for reading practice upon the basis of their reading ability and not upon the time spent in school. Pupils should be tested at the beginning of each year and grouped accordingly. Apply remedial measures whenever necessary.

VOCATIONAL INSTRUCTION

Teachers are expected to emphasize the importance of vocational instruction. Dressmaking, crochet work, knitting, hand loom weaving, elementary domestic science, gardening and care of poultry are recommended for girls, and elementary carpentry work, general shop, Indian handicraft, gardening and poultry raising for boys. At residential schools the care of live stock, auto mechanics and cultivation of land should be emphasized. Cultivation should conform to the requirements of the home of each pupil. This is especially true of residential schools where pupils come from different reserves.

PHYSICAL EDUCATION

Lay stress on physical activities that will strengthen the chest and neck. Special attention should be given to outdoor group games, supervised play and exercises, accompanied by singing, to afford variation and improve physique.

VOCAL MUSIC

Simple songs and hymns; the theme of the former to be interesting and patriotic; the tunes bright and cheerful.

RELIGIOUS INSTRUCTION

Scriptural reading, the Ten Commandments, the Lord's Prayer, the Life of Christ, etc.

CHARACTER TRAINING

Teachers will strive to develop the spirit of responsibility among the children, giving responsibility in turn, even in small things; gathering books, pencils, etc. for the smaller ones. Give greater responsibility as the child advances in age. Commend success and tactfully reprimand failures. Teachers will stress obedience, courtesy, cleanliness, self-respect, thrift, self-maintenance and patriotism. Cultivate honesty and the spirit of fair play. Teach respect of law, order, authority and public property. Explain the relation of the sexes as to labour, home and public duties.

HEALTH EDUCATION

The object of health education is to have the pupils form worth-while habits. Habits cannot be taught in the traditional way as book-learning, but must be acquired by constant practice. Methods must be worked out by the teacher, who will have the pupils make health posters, join classroom health activities and health games, etc. It is of the utmost importance that Indian pupils be taught to recognize the value of a well balanced diet. Recommend the use of meat, milk and vegetables. The teacher should stress the relationship of such diet to physical fitness, growth and general health.

Great care must be exercised by the teacher to see that the schoolroom is kept thoroughly clean. The floor should be swept daily and scrubbed frequently. The air in the schoolroom should be completely changed during recess and at the noon hour, even in the coldest weather, by the opening of windows and doors. Spitting on the floor, or inside the school building should not be allowed. Cleanliness in the classroom as well as in the surrounding buildings and school yard is a definite phase of health education. Great stress will be emphasized on these by the teacher.

GENERAL   Whenever possible the teachers will employ the activity programme. Teachers must keep in mind that the text-book is but an educational instrument. Pupils must be well grouped according to their ability. Objective achievement tests should be used as frequently as necessary.

This is, to say the least, a very sketchy programme of studies. But, as shown elsewhere, even this is not fully carried out especially with respect to the use of modern educational practices and the teaching of up-to-date occupational courses.

The denominational schools in Mackenzie District of the North West Territories, whether day schools or residential schools, are owned and operated by either the Anglican Church (Church of England in Canada) or the Roman Catholic Church. The Indian Affairs Branch of the Dominion Department of Mines and Resources does not own or operate any schools in the district. It delegates its responsibility for the education of Indian children to these churches and pays them grants for their services. For the year 1942-3 these grants amounted to $1,667.15 for the day schools and to $31,558 for the residential schools making a total of $33,225.15 for the North West Territories.[10] The total enrolment in the day schools for 1943-4 was 55 and in the residential schools for the same year was 115 pupils.

According to the official census returns of 1941, there were in the North West Territories 1,007 Indian children between the ages of five and fourteen years, inclusive. Moreover, according to the same census, there were in the North West Territories 443 Eskimo children between the ages of five and fourteen inclusive. This makes a total of 2,450 native children of school age in the North West Territories. Only 170 of these were receiving schooling from the denominational schools in 1943-4. Even admitting that many of them, especially the Eskimo, are highly nomadic and inaccessible, too large a proportion of them are receiving no schooling. No doubt compulsory education would be difficult to enforce, but wherever feasible it should be attempted. Indian parents are inclined to permit their children to be absent from school too readily. The R.C.M.P. should have the necessary authority to require school attendance whenever possible.

In approaching the problem of making adequate provision for a modern educational programme in the North West Territories, the requirements of each settlement in Mackenzie District should be ascertained through a comprehensive survey having regard not only for immediate demands but also for future possibilities. The present accommodation in the nearby Prairie Provinces should not be taken as a standard. Much of it is quite

[10]*Report of the Department of Mines and Resources for the Fiscal Year Ended March 31, 1943* (Ottawa, 1943), p. 150.

obsolete for modern educational requirements and it would be short-sighted, in inaugurating a new system in Mackenzie District, to take the average prairie school as a standard. For example, if the improved curriculum recommended herein is inaugurated in the North West Territories, considerable accommodation and equipment for practical courses would have to be provided. Outside the larger centres, relatively few schools on the prairies have adequate equipment.

Public Schools. The Ordinances of the North West Territories[11] make provision for a decentralized form of school administration consisting of a central authority (Department of Education) with wide regulation-making powers, and numerous local school authorities (elected school boards). For obvious reasons no such organization has been set up in what is now (1944) the North West Territories. Over this vast region the Indians are under the care of the Department of Indian Affairs, and there are not enough white children and children of mixed blood[12] to require any such organization. Recent developments at Yellowknife and Fort Smith involve problems of organization of public schools under these Ordinances.

Yellowknife. With the advent of modern methods of communication and transportation and mining development, there came a greater need for education for white children and for children of mixed blood who were not wards of the government. This need became particularly acute at Yellowknife where considerable gold mining developed. The result was that in 1941 a three-roomed public school was built and three qualified teachers engaged who taught Grades I-VII according to the Alberta course of studies. From the standpoint of instructional efficiency, this is one of the most successful educational institutions in the North West Territories. At the time of this visit in August, 1944, summer holidays were in effect and all the teachers except the Principal, Mrs. Christine May, were "out" in the provinces. Some very definite evidence concerning the instructional efficiency was available, however. From Grade III upward the pupils of this school wrote tests sent in by the Correspondence Branch of the Department of Education in Alberta. Their answers were sent out to Edmonton to be marked and the results were well above the average. Furthermore, several pupils from this school have gone out to schools in Alberta and elsewhere and have made a good showing.

It would seem, however, that a few modern touches would greatly improve the instructional efficiency of this school. Suitable utilization of modern testing materials should be part of its programme. Mental alertness tests, achievement tests, and personality ratings might be used to build up a cumulative record for each pupil. This record should include not only the results

[11]Consolidated Ordinances, 1898, chap. 75.

[12]The Census of 1941 shows 164 white children in the North West Territories, and 87 children of mixed blood not under the Indian Affairs Branch.

of these tests but also the usual school information together with a personal history record to contain information concerning the home environment and as much as possible about the out-of-school activities and interests of each pupil. All these should be adapted to suit the circumstances in Yellowknife. Nothing too elaborate should be attempted in the beginning, but the better the educational assessment of each pupil the greater should be the educational efficiency. It is not to be expected that the teachers in Yellowknife will be able to make expert statistical analyses and interpretations of all the assessment data procured, but they can utilize many of them in their raw form for diagnostic and remedial purposes and the data can be sent out to some of the educational research branches in the provinces if more technical interpretations are desired.

Moreover, it would seem that modern project and enterprise methods of teaching could be utilized to a considerable degree with these children, and the fullest possible use should be made of motion pictures and all other available visual material. A great variety of charts, maps, diagrams, film slides, art exhibits, music-appreciation records, etc., are particularly necessary in this remote environment. Of these there are too few in this school. Could not good use be made of the radio in this school?

Some attempt is being made at manual training and sewing in the Yellowknife school. Could not these projects be developed into very effective adaptations of general shop courses for the boys and home-making courses for the girls?

The teachers in this school, and indeed in all the schools of the district, should not only be encouraged but should be required and assisted to take summer courses out in the provinces or elsewhere every two or three years, or, better still, to take a sabbatical year every five years, or a combination of these plans. A teachers' convention, at public expense, for all teachers, whether denominational or non-denominational, who remain in the District, should be held every summer at some convenient centre. Such measures as these are essential in this remote area and would contribute greatly toward attracting the calibre of teachers required.

Since the enrolment in 1943-4 was down to something under fifty for the whole school, the school board were considering the idea of reducing their staff to **two** teachers. The Principal informed the writer that consideration also was being given to asking her to teach to the end of Grade XI; i.e., the senior room would include at least Grades VII-XI, inclusive of the Alberta programme. The writer recommended to her and to two members of the school board that if Grades X and XI were to be included in the teaching load of the school the three teachers should be retained. This would be wise even if correspondence courses were utilized for the senior grades because these pupils would benefit greatly from supervised study and other assistance which could be provided much better with three teachers than with two.

The Canadian Institute of International Affairs is sending Mrs. May a great deal of information on how to keep informed concerning the affairs of the day.   In fact that organization is sending similar information to all the schools in Mackenzie District.

Like all the other schools, Yellowknife school is deficient in supplementary reading and general reading and in library accommodation.   If there is any place where good reading material is needed and where good reading habits could be inculcated, the North West Territories should be that place.   No one, today, is expected to know everything, but everyone should be trained in the use of a library and how to find information.   Could not every school in Mackenzie District serve as a library centre?   Could not one of the Foundations try out, say, a Mackenzie River Valley library project?

The paucity of library material and library accommodation naturally brings up the question of school accommodation and equipment in general. Since Yellowknife school is now functioning on the junior high-school level and is giving some thought to including senior high-school work to the end of the junior matriculation level, it will be in order to mention a few of the accommodation requirements for a modern junior-senior high-school plant. In addition to whatever classrooms are necessary to accommodate the enrolment reasonably, such a school requires an auditorium, a gymnasium, a library, a science laboratory, a general shop, home-making accommodation, commercial course accommodation, a principal's office, a nurse's office, restrooms for the teachers, a natural history museum, to say nothing of modern toilet and lavatory accommodation.   No doubt it will be difficult, having regard for the resources of the community, to provide all this accommodation at Yellowknife, but it should be kept in mind for future planning.

What is actually to be found at Yellowknife is a three-room frame school building which has been erected on a site on the shore of Great Slave Lake about midway between the town of Yellowknife and the "Con" mine.   This means that the children from each of these places, as well as from the Negus mine, have to scramble over the rocks and muskegs or travel over the lake ice in winter for a distance of anywhere from one to three miles.   This may have had some effect on the attendance record.   No doubt some of the smaller children have too far to go to school, especially having regard for the northern climate and short winter days.

A suitable school site was not easy to find at Yellowknife where the terrain largely alternates between rocky outcroppings and muskegs.   At the site selected there is enough level ground to carve out a relatively small playground about only half of which is now in use for this purpose.   The outdoor toilets are far from satisfactory.   No attempt has been made at beautifying the school grounds.

The exterior of this school building is drab and unprepossessing.   It is covered with some sort of dark building paper material over which, the secretary-treasurer states, a further siding can be placed. Having regard to the fact that in severe weather the temperature in some of the classrooms is none too comfortable, this might be desirable. The classrooms are a fair size but the ceilings are low. The partitions are not very substantial and the interior decorations and wall pictures leave much to be desired. The light from outside is suitable but during a good portion of the school year electric lighting is necessary. Greater use could be made of indirect lighting. On the whole this building does not impress one as being very substantial. It appears to have been run up in a hurry to cope with immediate demands rather than from any long-range point of view.

Equipment and apparatus are insufficient especially now that more senior work, to the completion of the junior matriculation level, is to be undertaken. More maps, charts, diagrams, blackboard devices, etc., are necessary. The library and supplementary reading material are inadequate as is also the science laboratory accommodation and equipment. The playground and sports equipment is insufficient.

Every school should be an attractive place to which children would desire to go and which would not compare unfavourably with a high standard of living at home. Although the citizens at Yellowknife are to be commended for the initiative and enterprise shown in establishing this school in the wilderness, they are by no means at the point where they can rest on their oars.

Presumably the local school authority at Yellowknife is constituted under the School Ordinance of 1901 and its amendments, to which reference has already been made. Presumably also the Regulations of the Board of Education of the North West Territories as adopted March 15, 1898, and subsequent amendments, are still in force. Be this as it may, this school seemed to be operating much the same as if the school law and regulations of the nearby provinces were in force. School hours were similar. The premises and equipment were similar. The teachers held recognized provincial certificates. The Alberta Programme of Studies was being followed and Alberta tests used.

There is an elected local school board which secures the bulk of its revenue through a local municipal organization from taxation chiefly on property. The secretary of the Yellowknife school board stated that it cost them about $7,500 to operate their school for the 1943-4 school year. To help meet these expenditures the governing authorities at Ottawa had provided a grant of some $1,500, that is to say approximately 20 per cent. This is much the same proportion provided by the Department of Education in several of the provinces. It is recommended that the Ottawa authorities should provide at least 50 per cent of the cost of operating the schools under their jurisdiction. This is an up-to-date principle in school finance and is the common practice in England, Scotland, Denmark, and some other enlightened countries. If the local school boards in the provinces of Canada are going to be able to meet modern educational requirements, they too must be financed on some such basis without further delay.

Several residents of Yellowknife, including a couple of school trustees, emphasize that their school compares favourably with those of a similar type on the prairies. This can be admitted but the comparison is quite unfortunate. It is now pretty generally conceded that the schools on the prairies, which they are using for comparison, are themselves hopelessly obsolete and most of the provinces of Canada are struggling to replace them with something better. Elsewhere in this report there is recommended for the North West Territories a highly centralized form of school administration. Under this plan of organization the local school board in Yellowknife would act in an advisory capacity only. Such local advisory bodies throughout the North West Territories might be either elected or appointed or a combination of both of these methods, but they would not actually be in charge of the operation and administration of the school. This recommendation might not prove to be popular with the present school board in Yellowknife, but every effort should be made to induce it to concur and thus avoid setting up in the North West Territories an out-of-date school organization such as most of the other Canadian provinces are now struggling to modernize. Incidentally, a thorough revision and modernizing of School Ordinances and School Regulations for the North West Territories is long overdue.

Fort Smith. Having regard for the fact that 1939-40 was the first school year of operation, the public school at Fort Smith has made a satisfactory showing. This is evidenced by the fact that in 1944 the pupils wrote examinations sent in from, and marked by, the Correspondence Branch of the Department of Education in Alberta, with highly satisfactory results. Moreover the teacher was duly certificated. A small enrolment (eight white, and seven mixed blood) enabled her to give considerable individual attention to the pupils. This was particularly necessary in some cases, due to unsatisfactory scholastic foundation.

The school building, which has now been in use for three years, is somewhat superior to the average one-room rural school building on the prairies. It is a snugly built log building with indoor toilets for the girls in winter-time and a pipeless furnace which should keep it warm. The ceiling is too low. Indirect lighting would be an improvement over the present frosted electric bulbs. Up-to-date school desks and furniture are in use. The supplementary reading and library material is scanty. Maps, charts, wall-pictures, etc., are few. No doubt equipment and apparatus will be accumulated as the years go by. A school-ground improvement programme would be in order.

Since school finances are usually controlled by school law and regulations, it is interesting to note that there is no debenture debt on the non-denominational school at Fort Smith. This little building was built as a community enterprise. To operate this school for the 1943-4 school year, approximately $1,500 was required of which the teacher's salary amounted to $1,000. An interested parent provided her with board and lodging which was conservatively estimated at $300. To meet these expenditures the Ottawa authorities granted $700; fees from parents amounted to some $360 and the balance was raised by concerts, dances, and bingo games. The net result is that the building and equipment have been provided, that the school has been operated for a year, and at the conclusion thereof there is no outstanding indebtedness. All of which is highly commendable and typical of the spirit of the North. Highly commendable also is the almost 50 per cent contribution from the Ottawa authorities. It is not recommended, however, that the Fort Smith method of raising the other 50 per cent should be followed as a general policy. This is altogether too precarious a practice and the necessary school law and regulations should be enacted in order to obtain it on an equitable basis of taxation not only in Fort Smith but over the whole North West Territories.

In several other settlements of Mackenzie District, there are one or two white children and several children of mixed blood whose parents would prefer to send them to public schools, rather than to the denominational Indian schools. Their numbers do not, however, justify setting up schools like those at Yellowknife and Fort Smith. In several cases these pupils are following Alberta correspondence courses with the help of their parents or other members of the community. These conditions exist at Fort Simpson, Fort Providence, Hay River, and Fort Resolution. Would it not be possible to provide an itinerant schoolmaster to visit these communities successively for a month at a time to assist pupils taking correspondence courses? This would be of great assistance and inspirational value because correspondence courses without some help at critical moments are difficult to keep going. Board and lodging for the teacher could be provided by interested parents during the period of his visit to each settlement. The regular flights of Canadian Pacific Airlines would provide adequate transportation. Another itinerant teacher might be profitably employed to serve Fort McPherson, Arctic Red River, Fort Good Hope, and Fort Norman in a similar manner.

Adult Education. In the North West Territories adult education is likely to develop along two rather distinct lines: viz., adult education for the white residents and adult education for the natives.

With a little stimulation and leadership some very profitable adult-education activities could be developed at such centres as Norman Wells, Eldorado Mines, Yellowknife, and Fort Smith along the following lines:

(*a*) correspondence courses in all fields, e.g., occupational, commercial, vocational, technical, high school, university; (*b*) study circles, discussion groups, radio forums, etc., on any desired topic, e.g., current events, economics, foreign languages, conservation, etc.; (*c*) directed reading; (*d*) handicrafts and hobbies; (*e*) music and art appreciation. These are but a few examples. In the long winter nights with the wealth of technical and other highly educated personnel, many of them Scandinavian, at the mining and oil centres, there should be a most fertile field for adult education. Moreover, the white residents and perhaps some of the natives living in the various settlements down the Mackenzie might also form discussion groups, listening groups, study circles, etc.

At the request of the managers concerned, definite suggestions have been made for the development of adult-education activities at Norman Wells and Port Radium. A practical approach at such centres would be to make a survey to ascertain what members of the professional and technical staffs would be prepared: (*a*) to devote a night or two a week in assisting those taking correspondence courses to cope with their difficulties; (*b*) to devote a night or two a week actually to teaching courses in various subjects or leading study circles and discussion groups. Once the voluntary instructional staff available has been ascertained, a canvass might then be made of all personnel to discover what courses or study groups would have sufficient enrolment to justify their existence. A half-dozen to a dozen members usually constitute a satisfactory study or discussion group.

In Canada adult education has been too much a pastime for the intelligentsia. In the Scandinavian countries it developed as a movement among the masses. This was largely due to an economic urge. The average individual, in the initial stages at least, does not as a rule attend study circles regularly or exert himself in adult-education activities unless there is some immediate economic or social or other personal incentive. This must be kept in mind when organizing and carrying out any adult-education programme. Fullest possible use should be made of audio-visual aids and the radio.

Adult education for the Indians and persons of mixed blood is a more specialized undertaking. Here, particularly, the self-preservation and economic improvement incentives would have to be utilized. If the field counsellors, recommended elsewhere, are appointed to live among and move about with the native bands, they should be trained and experienced in the utilization of adult-education organization and study techniques. There are many things about improving their economic condition and coping with the oncoming white civilization that the natives should find of interest, especially if full use were made of sound movies and the radio. Could not white man's ideas concerning health, conservation, prospecting, fishing, etc., be shown to the natives even if they are unable to read and write? The Scandinavian folk high schools emphasize the use of the spoken word. The proposed school barges should be fitted up for use of adult-education purposes outside school hours. Could not some adaptation of a Danish folk high school be tried out on an experimental basis in some one or two of the present residential schools? The emphasis in the folk high school is not on book-learning.

Are there not some young and even older Indians, past school age, who would enjoy and learn a good deal from spending a few weeks in one of the residential schools even if they could not read and write? These schools are largely idle during the summer months. So are a good many natives. Why not try out some short courses for them on conservation, prospecting, motor mechanics, fur trading, and such other activities as would be of interest and profit to them. Some of them might even desire to learn to read and perhaps do a little arithmetic but these things do not need to be forced upon them. Sound pictures, the radio, and the spoken word should be able to do a very great deal for them.

Might not something of the kind be tried out during June, July, and August at, say, Aklavik and Fort Simpson? Would young adult male Indians and Eskimo like to come in and spend a few weeks in these schools which to them formerly were out of the question? Would there be sufficient enrolment if the grapevine and all other methods of disseminating the offer were used? Could these schools handle them with, of course, direction from someone on the spot who understood not only the project but also the natives? Frankly, the answers to these questions might only be forthcoming as a result of trial and error, but if these school plants could be utilized during the summer for short courses with a folk high-school spirit and approach, much might be accomplished for the vast proportion of Indian and Eskimo population who now receive no schooling. Such projects might also accelerate the accomplishment of the very fundamental objective of rehabilitating the native in his own self-respect.

Yellowknife might well form the location for another adult-education project in the way of a residential type of vocational or occupational school. People well-acquainted with the natives of the North West Territories advise that they can handle machinery very satisfactorily. The Eskimo are particularly capable in this respect. Even the Indians, after they are properly fed and gradually acclimatized, are capable of doing many types of work in the mining and petroleum industries. Moreover, all over this north country there shortly will be a great network of radio, meteorological, and other stations as well as airfields. Could not some of the natives be trained to carry out, under adequate supervision, much of the maintenance and operation of these developments? If such were the case, some white men could be relieved of the monotony and isolation of service in the far North. Could anything like the school forestry project of the Earl Grey Junior High School in Winni-

peg be developed from such a centre? In short, an occupational training centre
at Yellowknife should pay good dividends.

No doubt the proposed Director of Education for the North West Territories would develop many other suitable adult-education activities. Certainly
adult education should be one of his responsibilities. Wherever desirable and
feasible, could not the school be used as a community centre?

One of the greatest problems which will face the Director in inaugurating
and maintaining the proposed new educational system in the North West
Territories will be to secure and retain adequately trained suitable teachers
and social workers. Would it not be desirable for the governing body of the
North West Territories through the Director of Education for the North
West Territories to offer scholarships and bursaries to specially selected
natives as well as whites to enable them to take special training for service in
these capacities in the North West Territories? Some of this training could
be given in the North West Territories but, in the initial stages, much of it
would have to be taken "outside."

RECAPITULATION OF RECOMMENDATIONS ON EDUCATIONAL POLICY

(1) That a middle-of-the-way curriculum be developed; i.e., one which is
not too academic and which includes suitable occupational courses and
activities together with adequate instruction in health and hygiene.

(2) That the general principle of taking suitable white man's education
to the natives in their own environment as much as possible be tried out on
an experimental basis as soon as possible along the following lines: (a) that
a suitable school barge (or barges) be fitted up to be tried out during the
summer months at the rendezvous centres along the southern and eastern
shores of Great Slave Lake (health, conservation, adult education, etc., might
be included in the programme); (b) that a community centre project be tried
out at the site of the former Salt River Settlement, and that some similar
but not so elaborate project be tried out at some specially selected camp-site
among the Eskimo, e.g., in the Coppermine area; (c) that specially selected
natives, both Indian and Eskimo and of both sexes, after suitable training be
returned to their native environment, to live among and serve as teachers
and counsellors to their tribes and bands.

(3) That compulsory education be enforced in so far as the conditions of
the area will permit.

(4) That a Teachers' Convention and Institute be held annually in
Mackenzie District to which outstanding lecturers would be brought from
the "outside" at public expense.

(5) That a Mackenzie River library project similar to that of the Fraser
River Valley be carried out. Wherever feasible the schools should be utilized
for library centres.

(6) That so far as is practicable every school in Mackenzie District be utilized as a community centre.

(7) That itinerant schoolmasters be tried on two circuits: (*a*) to serve Fort Simpson, Fort Providence, Hay River, and Fort Resolution; (*b*) to serve Fort McPherson, Arctic Red River, Fort Good Hope, and Fort Norman.

(8) That short courses for adult natives (Indians, Eskimo, mixed-blood), even though they are illiterate, be tried during the summer months in as many of the residential schools (which usually are not in operation during the summer months) as possible. These courses should be largely occupational (motor mechanics, prospecting, mining, etc.) with some inspirational material and the utilization of motion pictures, radio, and such adult education techniques as can be adapted.

(9) That suitable adaptations of the Danish folk high school be tried out in one or two specially selected residential schools.

(10) That a fully-equipped occupational training centre be established at Yellowknife as soon as possible.

(11) That the governing body of the North West Territories offer scholarships and bursaries for selected natives and whites to take special training, both within the North West Territories and "outside" for service as teachers and social workers in the North West Territories. Some of the trading, mining, and other interests might also be induced to do likewise.

RECOMMENDATIONS CONCERNING THE ORGANIZATION AND ADMINISTRATION OF EDUCATION IN THE NORTH WEST TERRITORIES

(1) It is recommended that there should be one authority in control of all education (Indian, mixed blood, and white) which is supported by public funds in the North West Territories. Under present conditions this authority should be the governing body of the North West Territories acting through a Director of Education who must reside in the North West Territories.

In the North West Territories as elsewhere in Canada the Indian Affairs Branch is responsible for the education of Indian children who are wards of the government. In Mackenzie District it has been the practice of the Indian Affairs Branch to delegate the actual provision of educational accommodation and instruction to two religious denominations; viz., the Church of England in Canada (Anglican) and the Roman Catholic. There are no schools in the North West Territories operated by the Indian Affairs Branch itself. It should not, therefore, be difficult for the Indian Affairs Branch to delegate its responsibilities to the sole authority in education above-mentioned.

The responsibility for providing education for native children who are not wards of the government (including children of mixed blood) and of white children is placed upon the civil government of the North West Territories by chapter 75 of the 1898 Consolidated Ordinances[13] of the North West Territories with amendments to 1905 which presumably are still in force in the North West Territories as they exist today (1944). In fact, this Ordinance makes provision for a Department of Education, an Educational Council, Local School Districts, Separate Schools, etc. However, the number of these children[14] in the present-day North West Territories would not justify any such elaborate organization. For even these small numbers, however, there should be some definite legal organization and administrative provision because it is a generally accepted principle that every child in Canada, no matter what his race or creed, or the economic condition of his parents, should have an opportunity to secure, at public expense, as much education on the elementary and secondary levels as he is capable of assimilating. In the past it has been the practice for parents of white children to send them "out" to schools in the provinces at their own expense. More recently some parents have been utilizing the very excellent correspondence courses which the Correspondence Branch of the Department of Education of the Province of Alberta has been kind enough to provide at reasonable rates. It is the policy of the Hudson's Bay Company to assist its personnel financially in meeting the expense involved in either or both of these practices. Some few white children are also, at the expense of their parents, attending residential or day schools maintained in the North West Territories by the two religious denominations aforesaid. Some parents of mixed-blood children who are not wards of the government also are attempting to pay for the education of their children in a fashion similar to that of the whites.

Some recognized legal educational organization and administration should be provided under which not only all children will have an opportunity to secure an approved standard of education but that their parents and all the citizens of the North West Territories will regularly contribute their share of the cost through some form of taxation.

(2) It is recommended that the administration of education in the North West Territories should be of the highly centralized type. The degree of centralization should be subject to periodical review, say every ten years, with a view to reduction of centralization as much as possible.

In most of the Canadian provinces school administration is decentralized in form but highly centralized in fact. These administrations are decentralized in form because there is one central authority for the whole province (Department of Education) and many local school districts. Theoretically, because they are elected bodies, these local school authorities are supposed to carry a considerable responsibility and wield considerable authority. It is an

---

[13]*The School Ordinance*, 1901, chap. 29.

[14]The Census of 1941 shows that there are 87 half-breed and 164 white children between the ages of five and fourteen years inclusive, in the North West Territories.

open secret that they do little of either. Under present conditions it would be a mistake to set up such a decentralized form of school administration in the North West Territories. Some adaptation of the New Zealand system where practically everything is administered from the Department of Education with locally constituted bodies in an advisory capacity only, would be more suitable for the North West Territories. The local advisory bodies might be elected or co-opted or partly both. It should be emphasized that the present writer would not normally recommend such a high centralization of control but this is what he believes to be most suitable for the North West Territories at the present moment. As rapidly as circumstances permit, it should be evolved into a suitable adaptation of the present Alberta type of school administration. This recommendation means that the local groups now supporting the schools in Yellowknife and Fort Smith should be continued in an advisory capacity only. Other local advisory bodies should be constituted wherever a public school is operated.

(3) It is recommended that the resident Director of Education should have wide powers and a very free hand to organize and administer the educational system in the North West Territories within the limits of policy and regulations laid down by the governing body of the Territories.

In such an extensive and sparsely settled area he must have sufficient authority and responsibility to organize and administer the proposed system of education for the North West Territories without the necessity of constant references to Ottawa. He must, however, be amenable to his superior authority and duly sensitive to local opinion. This involves certain checks and balances. First, the governing body of the North West Territories to which he is directly responsible should carefully lay down the policy he must follow and he must refer to it for guidance whenever he is in doubt as to interpretation. Second, he must not overrule or ignore the recommendations of the Educational Advisory Council recommended elsewhere for the North West Territories except by way of an appeal to the governing body at Ottawa. Third, an appeal should lie to Ottawa concerning any difference between the Director and any local advisory body *not covered by regulations.* The objective of all this is to secure for the North West Territories a centralized system of school administration which will give the resident Director of Education ample authority to organize and administer but at the same time to keep him from becoming unduly bureaucratic. The fact that his administration will come up for review, say every ten years, with a view to reducing centralization as much as possible, should have a salutary and restraining influence.

The Director of Education must be very mobile. He must have a suitable motor-boat and an aeroplane with pilot at his service if he is to co-ordinate and supervise the proposed educational system on a modern basis. This is particularly true if some form of compulsory attendance is established.

(4) It is further recommended that an Educational Council be constituted to act in a purely advisory capacity to the Director of Education. This Council should not be clothed with legislative, judicial, or executive powers.

There is a sound general principle in educational administration that such matters as educational standards, teacher-training, text-books, curricula, examinations, etc., should be outside the pale of partisan politics. This Council should advise on such matters and its advice should be followed unless under most exceptional circumstances. It might properly consist of about nine members carefully selected from representative laymen and clerics who should serve without remuneration but should receive reasonable expenses. No single denominational or other interest should dominate it. It should be so chosen that a relatively small quorum (say five members) could meet on short notice. The Educational Council provided for in the 1901 School Ordinance embodies the general principle.[15] Neither the Director of Education nor any other civil servant should be a member.

(5) It is recommended that all teachers in any schools established in the North West Territories should be members of the federal Civil Service with special provision for a sabbatical year after each five years of teaching in the North West Territories.

Living conditions and the general environment in the North West Territories do not tend to attract the best type of teachers unless they are fired by missionary or religious zeal and of these there is an insufficient supply even at present under church auspices.

(6) It is recommended that all teachers in the North West Territories should hold at least first-class professional certificates and should have a year of special training for this type of work.

The teaching of Indian and Eskimo children so close to aboriginal conditions is just as specialized as the teaching of auxiliary classes or of kindergarten classes.

(7) It is further recommended that the legislation concerning education in the North West Territories be thoroughly revised and brought up-to-date having due regard for present conditions.

The School Ordinances[16] and Regulations[17] passed prior to 1905 and pre-

---

[15]*The School Ordinance*, 1901, chap. 29, secs. 8-11 inclusive.

[16]*The General Ordinances of the North West Territories in Force September 1, 1905 (Being the Consolidated Ordinances of the Territories 1898 and All Subsequent Public General Ordinances of the Legislature of the Territories Revised in Force at the Commencement of the Saskatchewan Act)*, ed. Reginald Rommer (Regina, 1907). (a) Schools, pp. 1008 to 1061; (b) School assessment, pp. 1061 to 1103; (c) School grants, pp. 1103 to 1108; (d) Treasury Department, sec. 29, p. 1171.

[17]*Regulations of the Board of Education for the North West Territories:*
(a) *For the Examination of Candidates for Certificates to Teach in the Schools of the Territories, Printed by Order of the Board of Education* (Regina, 1886), 10 pp.
(b) *General Regulations Adopted 15th March 1888, Printed by Order of the Board of Education* (Regina, 1889), 36 pp.

sumably still legally applicable to the North West Territories of today contain many excellent provisions as well as some wholly unsuitable at the present time. The former should be retained and incorporated with whatever further legislation is necessary to provide modern organization and administration of education in the North West Territories. No new Ordinances concerning education in the North West Territories have been passed since 1905. Certain Dominion Orders-in-Council have been passed under the Indian Act and some of these may be applicable to the North West Territories.[18]

[18]James Collins Miller, *National Government and Education in Federated Democracies, Dominion of Canada* (Philadelphia, 1940), pp. 272-93 incl. The author was a Professor in the University of Pennsylvania.

Part Ten

J. A. URQUHART

Eskimos of the Canadian Western Arctic*†

In Canada, the Eskimos inhabit the entire Arctic coast from the Yukon-Alaska boundary to the eastern limits of Canadian territory, the more southerly islands of the Arctic archipelago, and some of the islands in Hudson Bay. The people dealt with specifically in this section are those Eskimos who inhabit the western Canadian Arctic coast from the International Boundary east through Coronation Gulf to Queen Maud Gulf, King William Island, and Boothia Peninsula. From the common point of view, the land along the coast is barren but while the Eskimos go inland on their hunting expeditions, particularly for caribou, the greater portion of their time is spent upon the coast. One exception to this is in the Mackenzie delta where for some years a number of Eskimos have inhabited timbered country. Only a few do this, for as a rule Eskimos dislike being shut in by trees. Further, as a result of habits and experience extending over generations they are naturally at their best when securing their livelihood in the "barren lands" or on the sea.

On the coast itself there is a short season of open water in midsummer, but for eight or nine months of the year the sea is frozen over, and travelling thereon seems no different from travelling over flat land areas. In fact it is often necessary when travelling, if one is doubtful of his location, to dig through the snow to see whether there is soil or ice underneath. So that to all intents and purposes, the Arctic Ocean itself, for a period of at least eight months, provides a happy hunting ground for the Eskimo, and he travels and lives on it as if it were solid ground.

The Eskimos are a sturdy race with good physique, straight dark hair, and dark eyes, the eyes having a distinctly Asiatic slant, rather broad, flat faces, and with a skin which, when exposed to the continuous daylight of the spring

*This article refers only to Western Arctic Eskimos, the circumstances of those of the Eastern Arctic being quite different. It is reprinted from *Canada's Western Northland,* assembled by W. C. Bethune, of the Department of Mines and Resources, Ottawa, 1937. By permission.

†Dr. J. A. Urquhart, the author of this section, was formerly Medical Health Officer for the Northwest Territories Administration, Department of Mines and Resources, at Aklavik, and later at Fort Smith, N.W.T., and retired from the government service in 1944.

and early summer, "snowburns" to almost a black. Although fatter than the average European they are very active and possessed of great endurance. The women are little smaller than the men and are equally strong. Accustomed to hard work in their homes, many of them also hunt and trap as efficiently as the men.

Many people suppose that the Eskimos are a diminutive people. This is only partly true. In the Mackenzie delta and the western portion of the Canadian Arctic, many of them are tall, fine-looking people, some of the men standing over 6 feet tall and weighing over 200 pounds. Many of the women are 5 feet 7 inches in height, or over, with an occasional "six-footer" among them. Around Coronation Gulf and towards King William Island the Eskimos are shorter in height by as much as 6 inches, but they still have the same sturdy build and are capable of doing hard work for long hours. As a rule their faces are pleasant, with the characteristic grin or smile which is most noticeable when one first comes among them. Both men and women are highly intelligent, quick to imitate or learn, and with a mechanical turn of mind that permits them rapidly to take advantage of mechanical power and labour-saving devices. Their outlook on life is cheerful, their dispositions are friendly, and most of them have a keen sense of humour.

The type of habitation used by the Eskimos depends upon local and seasonal conditions. Whenever possible, the Eskimos have "permanent" homes in which they reside during the winter months, although the location of these homes may be changed every few seasons. While the Eskimos do not ordinarily live in timbered country, there is, within a wide radius of the mouths of many of the rivers, considerable drift-wood, which they salvage, and out of which they build log-houses. The drift-wood is also used for fuel. These houses are invariably one-roomed, with sleeping benches and sometimes beds at one end. The beds are usually made of poles covered with raw caribou skin and then sleeping robes. As often as not two families will occupy the one house. The stove is in the end opposite to the beds and the occupants share the housework. This is their permanent winter abode and trapping base, and if the country surrounding is good trapping country, two or three houses will be built at the same spot. The two factors on which the location of a house depends are, of course, available drift-wood, and, equally important, good fishing or sealing. Strangers are gladly welcomed and the banding together of three or four congenial families banishes loneliness from their midst.

On the coast the Eskimos move out on the ice to sealing grounds, and it is then that the snow-house is utilized by many of them. There are, of course, some locations where drift-wood is not available, and the snow-house is used throughout the entire winter. In other places, where caribou are not to be found, groups of families will maintain sealing camps on the ice, which they also use as a base for their trapping operations during the winter season.

These sealing camps may be from five to eighteen or twenty miles out on the ice and the hard, drifted snow which covers the Arctic ice-pack throughout the winter is the building material. Blocks of snow are cut out with a long snow-knife and the houses are built circular in shape, with a dome top, very much like a beehive. On the leeward side according to the prevailing wind a door is left, and this is protected by a snow entrance or porch. Some of these snow-houses are large enough to accommodate two or three families; others, of a more temporary nature, may be only big enough for two. A hole is left at the top for ventilation and while occasionally blubber is still used for heating, the modern Eskimo uses a Primus stove, burning coal-oil for both heating and cooking. The house is carefully chinked, and after a few hours with heat inside, the interior becomes encrusted with an icy coating. It is really warm and draught-free, and strong enough to bear the weight of a man on the top. In a short time the wind drifts snow about the houses and little can be seen except the vent pipe at the top. The entrance, which is invariably occupied by the dogs, closely resembles the entrance to a cellar. When there are a number of families they build their houses close together and usually have snow-covered communication passages between the houses.

Whether big or little, each house consists of one room, about half of it being occupied by a raised sleeping platform, which is covered with raw skins, more to keep out the cold from the snow and ice below than with any idea of softness. The entire family uses the same sleeping bench, and if there are visitors it is often quite crowded. Sleeping closely together they keep each other warm and thus a minimum of fuel is required. Coal-oil is expensive, but seal-oil, or blubber, is valuable not only as fuel but as food for themselves and their necessary dogs.

Naturally it is not easy to keep such a house clean, but the sealing camps must be shifted every few weeks. The Eskimos simply move to new ground, build new houses and thus avoid all the trouble of house-cleaning. All traces of the camps and their refuse disappear when the ice breaks up in the summer. No snow-house is occupied long enough for it to become germ ridden, and because it is used but once, probably accounts for the Eskimo's comparative freedom from many diseases.

With the onset of spring, when the season for foxes is over, the Eskimos move to temporary quarters which are occupied until the seasonal break-up. In the Mackenzie delta these temporary quarters consist of "ratting" camps, usually tents, where the natives remain, hunting muskrats and living under canvas until the season of open water arrives.

The summer existence of the natives depends largely upon their prosperity, and to a lesser degree upon location. Those who own whale-boats put them in order with the first open water and proceed to the whaling grounds where they fish for white whale. Here they either live in their boats or establish tents on shore. The white whale is taken by Eskimos in nets and by shooting. A small power-boat is capable of keeping up with a school while individual animals are shot in the open sea. The nets are very cumbersome and expensive and consequently their use is limited. In some localities the natives will make a "drive" of these porpoises, herding them into shallow water where they are stranded and easily dispatched. A successful whaling season means prosperity for all. The flesh of the white whale is used for food, both for human consumption and for dogs. The blubber, which is the really valuable part, has the oil extracted and this oil, or "ookchuk" forms part of practically every meal. It is stored up in barrels or sealskin bags for winter use, and the prosperity of any native is more or less gauged by the amount of oil he has.

Natives who have no whale-boats, live throughout the summer in tents, often made of skin, and carry on their fishing and whaling from the shore. Naturally, without this necessary equipment, their success is not so great. The seal is no very great factor to them during the early summer, as the animals are thin and sink rapidly if shot, rarely being recovered, but inasmuch as fish are plentiful the lack of seal meat is no hardship. The last month of the very short summer is usually spent in sealing. The animals are now fat, do not sink so rapidly and consequently are easily secured. At this time they use the meat as a staple article of diet. The oil from the blubber is not as choice as that of the white whale and though often eaten by the natives it is more often used as dog feed. The sealskin—and to avoid confusion it should be borne in mind that this is the hair seal[1] and not the valuable fur-bearer—is used extensively. From it the Eskimos make waterproof boots, and very often parkas (long outer smocks or snow shirts) when caribou skins are not procurable, and it is the skin of this seal that is used in the construction of the native kayaks or skin boats. The skin of the white whale is also used to make waterproof boots. It is, however, not nearly as durable, although beautifully white in colour, and is most commonly used for their best, or dress boots.

By the end of September, the Eskimos are back again at their winter quarters and now comes their very busy time. They fish assiduously during the entire month of October, and this is accomplished by setting their nets under the ice, for freeze-up occurs early in that month. The amount of fish required by an Eskimo family appears to us enormous. They eat huge amounts themselves and require large quantities for their dogs, and an Eskimo who starts the winter with less than 8,000 or 10,000 fish can look forward to lean days ahead. The fish they get are herring, white fish, and inconnu, and the natives prefer them in that order. A large proportion of the fish catch is eaten raw and frozen, and even to the white man's palate "quawk" or frozen fish is improved by being slightly "high." This custom of eating raw fish, while not natural to white men,

[1]Hair seal is the common term for the Harbour Seal, the Ringed Seal, the Greenland or Harp Seal, and the Bearded Seal.

is actually a very good thing for the Eskimos. They live in a country where there are few fresh vegetables and even though canned vegetables are available to a limited extent, the natives, not being accustomed to them, do not like them. It is obvious then that they must get their supply of "live" food containing vitamins from some other source, and this source is raw oil, raw fish, and raw meat. Scurvy is to them a disease unknown, and this is the explanation.

On the fifteenth of November the trapping season for the white fox opens and the natives then engage industriously in that pursuit. They have no use for the white fox skin themselves, but it has a ready market and might almost be called the currency of the country. After a successful trapping season, the Eskimo trapper is in a position to purchase clothing, especially underwear—far superior in his eye to anything made with skins—and this clothing, plus shirt and trousers, is commonly worn under his outer skin garments. The Eskimos are also developing a taste for flour and bread, butter, tea, and jam, and it is for the purchase of these supplies, which in the light of their changing ideas go far towards making their lives much more livable, that they trap the fox at all. In fortunate years they may even have an excess of fox pelts, and if this is sufficient they will purchase new rifles, ammunition, and even power-boats of some sort. All of their activities demand transport. The only possible means in the winter is the dog-team. Without dogs the natives are tied to their camps and can neither hunt nor trap. In the summer, possession of a power-boat ensures transportation to a good fishing ground, and is almost a guarantee of a really good whaling and sealing season, which, as has already been said, means actual prosperity to them.

The one food that Eskimos really crave, and which the country itself supplies, is fresh meat. Seal meat is the staple, but caribou meat, when obtainable, is the most prized. Caribou hunting for meat extends throughout the winter and organized expeditions of ten, twenty, or even more hunters are made from time to time for the purpose of securing meat. In addition, caribou skins make infinitely better fur clothing than can be obtained from any other source. The back sinew supplies the best thread and while sinew can be obtained from other sources such as foxes, the Eskimos much prefer caribou because a greater quantity can be obtained from one animal and the strands are longer and more easily worked.

In the above brief description, the Eskimos have been followed through the annual rotation of activities and it will be noticed that in the appropriate season, they do the particular job which enables them to prepare for the coming winter. It can thus be easily seen that the Eskimos in general live by the year rather than by the day or by the week. They have learned that they must take advantage of seasonal opportunities at the correct time, otherwise they will suffer a distinct shortage throughout coming months. Rarely is there an opportunity to recoup, following misfortune or negligence.

Following is a description in more detail of some of their activities. In general the men take the lead and do the hunting, fishing, and trapping, while the women cut up meat and fish for drying, tan skins, make clothing, and, in addition to the cooking and caring for the children, often assist in the actual trapping. On the whale-boats they "work their passage" as crew, and in any moving of camp the women do their full share, whether it be by actual back-packing in the summer or by handling a dog-team in the winter.

Caribou hunts are conducted in much the same manner in Eskimo territory as elsewhere. These animals are still numerous in the North West Territories but migrate seasonally and from time to time the route of migration is changed. The reason for this change of route varies. It may be that the head of the migration has been deflected through fright or lack of grazing along a particular route. From whatever cause, the effect is frequently serious to the natives who have been depending for their meat supply upon the arrival of caribou at the usual time. Practically every year at some point the migration fails to materialize and in that locality there will be a shortage of meat. The Eskimos there must then depend upon the sealing, or, if possible, change their location to conform to the movements of the caribou.

Fishing is conducted to a large extent with the ordinary gill nets, although in locations where there is a large run of fish, spearing is commonly resorted to, more especially if it is possible to construct a rock trap at a shallow point. This latter practice is quite common in the Coppermine area, where annually there are quite good runs of "salmon."[2] West of that area the rivers are muddy—and this applies particularly to the Mackenzie—and salmon do not come to muddy rivers.

Sealing provides more of interest. When there is open water the seals are often seen sleeping on cakes of ice. The hunter, after a cautious stalk, kills them by rifle fire. If he fails to shoot the animal through the head, it will flop about and slide into the water and be lost. The native who has a boat will watch for the seals coming up to breathe, shoot them through the head in the same manner and then hurry to get to them before they sink. All this may perhaps seem quite natural, but what does intrigue one is mid-winter sealing. There is no open water and nothing to be seen but the hard-packed snow covering the ice. Seals, however, cannot remain indefinitely under water without coming up to breathe, and during the winter months they keep holes open in the ice to which they come at regular intervals to renew their supply of air. The Eskimo uses a dog to locate these seal holes and a good sealing dog is as valuable to him as a good lead dog in his dog-team. He starts out over the ice in an area which experience has taught him is a good sealing ground, and the dog, when he comes to a seal hole, draws his master's attention to it. From that moment great care must be used. The Eskimo feels through the snow with a slender stick and locates the centre of the hole without breaking the snow covering. His next job is to erect a few blocks of snow to protect him from the

[2] Actually the Arctic Char.

wind. He then sets his slender indicator so that it just touches the water in the centre of the air hole and crouches over it with his seal spear in his hand. The spear head is detachable from the staff, but has a rawhide thong tied to it. The other end of the thong he fastens securely, often to his leg. Patience is now a virtue. The Eskimo may have to crouch over his tell-tale for a few minutes or it may be an hour or more until a movement of the indicator shows that a seal has come up to breathe. The moment this occurs he drives his spear through the crust with all of his force into the body of the seal. A moment or so later he is in possession of a good supply of meat, fat, and another sealskin. On a good day a native may take five or six seals, and on a poor day none at all. If he is lucky, all in the camp share in his good fortune. When the sealing is good, all feast equally. When it is poor they all go hungry to the same degree irrespective of who kills or who does not. In all of these hunting pursuits the Eskimos are highly skilled. They must be, to exist.

Let us now deal with the occupations of the women. Many of them, as we have said before, are adepts at the vocations of the men, but in addition to this they have their own occupations which require the greatest skill. They excel in the making of clothing. They first tan the hides and then make up the garments, doing all the sewing by hand, and with sinew. The sewing must be well done because the parkas and skin trousers must be windproof, while the water-boots which are so necessary in the spring, summer, and fall, must be sewn so that they are waterproof. The tanning of the skins is more or less crude and does not entirely eliminate odour, but it is otherwise efficient, giving a soft, pliable skin to work with. The Eskimo is very particular about his clothing. The parkas are always roomy as he must have great freedom of movement, and it is very amusing to see an Eskimo man try on a new parka. These are often quite nicely decorated with a pattern of different coloured pieces of fur around the edges. However his chief concern is not with the appearance of it. He slips the parka on over his head and then promptly goes through all the violent contortions he can think of to throw as much strain on the seams as possible. If it passes this test, well and good. If not, it is tossed back to the woman, who makes whatever alterations are necessary to make it perfect.

Throughout the winter when it is cold and dry, moose skin or deer skin soles are used for the mukluks or boots. With the advent of warmer weather, when the snow begins to get damp, waterproof boots of some sort must be available and these, of course, must be manufactured at home. For fancy wear the skin of the white whale is used for soles with either canvas, cloth, or fur tops. For hard wear, however, sealskin is much better and while the skin of any of the hair seals is good, the skin of the bearded seal is preferred because it is thicker and heavier. If it is merely damp underfoot, waterproof soles are used with some other material for the top. If, however, much water is about, the complete water-boot made of sealskin is used. This boot reaches to the knee and all of the seams, which are sewn with sinew, must be so well done that the seams themselves are completely waterproof. The women are clever at this and it is rare indeed for a water-boot to leak, and properly cared for they will last a full season. Much has been said of the women chewing boots. To turn the toe and heel, the skin must be crimped, and as they have no crimping machines, the women chew these crimps into both the heel and toe to make the boot fit perfectly. The completed article looks as neat as if it had been crimped by a machine, but the teeth of the older women show a certain amount of wear from performing this work.

The feminine side of their character is evidenced by their attempts at decoration, and it is remarkable indeed to see what they can do with the limited materials at hand. Bits of different coloured fur are cut up and made into a sort of mosaic pattern to trim the hem of a parka, while other coloured pieces are inset at the neck, shoulders, and sometimes in the arms. These, plus various bits of long-haired fur such as wolf or wolverine, make an attractive looking garment. The hood of the parka is trimmed with wolverine, if that fur is available. Many believe that the fur of the wolverine does not freeze or get frosted up. This is not correct. It does get coated with frost but the moment one gets indoors where it is warm the ice pulls off leaving a practically dry fur, whereas the fur of other animals is left wet and can be most uncomfortable.

The cooking is comparatively simple. A large proportion of the meat and fish is eaten raw and frozen, and when food is cooked, boiling or stewing is the favourite method.

The care of the babies presents a distinct problem. With the intense cold and the long winter, infants must be carefully protected. The Eskimo mother accomplishes this by wearing a very full and wide parka, usually, as a matter of fact, two parkas, one with the fur turned in and one with the fur turned out and when the Eskimo mother has to go outside with her child, she slips it, often scantily clad, onto her back under the parka. The hoods of the women's parkas are left with a distinct bulge in the back to provide room for the baby's head, so that when it is not too cold, by leaving the hood down, the infant can get a supply of fresh air. A sash tied around the parka at the waist converts it into a sack in which the baby lies comfortably, protected from the cold by a double lining of fur and warmed by its mother's body. There is even sufficient room in the parka for the mother to slide the baby around to the front without exposing it to the air when necessary to nurse it. In their homes the children play around on the floor, often with very little clothing on.

When the children are a little older and can run about they have an outfit which is an exact replica of that of their elders, and the youngsters, with their little fat faces and bulky fur clothing, resemble little woolly bears. They play as other children do, the only difference being in their games. Naturally their games are often imitations of the activities of their parents. The boys busy themselves setting snares, making miniature houses, and at the first moment they are big enough to do so, attempt to drive dogs. Usually the pups are made use of for this amusement. The result in most cases is that by the time the dog has reached a size and age where he can be worked in the dog-team, he has already been trained by the children, and for the parents it is merely a matter of appropriating the dog and putting him into harness. When a boy reaches the age of nine or ten he is sufficiently skilled in dog handling to have a little team of his own—not, of course, the team of six or seven dogs that is driven by his elders, but of two, and as he gets older, of three dogs. By this time he is capable of taking his little team and following along after his father when he goes on a short trap-line, and the little Eskimo boy has his own traps and will set trap for trap with his father. It is amusing in the extreme to see father and son come back from a trip over the trap-line that the youngster is sharing. He very often beats his father, having caught more fur and is as proud as would be a child in the outside world who had won a scholarship. This early training is essential to them. They eventually must support themselves by hunting, fishing, and trapping and it is in their youth that they really learn to do these well. The normal Eskimo boy of fourteen has a knowledge of animal lore that is nearly the equal of his father's. He knows where, when, and how to set a trap to get results. In addition to that he is a skilled dog handler and at that age is a real asset to his family. To all intents and purposes he is as much of a bread-winner as his father. The only thing he lacks is the physique which he will attain in a very few years. A certain amount of education is an advantage to him but he should not acquire this at the expense of his practical lessons in natural history.

The girls have their fun playing outside just as the boys do, but at the time when the boys go out on the trap-line, the girls stay at home and take over a large part of the care of the young children, and in addition to this learn the art of tanning skins, sewing, and cooking. In the fall, after the ice has become too thick to fish with nets, holes are kept open for the purpose of jigging for fish, and the whole family, men and women, boys and girls, assist in this. A tremendous amount of their time is spent on the ice adding to the needed store of food for man and dog.

The Eskimo is cheerful, easy to deal with, intelligent, quick to learn, and an admirable patient when sick. For generations he has wrested a living, mated, and reared a family in a country where only a hardy and intelligent race could survive. He is making a very good job of slowly assimilating a certain amount of civilization while still retaining his independence, his pride, and his ability to carry on and care for himself. The vast majority of them now appreciate the value of conserving the natural resources of the country in which they live, and co-operate in that work to a remarkable degree. The Eskimo is naturally law-abiding and even though he may not always quite understand the meaning and purpose of the law, his natural tendency is to obey it. His communal life has taught him that the wishes of the individual must be subordinate to the good of the majority and this has made him especially easy to deal with. For a number of years the government of Canada has been paying special attention to its Arctic citizens, in order to keep them independent, self-reliant, and self-supporting, and with this object in view has put forth continuous and unremitting efforts to preserve the natural resources of the country so that the Eskimos may continue to be the admirable race of people they now are.[3]

INDIAN AND ESKIMO POPULATION OF NORTH WEST TERRITORIES BY DISTRICTS, 1941*

	Indian		Eskimo	
	Male	Female	Male	Female
North West Territories	2,066	2,027	2,828	2,811
Aklavik and District	96	114	187	188
Arctic Red River	65	53		
Baffin Island				
East Coast			274	282
North Coast			182	164
Northwest Coast			208	297
South Coast			413	427
Baillie Island and Points East as far as Pearce Point.	5	6	123	119
Baker Lake and District			133	133
Banks Island			25	26
Boothia Peninsula			89	83
Chesterfield Inlet and District			543	491
Coppermine River and Coronation Gulf District			135	107
Dundas Harbour (Devon Island)				
Fort Good Hope and District	167	161		
Fort Liard and District	107	91		
Fort MacPherson and District	139	178		
Fort Norman and District	111	93		
Fort Providence and District	166	143		
Fort Rae and District	343	342		
Fort Reliance and District	45	42		
Fort Resolution and District	207	231	1	
Fort Simpson and District	171	161		
Fort Smith and District (incl. Indian Settlement)	151	120		
Fort Wrigley and District	39	44		
Great Bear Lake	74	92		
Hay River Settlement and District	77	68		1
Islands in Hudson Bay, James Bay (incl. Cape Smith)	6	3	163	167
Port Leopold (North Somerset Island)			8	7
Queen Maud (incl. King William Island)			140	126
Victoria Island	1		204	193
Yellowknife Settlement Area	96	85		

*Assembled by Nathan Keyfitz of the Dominion Bureau of Statistics.

[3]To supplement the natural resources on which Eskimos primarily depend, a herd of 2,370 reindeer was brought from Alaska to the Arctic coast of the North West Territories east of the Mackenzie River delta in 1935. This herd has increased rapidly, and large numbers of stock have been used for meat and hides. It is estimated that in 1947 the total number of deer contained in two herds will be approximately 7,000. The herding work is performed mainly by Eskimos under Government supervision (see *Canada's Western Northland* published by the Department of Mines and Resources, pp. 85-7).

Part Eleven

C. A. DAWSON

The New North-West

My research interest in the settlement of the new North-West dates back to the summer of 1929 when I was asked to make a preliminary study of the Peace River Country which was one of the "Frontiers of Settlement" studies published during the first half of the nineteen-thirties. During the following summer the field study was completed and the *Settlement of the Peace River Country* was published in 1934.[1] This study made familiar to the author the Alberta and British Columbia divisions of the Peace River region from Notikewin, seventy-five miles north of Grimshaw through the settlements of the Peace as far west as Fort St. John. Among many communities studied in this survey were Notikewin on the north-east fringe of settlement and Dawson Creek which forms the southern anchor of the Alaska Highway. The opening of the Alaska Highway, built between 1942 and 1944, together with the oil developments along the Mackenzie River and the mineral production of the Pre-Cambrian area just east of it, focused attention on this new North-West. The possibilities of settlement in this far north-western territory have received wide publicity. Among others, I spent the summer of 1944 in this great stretch of territory, which lies north of the Peace River and extends from a line drawn from Waterways to Coronation Gulf on the east (approximately the western boundary of the Pre-Cambrian Shield), to the Alaska Highway on the west. The northern boundary of the territory studied is the Arctic Ocean. My own part of this survey included also that part of Alaska served by the Alaska railroad and the highway network which lies between Fairbanks and Anchorage.

My task was to make a general overall survey of this far northern territory with a view to discovering the factors making for an extension of settlement in this vast territory which lies north of the well established districts of the Peace River Country. The mineral, agricultural, and other resources of this vast domain have been objects of marked interest by various governmental departments at Ottawa. Provincial departments, the exploratory efforts of corporations, and the widespread efforts of unattached individuals have done much to lay bare the resources of this northern wilderness. Despite these efforts, some of which go back many decades, little has been achieved beyond

[1]"Frontiers of Settlement" series, vol. VII, ed. W. A. MacKintosh and W. L. G. Joerg (Toronto, 1934).

the preliminary stages of investigation. Thus my own survey which depends so much on what other investigators have discovered, together with my limited observations during one summer, makes possible highly tentative conclusions concerning the potentialities for settlement in this new Northland. The time spent in Alaska was for the purpose of finding out in particular the special agricultural problems of the far North. These experiences of Alaskan farmers will be useful to those Canadians who now hope to establish agricultural settlements in our own North.

THE ALASKA HIGHWAY AND ITS ADJOINING TERRITORY

The Pioneer Military Road reached from Dawson Creek to Big Delta on the Richardson Highway in Alaska, a distance of 1,523 miles. For fifty-five miles north of Dawson Creek the road width is 36 feet, and a four-mile strip south of Whitehorse has a width of 30 feet. Otherwise the highway has an average width of 26 feet. The surface is now gravelled to an average width of 22 feet but is somewhat wider on the hair-pin turns that are a prominent feature of the Alaska Highway.[2] These facts apply to the highway at the end of 1944. The initial Pioneer Road was begun early in 1942 and pushed through directly without regard to cost within a period of eight months. Except for the section between Kluane Lake and the Alaska border, usable only when the ground was frozen, the Pioneer Road was an all year road. Greyhound buses were able to reach Whitehorse in December, 1942 and one year later there was a daily service between Dawson Creek and Fairbanks.[3] During 1942 the Pioneer Road was pushed through with a tremendous burst of energy by American army engineers. It took two more years to transform it into the Alaska Highway. The American army retained the chief responsibility for the whole project. However, they were aided in the transformation period by the Public Roads Administration engineers. The final result was a compromise between the army and the civil engineers of the latter body. Strategy demanded that the army push the road to its completion with utmost speed and with little regard for expense. In the light of this tremendous obligation placed on the army to get there quickly, the allegations of "wasted materials" are readily explainable. The civilian engineers strove for a permanent highway which would take some years longer than the army considered advisable. The result is the present Alaska Highway which permits buses to move over an all-gravelled highway from Dawson Creek to Fairbanks. Throughout much of its 1,600 miles it is a permanent highway. It still lacks certain permanent bridges across important rivers, and over extended areas the gravel is destined to sink into the muskeg. This will call for rerouting of

[2]For construction details, see S. C. Ells, "The Alaska Highway" (*Canadian Geographical Journal*, March, 1944, pp. 104-19).
[3]*Ibid.*, pp. 111-14.

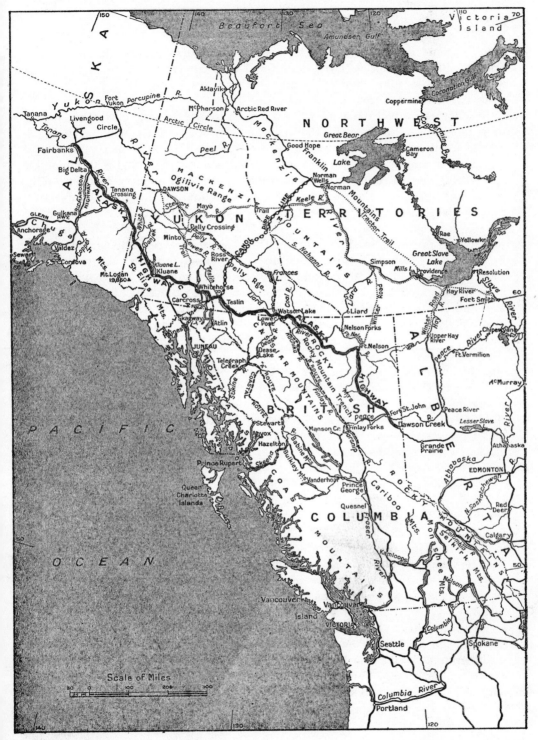

some sections and intensive refilling work in others. Certain temporary bridges will need to be replaced, additional steel culverts laid, and the highway drainage system extended in many other ways before the maintenance costs can be reduced to a tolerable level.

Bulldozers pushed the shallow rooted trees to one side and there they lie, for hundreds of miles along this thoroughfare. These tree trunks will need to be cleared for their salvageable wood and timber, as well as the reduction of the fire and drainage hazards they entail. Perhaps some additional $20 million will be required to complete the transformation of this military road into a permanent highway. For the present its construction is sufficiently advanced to meet the strategic needs for which it was built. In its present condition it became a Canadian possession on April 1, 1946 and came under the direct supervision of the Canadian army. This has been a project carried out jointly by the United States and Canada. Canada provided the right of way, made available local building materials, and facilitated the easy entry of men and mechanized equipment from the United States. Financially it was underwritten by the United States government, which expended approximately $200 million on the road and adjoining airfields in Canada. Recently the Canadian government has reimbursed the United States for the $76,800,000 the latter spent on airfields in Canada. The highway required the services of thousands of United States army engineers and a great many thousands of civilian workers employed by civilian contractors from the United States and Canada. At every one hundred miles along the highway may now be seen the well-equipped maintenance camps, with diesel powered electric light, complete sanitary systems, comfortable and efficient. They represent radiant points in the conquest of the wilderness from Dawson Creek to Big Delta.

The problem from this point is the permanent usefulness of the Alaska Highway. It is clear that the initial purpose of the highway was to service the airfields from Edmonton to Fairbanks. Before the Alaska Highway was begun these airports had been established as a result of Canadian experience in northern flying along a route which was eventually followed by the highway. The servicing of the airfields and emergency air-strips en route will likely continue to be an important reason for its maintenance. These flying-field establishments in peace-time, as in war, require both the movement of commodities by truck and car along the highway and the extension of flying security. For strategic reasons, this hook-up of the continental highway system extending to Fort St. John with that of Alaska can scarcely be allowed to disintegrate. Alaska has become of great strategic importance in planning the future security of Canada and the United States. An air-route together with a land-route would seem to be minimum requirements for the security of Alaska. No doubt the seaborne transportation will continue to be of the greatest importance, but it can be threatened in time of war. It is possible that we shall come to see that the safety of the far North-West will demand a railway connection from Prince George to a selected point on the Alaskan railroad. Such a railroad, already discussed by representatives of the United States and Canada, could serve not only as an additional security link for Alaska but could also service new exploitable areas through which it would have to pass in Canada.

The commercial and industrial usefulness of the highway has not yet been proved. As an adjunct to the airlines taking this northern route to Asia and intervening points, the highway has a servicing function. How much passenger and commodity transportation may be required beyond Alaska now lies mainly in the wishes of commercial companies. No doubt the highway can facilitate the exploration of mineral resources of the territory through which it passes, acting in conjunction with the aeroplane. Except for the Klondike, Mayo, and Whitehorse districts, along with widely distributed gold bearing creek gravels, the minerals lie undiscovered. If, as surmised, there should be important mineral discoveries in the Liard River valley, the highway can be useful in exploring and mining the minerals of such areas adjoining the highway and the feeder roads likely to stem from it. The application of new ways of conserving fur-bearing animals will help to increase the economic and social importance of the fur trade along the highway.

Another economic use of the highway will be its development into an attractive tourist route. Now, one can travel by car or motor bus from Dawson Creek to Anchorage in Alaska. However, this use of the highway must await the end of the war and the emergence of certain facilities without which tourist travel cannot develop. The highway has obvious natural advantages of which its scenic attractiveness may not be the most important. Scenically there is not much to intrigue travellers seeking eye-filling views until Fort Nelson is passed. Then, the road moves up through mountains to Summit Lake, 4,200 feet above sea-level, the highest point on the highway. Here, the road for long distances has been carved out of rocky benches high above forested river valleys, but here and there it follows along the edge of mountain streams whose gravel has been bulldozed into protective walls against seasonal floods. In the vicinity of Summit Lake, Steamboat Mountain, and Muncho Lake there is superb scenery. In this territory are to be found choice sites for hotels and tourist lodges. This is particularly true of the Muncho Lake district which the British Columbia government has set aside as a national park. Within its boundaries are included the two hot-springs across the first Liard River bridge 38 miles from Muncho Lake. This is the famed "Tropical Valley" where the vegetation is shoulder-high. While the highway was being built one hot-spring was enclosed for use by soldiers and civilian workers. The springs lie a quarter of a mile from the road-bed, and are connected with it by a boardwalk. Beyond Watson Lake the highway threads its way through the Cassiar Mountain Range and a subtle change in the character of the mountains is soon sensed. Many of their bare-surfaced pyramid shapes rise well above the snow-line. They impress the traveller with their bleak severity and he soon comes to know that he is in the hard land of the sourdough, where a livelihood is wrung from nature with great difficulty. Teslin Lake, more than sixty miles long and about two miles wide, marks the end of a rugged section of the road which now follows its shore. Johnston's Crossing on the Teslin River where it emerges from the north end of the lake affords an excellent site for a town with hotels, lodges, shops, and homes. At this point the Pipeline Road connects the Mackenzie River basin with the Alaska Highway, but the recent abandonment of this pipeline road has reduced the site importance of Johnston's Crossing. Here, as at Muncho Lake, there is an attractive landscape combined with good fishing and hunting. It might become in a short time a supply centre, for prospectors, trappers, survey and hunting parties. From Johnston's Crossing to Whitehorse the road passes through open valleys where there are no steep grades.

Whitehorse is the dominant centre on the Alaska Highway. It was the administrative centre for all those from the United States who were linked with highway maintenance, air-bases and other military establishments in highway territory. Situated on the beautiful Lewes River it is the junction point of the White Pass railroad and the steamboat traffic of the Yukon River system which is also an inland link between the White Pass and Alaska railroads. It is the central point in aeroplane traffic and is connected with Dawson City by river boats, by roads with Carcross in the Yukon and Norman Wells on the Mackenzie. Long before the war it was an important Yukon centre with a population of 754 according to the 1941 census taken prior to the Canol development. Its population was smaller during the winter months. During the years of highway building and other war projects, it became a city of several thousands in addition to those manning the military establishments in its vicinity. Overnight, it became a boom city, precipitating a crisis for postal and other local services. By the end of 1944 the "fever" had subsided and those who lived in Whitehorse began to take stock of its future possibilities. The war has brought a modern water and sewage system to its military establishments and the central business section of the town. Whitehorse will likely come into permanent possession of a large splendidly equipped military hospital. There are many other large buildings which were constructed during its boom days for the use of the United States armed forces and contractors from the United States and Canada. It possesses the refinery and storage facilities for the oil that was piped across the Mackenzie Mountains from Norman Wells. A local "garden city" on the upper level overlooking the refinery no longer houses refinery workers, for the refinery has been closed and its three hundred workers have departed. The Canadian Pacific Air Lines has built a number of comfortable homes for its employees. This town has possibilities as a centre for outfitters, for transportation, for the tourist business, for the refining and distribution of oil. It may settle down to be a town of two thousand, more or less, in the post-war period. An important factor in its growth is possible mineral development in its vicinity. The recent closing of the pipeline and refinery eliminates oil as a factor in the growth of Whitehorse for the present.

Its tourist attractiveness will be aided by its colourful history and its concentration of a variety of services growing out of its highly advantageous "cross-roads" position. It is located on a bench of level land slightly elevated above the high water level of the swift flowing Lewes River, about a mile below the spectacular Whitehorse Rapids. The old town and most of the recent additions to it are on the low-lying bench along the river's edge. Surrounding it is an upper level whose perpendicular frontage surrounds much of the town and gives it a walled-in appearance. On this upper bench are to be found the airfield and the "garden city" homes which overlook the main site. The views of the town from this upper level are most pleasing. In the background rise the permanently snow-crowned mountain peaks and past it flows one of the most beautiful rivers in the Northland. The boats running to Dawson City will afford the tourist a side trip of great interest and charm. Another side trip with great scenic attractiveness is by the White Pass railroad to Skagway on the Pacific coast 110 miles distant.

Beyond Whitehorse the scenery continues to be very pleasing and has increasing allure along the western boundary of Kluane Lake which is skirted by the Alaska Highway. Still farther west rise the lofty snow-clad peaks of Mount Logan and other giants of the magnificent St. Elias Mountain Range. Along the main route to Fairbanks and from there to Anchorage are vantage points of great interest and beauty. Especially interesting is the far-famed Matanuska Valley Settlement, forty-eight miles north of Anchorage. Placed in its superb physical setting is this stable agricultural community carved out of the wilderness by means of governmental subsidy and under the general supervision of the United States government. Of great interest, too, are the many glaciers close to Glen Highway and the great golden dome of Mount McKinley, the highest mountain on the North American continent, which can be seen at a great distance in clear weather. This summary has sketched certain features that lend allure to the Alaska Highway. No region has any monopoly in scenic appeal. Some will prefer the scenery of sections of the Rocky Mountains which lie hundreds of miles closer to continental centres of population from which any great movement of tourists must come. One can merely state that this far northern journey has a uniqueness owing to its own special charm and to the fact that for the first time is available an opportunity to travel the northern wilderness in comfort. Thousands have heard of the highway directly through their sons, daughters, fathers, mothers, and others. Wider still has been the publicity of the printed word and radio. One can readily surmise that thousands will want to see it for themselves at the earliest opportunity. They will want also to get a first hand experience of the way of life in our last North American frontier.

Despite the lure of the North yesterday, today, and tomorrow, the Alaska Highway will not be ready at war's end for a cavalcade of tourists. At present there is a maintenance camp every one hundred miles, sufficient for servicing the highway in war-time. Maybe most of these camps will be continued, but additional facilities will be required, such as hotels and lodges at sites selected to cater to the varied interests of those who spend days or weeks in this vast Northland. Very necessary also will be a competent personnel to cater to the wishes of the tourist public. With such vast distances of uninhabited wilderness to cover, a highway patrol system connected with the maintenance stations will be necessary in providing a minimum measure of security for travellers. The attractions of the highway, splendid as they are in many ways, need to be supplemented also by means of "feeder" roads, which permit side-trips into the most attractive nearby or distant terrain. Some of these already branch out from Whitehorse and Johnston's Crossing. Still others will be required at Muncho Lake, Kluane Lake, and at many other points which possess great natural advantages.[4] None travelling the circuitous road from Edmonton to Smith, skirting the Lesser Slave Lake, then passing through much uninteresting territory till the Peace River Country is reached, would view it as a satisfactory link between Edmonton and the Alaska Highway. Already a new route has been suggested, by way of Whitecourt direct to Grande Prairie, beyond which point there is now a good road to Dawson Creek. This will call for quite a long stretch of new road in an area where road-building should not be too difficult. A new road from Prince George to a southern point on the Alaska Highway would have a number of important uses among which would be a direct link between the latter and the highway network of British Columbia.

Subsidiary Agriculture in the Vicinity of the Highway

An earnest effort has been made by the Canadian Department of Agriculture to discover potential agricultural lands along the Alaska Highway. Not enough detailed work has been done to state specifically what districts are most suitable for cultivation. Thirty miles beyond Fort St. John arable lands become marginal and fade out for a long distance. It is possible that there is some agricultural land in the Fort Nelson area, the Liard River and

[4]The Haines cut-off between the port of Haines on Lynn Canal and the Alaska Highway has been re-opened and will have a maintenance crew during the summer months.

its tributaries, around Teslin Lake, and in the Takhini-Dezadeash valley just west of Whitehorse. The district around Mayo has agricultural possibilities. These agricultural lands are river flats and more elevated plateaus. In many instances these lands comprise small scattered patches of a few thousand acres while others like the Nelson plateau may contain a half-million acres. Preliminary surveys have indicated that there is enough arable land in the vicinity of the highway to meet the needs of any market which may be available at Whitehorse and any new centres which may develop. From our present knowledge one finds general agreement with the proposition: agriculture north of the Peace River country is likely to be limited to the local demands of northern communities. Agriculture is likely to develop only in the vicinity of communities based primarily on mining and other non-agricultural activities. The Dominion Department of Agriculture has done some initial work in setting up an experimental substation at Pine Creek, 102 miles west of Whitehorse. Its task is to discover what can be grown profitably in an area that may in time produce all the dairy and other farm products that the town of Whitehorse can consume.[5] A small number of farmers, if conditions are found to be suitable, may be placed on the arable land which lies between the town and the sub-station. If additional centres emerge to serve the combined interests of mineral exploration, forest protection, lumbering, hunting, fishing, trapping, highway maintenance, airfields personnel, and the tourist business, the extension of agriculture can be stepped up to meet increased local demand. The more the main elements just mentioned can be located at a few well selected sites close to available farmland, the more likely will farmsteads come into existence. Not a wide scattering of isolated farmsteads but clusters of them close to the more important highway centres will make their survival possible and family life endurable. Life in the North calls especially for communities large enough to afford basic health, educational, and other services. A few dozen farmers located at strategic points in relation to their local market seems to be all that this situation will warrant in the discernible future. Even these could only take up their places where and when the markets are available. The development of farmsteads near Whitehorse can be an initial test of the point of view just presented.

The Alaska Highway was an outcome of strategic necessity. Despite its industrial and commercial possibilities, it seems to many observers that the strategic factor will continue for a long time to be the chief reason for its maintenance. The development of industrial and commercial activities may help to lighten the load increasingly. At the outset the Canadian government will be expected to bear the burden of its completion,[6] and also its maintenance

[5]By August 1, 1945, twenty acres had been made ready for seeding and a number of buildings were to be found at this sub-station.

[6]See p. 288.

at an estimated $1,000 per mile. It should be emphasized that the security of
Alaska is closely associated with the defence of our own far North-West. The
Alaska Highway while in Canadian territory is of mutual concern to both the
United States and Canada. Plans for its maintenance may well become a
matter of further negotiation between both countries.

THE MACKENZIE BASIN

The western boundary of this region comprises the Mackenzie Mountains
and other Rocky Mountain Ranges to the south. Moving swiftly down
through their gorges are the Peace, Liard, and smaller rivers flowing eastward
to join the Mackenzie. These rivers are in part transportation links between
the area served by the Alaska Highway and the Mackenzie Basin. More
recently a new means of transportation and communication, the Pipeline
Road has been built across the Mackenzie Mountains from Johnston's Crossing
on the Alaska Highway to Canol on the Mackenzie. The closing of the pipeline may mean the disintegration of this road. On September 30, 1945, a
140-mile stretch east from Whitehorse could be travelled by surveying parties
under special permits. East from Pelly River many sections of the road
have been damaged heavily by washouts and slides, and can be travelled only
with great difficulty. The re-establishment of this road is very uncertain. The
eastern boundary of the Mackenzie Basin is the western edge of the Pre-
Cambrian Shield which runs across the extreme eastern part of Great Bear
Lake, cuts Great Slave Lake near Yellowknife and follows approximately the
eastern banks of Great Slave and Athabaska Rivers to Waterways. Centres
on the western edge of the Shield form an integral part of the economic development of the Mackenzie Basin whose water transportation system constitutes the chief means in moving products within the territory it drains. The
aeroplane has come into extensive use for carrying men, mail, and express
packages.

Until the recent exploration and production of minerals, the fur trade was
the basic industry of the Mackenzie Basin. In its exploitation, trading posts
like Fort Smith, Resolution, Hay River, Fort Simpson, Fort Norman, Good
Hope, Arctic Red River, McPherson, Aklavik, and a few other outposts have
become established. Except Fort Smith the centre of dominance of the Mackenzie transportation system, Fort Resolution and Aklavik, sixty-nine miles
from the Arctic coast, these centres have ordinarily less than fifty white
persons. There are in addition on an average from one hundred to three
hundred Indians and half-breeds in or not far distant from these various
centres. During the hunting and trapping season the majority of these
Indians are away from these centres. Usually they have Anglican and Catholic missions, in a few instances mission hospitals, a detachment of the Royal
Canadian Mounted Police, a post-office, sometimes a government radio

station, occasionally a resident medical officer who may also be the Indian Agent, a trading post, and some provision for education which is usually under the auspices of one or both the churches mentioned above. In larger centres like Smith are to be found offices of government which serve far-flung administrative districts. In Smith, too, is to be found the headquarters of one of the two chief river transportation companies. The other has moved recently to Bell Rock, eight miles down stream from Fort Smith.

THE NEW INDUSTRIAL TOWNS

The discovery of oil at Norman Wells, of pitchblende at Port Radium, and gold at Yellowknife has initiated a new stage in the development of this far northern region. Silver and other minerals have been found in the vicinity of the two chief mining centres, but to date, they have played but a minor role in the economic development of this region.[7] This war has caused an active interest in pitchblende but it has delayed gold mining which had made a promising beginning at Yellowknife on Great Slave Lake.

The requirements of war strategy have given a great impetus to the exploration and production of oil. Explorers had noted oil-seepages along the Mackenzie River many decades ago. Geological field work dates back to R. G. McConnell in 1887-8. A test drilling in 1920 found oil in commercial quantity, fifty miles north-west of Fort Norman. Three additional wells indicated a much larger productive area. In 1940 the present refinery equipment went into operation with a daily capacity of 840 barrels of crude oil. By 1943 its capacity had reached 1,100 barrels per day. This oil was used for local needs which included the mining camp requirements at Port Radium and Yellowknife. Such was the situation when the Canol Project was initiated by the United States War Department in 1942.[8] Negotiations between the United States and Canada led to the beginning of construction and further oil drilling in 1942. Operations directly connected with the drilling of oil wells and its initial production were carried out by the Imperial Oil Company, Limited under a contract with the United States government. This company had been active in the oil development of this region for many years and was thoroughly familiar with local conditions.[9] Consequently, at the end of 1944, fifty-six wells were producing oil in the Norman Wells field. Altogether sixty-seven wells were drilled by the Canol Project, of which sixty found oil in commercial quantity. This field is confined to Goose Island, Bear Island, and immediate vicinity. The depths of

[7] Exploratory efforts have revealed the presence also of lead, zinc, nickel, copper and coal.

[8] J. S. Stewart, "Petroleum Possibilities in Mackenzie River Valley, N.W.T." (*Transactions of the Canadian Institute of Mining and Metallurgy*, vol. XLVII, 1944, pp. 152-8).

[9] Wartime Information Board, "Defence Projects in Northwest Canada," mimeographed report, 1943, p. 8.

these wells range from approximately 1,300 feet for vertical drilling to 2,400 feet for directional drilling (slanted to tap oil under the Mackenzie River).[10] The oil is forced by natural gas pressure into the Norman Wells storage tanks and refinery. It was pumped across the Mackenzie Mountains to the Whitehorse refinery.

It has been reported in press releases that the Canol Project cost the United States government $134 million. Some of this expenditure went into well-drilling exploration. Much of it went into pipe-laying from Norman Wells to Whitehorse, Fairbanks and other points. To lay a pipeline between Norman Wells and Whitehorse, a very expensive road-building project through a mountain wilderness was necessary. This road, connecting the Mackenzie Basin with the Alaska Highway was a difficult engineering a-chievement. Its builders had to contend with glacial ice and mountain streams, problems more difficult than those faced in building the Alaska Highway. The Pipeline Road did not reach the stage where it is easy to main-tain, but for most of its length a permanent road had been built. Through the pipeline to the Whitehorse refinery the annual flow of 800,000 barrels of oil was possible. The pipeline is 6 inches in diameter for a distance of 120 miles east of Whitehorse and the remainder is 4 inches in diameter. It met the military demands for which it was constructed, a guaranteed emergency supply of aviation gasoline, motor gasoline, and light diesel fuel. That such a venture cost a vast sum which need not have been expended at that time, if the United Nations had known that their northern oil needs could have been met by tankers, is obvious. But such knowledge was not extant in 1942 and this great enterprise was a necessary phase of the expanding war enter-prises of that period. To call it a military "boner" from the vantage ground of the present is partisan nonsense. No doubt there was vested interested private opposition to the Canol Project in 1942, but there was no important public opposition until two years later, when the need for such a project no longer existed.

The future of oil development in the Mackenzie Basin is by no means clear at this time. The Canol Project was discontinued March 8, 1945 by order of the government of the United States. The drilling for oil on Canol account came to an end. Furthermore the pipeline from Norman Wells to White-horse and the refinery in the latter town were closed. Sixty-seven wells had been drilled under the Canol Project, of which sixty produced oil in commercial quantity. These are in addition to the four original wells mentioned above. Most of these wells have been capped but a few have been left flowing to supply the requirements of the Mackenzie Basin. In 1944 the Imperial Oil Company hoped to extend Mackenzie reserves from an estimated 30 million barrels to possibly 300 million barrels. During the past year, the

[10]Stewart, "Petroleum Possibilities," pp. 163-4.

Norman Exploration, a subsidiary of Imperial Oil, has made a great effort to extend the Norman Wells pocket. Drilling has been carried on quite far afield but no extension of the Norman Wells oil-field is in the offing. The present estimated recoverable reserve is approximately 36 million barrels. Despite extended drilling there has been no expansion of the oil-field beyond the immediate vicinity of Norman Wells. If the present Mackenzie recoverable reserves could be extended to 300 million barrels, it seems quite probable that a determined effort would be made to pipe this oil to the outside market on the Pacific coast. The future of the Norman Wells oil development is uncertain at the writing of this report. Meanwhile the work of exploration is going on. The Norman Wells refinery will be kept open to supply the mining and other communities in the Mackenzie valley.[11] In 1944 the population of Norman Wells was 600 with a possible extension to 1,000 persons if the community should come to be based on families rather than individuals. As a result of the withdrawal of the United States from this area of oil development together with its restricted present known oil reserves, the population of Norman Wells dropped to 352 whites by 1946. There are in addition 20 persons under the general category of wives and children.

The disposition of the Canol Project is based on the following agreement: The Canadian government has the first option on the purchase of existing facilities. In the event that neither the Canadian government nor a private company is interested, the disposition may be referred to the Permanent Joint Board on Defense.[12]

It may be presumed that the Imperial Oil Company of Canada backed financially by oil interests in the United States is in the best position to take over the future exploration of the Norman Wells oil region.

The nearest newly established centre of permanent importance is Port Radium on the eastern side of Great Bear Lake. The discovery of pitchblende by Gilbert LaBine and his partner Charles St. Paul in 1930 was stimulated by reading a report made thirty years earlier by the late James Mackintosh Bell and Dr. Charles Camsell, former Deputy Minister of Mines and Resources. This report included a statement that the rocks facing the shore of Echo Bay were stained with cobalt bloom. Trained in the Cobalt region, such a clue was all that LaBine needed to encourage his initial exploration. The samples taken to Ottawa were tested by the Bureau of Mines and it was clear that high quality pitchblende, the radium bearing ore, had been discovered. During 1933, Eldorado Gold Mines, Limited, erected a milling plant on the property

[11]Note greater detail in a paper by Dr. Charles Camsell—"Mineral Development in the Northwest and Yukon Territories" (*Transactions of the Canadian Institute of Mining and Metallurgy*, Sept. 1945).

[12]Wartime Information Board, "Defence Projects in Northwest Canada," mimeographed report, 1943, p. 39.

and a refinery at Port Hope. When the war began the production of radium in Canada was well on its way. Because of disturbed world markets the Port Radium mine closed down in 1940, but new uses for the constituents of pitch-blende (immediately in connection with the development of the atomic bomb) caused this mining enterprise to be reopened in 1942.[13] It has been a crown company of the Canadian government since January, 1944.

This remote northern community is carried on by a work force of two hundred persons, seven of whom are living with their families. That it will be transformed into a permanent centre with a population of five hundred persons (as it becomes based on families rather than individuals) seems very probable. Its limited transportation to the world outside increases its sense of isolation. After one year on the job an employee is permitted a trip to the outside by aeroplane and thereafter a similar annual trip. The Canadian Pacific Air Lines operates one plane a week from Edmonton carrying mail and passengers. The company operates two Norseman planes which supplement the regular weekly passenger and mail services. Much of the time of these planes is utilized during the summer months in servicing geologists and miner-alogists in the Port Radium area. They also freight fresh meat from the Burns cold storage plant at Yellowknife. These planes are most essential in making emergency trips to various centres, particularly Edmonton. In the far North the aeroplane continues to be the chief means by which men are transported, but, in the main, the products of the mine and the supplies that make its operation possible are water-borne. Freight is carried by barges and the diesel powered boats which push them across Great Bear Lake, by the still smaller boats and barges used on the upper and lower sections of Great Bear River, and by truck across the eight mile portage near its mid point. Larger packet-boats and barges ply between Fort Norman at the mouth of Great Bear River and Fort Smith on Great Slave River. This latter centre is separated from Fitzgerald by a sixteen mile portage. From there packet-boats and barges carry freight on the upper part of Slave River, across Lake Athabaska and along the Athabaska to Waterways from which the railroad conveys freight and passengers to Edmonton. It is said by those familiar with this tortuous transportation route that articles have to be transferred thirteen times between Edmonton and Port Radium. This makes freight carriage an expensive business which is not likely to be reduced greatly in the discernible future. This is one of the factors setting limits on any great expansion of settlement in the far North. Mines must be exceedingly rich and other resources in great demand to warrant their production.

If traffic makes it feasible one would expect improvements in services and a lowering of the freight rates between Edmonton and Waterways. Improve-ments of the transportation facilities on the Athabaska, Slave, Mackenzie,

[13]Canadian Department of Mines and Resources, "The Northwest Territories," pp. 30-1.

Great Bear, and other rivers have been made by the departments of government responsible for such work. Nevertheless it is well known that river channels can be improved by blasting out rocks. Beacon lights and other devices for aiding water transportation might be installed throughout the entire Mackenzie Basin. No doubt diesel driven boats with greater power and more suitable in design will emerge as traffic continues to expand. The rivers and lakes will continue to bear most of the tonnage which enters and leaves this vast northern region. The overdue systematic survey of the facilities of water-borne traffic with a view to improving their efficiency and adjusting freight rates is to be found in the part on transportation in this volume.[14] In view of the powerful loading machinery operated by the United States forces at such transfer points as Fort Smith, the freight transfer devices in operation throughout most of the Mackenzie Basin would appear to be outmoded. One of the most patent examples of this is the handling of freight at Great Bear River portage where heavy freight is "bulled" on and off carriers by hand.[15] Adjuncts to water-borne traffic may be an overland truck road over all or part of the Great Bear River route between Fort Norman and the eastern end of Great Bear Lake. At present oil is pumped from barge to tank three times and is loaded by gravity flow three times between Norman Wells and Port Radium. These transfers of oil and other freight will be reduced by a supplementary truck highway now under construction.

GOLD MINING AT YELLOWKNIFE

Yellowknife, situated on the northern shore of Great Slave Lake, is connected directly with Port Radium by the Canadian Pacific Air Lines and indirectly by the Mackenzie River system. This mining town has mushroomed since 1935 after gold was discovered in its vicinity. Since then many claims have been staked and a few mines are in various stages of development. The most completely established mine is the "Con," a property of the Consolidated Mining and Smelting Company of Canada, which was an important producer before the war. Among other mines are the Negus, Ptarmigan, and the Rycon. The Giant Yellowknife is now being developed into a mine. The war has kept back gold mining in this section. The Consolidated and one or two other mines were able to retain only a few dozen miners for maintenance and incidental development during the past two years. However the author sensed the symptoms of gold-rush fever in late August, 1944. The C.P.A.

[14] The Northern Transportation Company was inaugurated by the Eldorado Mines because its officials could not obtain what they deemed a satisfactory arrangement with the line operated by the Hudson's Bay Company.

[15] The author spent one week en route from Fort Norman to Port Radium by the river and lake boats. Two days were spent at the portage. This made possible first hand observation of freighting difficulties over this part of the Mackenzie route.

planes were crowded. Strange faces were to be seen on the streets of Yellow-knife. Little knots of men in hotel lobbies, rooms, on street corners, and in restaurants were talking excitedly about gold prospects. Entrepreneurs were ready to "jump the gun" at the first sign of the war's end. Since then the gold fever has increased greatly and a new boom is on. Three thousand persons were active in the actual mining development of the Yellowknife region in 1945. Certain mining stocks have sold freely and risen rapidly on the market. No doubt others will do likewise.

Transportation difficulties are not so great as at Port Radium, but they nevertheless constitute a severe handicap in mining development. While gold bricks may be flown out by plane, the machinery and other supplies must come in from the head of steel at Waterways by a long, arduous four months of the year water route. In order that Yellowknife may be able to compete with gold mining areas elsewhere, its gold deposits will have to be of a very high grade.[16] While the initial returns have been encouraging, many millions will have to be put into the ground before Canada can know with assurance the extent of mineral wealth in this area. The chief reason for population expansion in the Great Slave area will be the warrantable development of gold mining, and the enterprises subsidiary to it. As mentioned above, Burns Company have anticipated its future development by the establishment of a large cold storage plant which is the chief outlet for fresh meat and vegetables. Since agricultural lands are limited in this area, practically all food products must come in by rail and water from outside.[17] One other primary industry is in sight, namely the development of the fresh fish industry of Great Slave Lake. This lake was surveyed by Dr. Rawson for the Fisheries Department in 1944 and it has been estimated that five million pounds of fish could be taken from the lake each year without depleting its fish population. The most important of its fish is the lake trout. These were filleted, quick frozen and sold in the city markets of Canada and the United States in 1945.

The development of mining, fishing, and trapping and a subsidiary agriculture in the vicinity of Yellowknife calls for not only the improvement of water transportation but also the extension of rail and road transportation. A railroad could be built from Grimshaw on the E. D. and B. C. Railway to Notikewin or even as far as the Keg River. This railroad would serve the well-settled agricultural Battle River area and its northern extension. From this steel head a permanent road is planned to Hay River on the south shore of Great Slave Lake. The present winter road from Grimshaw to Hay River with its caterpillar trains did not seem sufficient to serve the mining and potential fisheries development of the Great Slave district. An all year

[16]See Part IV on mineral industry of the North West Territories by E. L. Bruce.

[17]The relation of subsidiary agriculture to this and similar communities will be discussed below.

road will supplement the basic but summer seasonal river transportation.
On this highway diesel engined conveyors might be a very useful substitute
for railway trains until the development of northern communities warrants
such an expensive undertaking as the building of a railway line to and eventually beyond Great Slave Lake.

One of the great needs of northern mining communities such as Yellowknife
is nearby agricultural production. While there are plots totalling approximately 200 acres suitable for cultivation in the vicinity of Yellowknife, this
acreage needs to be supplemented by a much larger agricultural area to be
found across Great Slave Lake in the Hay River valley.[18] It is quite possible
that agricultural communities can be developed near the outlet of the Hay
and perhaps also in other portions of the valley of the Hay. The building of
a permanent road from Notikewin to Hay River post will not only aid the
servicing of Yellowknife and other northern centres but will also facilitate
the development of agriculture in the Hay River valley. This will be agriculture depending fundamentally on a northern market. Thus, about the
dominant activity of mining will be clustered agriculture and transportation
facilities by water, land, and air. Associated in this industrial complex and
gaining by this association are the fur trade and the new fishing industry on
Great Slave Lake. The feasible expansion of each unit in this complex will
depend on the cumulative interdependence of all the units mentioned as well
as that of other institutions providing services necessary for the retention of
permanent settlers in these newer northern communities. Among many
items about which new dwellers in the North are becoming increasingly
vociferous are secular schools, an extension of medical services, and responsible local government to which they may elect representatives of their own
choosing.

Last to be discussed in this section are the twin towns of McMurray and
Waterways. The latter, the northern terminal of the railroad line from
Edmonton, is located on Clearwater River near its junction with the Athabaska. Its location three miles from McMurray is just one more example of
railroad builders selecting a town site a short distance from an older established
town for the dual purposes of reducing their costs for a right of way and making
some real estate profit from their newly created town site. There are local
explanations that the river at Waterways is more suitable for the docking of
river boats. However the United States engineers anticipated no such difficulty for they pushed the railroad on to Prairie, which lies between these
towns and built wharves and docked craft very much closer to McMurray.
Their location at the end of steel where goods are trans-shipped to river boats
and barges made them important centres before the war but the heavy freight

[18]J. Lewis Robinson, "Land Use Possibilities in Mackenzie District, N.W.T." (*Canadian Geographical Journal*, July, 1945, p. 32).

shipments for the Canol project gave them added importance during recent years. Trading and transportation agencies occupy places of first importance in the economic life of these twin towns. The widely publicized Tar Sands lie in the valleys of the Horse, and other tributaries of the Athabaska River. It is quite clear that vast oil reserves exist in this area but just how much potential oil lies here is not definitely known.

The Canadian government has taken over the facilities for extracting the oil from the sand at Abasand a short distance over the hill from McMurray. Between one and two hundred men were engaged at the processing plant in 1944 where the experimental efforts to find an economic means of separating oil from these tar sands were going on. Should this become a big industry the twin towns would develop into an industrial city. This will not likely take place at present when large reserves of flowing oil exist in other regions.[19] Nevertheless this great oil reserve may some day come into its own. Another concern, the Roofing and Asphalt Company, is experimenting with the possible use of these tar sands in constructing roads and buildings. About twenty-five men are employed in this activity. Still another industry, that of mining salt, employs fifty workers at Waterways. This salt deposit underlies an outer section of the town of Waterways. Not far away is a small fish-packing plant. The economic base of these twin towns has brought together a combined permanent population of five hundred. This is considerably augmented at times by migratory Indians. Owing to their location at a break in transportation and at the gateway to the recent industrial expansion taking place farther north, these towns can expect a gradual increase in their permanent population. Although these centres lie south of the territory selected for this survey, they have been included because they form such an important link in the transportation chain which connects the new North-West with the world outside.

Agriculture and Lumbering in the New North-West

Brief references to agriculture and lumber have been mentioned above. At this point a more extended systematic treatment of these topics will be attempted.

Since 1943 the Dominion Department of Agriculture has been making reconnaissance surveys to ascertain agricultural possibilities in the Yukon and Mackenzie Districts. Dr. A. Leahey and his associates have taken stock of the gardens and the few farmlets in the North which are to be found from Smith to Aklavik. A partial list of products includes potatoes, turnips, cabbage, cauliflower, beets, carrots, beans, peas, onions, small fruits, celery, hay, oats, and barley. Tomatoes are grown but they do not ripen in the open as a general rule in the communities north of Fort Smith. Flower gardens growing

---

[19] On June 16, 1945, the experimental plant at Abasand was destroyed by fire.

many of the annuals and perennials of southern Canada are to be found in all settlements in the far North-West. It would seem that the urge to grow things is often greatest when the handicaps of nature are most apparent. For in this Northland the growing season is short, but there is some compensation in the great extension of summer daylight.

The MacKenzie Valley's frost free period varies with topography and air drainage. The extreme range is a minimum of 44 days at Fort Norman and a maximum of 92 days at Fort Resolution. Latest spring frosts usually occur around mid June at most stations . . . spring planting in MacKenzie district usually precedes the average last spring frost; it is done in the third week of May in the Great Slave Lake Area and carried out during the last part of May, at the lower MacKenzie River posts. Fall frosts vary from early August to early September and are instrumental in killing grain crops in certain seasons. At most stations there is a range of 50 to 60 days from the time the earliest fall frost has been recorded to the time of the latest fall frost. This precarious situation is the key to the future of agriculture in the Mac-Kenzie Valley, and has been one of the factors placing the present northern limit of successful grain growth at Fort Simpson.[20]

Rainfall too, is limited, ranging from 10 to 13 inches where agricultural soils are available.[21] There is some compensation for this light rainfall in the presence of permanently frozen soil where it is estimated that thawing extends from 3 to 10 feet under cultivated land. With increase in cultivation the thawing deepens and a limited moisture problem increases.

There are limited agricultural lands in the vicinity of the settlements along the Mackenzie and its tributaries. In the main, they cannot provide sufficient vegetable and dairy products to meet local needs. A few such as Fort Norman and Fort Nelson provide a small surplus in potatoes. The new mining centres like Norman Wells, Eldorado, and Yellowknife have a very small available local agricultural acreage. They must depend mainly on agricultural and dairy products from regions outside or from larger productive areas within the Mackenzie District, but some distance away. However, these potential areas are near enough to cut down greatly food freight cost and greatly to extend the consumption of fresh vegetables and dairy products in these new industrial communities. To make a start in this direction one distinctive agricultural community might be inaugurated in the lower Hay River valley and another in the vicinity of Fort Simpson utilizing the river bottom land and suitable terraces in the lower Liard valley. The addition of a dozen families in each of these districts could supply the present limited northern market. Additional families could be added when this was warranted by increased market demands in the far North. No doubt more intensive soil surveys by the Canadian Department of Agriculture will make more specific the boundaries of the areas most suitable for the settlement of families who will concentrate on the production of agricultural products.

[20]J. Lewis Robinson, "Land Use Possibilities in Mackenzie District," p. 36.
[21]See Part III, p. 106.

Besides the agricultural sub-station west of Whitehorse, others will be necessary in the Yukon, and Mackenzie valley districts, to do pioneer experimental work on which northern agriculture may be scientifically based. It is assumed that the development of two such initial agricultural communities as those just suggested for the lower Hay and Liard valleys will require educational, health, religious, and other institutional facilities necessary to a standard of living that will make for permanent settlement. The establishment of such communities will require organization and subsidization. The homestead policies in such districts as the settled portions of the Peace River laid great hardships on the individual settler and provided a costly means of selecting the eventual permanent settler. In facing the added hazards of climate, land clearing cost, and market distances, settlement of agricultural communities in the far North requires a special type of financial aid and organization sponsored in this instance by the Canadian government. For coping with agricultural settlement in the new North-West, Canada can learn from the experiments carried on by other countries, particularly the United States and Russia. In this connection the author spent some time in the agricultural communities in the Tanana and Matanuska valleys in Alaska.

AGRICULTURE IN THE MATANUSKA VALLEY[22]

The Matanuska Valley project was undertaken by the United States government in 1935, as a means of rehabilitating a few of the unemployed families in the United States and had as its purpose, also, the development of agriculture in Alaska. Trappers, miners, and farmers had homesteaded in various parts of the valley, but they had not succeeded in building a stable agricultural community. At the time this colonization project was initiated there were about seventy-five of these homestead farms in a more or less "going" condition.[23] In 1943 there were about 250 farms in the valley, 144 of which had been established by the Corporation. There were about 140 of the colonist families on the job in 1944. Less than half of these were expected to remain permanent settlers. However, it was apparent that select families would be available in sufficient numbers to succeed them as permanent settlers.

[22]In studying the Alaskan situation information was given generously by Colonel O. F. Ohlson, Manager of the Alaska Railroad and President of the Alaska Rural Rehabilitation Corporation which was the agency set up by the United States Government to finance and direct the Matanuska Colonization Project. Particular mention must be made of the frank statements of fact and the ready cooperation in this study by Dr. Herbert C. Hanson, General Manager of the Corporation just cited. Much aid was given, too, by Mr. Roland Snodgrass, Manager of the Matanuska Valley Farmers' Cooperative Association.

[23]Dr. H. C. Hanson, "Agriculture in the Matanuska Valley," United States Department of the Interior, 1943, p. 1.

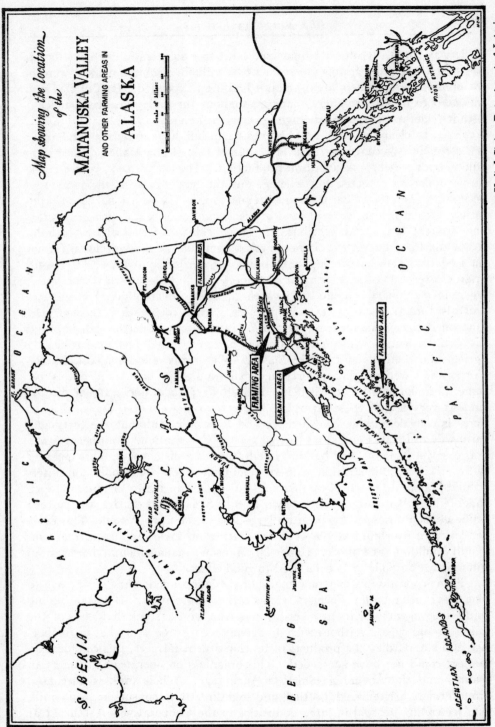

Map showing the location of the MATANUSKA VALLEY AND OTHER FARMING AREAS IN ALASKA

Scale of Miles:

United States, Department of Interior

It was stated by officials connected with this colonization project that it had cost the United States government $5 million. Some outsiders were of the opinion that a much larger amount had been expended. Part of this sum was used to build permanent roads throughout the valley and to connect it with its chief market at Anchorage, forty-eight miles away. Much more of it was used to clear the land, build homes, farm buildings, buildings at Palmer the community's centre located on a spur of the Alaska Railroad, and farm equipment needed for agricultural production. The Corporation possesses the farms under an amortisation scheme, but the farms pass to the individual occupants when they clear their indebtedness to the Corporation. The Corporation cleared fifteen acres of land at the outset to give the farmers a start and brought in a group of transient workers ahead of the settlers to build roads and farm buildings. It now makes available to the individual farmer for a relatively low cost the use of its bulldozer, scarifier, pulverizer, large seed-grain clearer, and other expensive machinery. It has also a "clearance farm" where its machinery is housed and where surplus food is produced to feed farm animals turned back by certain farmers. The Corporation through Dr. Hanson is the government's collector of indebtedness but through him and his staff it selects new farmers for its land and gives much technical advice on agricultural methods suitable in Alaska. The farms made available by the Corporation were originally forty acres in extent but have tended to grow larger although every effort is being made to keep them under 160 acres. At present very few of these farms are larger than one hundred acres. Eighty acres is considered the ideal acreage and it is now said that the forty-acre farm was an initial blunder on the part of the Corporation. Another mistake was over-building of farm buildings and other establishments. This together with unwise administration caused indebtedness on the small and inter-mediate farms to reach 15 to 18 thousand dollars in many instances. Such indebtedness had to be written down to 6 to 8 thousand dollars, the current value of such farms. This meant a large loss to the Corporation. This same tendency to overbuild at the outset and write off losses applies to the community buildings at Palmer. Under Dr. Hanson's management a more careful administration policy has been used to good effect.

The corporation farmers and many of the independent outsiders belong to the Matanuska Valley Farmers' Cooperative Association. It is the buying and selling agency for its member farmers who receive stock dividends of the conventional type. Without such an agency to organize a market in Anchorage and standardize the products of its constituent farmers, this colonization project could not have succeeded. This organization operates a creamery in Palmer and the Anchorage dairy in Anchorage. Whole milk is purchased from farmers, pasteurized, bottled, and sold directly to consumers, while milk and ice-cream are sold in large quantities in the Cooperative's restaurant at

Palmer; an additional 800 gallons is carried by truck each day to Anchorage. The Cooperative also operates a general store, restaurant, garage, cabinet shop, and cold storage facilities. Its pea-sheller and bulldozer are widely used by the farmers. Its chicken houses like some other colonization ventures were among the initial building blunders. The Cooperative, more or less compulsory at the outset, should have been allowed to grow gradually. It passed through a difficult period to its present state of efficiency. As an organization it found itself with too many establishments and it is now conceded that the colonization project should have started with a few basic essentials and gradually accumulated additional establishments. The settlers now possess first class educational facilities, a hospital, churches, and other associations that contribute to a tolerable rural standard of living. Furthermore 90 per cent of the farms have electricity provided by an independent corporation.

Matanuska and its adjoining river valleys were selected for this colonization project because this area at the head of Cook Inlet possesses a relatively moderate climate for its location so far north,[24] proximity to a railway connecting it with Anchorage, and fertile soil. Tree clearance, as in certain sections which may be settled in Liard valley, is costly. It is estimated that $150 is needed to prepare one acre of land for its initial seeding. The bulldozer pushes out the trees from which logs and wood are taken and the scarifier tumbles the stumps into piles for burning. This machine helps to shake the top soil from the stumps and to give it a more even distribution than could be achieved by the bulldozer. The colony's position on the railroad and a good highway also connecting Palmer with Anchorage, a seaport of approximately 8,000, make its agricultural achievement possible. Even the colony's position would not have done this had not the Cooperative developed the market and organized the settlers to use it. At this point it should be mentioned that the war gave a great impetus to the colony's market by the presence of thousands of service men at camps in the vicinity of Anchorage. For instance the Cooperative's pea-sheller was often used to market 1,800 pounds of new peas for a single delivery to Camp Richardson. The community besides providing fresh vegetables and dairy products for the armed services constituted a civilian centre readily available and extensively used by these men so far away from their homes in the south. The strategic importance of this new Alaskan agricultural settlement is obvious and although this aspect was not mentioned it was, no doubt, in the minds of those who conceived this project. While this settlement venture might have achieved its aim with a much smaller budget, some such plan was essential if stable settlement was to be established. This organization helped rehabilitate the struggling homesteaders and proved itself the catalyst in Alaska's agricultural expansion.

[24]It has on the average a growing season of 108 days. See Hanson, *ibid.*, p. 3.

In contrast, homesteading has remained the chief mode of farm development in the Tanana valley where market opportunities in Fairbanks and at Ladd Field are quite equal to those available to the Matanuska settlers. Here one finds on the outskirts of Fairbanks two well-equipped dairy farms each with herds of thirty-five to fifty milch cows. There are two potato growers, one with a forty-acre crop and the other with twenty acres. There are many less specialized farms with small acreages of potatoes and other crops. In the vicinity of Fairbanks there are about twenty-five farms with forty acres broken and there are many others in the crude homestead stage. The whole agricultural effort here is spotty, unorganized, and generally ineffective despite the stimulus of war-time market demands which these farmers were not (nor are they yet) organized to utilize. Here too the soil is fairly fertile and it produces about the same variety of dairy, vegetable, and cereal crops to be found in the Matanuska valley. Some rudimentary organization of the local market has taken place as the result of war-time demand and a co-operative appears to be in the making.[25] Some of the chief devices which might be used for agricultural expansion in the Canadian far North-West are now being employed in the Matanuska rather than in the Tanana valley. However, because many of the hazards to permanent settlement prevail throughout the North much can be learned from the whole agricultural situation in Alaska. Its agricultural expansion is much greater than that in the Yukon and the North West Territories and its experimental station work has covered many years. Its products are quite similar to those now grown in such meagre fashion in the Yukon and the North West Territories. Canada can learn much from the agricultural experiments in Alaska. One of the more obvious of these lessons is agricultural production for the nearby local market rather than competing for distant markets outside. Some of the earlier enthusiasts thought that they could export potatoes to the distant states. Such thoughts with respect to potatoes and other items have been cast aside.

It has already been suggested that the lower Hay River and Liard valleys have enough land for the northern market. In these valleys might be now organized at least two small communities given over primarily to agriculture. A government hospital might be associated with such a project in the Fort Simpson area. While here and there individual entrepreneurs, such as the two dairy farmers near Fairbanks and the vegetable growers at Yellowknife, get established because of an early start coupled with a special insight and often considerable capital, they do not represent the main trend in the establishment of stable agricultural communities. Such settlements in northern

[25]Dean Gasser of the Agricultural Section of the University of Alaska took the writer to many of the Tanana valley farms and gave freely of his time and knowledge of the local situation. His capable leadership would have achieved much more in this district if even part of the aid given Matanuska had been available.

districts require financial aid far beyond the resources of the average individual settler. Roads are required at the outset. Schools, churches, local medical services, and other essentials must be provided long before such communities can provide them out of local resources. Pioneering is not dead in Canada, but the persons who would build stable communities in the far North-West are sensible enough to know what scientific equipment in machines and organization are required for this purpose. They are wise enough to insist on adequate aid in the northward march of Canada. With greater thoughtfulness and caution similar Canadian projects can be done far more cheaply and effectively than that in Matanuska. Such is the value of the experience of others, if we have the wisdom to profit from it. These suggested community settlements of agriculturists would leave room for the two or three families who might live close by the old trade centres and the river industrial towns in this Northland. These close-by farmers can make use of the institutional facilities now existing and likely to be improved.

References to what Russia has accomplished do not always meet with favour among the more extremely individualistic among us. There is one attitude that is very common among most of those who are extremely anxious to see the northward march of settlement in Canada; they claim that if the Russian north has permitted far greater population expansion than that of Canada it is because Canada has neglected its far northern sections. Doubtless there is some truth in this, but there is also an implicit assumption that like parallels of latitude signify marked similarity in settlement opportunities. The far north in Russia has much in common with that in Canada, but her more urgent need to use Arctic waters for transportation coupled with certain geographic variations from that of northern Canada presents a somewhat different settlement situation. This requires careful detailed comparative study before any mature conclusions can be drawn.[26] There is still another naïve assumption that what can be done under the highly organized Russian system can also be achieved by our old highly individualistic methods of pioneering. We need not become Sovietized in order to expand our very thin line of northern population, but we do require the free use of scientific knowledge and carefully planned organization to achieve the possible in our own far North. Even with adequate aid and understanding, Canada in the light of present evidence, can expect not more than a four or five thousand increase in her present relatively permanent population of the Yukon and North West Territories during the next decade. Farming and lumbering in Alaska, Yukon, and the North West Territories seem destined to remain subsidiary enterprises. Forest growth is extensive in these northern areas,

[26]Among the books which make an important contribution to an understanding of northern Russia are—George B. Cressey, *Asia's Lands and Peoples* (New York, 1944); F. A. Taracouzio, *Soviets in the Arctic* (New York, 1938).

but for the most part it is useful chiefly for supplying rough boards, mining timber and wood.[27] Oil production, the mining of gold and other precious metals, and in some degree the rehabilitation of fur production and the growth of the tourist business will be the dominant factors in determining the northward expansion of population. In the Yukon and Alaska defence policies will continue to play a role in maintaining northern settlement. To these the mining of coal and fisheries may be added in Alaska. Fisheries will have a relatively small importance in Yukon and the North West Territories. Nevertheless each of these items is important as it fits into the whole configuration. Will agricultural production continue to be limited to the market provided by the small population concentrations of the far North? In the main this will likely continue. There is, however, one section in which there is an exception to this general expectation, i.e. the Hay River valley and its contiguous agricultural land. A railroad extension to the Keg River would stimulate a northward expansion of the Peace River region. Subsidized agriculture on the lower Hay River might expand eventually to the south along the planned permanent highway from the end of steel to the village of Hay River. Such a development might eventually extend outside markets to the lower Hay River and possibly to the lower Liard River valleys.

INDIANS IN THE NEW NORTH-WEST

This article concludes with a brief mention of the Indians in the new North-West.[28] There are about 4,000 Indians in the North West Territories and somewhat less than half that number in Yukon. They are widely scattered and represent various degrees of race mixture. Many of them have been to schools of the white man and have come in contact with white civilization in many other ways particularly in recent years. More and more they are trying to adopt the ways of white people in clothes, entertainment, and in many other matters. Numbers of them follow the white man's occupations which have increased during the war years. War projects together with the expansion of mining activities in the North have brought new people into the area which in turn has brought a new awareness of the extent and nature of Indian problems. A new restlessness is beginning to pervade the Indian mind. Many of them want new rights and responsibilities. They want to move away from all that is involved in being wards of the Canadian government.

Recent visitors to the North from the United States and Canada have been appalled by their ill-health and meagre health facilities. Their education under the whole educational set-up in Yukon and the North West Territories is coming under critical review. Matters of health and education are closely

---

[27]The growth of spruce in the Liard valley is in some measure an exception. For a long time this spruce will be used locally and farther north if it is used at all.

[28]Eskimos deserve equal attention, but they did not come within the writer's observation.

integrated with the Indian's economic situation. The old hand-to-mouth trading arrangements with the Hudson's Bay Company and other traders call for a severe scrutiny from the standpoint of their effect on the Indian's initiative and ambition. They have tended to make him dull and ambitionless. He is losing many of his old crafts and now requires not only the white man's substitutes, but the development of the educational facilities and economic opportunities which will create goals about which his life can be hopefully organized. Too long has he been the ward of somebody politically, educationally, and religiously. It is about time he was getting a new incentive to do something on his own. A new type of economic and educational organization might be established along the lines of modern co-operatives under the governmental direction. This would give a new goal to Indian education. It seems rather likely that the Indian is destined to intermarry more freely with other races and become more closely woven into the economic and social fabric of the new North-West. It seems to be the time to get a new slant on his problems and to give him a new deal. This brief statement about the Indians of the Yukon and the North West Territories applies to Indians right across Canada. An independent outside survey of the Indian and his problems as preparation for a new Indian programme should be undertaken at once.

21

Part Twelve

ELAINE ALLAN MITCHELL

Bibliography of the Canadian North

THE exact boundaries of the Canadian North are indefinite, but for the purposes of this bibliography the region is considered as comprising the North West Territories and the Yukon, together with the largely undeveloped lands in northern British Columbia and Alberta lying to the south of the sixtieth parallel and the Arctic fringes of southern Hudson and James Bays. Because of the limitations of space the bibliography is highly selective and indeed is little more than an indication of material which, it is hoped, will provide further sources of research for the reader of this book. Accordingly the emphasis has been placed on scientific and governmental publications, historical material being largely represented by the accounts of the explorers together with a few of the more recent books on the Canadian North. Since a good deal of important material appears in periodical form a selection of articles has been included, but only the more valuable from a scientific standpoint.

In a bibliography of this type whole sections of material have had to be omitted almost entirely,[1] but listings are available to the reader in the bibliographies appended to scholarly works dealing with the particular subject,[2] some of which appear below. Other sources will be found in the "Bibliographies and Indexes" section of this bibliography. It has also been found impossible to include the valuable reports of the Canadian Geological Survey,[3] but their titles are available in the various indexes published by the Survey and in Ferrier's *Catalogue and Guide* to its publications. Because of its arrangement and scope the latter, which covers the period from 1845 to 1917, is especially useful. A new list of publications of the Geological Survey, for the years from 1909 to 1946, has just been issued by the Department of Mines and Resources. Current Geological Survey publications appear in the bibliographies of the *Canadian Journal of Economics and Political Science,* generally under the "Mining" section. The new North-West has lately come in for a good deal of attention as the papers for the nineteen-forties will show.

For the newer books on the Canadian North a number of bibliographical sources are available. H. A. Innis's articles entitled "Recent Books on the North American Arctic," eleven of which have appeared in the *Canadian Historical Review* since 1934, cover this period effectively, and bibliographies in the *Review,* in the *Canadian Journal of Economics and Political Science,* and in the *Polar Record* provide a continuous source of new material and have the advantage of listing periodical articles and government pamphlets as well as books. In addition, book reviews in all three of these periodicals and also in the *Beaver* will be found helpful. Of great value in a specialized field are the annual contributions of T. F. McIlwraith to the *Canadian*

---

[1] E.g., that relative to the fur-trading companies.

[2] E.g., McKay's *The Honourable, Company* Crouse's *The Search for the North-west Passage* and *In Quest of the Western Ocean;* also books on general exploration like Mirsky's *To the North!,* books on the Eskimos such as Weyer's and Birket-Smith's, and books on the polar regions in general like Joerg's *Geography of the Polar Regions.* See *infra* for complete listings.

[3] Except for a few.

Historical Review entitled "List of Publications in Canadian Ethnology, Anthropology, and Archaeology." This annotated bibliography has been appearing since 1925 and includes periodical material.

ADAMS, JOHN T. *Settlements of the Northeastern Canadian Arctic.* (Geographical Review, XXXI (1), Jan., 1941, 112-26).

ALBRIGHT, W. D. *Crop Growth in High Latitudes* (Geographical Review, XXIII (4), Oct., 1933, 606-20).

———————— *Gardens of the Mackenzie* (Geographical Review, XXIII (1), Jan., 1933, 1-22).

Alaska and Canada. *Exchange of Notes (March 17 and 18, 1942) between Canada and the United States of America Recording an Agreement Providing for the Construction of a Military Highway to Alaska, in Force March 18, 1942.* (Treaty Series, 1942, no. 13.) Ottawa: King's Printer. 1944.

Alaska Highway.[1] United States Congress, 77th, 2nd session. Senate. *Alaska Highway, Hearings before a Sub-Committee of the Committee on Foreign Relations . . . On S. Res. 253, a Resolution Providing for Enquiry into the Location of the Alaska Highway on the So-Called C or Prairie Route, June 1, 12 and 16, 1942.* Washington. 1942.

ALLEN, EDWARD WEBER. *The Halibut Commission, Its Legal Powers and Functions.* (International Fisheries Commission, Circular no. 1.) Seattle, Washington. 1936.

———————— *North Pacific: Japan, Siberia, Alaska, Canada.* New York: Professional and Technical Press. 1936.

AMUNDSEN, ROALD. *The Northwest Passage.* London: A. Constable and Co.; New York: E. P. Dutton. 1908.

———————— *Scientific Results of the Norwegian Arctic Expedition in the Gjøa, 1903-1906.* 3 pts. Oslo, Norway: Cammermeyers Boghandel.

ANDERSON, R. M. *The Present Status and Future Prospects of the Larger Mammals of Canada* (Scottish Geographical Magazine, XL, Nov. 15, 1924, 321-31).

———————— *Recent Explorations on the Canadian Arctic Coast* (Geographical Review, IV (4), Oct., 1917, 241-66).

ANDREWS, G. S. *Alaska Highway Survey in British Columbia* (Geographical Journal, C (1), July, 1942, 5-22).

Anonymous. *An Account of a Voyage of Discovery to the Arctic Regions, in Search of a North-West Passage. Performed by His Majesty's Ships, Hecla and Griper, under the Command of Capt. Parry, R.N. By an Officer Employed on the Expedition.* London. 1821.

———————— *The Geographical Work of the Canadian Arctic Expedition* (Geographical Journal, LXIII (6), June, 1924, 508-25).

———————— *The Geographical Work of the Canadian Arctic Expedition* (Geographical Journal, LXV (4), Apr., 1925, 340-2).

ANTEVS, ERNST. *The Last Glaciation, with Special Reference to the Ice Retreat in Northeastern North America.* (American Geographical Society, Research series, no. 17.) New York: American Geographical Society. 1928.

Arctic Manual. Vols. I and II. Prepared under the direction of the Chief of the Air Corps, United States Army. Washington: Government Printing Office. Nov. 6, 1940.

Arctic Manual. (United States War Department, Technical Manual, TM 1-240.) Washington. Jan. 17, 1944. (Supersedes TM 1-240 of 1st April, 1942).

Arctic Pilot. 3 vols. London: Admiralty, Hydrographic Department. 1931-4.
Supplement—Relating to the Arctic Pilot. 2 vols. London. 1941-2.

ARMSTRONG, ALEXANDER. *A Personal Narrative of the Discovery of the North-West Passage with Numerous Incidents of Travel and Adventure during Nearly Five Years' Continuous Service in the Arctic Regions while in Search of the Expedition under Sir John Franklin.* London: Hurst and Blackett. 1857.

___

[1]For other United States Government publications on the Alaska Highway see Grace Hadley Fuller, *Alaska: A Selected List of Recent References* (United States Library of Congress, Division of Bibliography, Washington, 1943, pp. 134-5).

ARMSTRONG, NEVILL A. D. *Yukon Yesterdays: Thirty Years of Adventure in the Klondike, Personal Memories of the Famous Klondike Gold Rush, First Hand Accounts of Lucky Strikes, Stories of Dawson in the Wild Nineties, Together with Adventures in Mining, Exploring, and Big Game Hunting in the Unknown Sub-Arctic.* London: John Long. 1936.

BACK, Sir GEORGE. *Narrative of an Expedition in H.M.S. Terror in 1836-7, Undertaken with a View to Geographical Discovery on the Arctic Shores.* London: John Murray. 1838.

———— *Narrative of the Arctic Land Expedition to the Mouth of the Great Fish River and Along the Shores of the Arctic Ocean in the Years 1833, 1834, and 1835.* London: John Murray. 1836.

BALL, M. W. *Development of the Athabaska Oil Sands* (Transactions of the Canadian Institute of Mining and Metallurgy, XLIV, 1941, 58-91).

BANKSON, RUSSELL A. *The Klondike Nugget.* Caldwell, Idaho: Caxton Printers. 1935.

BARROW, JOHN. *Voyages of Discovery and Research within the Arctic Regions from the Year 1818 to the Present Time.* London. 1846.

BARTLETT, R. A. *The Last Voyage of the Karluk, Flagship of Vilhjalmur Stefansson's Canadian Arctic Expedition of 1913-16.* Boston. 1916.

BELCHER, Sir EDWARD. *The Last of the Arctic Voyages: Being a Narrative of the Expedition in H.M.S. Assistance . . . 1852-4.* 2 vols. London. 1855.

BELL, CHARLES NAPIER. *Our Northern Waters: A Report Presented to the Winnipeg Board of Trade Regarding the Hudson's Bay and Straits: Being a Statement of Their Resources in Minerals, Fisheries, Timber, Furs, Game and Other Products, also Notes on the Navigation of These Waters, Together with Historical Events and Meteorological and Climatic Data.* Winnipeg: James E. Steen. 1884.

BELL, JAMES MACKINTOSH. *Far Places.* Toronto: Macmillan Co. of Canada. 1931.

———— *Great Slave Lake* (Geographical Review, XIX (4), Oct., 1929, 556-80).

BELL, ROBERT. *On the Commercial Importance of Hudson's Bay with Remarks on Recent Surveys and Investigations* (Proceedings of the Royal Geographical Society, and Monthly Record of Geography, no. 10, Oct., 1881).

———— *Report on Hudson's Bay and Some of the Lakes and Rivers Lying to the West of It.* (Geological and Natural History Survey of Canada, Report of Progress, 1879-80.) Montreal. 1881.

———— *Rising of the Land around Hudson Bay* (Smithsonian Institution, annual report, 1897, Washington, 1898, 359-67).

BELLOT, J. R. *Memoirs of Lieutenant Joseph René Bellot, with His Journal of a Voyage in the Polar Seas, in Search of Sir John Franklin.* 2 vols. London: Hurst. 1855.

BENNETT, P. M. *The British Canadian Arctic Expedition* (Geographical Journal, XCV (2), Feb., 1940, 109-20).

BENTHAM, ROBERT. *Structure and Glaciers of Southern Ellesmere Island* (Geographical Journal, XCVII (1), Jan., 1941, 36-45).

BENTHAM, ROBERT and JENNESS, DIAMOND. *Eskimo Remains in S.E. Ellesmere Island* (Royal Society of Canada, Transactions, XXXV, sec. 2, May, 1941, 41-55).

BÉRIAULT, YVON. *Les Problèmes politiques du nord canadien: Le Canada et le Gröenland; A qui appartient l'Archipel arctique?* Préface de M. MAURICE OLLIVIER. Montréal: Éditions Bernard Valiquette; Ottawa: Université d'Ottawa. École des Sciences Politiques. 1942.

BERNIER, J. E. *Report on the Dominion Government Expedition to the Arctic Islands and the Hudson Strait on Board the C.G.S. "Arctic", 1906-1907.* Ottawa: Department of Marine and Fisheries. 1909.

———— *Report on the Dominion Government Expedition to the Northern Waters and Arctic Archipelago of the D.G.S. "Arctic" in 1910, under the Command of J. E. Bernier, Officer in Charge and Fishery Officer.* Ottawa: Department of Marine and Fisheries. [1915].

BERNIER, J. E. *Report on the Dominion of Canada Government Expedition to the Arctic Islands and Hudson Strait on Board the D.G.S. "Arctic"* [*1908-1909*]. Ottawa: Department of Marine and Fisheries. 1910.

BEST, GEORGE. *A True Discourse of the Late Voyages . . . of Martin Frobisher.* London. 1578. (Edited by RICHARD COLLINSON for the Hakluyt Society, London, 1867, Hakluyt Society Publications, no. 38; and by Vilhjalmur Stefansson with the collaboration of Eloise McCaskill, 2 vols., London: Argonaut Press, 1938.)

BETHUNE, W. C. *Canada's Eastern Arctic: Its History, Resources, Population, and Administration.* Ottawa: Department of the Interior. 1935.

——————— *Canada's Western Northland: Its History, Resources, Population, and Administration.* Ottawa: Department of Mines and Resources, Lands, Parks and Forests Branch. 1937.

BIRKET-SMITH, KAJ. *Anthropological Observations on the Central Eskimos.* (Report of the Fifth Thule Expedition, 1921-4, vol. III, pt. 1.) Copenhagen: Gyldendalske Boghandel, Nordisk Forlag. 1940.

——————— *The Caribou Eskimos: Material and Social Life and Their Cultural Position.* (Report of the Fifth Thule Expedition, 1921-4, vol. V, pts. 1 and 2.) Copenhagen. 1929.

——————— *Contributions to Chipewyan Ethnology.* (Report of the Fifth Thule Expedition, 1921-4, vol. VI, pt. 3.) Copenhagen. 1930.

——————— *The Eskimos.* Translated from the Danish by W. E. CALVERT, the translation revised by Professor C. DARYLL FORDE. With a foreword by DIAMOND JENNESS. London: Methuen and Co. 1936.

——————— *Geographical Notes on the Barren Grounds.* (Report of the Fifth Thule Expedition, 1921-4, vol. I, pt. 4.) Copenhagen. 1933.

BLANCHET, G. H. *The Great Slave Lake Area.* Ottawa: Department of the Interior. 1926.

——————— *Keewatin and Northwestern Mackenzie: A General Survey of the Life, Activities, and Natural Resources of This Section of the Northwest Territories.* Ottawa: Bureau of Northwest Territories and Yukon Affairs. 1930.

——————— *Preliminary Report on the Aerial Mineral Exploration of Northern Canada.* Ottawa: Bureau of Northwest Territories and Yukon Affairs. 1930.

BOAS, FRANK. *The Central Eskimo.* (Bureau of American Ethnology, 6th annual report.) Washington. 1888.

——————— *The Eskimo of Baffin Land and Hudson Bay.* (American Museum of Natural History, Bulletin XV.) New York. 1907.

——————— *Ethnological Problems in Canada* (Congrès Internationale des Américanistes, XV sess. T.I. Quebec. 1907 (b)).

BODFISH, HARTSON H. *Chasing the Bowhead.* As told by Captain HARTSON H. BODFISH and recorded for him by JOSEPH C. ALLEN. Cambridge: Harvard University Press. 1936.

BOSTOCK, H. S. *The Mining Industry of the Yukon, 1934.* (Canada, Department of Mines, Bureau of Economic Geology, Geological Survey Memoir 178.) Ottawa: King's Printer. 1935. (One in a series.)

BRAITHWAITE, JOHN. *Supplement to Captain Sir John Ross's Narrative of a Second Voyage.* London. 1835.

BRAY, REYNOLD. With comments by T. H. MANNING. *Notes on the Birds of Southampton Island, Baffin Island, and Melville Peninsula* (Auk, LX (4), Oct., 1943, 504-36).

British Polar Year Expedition, Fort Rae, N. W. Canada, 1932-33. Vol. I. *Discussion of Results: Meteorology, Terrestrial Magnetism and Aurora, Atmospheric Electricity.* Vol. II. *Tables.* Published under the direction of the British National Committee for the Polar Year. London: Royal Society, Burlington House. 1937.

BROWN, R. N. RUDMOSE. The Polar Regions. New York: E. P. Dutton and Co. 1927.

BROWN, W. E. *Motor Tractors* (Polar Record, II (11), Jan., 1936, 90-8).

BURPEE, LAWRENCE J. *The Search for the Western Sea: The Story of the Exploration of North Western America.* 2 vols. Toronto. 1908. Revised edition, Toronto: Macmillan Co. of Canada. 1935.

Burwash, E. M. J. and Burwash, L. T. *Travelling in Canada* (in Brouwer, H. A., ed., *Practical Hints to Scientific Travellers*, 1929, VI, 1).

Burwash, L. T. *Across Arctic Canada, 1925-1926* (Geographical Journal, LXXIV (6), Dec., 1929, 553-68).

———————— *Canada's Western Arctic, Report on Investigations in 1925-6, 1928-9 and 1930.* Ottawa: Department of the Interior, Northwest Territories and Yukon Branch. 1931.

———————— *Coronation Gulf Copper Deposits.* Ottawa: Department of the Interior. 1930.

———————— *The Eskimo, Their Country and Its Resources.* Economic Survey of the East Coasts of Hudson Bay and James Bay from Richmond Gulf to Rupert House, Including the Belcher and Other Adjacent Islands. Typed copy in Library, Department of Mines and Resources, Lands, Parks and Forests Branch. Ottawa. 1927.

———————— *Mining Development in the Mackenzie District, 1922.* Ottawa: Department of the Interior, Northwest Territories and Yukon Branch. 1923.

Butler, W. F., Colonel (later General Sir). *The Great Lone Land: A Narrative of Travel and Adventure in the North-West of America.* London. 1872; Toronto. 1910.

———————— *The Wild North Land: Being the Story of a Winter Journey, with Dogs, across Northern North America.* Montreal: Dawson. 1874; London. 1874; Toronto. 1910.

Cadzow, Donald A. *Archaeological Work with the Putnam Baffin Island Expedition* (Indian Notes, V (1), Jan., 1928, 98-106).

Cameron, T. W. M. *The Feeding of Dogs in the Canadian Arctic* (Canadian Journal of Comparative Medicine, July, 1938). Reprint. (The substance of a lecture given annually to the Royal Canadian Mounted Police proceeding to the Eastern Arctic).

Camsell, Charles and Malcolm, W. *The Mackenzie River Basin.* (Canada, Geological Survey Memoir 108, pp. 99-104). Ottawa. 1921.

Canada,[2] British Columbia-Yukon-Alaska Highway Commission. *Report on the Proposed Highway Through British Columbia and the Yukon Territory to Alaska, August, 1941.* Ottawa: King's Printer. 1942.

Canada, Department of the Interior. *Canada's Arctic Islands: Canadian Expeditions 1922 and 1923, 1924, 1925 and 1926.* Ottawa: Northwest Territories and Yukon Branch. 1927.

———————— *Canada's Eastern Arctic.* Ottawa: King's Printer. 1934.

———————— *Lower Athabaska and Slave River District.* Ottawa: Natural Resources Branch. 1921.

———————— *The Northwest Territories, 1933.* Ottawa: King's Printer. 1933.

———————— *The Yukon Territory.* Ottawa: King's Printer. 1907. New editions printed 1909, 1916, and 1926. (Now out of print).

Canada, Department of Marine. *Navigation Conditions in Hudson Bay and Strait during Season of Navigation.* 6 vols. Ottawa: King's Printer. 1931-6. (For later reports see Canada, Department of Transport).

Canada, Department of Mines and Resources. *Canada's Reindeer.* Ottawa: Bureau of Northwest Territories and Yukon Affairs. 1940.

[2]Canada, Government Publications. For regular government publications the reader is referred to the lists which appear annually in the *Canada Year Book,* to the *Catalogue of Official Publications of the Parliament and Government of Canada* issued annually (with supplements monthly or as required) and to Marion Higgins, *Canadian Government Publications, 1935.* The papers given here are a few for which the authors are not listed, others appear elsewhere under the authors' names, but the list as included in this bibliography is by no means complete and is intended only to illustrate the type of material available in government publications.

Canada, Department of Mines and Resources. *The Northwest Territories: Administration, Resources, Development.* Ottawa: Bureau of Northwest Territories and Yukon Affairs. 1944.

———————————————————— *An Outline of the Canadian Eastern Arctic: Its Geography, Peoples and Problems.* Ottawa: Bureau of Northwest Territories and Yukon Affairs. 1944.

———————————————————— *Sailing Directions for the Hudson Bay Route.* (Hydrographic and Map Service). Ottawa: King's Printer. 1940.

———————————————————— *The Yukon Territory, Administration, Resources, Development.* Ottawa: King's Printer. 1944.

Canada, Department of Naval Service. *Reports of the Canadian Arctic Expeditions, 1913-18.* 14 vols. Ottawa: King's Printer. 1917-28.

Canada, Department of Transport. *Canadian Polar Year Expeditions, 1932-33.* 2 vols. Division of Meteorological Service of Canada, Air Service Branch. Ottawa: King's Printer. 1939-40.

———————————————————— *Churchill and the Hudson Bay Route.* Ottawa: King's Printer. 1939.

———————————————————— *Meteorology of the Canadian Arctic.* Division of Meteorological Service of Canada, Air Service Branch. Ottawa: King's Printer. 1944.

———————————————————— *Navigation Conditions on the Hudson Bay Route from the Atlantic Seaboard to the Port of Churchill.* Ottawa: King's Printer. 1937-41. (For earlier reports see Canada, Department of Marine).

Canada, Hudson Strait Expedition. *Report of the Hudson Strait Expedition, 1927-28.* N. B. McLean, Officer in Charge. Ottawa: King's Printer. 1929.

CHAMBERLAIN, A. F. *Eskimo Race and Language.* (Proceedings of the Canadian Institute, VI, 3rd series, 1887-8, 261-314). Toronto: Copp Clark. 1889.

CHAMBERS, E. J. *The Great Mackenzie Basin.* (Reports of the Select Committee of the Senate, Sessions 1887 and 1888. A Summary of the Reports of the "Schultz Committees"... edited by Captain ERNEST J. CHAMBERS). Ottawa: Select Committee on the Natural Food Products of the Northwest Territories. 1919.

CHAPPELL, Lieutenant EDWARD, R. N. *Narrative of a Voyage to Hudson's Bay in H.M.S. Rosamond, Containing Some Account of the N.E. Coast of America, and of the Tribes Inhabiting That Remote Region.* London: J. Mawman. 1817.

CHITTY, D. and others. *Canadian Arctic Wild Life Enquiry 1935 to 1942.* Series published in the *Journal of Animal Ecology.*

———————————————————— *The Snowshoe Rabbit Enquiry.* Series published since 1933 in the *Canadian Field-Naturalist.*

CHRISTY, MILLER (i.e. ROBERT MILLER) (ed.). *The Voyages of Captain Luke Foxe of Hull. and Captain Thomas James of Bristol, in Search of a Northwest Passage, in 1631-32: With Narratives of the Earlier Northwest Voyages of Frobisher, Davis, Weymouth, Hall, Knight, Hudson, Button, Gibbons, Bylot, Baffin, Hawkridge, and Others.* (Hakluyt Society Publications, nos. 88, 89). London: The Hakluyt Society. 1894.

CLARKE, C. H. D. *Biological Investigations of Thelon Game Sanctuary.* (National Museum of Canada, Bulletin no. 96, Biological series, no. 25). Ottawa. 1940.

———————————————————— *Notes on the Status and Distribution of Certain Mammals and Birds in the Mackenzie River and Western Arctic Area in 1942 and 1943* (Canadian Field-Naturalist, LVIII (3), May-June, 1944, 97-103).

CLUTTERBUCK, H. M. *Akpatok Island (Hudson Strait): The Oxford University Exploration Club's Expedition, 1931* (Geographical Journal, LXXX, (3), Sept., 1932, 211-33).

COATS, WILLIAM. *The Geography of Hudson's Bay: Being the Remarks of Captain W. Coats, in Many Voyages to That Locality, Between the Years 1727 and 1751.* With an appendix containing extracts from the log of Captain Middleton on his voyage for the discovery of the North-West Passage, in H.M.S. "Furnace," in 1741-2. Edited by JOHN BARROW. (Hakluyt Society Publications, no. 11). London: The Hakluyt Society. 1852.

COCHRANE, H. G. *Petroleum Possibilities North of Sixty-One* (Oil and Gas Journal, XLIII (11), Nov., 1944, 42-4).

COCKFIELD, W. E. and BELL, A. H. *Whitehorse District, Yukon.* (Canada, Geological Survey Paper 44-14). Ottawa. 1944.

COGHILL, F. S. *Flying Operations of the Hudson Strait Expedition* (Canadian Defence Quarterly, VII (2), Jan., 1930, 193-207).

COLLINSON, RICHARD. *Journal of H.M.S. Enterprise, on the Expedition in Search of Sir John Franklin's Ships in Behring Strait, 1850-55.* Edited by T. B. COLLINSON. London: Sampson Low, Marston, Searle and Rivington. 1889.

CRAIG, J. D. *Canada's Arctic Islands: Log of Canadian Expedition, 1922.* With an appendix, *Aviation in the Arctic,* by Major R. A. LOGAN. Ottawa: Department of the Interior, Northwest Territories and Yukon Branch. 1923.

CROUSE, NELLIS M. *In Quest of the Western Ocean.* New York: William Morrow and Co. 1928.

———————— *The Search for the Northwest Passage.* New York: Columbia University Press. 1934.

CURTIN, WALTER R. *Yukon Voyage: Unofficial Log of the Steamer Yukoner.* Caldwell, Idaho: Caxton Printers. 1938.

CYRIAX, RICHARD J. *Captain Hall and the So-Called Survivors of the Franklin Expedition* (Polar Record, IV (28), July, 1944, 170-85).

———————— *Sir James Clark Ross and the Franklin Expedition* (Polar Record, III (24), July, 1942, 528-40).

———————— *Sir John Franklin's Last Arctic Expedition: A Chapter in the History of the Royal Navy.* London: Methuen and Co. 1939.

DALL, W. H., DAWSON, G. M., and OGILVIE, W. *The Yukon Territory.* (Extracts of Reports). London: Downey and Co. 1911.

DAVIDSON, GORDON CHARLES. *The North West Company.* (University of California Publications in History, vol. VII). Berkeley: University of California Press. 1919.

DAVIES, RAYMOND ARTHUR. *Arctic Eldorado.* Toronto: Ryerson Press. 1944.

DAVIS, MARY LEE. *Sourdough Gold: The Log of a Yukon Adventure.* Boston: W. A. Wilde Co. 1933.

DAWSON, C. A. and MURCHIE, R. W. *The Settlement of the Peace River Country. A Study of a Pioneer Area.* (*Canadian Frontiers of Settlement,* edited by W. A. MACKINTOSH and W. L. G. JOERG, vol. VI). Toronto: Macmillan Co. of Canada. 1934.

DAWSON, GEORGE M. *Report on an Exploration in the Yukon District, N.W.T., and Adjacent Northern Portion of British Columbia, 1887 . . . with Extracts Relating to the Yukon District from a Report on an Exploration in the Yukon and Mackenzie Basins, 1887-88 by R. C. McConnell.* Ottawa: King's Printer. 1898.

DEBENHAM, FRANK. *The Polar Regions.* London: Benn. 1930.

DOBBS, ARTHUR. *An Account of the Countries adjoining to Hudson's Bay, in the North-West Part of America... With an Abstract of Captain Middleton's Journal, and Observations upon His Behaviour During His Voyage and Since His Return... The Whole Intended to Shew the Great Probability of a North-West Passage, so Long Desired; and Which (if Discovered) Would be of the Highest Advantage to These Kingdoms.* London: J. Robinson. 1744. (No. 3 of 9 on the literary side of the Dobbs-Middleton controversy).

Dog Transportation. (United States War Department Field Manual, FM 25-6). Washington: Government Printing Office. 1944. (Superseded FM 25-6, *Dog Team Transportation,* January 4, 1941).

DOUGLAS, GEORGE M. *Lands Forlorn.* New York: Putnam. 1914.

DOWNES, P. G. *Sleeping Island: The Story of One Man's Travels in the Great Barren Lands of the Canadian North.* New York: Coward-McCann; Toronto: Longmans Green and Co. 1943.

DRAGE, THEODORE SWAINE. *An Account of a Voyage for the Discovery of a North-West Passage by Hudson's Streights, to the Western and Southern Ocean of America. Performed in the Year 1746 and 1747, in the Ship California, Capt. Francis Smith, Commander. By the Clerk of the California.* London: Jolliffe. 1748.

DUMAN, MAXIMILIAN GEORGE. *The Genus Carex in Eastern Arctic Canada.* (Catholic University of America Biological series, no. 36). Washington. 1941. (Ph.D. thesis obtainable from the Librarian, Mullen Library, Catholic University of America, Washington, D.C.)

DUNBAR, M. J. *Food of Seals in Canadian Eastern Arctic* (Canadian Journal of Research, XIX (5), May, 1941, section D, 150-5).

DUTILLY, Rev. ARTHÈME, O.M.E. *A List of Insects of the Mackenzie River Basin* (Canadian Field-Naturalist, LX (2), Mar.-Apr., 1946, 35-44).

ELLIS, HENRY. *A Voyage to Hudson's Bay, by the Dobbs Galley and the California in the Years 1746 and 1747 for Discovering a North-West Passage.* London. 1748. (No. 9 of 9 on the Dobbs-Middleton controversy).

ELLS, S. C. *Bituminous Sands of Northern Alberta: Occurrence and Economic Possibilities. Report on Investigation to End of 1924.* Ottawa: Bureau of Mines. 1926.

ELLSWORTH, LINCOLN (ed.). *Air Pioneering in the Arctic: The First Two Polar Flights of Roald Amundsen and Lincoln Ellsworth. Part I. The 1925 Flight from Spitsbergen to 88° North. Part II. The First Crossing of the Polar Sea, 1926.* New York: National Americana Society. 1929.

ELTON, CHARLES. *Voles, Mice and Lemmings: Problems in Population Dynamics.* Oxford: Clarendon Press. 1942.

The Eskimo Kayak. (Polar Record, I (7), Jan., 1934, 52-62).

FERGUSON, ROBERT. *Arctic Harpooner: A Voyage on the Schooner Abbie Bradford, 1878-1879.* Edited by D. L. STAIR. Philadelphia: University of Pennsylvania Press. 1938.

FINNIE, RICHARD. *Canada Moves North.* Toronto: Macmillan Co. of Canada. 1942.

——————— *Canol, the Sub-Arctic Pipeline and Refinery Project Constructed by Bechtel-Price-Callahan for the Corps of Engineers, United States Army, 1942-1944.* San Francisco, California. 1945.

FISCHER, MØLLER K. *Skeletal Remains of the Central Eskimos.* (Report of the Fifth Thule Expedition, 1921-4, vol. III). Copenhagen: Gyldendalske Boghandel, Nordisk Forlag. 1940.

FISHER, ALEXANDER. *A Journal of a Voyage of Discovery to the Arctic Regions, in His Majesty's Ships, Hecla and Griper, in the Years 1819-1820.* London: Longman. 1821.

——————— *Journal of a Voyage of Discovery to the Arctic Regions Performed between the 4th of April and the 18th of November, 1818, in His Majesty's Ship Alexander, Wm. Edw. Parry, Esq., Lieut. and Commander.* London: Phillips. 1819.

FLAHERTY, R. J. *The Belcher Islands of Hudson Bay: Their Discovery and Exploration* (Geographical Review, V (6), June, 1918, 433-58).

FRANKLIN, Sir JOHN. *Narrative of a Journey to the Shores of the Polar Sea in 1819-22.* London: John Murray. 1823.

——————— *Narrative of a Second Expedition to the Shores of the Polar Sea in the Years, 1825, 1826 and 1827 ... Including an Account of Progress of a Detachment to the Eastward by John Richardson.* London: John Murray. 1828.

FREUCHEN, PETER. *Arctic Adventure: My Life in the Frozen North.* New York: Farrar and Rinehart; Toronto: Oxford University Press. 1935.

GIBSON, ROY A. *Canada's Reindeer Herd.* Ottawa: Department of Mines and Resources, Northwest Territories Administration. 1938.

GIBSON, WILLIAM. *Sir John Franklin's Last Voyage* (Beaver, outfit 268 (1), June, 1937, 44-75.) Reprinted.

——————— *Some Further Traces of the Franklin Retreat* (Geographical Journal, LXXXIX (5), May, 1932, 402-8).

GILBERT, WALTER E. *Arctic Pilot: Life and Work on North Canadian Air Routes.* As told to KATHLEEN SHACKLETON. London, New York, etc.: Thomas Nelson and Sons. 1940. 1945.

GODSELL, PHILLIP H. *Arctic Trader: The Account of Twenty Years with the Hudson's Bay Company.* New York: G. P. Putnam's Sons. 1934. Sixth and revised edition, Toronto: Macmillan Co. of Canada. 1943.

GOODSIR, R. A. *An Arctic Voyage to Baffin's Bay and Lancaster Sound, in Search of Friends with Sir John Franklin.* London: Van Voorst. 1850.

GRAHAM, ANGUS (recorded by). *The Golden Grindstone: The Adventures of George M. Mitchell.* Toronto: Oxford University Press. 1935.

GREELY, General ADOLPHUS W. *International Polar Expedition: Report on the Proceedings of the United States Expedition to Lady Franklin Bay, Grinnell Land.* 2 vols. Washington: Government Printing Office. 1888.

———————————— *Three Years of Arctic Service: An Account of the Lady Franklin Bay Expedition of 1881-4 and the Attainment of the Farthest North.* 2 vols. New York. 1886.

GREGG, W. K. *Aeronautical Meteorology.* New York. 1930.

GRIFFIN, HAROLD. *Alaska and the Canadian Northwest, Our New Frontier.* New York: Norton. 1944.

GUNNING, H. C. *Sulphide Deposits at Cape Smith, E. Coast of Hudson Bay.* (Canada, Geological Survey, Summary Report, 1933, 139D-154D). Ottawa: King's Printer. 1934.

HADWEN, SEYMOUR. *A Visit to the Mackenzie River Delta: Progress of Our Reindeer Herds* (Bulletin of the Ontario Research Foundation, VI (12), Dec., 1939, 1-4). Summary of a report to the Dominion Department of Mines and Resources, 1939.

HAIG-THOMAS, DAVID. *Expedition to Ellesmere Island, 1937-38* (Geographical Journal, XCV (4), Apr., 1940, 265-77).

———————————— *Tracks in the Snow.* London: Hodder and Stoughton; Toronto: Musson Book Co. 1939.

HALL, C. F. *Arctic Researches, and Life Among the Esquimaux.* New York: Harper and Bros. 1865.

———————————— *Life with the Esquimaux: The Narrative of Captain Charles Francis Hall, of the Whaling Barque "George Henry," from the 29 of May 1860 to the 13 Sept. 1862...* 2 vols. London. 1864.

———————————— *Narrative of the North Polar Expedition, U.S. Ship Polaris.* Edited by Rear-Admiral C. F. Davis. Washington: Government Printing Office. 1876.

———————————— *Narrative of the Second Arctic Expedition . . . to Repulse Bay, . . . 1864-9.* Edited by J. E. Nourse. Washington. 1879.

HANBURY, DAVID. *Sport and Travel in the Northland of Canada.* London: Arnold. 1904.

HARPER, ALLAN G. *Canada's Indian Administration: Basic Concepts and Objetives (sic)* (América indígena, V (2), Apr., 1945, 119-32).

HAWLEY, J. E. *The Association of Gold, Tungsten, and Tin at Outpost Islands, Great Slave Lake* (University of Toronto Studies, Geological Series, no. 42, 1930, 53-66).

HAYES, ISAAC I. *An Arctic Boat Journey, in the Autumn of 1854.* Boston. 1860.

———————————— *The Open Polar Sea . . . Voyages of Discovery Towards the North Pole in the Schooner United States.* New York: Hurd and Houghton. 1867.

———————————— *Physical Observations in the Arctic Seas . . . Made on the West Coast of North Greenland, the Vicinity of Smith Strait and the West Side of Kennedy Channel, during 1860 and 1861.* (Reduced and discussed at the expense of the Smithsonian Institution, Smithsonian Contributions to Knowledge, vol. V, Art. 5, Smithsonian publication, 196.) Washington: Smithsonian Institution. 1867.

HEARNE, SAMUEL. *A Journey from Prince of Wales's Fort in Hudson's Bay to the Northern Ocean. Undertaken by Order of the Hudson's Bay Company, for the Discovery of Copper Mines, a North-West Passage, etc., in the Years 1769-1772.* 1st ed. London: Strahan and Cadell. 1795. New edition published by the Champlain Society, Toronto, 1911, with introduction and notes by J. B. Tyrrell.

HENDERSON, J. F. and JOLLIFFE, A. W. *Relation of Gold Deposits to Structure, Yellowknife and Gordon Lake Areas, Northwest Territories* (Canadian Mining and Metallurgical Bulletin, XLII, June, 1939, 314-36).

HERSHEY, BURNET. *The Air Future: A Primer of Aeropolitics.* New York: Duell, Sloan and Pearce; Toronto: Wm. Collins and Sons. 1943.

HOARE, W. H. B. *Conserving Canada's Musk-Oxen: Being an Account of an Investigation of the Thelon Game Sanctuary, 1928-9.* Ottawa: Department of the Interior, Northwest Territories and Yukon Branch. 1930.

HOBBS, WILLIAM HERBERT. *The Boundary of the Latest Glaciation in Arctic Canada* (Science, n.s., CI (2631), June 1, 1945, 549-51).

HOLDRIDGE, DESMOND. *Northern Lights.* New York: Viking Press; Toronto: Macmillan Co. of Canada. 1939.

HONE, E. *The Present Status of the Musk-Ox.* (Special Publication of the American Committee for International Wild Life Protection, no. 5). 1934.

HOOPER, WILLIAM HULME. *Ten Months Among the Tents of the Tuski, with Incidents of an Arctic Boat Expedition in Search of Sir John Franklin, as Far as the Mackenzie River and Cape Bathurst.* London: John Murray. 1853.

Hudson Bay. *Surface Water Supply of Canada, Arctic and Western Hudson Bay Drainage, Climatic Years 1937-8 and 1938-9.* (Water Resources Paper, no. 83). Ottawa: Department of Mines and Resources. 1943.

HUNTSMAN, A. G. *Biological and Oceanographic Conditions in Hudson Bay* (Canadian Biology and Fisheries, VI (21), 1931).

INGLEFIELD, E. A. *A Summer Search for Sir John Franklin with a Peep into the Polar Basin.* London. 1853.

INGSTAD, HELGE. *The Land of Feast and Famine.* New York: A. A. Knopf. 1933.

INNIS, HAROLD A. *The Fur Trade in Canada: An Introduction to Canadian Economic History.* With a preface by R. M. McIver. New Haven: Yale University Press. 1927.

———————— *The Fur Trade of Canada.* (University of Toronto Studies, History and Economics series, vol. V). Toronto: University of Toronto Library. 1927.

———————— *The Hudson Bay Railway* (Geographical Review, XX (1), Jan., 1930, 1-30).

———————— *Recent Books on the North American Arctic* (Canadian Historical Review, XV, Sept., 1934; XVI, June, Dec., 1935; XVII, June, Dec., 1936; XIX, June, 1938; XX, Mar., 1939; XXI, June, 1940; XXII, June, 1941; XXIII, Dec., 1942; XXV, Mar., 1944).

———————— *Settlement and the Mining Frontier.* (*Canadian Frontiers of Settlement,* edited by W. A. MACKINTOSH and W. L. G. JOERG, vol. IX). Toronto: Macmillan Co. of Canada. 1936.

International Ice Patrol. *The Marion Expedition.* See *Ricketts* and *Smith,* ff.

JACKSON, ALEXANDER YOUNG. *The Far North: A Book of Drawings by A. Y. Jackson,* with an Introduction by Dr. F. G. Banting and Descriptive Notes by the Artist. Toronto: Rous and Mann. 1927.

JAMES, BESSIE ROWLAND (ed.). *Six Came Back: The Arctic Adventure of David L. Brainard.* Indianapolis, New York: Bobbs-Merrill Co.; Toronto: McClelland and Stewart. 1940.

JENNESS, DIAMOND. *The Life of the Copper Eskimos.* (Report of the Canadian Arctic Expedition, 1913-18, vol. XII.) Ottawa: King's Printer. 1922.

———————— *A New Eskimo Culture in Hudson Bay* (Geographical Review, XV (3), July, 1925, 428-37).

———————— *Origin of the Copper Eskimos and Their Copper Culture* (Geographical Review, XIII (4), Oct., 1923, 540-51).

———————— *The People of the Twilight.* With an introduction by FRIDTJOF NANSEN. New York: Macmillan Co. 1928.

———————— *Physical Characteristics of the Copper Eskimos.* (Report of the Canadian Arctic Expedition, vol. XII.). Ottawa. 1923.

———————— (ed.). *The American Aborigines, Their Origin and Antiquity: A Collection of Papers by Ten Authors.* (Published for presentation at the Fifth Pacific Science Congress, Canada, 1933.) Toronto: University of Toronto Press. 1933.

Jeremie's Narrative. *Twenty Years of York Factory, 1694-1714.* Translated from the French edition of 1720, with notes and introduction by R. DOUGLAS, and J. N. WALLACE. Ottawa: Thorburn and Abbott. 1926.

JOERG, W. L. G. *The Geography of the Polar Regions.* (American Geographical Society, special publication, no. 8.) New York: American Geographical Society. 1928.

———————— *Problems of Polar Research.* A series of papers by thirty-one authors, edited by W. L. G. JOERG. (American Geographical Society, special publication, no. 7.) New York: American Geographical Society. 1928.

JOHNSTON, V. KENNETH. *Canada's Title to Hudson Bay and Hudson Strait* (British Year Book of International Law, Oxford Press, 1934, 1-20).

———————— *Canada's Title to the Arctic Islands* (Canadian Historical Review, XIV, 24-41).

JOLLIFFE, A. W. *Mineral Possibilities of N.W.T.* (Canadian Mining and Metallurgical Bulletin, XL, Nov., 1937, 663-77).

KANE, ELISHA KENT. *Arctic Explorations: The Second Grinnell Expedition in search of Sir John Franklin, 1853-5.* 2 vols. Philadelphia and London. 1856-7.

———————— *The U.S. Grinnell Expedition in Search of Sir John Franklin.* New York. 1853.

KIDD, D. F. *Great Bear Lake-Coppermine River Area, Mackenzie District, Northwest Territories.* (Canada, Geological Survey, Summary Report for 1931, pt. C, 47-69). Ottawa: King's Printer. 1932.

———————— *Rae to Great Bear Lake, Mackenzie District, N.W.T.* (Canada, Geological Survey Memoir 187.) Ottawa: King's Printer. 1936.

KINDLE, E. M. *Arrival and Departure of Winter Conditions in the Mackenzie River Basin* (Geographical Review, X (6), Dec., 1920, 388-99).

———————— *Canada North of Fifty-Six Degrees: The Land of Long Summer Days.* Ottawa: Department of the Interior, Northwest Territories and Yukon Branch. 1928.

KING, RICHARD. *The Franklin Expedition from First to Last.* London: John Churchill. 1855.

———————— *The Franklin Expedition, to His Grace, the Duke of Newcastle . . . a Letter of Appeal.* London: John Churchill. 1860.

———————— *Narrative of a Journey to the Shores of the Arctic Ocean, in 1833, 1834, and 1835 under the Command of Capt. Back, R. N.* London: Bentley. 1836.

KITTO, F. H. *Athabaska to the Bay. Report of a Reconnaissance Expedition, Chiefly by Canoe, from Edmonton and McMurray across the Northern Parts of Alberta, Saskatchewan, and Manitoba to Port Nelson and Churchill on Hudson Bay, 1918.* Ottawa: National Development Bureau. 1919.

———————— *The Hudson Bay Region.* Ottawa: Department of the Interior. 1929.

———————— *The Northwest Territories, 1930.* Ottawa: Department of the Interior, Northwest Territories and Yukon Branch. 1930.

———————— *The Peace River District, Canada: Its Resources and Opportunities.* Ottawa: National Development Bureau. 1918. 1920. Revised edition issued in 1928 under the title *The Peace River Country, Canada.*

———————— *Yukon; Land of the Klondike.* Ottawa: Department of the Interior, Natural Resources Intelligence Branch. 1929. 1930.

KIZER, BENJAMIN H. *The U.S.-Canadian Northwest: A Demonstration Area for International Postwar Planning and Development.* Princeton: Princeton University Press; Toronto: Ryerson Press. 1943.

KNIGHT, Captain. *The Founding of Churchill: Being the Journal of Captain James Knight, Governor-in-Chief of Hudson Bay from 14th July to 13th Sept., 1717.* Edited by JAMES F. KENNEY. Toronto: J. M. Dent and Sons. 1932.

KOEPPE, C. E. *The Canadian Climate.* Bloomington, Illinois. 1931.

KORTRIGHT, FRANCIS H. *The Ducks, Geese and Swans of North America.* Washington: American Wildlife Institute. 1943.

LANKS, HERBERT C. *Highway to Alaska.* New York: D. Appleton-Century. 1944.

LARSEN, H. A. *Royal Canadian Mounted Police, 1945. Reports and Other Papers Relating to the Two Voyages of the R.C.M. Police Schooner "St. Roch" through the North-West Passage from (1) Vancouver, B.C. to Sydney, N.S. (1940-42) (2) Dartmouth, N.S. to Vancouver, B.C. (1944) under the Command of Regimental Number 10407 Staff/Sergeant H. A. Larsen (now Sub-Inspector).* Ottawa: King's Printer. 1945.

LAYTHA, EDGAR. *North Again for Gold: Birth of Canada's Arctic Empire.* New York, Toronto: Frederick A. Stokes Co. 1939.

LEECHMAN, DOUGLAS. *Eskimo Summer.* Toronto: Ryerson. 1946.

LEPPARD, H. M. *The Settlement of the Peace River Country* (Geographical Review, XXV (1), Jan., 1935, 62-78).

LETHBRIDGE, T. C. *Archaeological Data from the Canadian Arctic* (Journal of the Royal Anthropological Institute, LXIX (2), 1939, 187-233).

LLOYD, TREVOR. *The Mackenzie Waterway: A Northern Supply Route* (Geographical Review, XXXIII (3), July, 1943, 415-34).

——————— *Oil in the Mackenzie Valley* (Geographical Review, XXXIV (2), Apr., 1944, 275-307).

LORD, C. S. *Mineral Industry of the Northwest Territories.* (Canada, Geological Survey Memoir 230.) Ottawa: King's Printer. 1941.

LOW, A. P. *Report on the Dominion Government Expedition to Hudson Bay and the Arctic Islands on Board the D.G.S. "Neptune," 1903-4.* Ottawa. 1906.

LYON, Captain G. F. *A Brief Narrative of an Unsuccessful Attempt to Reach Repulse Bay, through Sir Thomas Rowe's "Welcome" in H.M.S. Griper, 1824.* London. 1825.

——————— *The Private Journal of Capt. Lyon of H.M.S. Hecla, during the Recent Voyage for the Discovery of a North West Passage, under Captain Parry.* London. 1824.

McCLINTOCK, FRANCIS LEOPOLD. *A Narrative of the Discovery of the Fate of Sir John Franklin and His Companions.* London. 1859. (Also published under the title, *Voyage of the Fox in the Arctic Seas.*)

——————— *Meteorological Observations in the Arctic Seas, Made on Board the Arctic Searching Yacht "Fox" in Baffin Bay and Prince Regent's Inlet, in 1857, 1858 and 1859.* (Reduced and discussed at the expense of the Smithsonian Institution, by CHARLES A. SCHOTT. Smithsonian Contributions to Knowledge, vol. XIII, Art. 3, Smithsonian Institution Publication 146.) Washington: Smithsonian Institution. 1862.

McCLURE, ROBERT L. *The Discovery of the North-West Passage by H.M.S. "Investigator," 1850-4.* Edited by Commander SHERARD OSBORN, from the logs and journals of Captain ROBERT McCLURE. London: Longman. 1857.

——————— *Proceedings of Capt. McClure of H.M. Discovery Ship "Investigator" in Search of the Expedition under Sir John Franklin, from August 1850 to April 1853.* (Parliamentary Papers.) London. 1854.

McCORMICK, R. *Narrative of a Boat Expedition up the Wellington Channel in the year 1852, under the Command of R. M'Cormick, R.N., F.R.C.S., in H.M.B. "Forlorn Hope" in Search of Sir John Franklin.* London. 1854.

——————— *Voyages of Discovery in the Arctic and Antarctic Seas, and Round the World: And of an Open-Boat Expedition in Search of Sir John Franklin in Her Majesty's Boat "Forlorn Hope."* 2 vols. London. 1884.

McDIARMID, F. A. *Geographical Determinations of the Canadian Arctic Expedition* (Geographical Journal, LXII (4), Oct., 1923, 293-302).

M'DOUGALL, G. F. *The Eventful Voyage of H.M. Discovery Ship "Resolute" to the Arctic Regions in Search of Sir John Franklin and the Missing Crews of H.M. Discovery Ships "Erebus" and "Terror," 1852, 1853, 1854 . . . to Which is Added an Account of Her Being Fallen in with by an American Whaler . . .* London: Longman. 1857.

MACFARLANE, R., Chief Factor of the Hudson's Bay Company. *Notes on Mammals Collected and Observed in the Northern Mackenzie River District, Northwest Territories, with Remarks on Explorers and Explorations of the Far North.* Washington: Smithsonian Institution. 1905; Toronto: Briggs and Co. 1908.

McGuire, J. A. *In the Alaska-Yukon Gamelands.* Cincinnati: Stewart and Kidd Co. 1921.

MacInnis, Tom (ed.). *Klengenberg of the Arctic: An Autobiography.* London: Jonathan Cape. 1932.

MacKay, Douglas. *The Honourable Company: A History of the Hudson's Bay Company.* Toronto: McClelland and Stewart. 1936.

Mackenzie, Alexander. *Voyages from Montreal, on the River St. Lawrence, through the Continent of North America, to the Frozen and Pacific Oceans in the Years 1789 and 1793. With a Preliminary Account of the Rise, Progress, and Present State of the Fur Trade of that Country.* London: T. Cadell. 1801. Numerous editions, the latest in *Masterworks of Canadian Authors,* edited by John W. Garvin, vol. III. Introduction by Charles W. Colby. Toronto: The Radisson Society of Canada. 1927.

MacLean, Thomas Archibald. *Lode Mining in the Yukon: An Investigation of Quartz Deposits in the Klondike Division.* Ottawa: Bureau of Mines. 1914.

McLearn, F. G. *Geography and Geology of Peace River Foothills* (Royal Society of Canada, Transactions, sec. 4, May, 1940, 63-74).

McMillan, Donald Baxter. *Four Years in the White North.* New York: Harper. 1918.

Manning, T. H. *Blue and Lesser Snow Geese on Southampton and Baffin Islands* (Auk, LIX (2) Apr., 1942, 158-75).

———————— *The Foxe Basin Coasts of Baffin Island* (Geographical Journal, CI (5, 6), May-June, 1943, 225-51).

———————— *Hunting Implements and Methods of the Present-Day Eskimos of Northwest Hudson Bay, Melville Peninsula, and South-West Baffin Island* (Geographical Journal, CIII (4), Apr., 1944, 137-52).

———————— *Notes on the Coastal District of the Eastern Barren Grounds and Melville Peninsula from Igloolik to Cape Fullerton* (Canadian Geographical Journal, XXVI (2), Feb., 1943, 84-105).

———————— *Notes on the Mammals of South and Central West Baffin Land* (Journal of Mammalogy, XXIV (1), Feb., 1943, 47-59).

———————— *Remarks on the Physiography, Eskimo, and Mammals of Southampton Island* (Canadian Geographical Journal, XXIV (1), Jan., 1942, 16-33).

———————— *Some Notes on Southampton Island* (Geographical Journal, LXXXVIII (3), Sept., 1936, 232-42).

———————— and E. W. *The Preparation of Skins and Clothing in the Eastern Canadian Arctic* (Polar Record, IV (28), July, 1944, 156-69).

Manning, Mrs. Tom. *Igloo for the Night.* London: Hodder and Stoughton. 1943; Toronto: University of Toronto Press. 1946.

Markham, Admiral Sir Albert H. *The Great Frozen Sea...Voyage of the Alert.* London: Daldy, Isbister and Co. 1878.

———————— *A Whaling Cruise to Baffin Bay and the Gulf of Boothia.* London: Sampson Low, Marston, Low and Searle. 1874.

Mathiassen, Therkel. *Archaeological Collections from the Western Eskimos.* (Report of the Fifth Thule Expedition, 1921-4, vol. X, pt. 1.) Copenhagen: Gyldendalske Boghandel, Nordisk Forlag. 1930.

———————— *Archaeology of the Central Eskimos. I. Descriptive Part. II. The Thule Culture and Its Position within the Eskimo Culture.* (Report of the Fifth Thule Expedition, 1921-4, vol. IV, pts. 1 and 2.) Copenhagen: Gyldendalske Boghandel, Nordisk Forlag. 1927.

———————— *Contributions to the Physiography of Southampton Island.* (Report of the Fifth Thule Expedition, 1921-4, vol. I, pt. 2.) Copenhagen. 1931.

———————— *Eskimo Relics from Washington Land and Hall Land* (Meddelelser om Grønland, København, 1926, Bd. 71, 181-216).

———————— *Material Culture of the Iglulik Eskimos.* (Report of the Fifth Thule Expedition, 1921-4, vol. VI, pt. 1.) Copenhagen. 1928.

———————— *The Question of the Origin of Eskimo Culture* (American Anthropologist, XXXII (4), Oct.-Dec., 1930, 591-607).

22

MIDDLETON, CHRISTOPHER. *Attempts Made for the Discovery of a Passage into the South Seas by the North-West...* (In Harris's *Collection of Voyages*, vol. II, 1748).

—————————— *A Vindication of the Conduct of Captain Christopher Middleton in a Late Voyage on Board His Majesty's Ship, the Furnace, for Discovering a North-West Passage to the Western American Ocean. In Answer to Certain Objections and Aspersions of Arthur Dobbs, Esq...* London: Jacob Robinson. 1743. (No. 2 of 9 on the Dobbs-Middleton controversy. For a complete list see McKay, *The Honourable Company*, pp. 78-9).

MILLER, MAX. *The Great Trek: The Story of the Five-Year Drive of a Reindeer Herd through the Icy Wastes of Alaska and Northwestern Canada.* Garden City, N.Y.: Doubleday, Doran and Co. 1936.

MILLWARD, A. E. (ed.). *Southern Baffin Island: An Account of Exploration, Investigation, and Settlement during the Past Fifty Years.* With an appendix *The Crossing of Baffin Island to Foxe Basin by Bernard A. Hantzch in 1910,* translated by M. B. A. ANDERSON. Ottawa: Department of the Interior, Northwest Territories and Yukon Branch. 1930.

MIRSKY, JEANNETTE. *To the North! The Story of Arctic Exploration from Earliest Times to the Present.* New York: The Viking Press. 1934.

MORAN, J. F. *Local Conditions in the Mackenzie District, 1922.* Ottawa: Department of the Interior, Northwest Territories and Yukon Branch. 1923.

MORRELL, W. P. *The Gold Rushes.* (The Pioneer Histories series.) London: Adam and Charles Black; Toronto: Macmillan Co. of Canada. 1940.

MORTON, A. S. *A History of the Canadian West to 1870-1: Being a History of Rupert's Land (the Hudson's Bay Territory) and of the Northwest Territory (Including the Pacific Slope).* London: Nelson. n.d.

MUNK, JENS. *The Expedition of Captain Jens Munk to Hudson's Bay...in 1619-20.* (Vol. II of GOSCH, C.C.C. *Danish Artic Expeditions, 1605-20,* 2 vols., Hakluyt Society Publications, nos. 96, 97.) London: The Hakluyt Society. 1897.

MUNN, HENRY TOKE. *Prairie Trails and Arctic By-Ways.* London: Hurst and Blackett. 1932.

MURRAY, ALEXANDER HUNTER. *Journal of the Yukon, 1847-8.* Edited with notes by L. J. BURPEE. (Publications of the Canadian Archives, no. 4.) Ottawa. 1910.

NARES, Captain Sir GEORGE S. *Narrative of a Voyage to the Polar Sea during 1875-6 in H.M. Ships "Alert" and "Discovery."* 2 vols. London: Sampson Low, Marston, Searle and Rivington. 1878.

Nares Expedition, 1875-76. *Arctic Expedition: Results Derived from the Arctic Expedition, 1875-76.* I. *Physical Observations,* by Captain GEORGE S. NARES, R.N. and Captain FEILDEN, etc. II. *Medical Report on the Eskimo Dog Disease,* by Fleet Surgeon B. MINNIS. London: George Edward Eyre and William Spottiswoode. 1878.

OGILVIE, WILLIAM. *Early Days on the Yukon.* Ottawa: Thorburn and Abbott; New York: John Lane Co. 1913.

—————————— *Klondike Official Guide.* Toronto: Hunter-Rose Co. 1898.

OSBORN, Captain SHERARD. *Stray Leaves from an Arctic Journal: Or, Eighteen Months in the Polar Regions, in Search of Sir John Franklin's Expedition, in the Years 1850-1.* London. 1852.

OSGOOD, CORNELIUS B. *The Ethnography of the Great Bear Lake Indians* (National Museum of Canada, Annual Report for 1931, Bulletin no. 70, 31-97). Ottawa. 1932.

OSTERMANN, H. (ed.). *The Mackenzie Eskimos.* After KNUD RASMUSSEN's posthumous notes. (Report of the Fifth Thule Expedition, 1921-4, vol. X, pt. 2.) Copenhagen: Gyldendalske Boghandel. 1942.

PARRY, WILLIAM EDWARD. *Journal of a Voyage for the Discovery of a North-West Passage from the Atlantic to the Pacific, 1819-20, in H.M.S. Hecla and Griper.* London. 1821.
The North Georgia Gazette and Winter Chronicle. London. 1821.
Journal of a Second Voyage...1821-3. In H.M.S. *Fury and Hecla.* London. 1824.
Appendix to Captain Parry's Journal of a Second Voyage. London. 1825.
Journal of a Third Voyage, 1824-5. In H.M.S. Hecla and Fury. London. 1826.

Narrative of an Attempt to Reach the North Pole, in Boats Fitted for the Purpose and Attached to H.M.S. Hecla, 1827. London. 1828.
Together, 6 vols. in 5. London: John Murray. 1821-8.

PAYNE, F. F. *Eskimo of Hudson's Strait* (Proceedings of the Canadian Institute, vol. VI, 3rd series, 1887-88, 213-30). Toronto: Copp Clark. 1889.

PEARCE, RICHARD. *Marooned in the Arctic: Diary of the Dominion Explorers' Expedition to the Arctic, August to December, 1929.* Toronto. 1931.

PETITOT, ÉMILE. *On the Athapaskan District of the Canadian Northwest Territories.* (Proceedings of the Royal Geographical Society, vol. V.) London. 1883.

PIKE, WARBURTON. *The Barren Grounds of Northern Canada.* London: Macmillan Co. 1891.

———— *Through the Subarctic Forest. A Record of a Canoe Journey from Fort Wrangel to the Pelly Lakes and Down the Yukon River to the Behring Sea.* London. 1896.

PLISCHKE, ELMER. *Trans-Arctic Aviation* (Economic Geography, XIX (3), July, 1943, 283-91).

Polar Record. Edited by F. DEBENHAM. (Printed in Great Britain for the Scott Polar Research Institute.) Cambridge: At the University Press. First published January, 1931. Semi-annual.

Polar Times. New York. Vol. I (1935-40). Official Publication of the American Polar Society. Semi-annual.

POLUNIN, NICHOLAS. *Botany of the Canadian Eastern Arctic.* Part I. *Pteridophyta and Spermatophyta.* (National Museum of Canada, Bulletin no. 92.). Ottawa: King's Printer. 1940.

———— *The Isle of Auks.* London: E. Arnold. 1932.

PORSILD, A. E. *The Alpine Flora of the East Slope of Mackenzie Mountains, Northwest Territories.* (National Museum of Canada, Bulletin no. 101, Biological series, no. 30.) Ottawa: King's Printer. 1945.

———— *Birds of the Mackenzie Delta* (Canadian Field-Naturalist, LVII (2,3), Feb.-Mar., 1943, 19-35).

———— *Emergency Food in Arctic Canada.* (National Museum of Canada, special contribution no. 45-1.) Ottawa: Department of Mines and Resources, Mines and Geology Branch. 1945. (mimeo.)

———— *Reindeer Grazing in Northwest Canada: Report of an Investigation of Pastoral Possibilities in the Area from the Alaska-Yukon Boundary to the Coppermine River.* Ottawa: Department of the Interior, Northwest Territories and Yukon Branch. 1929.

———— *The Reindeer Industry and the Canadian Eskimo* (Geographical Journal, LXXXVIII (1), July, 1936, 1-19).

PREBLE, E. A. *A Biological Investigation of the Athabaska-Mackenzie Region.* (United States Department of Agriculture, Biological Survey, North American Fauna, no. 27.) Washington. 1908.

———— *A Biological Investigation of the Hudson Bay Region.* (United States Department of Agriculture, Biological Survey, North American Fauna, no. 22.) Washington. 1902.

Proposed Pacific-Yukon Highway Connecting Washington-B.C.-Yukon Territory-Alaska. Alaska Road Commission, Territory of Alaska, Juneau, Alaska. April 1, 1931.

PUTNAM, GEORGE PALMER. *The Putnam Baffin Island Expedition* (Geographical Review, XVIII (1), Jan., 1928, 1-40).

QUIMBY, GEORGE I. JR. *The Manitunik Eskimo Culture of East Hudson's Bay* (American Antiquity, VI (2), Oct., 1940, 148-65).

RAE, JOHN. *Narrative of an Expedition to the Shores of the Arctic Sea in 1846 and 1847.* London: Boone. 1850.

———— *Practical Hints for Arctic Travelling* (Bulletin of the American Geographical Society, IX, 1877, 149-53).

———— *Report of the Arctic Searching Expedition under His Command.* (Parliamentary Papers.) London. 1855.

RAND, A. L. *Mammal Investigations on the Canol Road, Yukon and Northwest Territories, 1944.* (National Museum of Canada, Bulletin no. 99, Biological series, no. 28.) Ottawa: King's Printer. 1945.

———— *Mammals of Yukon.* (National Museum of Canada, Bulletin no. 100, Biological series, no. 29.) Ottawa: King's Printer. 1945.

———— *The Southern Half of the Alaska Highway and Its Mammals.* (National Museum of Canada, Bulletin no. 98, Biological series, no. 27.) Ottawa: King's Printer. 1944.

RASMUSSEN, KNUD. *Across Arctic America: Narrative of the Fifth Thule Expedition.* New York and London: G. P. Putnam's Sons. 1927.

———— *Intellectual Culture of the Copper Eskimos.* (Report of the Fifth Thule Expedition, vol. IX.) Copenhagen. 1932.

———— *Intellectual Culture of the Iglulik Eskimos.* (Report of the Fifth Thule Expedition, vol. VII, pt. 1.) Copenhagen. 1929.

———— *The Netsilik Eskimos: Social Life and Spiritual Culture.* (Report of the Fifth Thule Expedition, vol. VIII.) Copenhagen. 1931.

———— *Observations on the Intellectual Culture of the Caribou Eskimos.* (Report of the Fifth Thule Expedition, vol. VII.) Copenhagen. 1929.

RAUP, HUGH M. *Botanical Investigations in Wood Buffalo Park.* (National Museum of Canada, Bulletin no. 74, Biological series, no. 20.) Ottawa: King's Printer. 1935.

———— *Forests and Gardens Along the Alaska Highway* (Geographical Review, XXXV (1), Jan., 1945, 22-48.)

———— *Phytogeographic Studies in the Peace and Upper Liard Regions, Canada: With a Catalogue of the Vascular Plants.* (Harvard University, Arnold Arboretum, contributions no. 6.) Jamaica Plain, Mass.: Arnold Arboretum. 1934.

Report of the Royal Commission Appointed by Order-in-Council of Date May 20, 1919, to Investigate the Possibilities of the Reindeer and Musk-Ox Industries in the Arctic and Sub-Arctic Regions of Canada. Ottawa: King's Printer. 1922.

RICKETTS, NOBLE G. and TRASK, PARKER D. *The Marion Expedition to Davis Strait and Baffin Bay under Direction of the United States Coast Guard 1928: Scientific Results. Part I. The Bathymetry and Sediments of Davis Strait.* (United States Treasury Department, Coast Guard bulletin, no. 19.) Washington. 1932.

ROBERTS, BRIAN. *Game Conservation in Arctic Canada* (Polar Record, III (23), Jan., 1942, 499-509).

ROBSON, JOSEPH. *An Account of Six Years' Residence in Hudson's Bay, from 1733 to 1736 and 1744 to 1747.* London. 1752.

ROSS, JOHN. *Narrative of a Second Voyage in Search of a North-West Passage, and of a Residence in the Arctic Regions during the Years 1829-33. Including the Reports of Commander, now Captain James Clarke Ross ... and the Discovery of the Northern Magnetic Pole.* London: Webster. 1835.

———— *A Voyage of Discovery, Made under the Orders of the Admiralty, in H.M.S. Isabella and Alexander, for the Purpose of Exploring Baffin's Bay and Inquiring into the Probability of a North-West Passage.* London: Murray. 1819.

ROWLEY, GRAHAM. *The Dorset Culture of the Eastern Arctic* (American Anthropologist, XLII (3), July-Sept., 1940, 490-9).

SEEMANN, BERTHOLD C. *Narrative of the Voyage of H.M.S. Herald.* 2 vols. London. 1853.

SEIDENFADEN, GUNNAR. *Modern Arctic Exploration.* Preface by PETER FREUCHEN. Translated from the Danish by NAOMI WALFORD. London: Jonathan Cape. 1939.

SETON, ERNEST THOMPSON. *The Arctic Prairies: A Canoe-Journey of 2000 Miles in Search of the Caribou, Being an Account of a Voyage to the Region North of Aylmer Lake.* New York: Scribner's. 1911. New edition, New York: International University Press. 1943.

SHACKLETON, EDWARD. *Arctic Journeys: The Story of the Oxford University Ellesmere Land Expedition 1934-5.* With a preface by the Right Honourable the Lord TWEEDSMUIR. London: Hodder and Stoughton; Toronto: Musson Book Company. 1937.

SIMMONS, H. G. *A Survey of the Phytogeography of the American Archipelago with Some Notes about Its Exploration.* (Lunds University Arsskrift, n.s., sec. 2, vol. IX, no. 19.) Lund. 1913.

SIMPSON, ALEXANDER. *Life and Travels of Thomas Simpson, the Arctic Discoverer.* London: Richard Bentley. 1845.

SIMPSON, DR. G. C. *Meteorology in Polar Regions* (Geographical Journal, LXXIV (3), Sept., 1929, 258-70).

SIMPSON, THOMAS. *Narrative of the Discoveries on the North Coast of America Effected by the Officers of the Hudson's Bay Company During the Years 1836-9.* London: Richard Bentley. 1843.

SMITH, EDWARD H. *The Marion Expedition to Davis Strait and Baffin Bay, 1928. Scientific Results.* Part III. *Arctic Ice.* (United States Treasury Department, Coast Guard bulletin, no. 19.) Washington. 1931.

SMITH, EDWARD H., SOULE, FLOYD M., and MOSBY, OLAV. *The Marion and General Greene Expeditions to Davis Strait and Labrador Sea, under the Direction of the United States Coast Guard, 1928-1931-1933-1934-1935. Scientific Results.* Part II. *Physical Oceanography.* (United States Treasury Department, Coast Guard bulletin, no. 19.) Washington. 1937.

SMITH, F. C. GOULDING. *The Canadian Hydrographical Survey of the Hudson Bay Route* (Geographical Journal, LXXXVII (2), Feb., 1936, 127-40).

SOPER, J. DEWEY. *Birds of Wood Buffalo Park and Vicinity, Northern Alberta and District of Mackenzie, N.W.T., Canada* (Transactions of the Royal Canadian Institute, XXIV (1), Oct., 1942, 19-97).

———————— *Explorations in Foxe Peninsula and along the West Coast of Baffin Island* (Geographical Review, XX (3), July, 1930, 397-424).

———————— *History, Range and Home Life of the Northern Bison (Wood Buffalo Park, Northern Alberta and District of Mackenzie, N.W.T., Canada)* (Ecological Monographs, II, Oct., 1941, 347-412).

———————— *The Lake Harbour Region, Baffin Island* (Geographical Review, XXVI (3), July, 1936, 426-38).

———————— *Life History of the Blue Goose, Chen Caerulescens (Linnaeus)* (Proceedings of the Boston Society of Natural History, XLII (2), Nov., 1942, 121-225).

———————— *Local Distribution of Eastern Canadian Arctic Birds* (Auk, LVII (1), Jan., 1940, 13-21).

———————— *The Mammals of Southern Baffin Island, Northwest Territories, Canada* (Journal of Mammalogy, XXV (3), Aug., 1944, 221-54).

STEELE, HARWOOD. *Policing the Arctic: The Story of the Conquest of the Arctic by the Royal Canadian (Formerly North-West) Mounted Police.* Toronto: Ryerson. 1935.

STEFANSSON, VILHJALMUR. *Arctic Manual.* New York: Macmillan Co. 1945.

———————— *The Friendly Arctic, the Story of Five Years in the Polar Regions.* New York: Macmillan Co. 1921. New edition, New York, Toronto: Macmillan Co., 1943.

STEWART, J. S. *Petroleum Possibilities in Mackenzie River Valley, Northwest Territories* (Transactions of the Canadian Institute of Mining and Metallurgy, XLVII, 1944, 152-71).

STOCKWELL, C. H. and KIDD, D. F. *Metalliferous Mineral Possibilities of the Mainland Part of the Northwest Territories.* (Canada, Geological Survey, Summary Report for 1931, part C, 70-85.) Ottawa: King's Printer. 1932.

SUTTON, GEORGE MIKSCH. *Eskimo Year: A Naturalist's Adventures in the Far North.* New York: Macmillan Co.; Toronto: Macmillan Co. of Canada. 1934.

SVERDRUP, OTTO. *New Land. Four Years in the Arctic Regions.* Translated from the Norwegian. 2 vols. London: Longmans, Green. 1904.

THOMAS, L. O. *Mineral Possibilities of Areas Adjacent to the Alaska Highway.* Part II. *British Columbia, Section D, Liard River Area* (Transactions of the Canadian Institute of Mining and Metallurgy, XLVII, 1944, 228-43).

Thule Expedition (Fifth) Reports. 10 vols. Copenhagen: Glyldendalske Boghandel, Nordisk Forlag. 1927-42.

TURNER, LUCIEN M. *Ethnology of the Ungava District, Hudson Bay Territory.* (Bureau of American Ethnology, Eleventh Annual Report, 1889-90, 159-350.)   Washington. 1894.

TYRRELL, JAMES W.   *Across the Sub-Arctics of Canada.*   Toronto: Briggs.   1897.

TYRRELL, JOSEPH BURR (ed.). *Documents Relating to the Early History of Hudson Bay.* (Publications of the Champlain Society, XVIII.) Toronto: The Champlain Society. 1931.

———————————— *Journals of Samuel Hearne and Philip Turnor.* (Publications of the Champlain Society, XXI.) Toronto: The Champlain Society. 1934.

UMFRÉVILLE, EDWARD. *The Present State of Hudson's Bay, Containing a Full Description of That Settlement and the Adjacent Country* ... London: Stalker. 1790

United States Navy Department. *Scientific Results of the United States Arctic Expedition. Steamer Polaris. C. F. Hall, Commanding. Vol. I. Physical Observations by Emil Bessels, Chief of the Scientific Department, United States Arctic Expedition.* Washington: Government Printing Office. 1876.

WAGER, HAROLD. *Growth and Survival of Plants in the Arctic* (Journal of Ecology, XXVI (2), Aug., 1938, 390-410).

WAKEHAM, WILLIAM. *Report of the Expedition to Hudson Bay and Cumberland Gulf in the Steamship "Diana"* ... *1897.* Ottawa: Department of Marine and Fisheries. 1898.

WEEKS, L. J. *Cumberland Sound Area, Baffin Island.* (Canada, Geological Survey, Summary Report for 1927, Part C, 83-95.) Ottawa. 1928.

——————————— *Rankin Inlet Area, W. Coast of Hudson Bay.* (Canada, Geological Survey, Summary Report for 1931, Part C, 37-46.) Ottawa. 1932.

WEIGERT, HANS W. and STEFANSSON, VILHJALMUR (eds.). *Compass of the World: A Symposium on Political Geography.* New York: Macmillan Co. 1944.

WEYER, EDWARD M. JR. *The Eskimos.* New Haven: Yale University Press. 1932.

WORDIE, J. M. *An Expedition to Melville Bay and Northeast Baffin Land* (Geographical Journal, LXXXVI (4), Oct., 1935, 297-316).

WRIGHT, JOHN. *Southeast Ellesmere Island* (Geographical Journal, XCV (4), Apr., 1940, 278-91).

YOUNG, SIR ALLEN. *Cruise of the Pandora.* London: W. Clowes and Sons. 1876.
——————————— *The Two Voyages of the "Pandora" in 1875 and 1876.* London. 1879.

Bibliographies and Indexes

BROWN, ANN DUNCAN (comp.). *Selected List of Recent Books and Pamphlets on Canada.* Washington: United States Library of Congress, Division of Bibliography. 1941.

Canada, Department of Public Printing and Stationery. *Catalogue of Official Publications of the Parliament and Government of Canada.* Issued annually with supplements monthly or as required.

The Canadian Catalogue of Books Published in Canada, about Canada, as well as Those written by Canadians with the Imprint of—Compiled by the Toronto Public Library. Published annually since 1923.

Canadian Historical Review. *Index. Vols. I-X, 1920-1929.* Toronto: University of Toronto Press. 1930.

——————————— *Index. Vols. XI-XX, 1930-1939.* Toronto: University of Toronto Press. 1944.

——————————— *List of Recent Publications Relating to Canada,* appearing in each quarterly issue, classified.

Canadian Journal of Economics and Political Science. *Bibliography of Current Publications in Canadian Economics,* appearing in each quarterly issue, classified.

——————————— *Decennial Index. Vols. I-X, 1935-1944.* Toronto: University of Toronto Press. 1945.

The Canadian North West. *A Bibliography of the Sources of Information in the Public Reference Library of the City of Toronto, Canada, in Regard to the Hudson's Bay Company, the Fur Trade and the Early History of the Canadian North West.* Toronto: Public Library. 1931.

Canadiana, 1698-1900, in the Possession of the Douglas Library, Queen's University, Kingston, Ontario. Kingston. 1932.

Carnegie Endowment for International Peace, Library. *The Arctic and Antarctic Regions: With Special Reference to Territorial Claims.* Compiled by M. A. Mathews. (Brief Reference List, no. 18.) Washington, D.C.: The Library. 1940. (mimeo.)

FERREL, JAMES. *Annotated Bibliography of the Polar Regions.* Parts I-II. (United States Works Progress Administration sponsored by the Explorers' Club of America.) New York. 1938-9. (mimeo.)

———————— *Bibliography of Greenland. Section on Medicine and Health. The Annotated Bibliography of the Polar Regions.* (Sponsored by the United States Department of State. Co-sponsored by the United States Department of War,—under the guidance of the Bibliography Committee of the Explorers' Club. Prepared by W.P.A. Official Project number 165-2-97-69 W.P.1.) New York. Oct., 1942. (This forms the only section yet published of the *Annotated Bibliography of the Polar Regions.*)

FERRIER, W. F., assisted by DOROTHY J. FERRIER. *Annotated Catalogue of and Guide to the Publications of the Geological Survey of Canada, 1845-1917.* Ottawa: King's Printer. 1920.

FULLER, GRACE HADLEY (comp.). *Alaska: A selected List of Recent References.* Washington: United States Library of Congress, Division of Bibliography. 1943. (Compiled mainly as a supplement to JAMES WICKERSHAM's *Bibliography of Alaskan Literature, 1724-1924.* Like Wickersham's comprehensive work it is useful for material common to Alaska and the Canadian North-West.)

Geological Survey of Canada. *Catalogue of Publications of the Geological Survey, Canada.* (Revised to January 1, 1909.) Ottawa: King's Printer. 1909. (Supersedes all previous lists.)

———————— *General Index to Reports 1885-1906.* Compiled by F. J. NICOLAS. Ottawa: King's Printer. 1908.

———————— *General Index to the Reports of Progress, 1863 to 1884.* Compiled by D. B. DOWLING. Ottawa: King's Printer. 1900.

———————— *Index to Memoirs, 1910-1926, Bulletins 1913-1926, Summary Reports of 1917-1926, Sessional Papers (Administrative) 1921-1926.* Compiled by F. J. NICOLAS. Ottawa: King's Printer. 1932.

———————— *Index to Separate Reports 1906-1910 and Summary Reports 1905-1916.* Compiled by F. J. NICOLAS. Ottawa: King's Printer. 1923.

———————— Publications (1909-1946 inclusive) of the Geological Survey and the National Museum. Ottawa. 1946. Pp. ciii (mimeo.).

HIGGINS, M. V. *Canadian Government Publications: A Manual for Libraries.* With an introduction by G. K. LOMER. Chicago: American Library Association. 1935.

Hudson's Bay Company. *Books Relating to the Hudson's Bay Company* (Beaver, outfit 260 (6), Dec., 1934, 55-60).

———————— *Hudson's Bay Company: A Selected Bibliography.* Winnipeg: Hudson's Bay House. 1936.

———————— *List of Books Relating to the Hudson's Bay Company.* Issued by the Company. January, 1935.

INNIS, HAROLD A. *Recent Books on the North American Arctic.* Appearing in the Canadian Historical Review. See under Innis, Harold A., above.

KIDDER, ALFRED VINCENT, with the aid of BRITTEN, Mrs. MARION HALE, and CHADWICK, Mrs. IDA S. *General Index: American Anthropologist Current Anthropological Literature, and Memoirs of the American Anthropological Association 1888-1929.* Compiled under the auspices of the Division of Anthropology and Psychology, National Research Council and Phillips Academy, Andover, Mass. (American Anthropologist, XXXII (3), part II, Menasha, Wis., 1930).

McIlwraith, T. F. *List of Publications in Canadian Ethnology, Anthropology, and Archaeology.* Appearing annually since 1925 in the Canadian Historical Review, *List of Recent Publications Relating to Canada.*

Maggs Bros., London. *Canada, Newfoundland, Labrador and the Canadian Arctic: A Selection of Six Hundred and Fifty Books, with 44 Illustrations.* London: Maggs Bros. 1939. (Book catalogue but useful for older historical material on the Canadian North).

Murdock, George Peter. *Ethnographic Bibliography of North America.* (Yale Anthropological Studies, vol. I.) New Haven, Conn.: Yale University Press; London: Oxford University Press. 1941. (Arctic and sub-Arctic regions occupy some twenty to thirty pages of the bibliography).

Polar Record. Published semi-annually by the Scott Polar Institute, Cambridge, with extensive bibliographies.

Staton, F. M. and Tremaine, M. (eds.). *A Bibliography of Canadiana: Being Items in the Public Library of Toronto, Canada, Relating to the Early History and Development of Canada.* With an introduction by George H. Locke. Toronto: Public Library. 1934.

Towne, Jackson E. (comp.). *A Bibliography of Polar Exploration: A Suggested List of Modern Books for the Larger American Library* (Bulletin of Bibliography, Jan.-Apr., 1936, 167-8).

Wickersham, James. *A Bibliography of Alaskan Literature, 1724-1924.* Cordova, Alaska: Cordova Daily Times. 1928.

Wright, John Kirtland. *Aids to Geographical Research: Bibliographies and Periodicals.* (American Geographical Society Publication, Research series, no. 10.) New York: American Geographical Society. 1923. (Out of print).

INDEX

Index

Abasand, 49, 51, 302

Abbott, J. W., 178

Agriculture: near Alaska Highway, 292-4; causes for increased interest in, 157, 177, 302-4; future prospects for, 105, 169, 181, 308-9; and government research, 25, 171-3, 177-8, 293, 302; in Laurentian Shield, 180; in Mackenzie District, 126, 158-73, 303; in Matanuska Valley, 304-7; and mining, 177, 301; northern points at which conducted, 169-70; and possible crops, 170, 172, 302-3; in Takhini-Dezadeash Valley, 178-80; in Tanana Valley, 308; and transportation, 168-9; in Yukon Territory, 173-80

Aklavik, 23, 26, 40, 42, 44, 45, 46, 47, 57, 79, 80-2, 141, 153, 168, 170, 234, 252

Alaska, 26, 30, 33, 34, 82, 286, 294, 304-9

Alaska Highway, 89, 199-201: agriculture near, 292-4; construction of, 16, 30-1, 199-200, 286-8; geographical notes on, 98-101; need of feeder roads to, 292; permanent value of, 107, 200, 288-92; and tourist trade, 107, 289-92

Alberta Northern Railway, 125

Albright, W. D., 172; "Gardens of the Mackenzie," 172 n.

Anderson, J. W., "Trading North of Hudson Bay," 136 n.

Anderson, R. M., "The Game and Fur-Bearing Mammals of Western North America," 140 n.

Arctic exploration, 27, 29, 48, 111, 135, 167, 203, 209; see also Hudson's Bay Company and North West Company

Arctic Red, 39, 42, 72, 75-6, 146, 150, 170

Arsenopyrite, 120, 121, 122

Athabaska District, 5

Athabaska River, transportation on, 213-14

Baker Lake, 180

Baldonnell, 103

Bear Creek, 97

Beaverlodge, 171, 172

Bell, James Mackintosh, 297

Bell, John, 76, 191

Bonanza Creek, 95, 97

Borden, R. L., 10

Brink, A. V., 172

British Columbia, northern: agriculture in, 173-80; and annexation of Yukon, 32-3

Browning's Farm, 63

Burnt Islands, 58

Burwash, L. T., 27

Butler, L., "Fur Cycles and Conservation," 154 n.

Campbell, Robert, 191

Camsell, C., 27, 297; "Mineral Development in the Northwest and Yukon Territory,"

297 n.; "Natural Resources and Their Conservation," 139 n.; and Malcolm, W., *Geological Survey Bulletin on Mackenzie River*, 70 n., 79 n.

Canada, Department of the Interior, *The Yukon, Its History and Resources*, 6 n.

Canada, Department of Mines and Resources, *Canada's Western Northland*, 45 n.; 282 n.; *The Northwest Territories*, 20 n., 23 n., 24 n., 25 n., 26 n., 27 n., 28 n., 31 n., 32 n., 139 n.; *An Outline of the Canadian Eastern Arctic*, 24 n., 28 n.; *The Yukon Territory*, 12 n., 14 n., 15 n., 16 n.

Canada, Wartime Information Board, "Defence Projects in Northwest Canada," 295 n., 297 n.

Canadian Pacific Air Lines, 53, 186, 192, 201-2, 220-4, 298

Canol Project, 30, 89, 202, 207, 295: cost of, 296; post-war future of, 31; terms of agreement, 31

Cape Dorset, 180

Carcross, 14, 189

Carmacks, 92, 93, 178, 191

Catel Telephone System, 30

Chalcopyrite, 120

Champagne, 180

Chesterfield Inlet, 180

Chipman, K. and Cox, J., *Report of the Canadian Arctic Expedition, 1913-1918*, 127 n.

Clarke, C. H. D., "A Biological Investigation of the Thelon Game Sanctuary," 148 n.; "Mammals and Birds in the Mackenzie River and Western Arctic Area," 150 n.

Climate: at Aklavik, 79; at Good Hope, 73; in Mackenzie District, 42-6, 160-2; and precipitation, 45, 57

Coal, 24, 68, 93, 191

Cobalt, 114

Coffee Creek, 94

Copper, 24, 120, 123, 127-8

Coppermine, 23, 207

Coronation Gulf, 111

Cox, J.: see Chipman, K. and

Cressey, G. B., *Asia's Lands and Peoples*, 309 n.

Cumberland House, 135

Cumming, A. L., 27

Dawson, C. A., *Settlement of the Peace River Country*, 285 n.

Dawson City, 13, 14, 15, 16, 94-7, 188-9

Dawson Creek, 30, 45, 100, 104-5

Denmark, D. E., "Beaver Conservation by the Hudson's Bay Company," 146 n.

Dewdney, A. S., 171

Distributor, the, 57, 58, 74, 83, 211, 216, 218

337